Fodor's

NOVA SCOTIA & ATLANTIC CANADA

10th Edition

Where to Stay and Eat for All Budgets

Must-See Sights and Local Secrets

Ratings You Can Trust

Fodor's Travel Publications   New York, Toronto, London, Sydney, Auckland
www.fodors.com

FODOR'S NOVA SCOTIA & ATLANTIC CANADA
Editor: Caroline Trefler

Editorial Production: Astrid deRidder
Editorial Contributors: Wanita Bates, Jeff Bursey, Joyce Eisenberg, Amy Pugsley Fraser, Sandra Phinney, Amy Wang
Maps & Illustrations: Bob Blake and Rebecca Baer, *map editors*; David Lindroth, Mark Stroud, Henry Colomb, *cartographers*
Design: Fabrizio LaRocca, *creative director*; Guido Caroti, Siobhan O'Hare, *art directors*; Tina Malaney, Chie Ushio, Ann McBride, *designers*; Melanie Marin, *senior picture editor*; Moon Sun Kim, *cover designer*
Cover Photo: Peggy's Cove: Garry Black/Materfile
Production/Manufacturing: Matthew Struble

10th Edition

ISBN 978-1-4000-1906-9

ISSN 1558-8173

SPECIAL SALES
This book is available at special discounts for bulk purchases for sales promotions or premiums. Special editions, including personalized covers, excerpts of existing books, and corporate imprints, can be created in large quantities for special needs. For more information, write to Special Markets/Premium Sales, 1745 Broadway, MD 6-2, New York, New York 10019, or e-mail specialmarkets@randomhouse.com.

AN IMPORTANT TIP & AN INVITATION
Although all prices, opening times, and other details in this book are based on information supplied to us at press time, changes occur all the time in the travel world, and Fodor's cannot accept responsibility for facts that become outdated or for inadvertent errors or omissions. So **always confirm information when it matters,** especially if you're making a detour to visit a specific place. Your experiences—positive and negative—matter to us. If we have missed or misstated something, **please write to us.** We follow up on all suggestions. Contact the Nova Scotia & Atlantic Canada editor at editors@fodors.com or c/o Fodor's at 1745 Broadway, New York, NY 10019.

PRINTED IN THE UNITED STATES OF AMERICA
10 9 8 7 6 5 4 3 2 1

Be a Fodor's Correspondent

Your opinion matters. It matters to us. It matters to your fellow Fodor's travelers, too. And we'd like to hear it. In fact, we need to hear it.

When you share your experiences and opinions, you become an active member of the Fodor's community. That means we'll not only use your feedback to make our books better, but we'll publish your names and comments whenever possible. Throughout our guides, look for "Word of Mouth," excerpts of your unvarnished feedback.

Here's how you can help improve Fodor's for all of us.

Tell us when we're right. We rely on local writers to give you an insider's perspective. But our writers and staff editors—who are the best in the business—depend on you. Your positive feedback is a vote to renew our recommendations for the next edition.

Tell us when we're wrong. We're proud that we update most of our guides every year. But we're not perfect. Things change. Hotels cut services. Museums change hours. Charming cafés lose charm. If our writer didn't quite capture the essence of a place, tell us how you'd do it differently. If any of our descriptions are inaccurate or inadequate, we'll incorporate your changes in the next edition and will correct factual errors at fodors.com immediately.

Tell us what to include. You probably have had fantastic travel experiences that aren't yet in Fodor's. Why not share them with a community of like-minded travelers? Maybe you chanced upon a beach or bistro or B&B that you don't want to keep to yourself. Tell us why we should include it. And share your discoveries and experiences with everyone directly at fodors.com. Your input may lead us to add a new listing or highlight a place we cover with a "Highly Recommended" star or with our highest rating, "Fodor's Choice."

Give us your opinion instantly at our feedback center at www.fodors.com/feedback. You may also e-mail editors@fodors.com with the subject line "Nova Scotia & Atlantic Canada Editor." Or send your nominations, comments, and complaints by mail to Nova Scotia & Atlantic Canada Editor, Fodor's, 1745 Broadway, New York, NY 10019.

You and travelers like you are the heart of the Fodor's community. Make our community richer by sharing your experiences. Be a Fodor's correspondent.

Happy Traveling!

Tim Jarrell, Publisher

CONTENTS

CLOSE UPS

MAPS

ABOUT THIS BOOK

Our Ratings

Sometimes you find terrific travel experiences and sometimes they just find you. But usually the burden is on you to select the right combination of experiences. That's where our ratings come in.

As travelers we've all discovered a place so wonderful that its worthiness is obvious. And sometimes that place is so unique that superlatives don't do it justice: you just have to be there to know. These sights, properties, and experiences get our highest rating, **Fodor's Choice** indicated by orange stars throughout this book.

Black stars highlight sights and properties we deem **Highly Recommended** places that our writers, editors, and readers praise again and again for consistency and excellence.

By default, there's another category: any place we include in this book is by definition worth your time, unless we say otherwise. And we will.

Disagree with any of our choices? Care to nominate a place or suggest that we rate one more highly? Visit our feedback center at www.fodors.com/feedback.

Budget Well

Hotel and restaurant price categories from ¢ to $$$$ are defined in the opening pages of each chapter. For attractions, we always give standard adult admission fees; reductions are usually available for children, students, and senior citizens. Want to pay with plastic? **AE, D, DC, MC, V** following restaurant and hotel listings indicate whether American Express, Discover, Diners Club, MasterCard, and Visa are accepted.

Restaurants

Unless we state otherwise, restaurants are open for lunch and dinner daily. We mention dress only when there's a specific requirement and reservations only when they're essential or not accepted—it's always best to book ahead.

Hotels

Hotels have private bath, phone, TV, and air-conditioning and operate on the European Plan (aka EP, meaning without meals), unless we specify that they use the Continental Plan (CP, with a Continental breakfast), Breakfast Plan (BP, with a full breakfast), or Modified American Plan (MAP, with breakfast and dinner) or are all-inclusive (including all meals and most activities). We always list facilities but not whether you'll be charged an extra fee to use them, so when pricing accommodations, find out what's included.

Many Listings
- ★ Fodor's Choice
- ★ Highly recommended
- ⊠ Physical address
- ✦ Directions
- ⌂ Mailing address
- ☎ Telephone
- 🖷 Fax
- ⊕ On the Web
- ✍ E-mail
- 🎟 Admission fee
- ⊗ Open/closed times
- Ⓜ Metro stations
- ▭ Credit cards

Hotels & Restaurants
- 🏨 Hotel
- ⏘ Number of rooms
- ⚴ Facilities
- ⦿ Meal plans
- ✕ Restaurant
- ⦸ Reservations
- ⦰ Smoking
- 🕌 BYOB
- ✕🏨 Hotel with restaurant that warrants a visit

Outdoors
- 🏌 Golf
- ⛺ Camping

Other
- ♨ Family-friendly
- ⇨ See also
- ⊠ Branch address
- ☞ Take note

WHAT'S WHERE

NOVA SCOTIA 	Nova Scotia has an abundance of lighthouses and pristine beaches. It's also famous for its apple orchards and award-winning wines. The legendary Cabot Trail is impressive and the *ceilidhs* (Gaelic music and dance) in Cape Breton make for unique experiences. And don't forget the festivals—over 600 to choose from! If you fancy city life, Atlantic Canada's largest city—Halifax—is cosmopolitan and hip. And Nova Scotians are known for their friendliness.
NEW BRUNSWICK 	New Brunswick has the highest tides in the world. They rise and fall a full 48 feet, twice a day—one of the marine wonders of the world. If you like wilderness and adventure with your water, New Brunswick scores an A+ with choices from whale watching to canoeing, salmon fishing, mountain climbing, and more. You can also experience world-class cultural and historic attractions, and top them off with culinary tastes to temp your palate.
PRINCE EDWARD ISLAND	Prince Edward Island, "the Gentle Island," is Canada's smallest province but has a huge heart. It's a photographer's haven and a feast for the senses. Home to Anne of Green Gables and the Fathers of Confederation, PEI also has more golf courses per square mile than anywhere else in Canada. And if you have an interest in theater, music, and fine arts this is the place to be.
NEWFOUNDLAND & LABRADOR 	Newfoundland and Labrador is where you can kayak between icebergs, retrace the paths of the Vikings, or just follow your nose and take a chance on getting lost. (What better way to find yourself!) It's a tiny nation of big celebrations. And the people here are funny, so get used to laughing—a lot. Nightlife in St. John's is wild and wooly; nightlife in the outports is, err, well, peaceful and heavenly.

PROVINCE PICKER

Not sure which of the Atlantic provinces is right for you? Nova Scotia? New Brunswick? Prince Edward Island? Newfoundland and Labrador? Which ever you choose you'll undoubtedly find friendly people and stunning scenery, but not every province might have that unique mix of attributes that makes it perfect for you. Use this chart to compare how each province will measure up to your idea of the perfect vacation. If you're looking for big cosmopolitan cities and super-hopping nightlife, though, you might be better off in a different part of the world.

	NOVA SCOTIA	NEW BRUNSWICK	PRINCE EDWARD ISLAND	NEWFOUNDLAND & LABRADOR
Cold-water beaches	◐	○	○	○
Warm water beaches	◐	●	●	○
Water sports	●	●	●	●
Spas	◐	◐	◐	◐
Scenic drives	●	●	●	●
Art & Crafts galleries	●	●	●	●
Rugged coastline	●	◐	◐	●
Museums	●	●	●	◐
Lobster	●	●	●	●
Iceberg-watching	○	○	○	●
Bird-watching	●	◐	●	●
Golfing	●	●	●	◐
Wineries & Distilleries	●	○	○	○
Urban life	●	●	●	◐
Lighthouses	●	●	●	●

KEY: ● Noteworthy   ◐ Some   ○ Little or None

QUINTESSENTIAL
NOVA SCOTIA & ATLANTIC CANADA

Lobster

Welcome to the crustacean pride of Atlantic Canada, where you can buy lobster right off the boats that "bring her in." Don a bib and sup in fishing villages, in view of lighthouses and historic fortresses, at colorful down-home eateries, or in haute-cuisine restaurants. In some places, you can board a fishing boat, learn how to haul traps, cook and shell lobster, then settle down for a huge, satisfying feast. Best of all don't miss the region's famed lobster suppers: in community halls or church basements, you'll want to return again and again to get your fill of these delicious, unpretentious gatherings, which often come with fresh, piping-hot bread, seafood chowder, mussels, salads, strawberry shortcakes, and home-baked pies for dessert. More than a meal, it's an experience.

Lighthouses

Nowhere is the marine heritage of Atlantic Canada more evident than in the more than 400 lighthouses that stand sentry in the four provinces. For centuries, these trusty sentinels have guided seafarers into port. Today, they weave a tale of the region's history and culture with up-close and personal glimpses into the area's lifestyle; many house museums, craft shops, or restaurants.

Nova Scotia holds the distinction as the birthplace of Canadian lighthouses, at Louisbourg, where the French built a light in 1734, and of having North America's oldest operating lighthouse in the granite guide on Sambro Island, guarding Halifax Harbour since 1758. Newfoundland's Cape Spear National Historic Site (the far east of the western world) is the oldest remaining in the province; just southeast of St. John's, the 1835 structure also features seaside trails,

If you want to get a sense of life in Atlantic Canada, start by familiarizing yourself with some of its simple pleasures. These are a few highlights that will send you home in quiet awe, with a spring in your step, downright stuffed (and happy)—or all of the above.

perfect for looking for whales, seabirds, and icebergs. Swallowtail Lighthouse on Grand Manan Island is one of New Brunswick's most photographed lighthouses, affording amazing views, with ferries, fishing boats, and whale-watching vessels sailing in and out of the harbor, while at the opposite end of the province, the lighthouse on Miscoe Island at the northern tip of the Acadian Peninsula offers scenery and the only rotating fresnel lens in New Brunswick. PEI's Cape Bear lighthouse, 1881, was where Thomas Bartlett heard the first distress signal from the Titanic as it sank off the coast of Newfoundland. Point Prim, built in 1846, is the island's oldest lighthouse, and one of the few constructed of brick in Canada; it's covered with wooden shingles now but the brick can be seen from the interior.

Slower Pace of Life

Gently ease your foot off the gas pedal and let go of that vacation checklist: in Atlantic Canada, no one is in a big hurry to get anywhere. Visitors will find a down-home flavor to the region, where communities are close-knit and families tight. They go for walks on the beach, or spend an afternoon at a fiddler's matinee. They stop and talk with neighbors and friends—and are apt to strike up a conversation with you, too. Folks are friendly and quick-witted, and go out of their way to make you feel at home. If a local grocery store is out of a hiking-trail map, chances are the clerk will photocopy his own for you. Ask for directions, and most likely you'll come away with advice on hidden back roads, great restaurants, and foot-stomping-good local dances. One piece of advice: you'll probably enjoy yourself most if you pick one province rather than try to see too much.

IF YOU LIKE

Beaches

Just for a minute picture the sun slowly sinking into the sea. The surf crashes lazily against the shore, as the sky is bathed in brilliant hues of red, orange, gold, and yellow. Welcome to the pleasures of the beach in Atlantic Canada. Canada's four easternmost provinces are all shaped by the shoreline, and you'll find everything from pebble beaches and dunes to freshwater strands and secluded coves. In fact, there are so many to choose from that it's possible to be the only human strolling along a mile of sand.

All of **Prince Edward Island** is a haven for beach lovers. Fringed with shifting dunes, the red sand reaches to the warmest waters north of the Carolinas, drawing clam diggers, beach walkers, wind surfers, birdwatchers, and sun worshippers alike. The **east coast of New Brunswick** offers some of the best swimming beaches, enhanced by the warm waters of the Northumberland Strait. **Parlee Beach** in Shediac is ever popular, attracting large crowds to its gorgeous long sand beach. **Cape Breton Island's western shoreline** is fantastic, and includes some little-known gems framed by dramatic mountain vistas. Crashing waves entice surfers to **Lawrencetown Beach,** near Halifax, whereas **Nova Scotia's south shore** has lovely protected coves and long stretches of powdery white sand. Coastal inns, bed-and-breakfasts, and seaside cottages dot this roadside. **Newfoundland & Labrador's rugged coastline** and cooler temperatures draw more people *on* the water than *in* it. Sea kayaking, sailing, and canoeing are popular activities—and watching birds, whales, dolphins, and porpoises isn't a bad way to spend the day, either.

Scenic Drives

Turquoise waters, cliffs plunging to the sea, curving mountain roads, rolling farm country, tranquil rivers, bustling cityscapes, quaint main streets in small towns: yes, with this scenery, it's no wonder Atlantic Canada is continually thought of by locals and visitors alike as one of the world's most beautiful places. Even by car, you're apt to discover this stunning scenery. Many roads follow the coast, providing sweeping ocean vistas, views of remote lighthouses on rugged shores, and glimpses of fishing boats tied up to the wharf.

The **Cabot Trail,** a coastal highway on Cape Breton Island, is regarded as one of the most scenic drives in the world, winding its way up mountains, through small fishing villages, and past whale-watching centers, all the while providing spectacular ocean views. In New Brunswick, the awesome hand of nature can be easily experienced on a road trip through **Fundy National Park,** through Alma to Cape Enrage, and on to Hopewell Rocks, where the awesome Bay of Fundy tides have carved gigantic rock formations that project out of the ocean floor when the tide is out. Compact, pastoral Prince Edward Island is chock-a-block full of breathtaking views: the **Blue Heron Drive** passes the white beaches of the North Shore, national parks, Acadian villages, and the red cliffs of the South Shore. Likewise, Newfoundland's splendid, celebrated scenery can be experienced all through the province; in particular, the **Discovery Trail,** near Clarenville, passes some of the province's most beautiful and historic communities.

The Great Outdoors

Don your hiking boots, pick up a paddle, and pump up your cycle—when it comes to outdoor activity, the Atlantic provinces make for a wonderful playground. More than 3,000 shipwrecks lie off the coast of Nova Scotia, making it particularly attractive for divers. Whale-watching trips are available from Newfoundland, Nova Scotia, and New Brunswick. Boat, kayak, and canoe rentals are widely available. Anglers can find their catch, too. (Check locally as restrictions, seasons, license requirements, and catch limits vary from province to province.) Numerous provincial and national parks provide days of exploration, camping, and wonderful hiking trails.

View wildlife, and feel like you're hiking in the clouds on some of the trails in **Cape Breton Highlands National Park;** canoe and hike amid the splendid **Kejimkujik Park** in Nova Scotia; take advantage of the warm waters off **Prince Edward Island National Park** to swim, canoe, and windsurf; and hike into **Greenwich,** Prince Edward Island National Park, to stroll the rare system of parabolic sand dunes. At New Brunswick's **Kouchibouguac National Park** on the northeastern shore, sand dunes and grasses protect endangered piping plovers, and **Fundy National Park** is one of the province's top attractions. Rent a cycle and explore quiet back roads, or PEI's pastoral **Confederation Trail,** a flat, tip-to-tip recreational path that follows the former railroad route. The more adventurous may want to challenge themselves on the **Cabot Trail.** Newfoundland's **Gros Morne National Park,** a UNESCO World Heritage Site, offers rugged hiking and camping amid stunning fjord scenery.

Shopping for Crafts

So, you're looking to shop? Perfect. The residents of Atlantic Canada are consummate craftspeople, and the region abounds with potters, painters, glassblowers, weavers, photographers, and writers. You never know where you might find that little something. Folk artists can be found in city centers and in quiet, off-the-beaten-path countryside studios; many artisans work from home or from restored barns and farmhouses. **Look for road signs** if you're driving through.

Good buys include hooked rugs, quilts, pottery, and pewter in New Brunswick and Nova Scotia; and pottery on PEI; and hand-knit clothing in Newfoundland. In Nova Scotia, shoppers can fill their bags with individually handcrafted pewter goblets from **Amos Pewter** in Mahone Bay, or gorgeous stemware from **Nova Scotian Crystal** on the Halifax waterfront, each piece created by Canada's only maker of mouth-blown, hand-cut crystal. While in New Brunswick, be sure to visit **Handworks Gallery** on King Street in Saint John's historic uptown. The gallery represents over 80 of the province's best artists and craftspeople: think quality, one-of-a-kind items from jewelry and blown glass, to pottery, photography, and wood turning. In PEI, hit up **Island Craft Shop,** an artisans' retail co-operative in downtown Charlottetown operated by the PEI Craft Council. The shop is brimming with gift ideas from wooden whale-shaped salad servers to antique beach-glass-trivet tiles. While in Newfoundland, look for unique tea cozies and canvas floor cloths at the **Craft Council Shop** in St. John's.

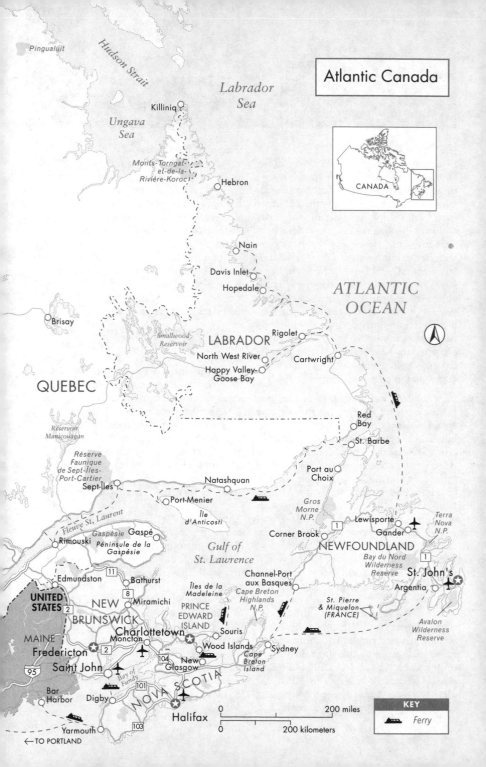

Atlantic Canada

CANADA

Pingualuit

Hudson Strait

Labrador Sea

Killiniq

Ungava Sea

Monts-Torngat-et-de-la-Rivière-Koroc

Hebron

ATLANTIC OCEAN

Nain

Davis Inlet

Hopedale

Brisay

Smallwood Reservoir

LABRADOR

Rigolet

North West River

Cartwright

Happy Valley-Goose Bay

QUEBEC

Réservoir Manicouagan

Red Bay

St. Barbe

Réserve Faunique de Sept-Îles-Port-Cartier

Port au Choix

Sept-Îles

Natashquan

Terra Nova N.P.

Port-Menier

Île d'Anticosti

Gros Morne N.P.

Lewisporte

Fleuve St. Laurent

Gaspé

Corner Brook

Gander

Gaspésie

Rimouski

Péninsule de la Gaspésie

Gulf of St. Lawrence

NEWFOUNDLAND

Bay du Nord Wilderness Reserve

St. John's

Edmundston

11

Bathurst

Îles de la Madeleine

Channel-Port aux Basques

Argentia

UNITED STATES

8

Miramichi

Cape Breton Highlands N.P.

St. Pierre & Miquelon (FRANCE)

Avalon Wilderness Reserve

MAINE

NEW BRUNSWICK

Charlottetown

Souris

2

PRINCE EDWARD ISLAND

Fredericton

Moncton

Wood Islands

Sydney

95

Saint John

2

104

New Glasgow

Cape Breton Island

Bay of Fundy

Bar Harbor

101

Digby

NOVA SCOTIA

Halifax

103

0   200 miles

0   200 kilometers

Yarmouth

KEY

← TO PORTLAND

Ferry

WHEN TO GO

Summer draws the most visitors to Atlantic Canada due to the fabulous warm ocean beaches, endless activities such as sailing and kayaking, scenic hiking trails, and waterfront restaurants serving succulent lobster. Festivals abound in summer. Fall brings explosions of color to the trees with its vibrant reds, yellows, and golds—generally, colors start to emerge in late September and remain until the end of October. Fall is also the best time of the year to view many species of whales, and it's a great time to travel here as the roads are less congested and the scenery is spectacular. The sea seems to transform into a deep blue that contrasts with the patchwork quilt of the forest. There's lots to do in the dead of winter, too, including downhill and cross-country skiing. In Labrador you can ride a dogsled to view the largest caribou herd in the world. Weather in March and early April can be unpredictable and is sometmes downright wet and muddy. Spring brings to life colorful wild lupines and fragrant apple blossoms, and this is when maple syrup flows from the trees, and the fishing poles come out again.

High season is summer and early autumn, but remember that one of the pleasures of Atlantic Canada is that it remains a fairly undiscovered tourist destination, so you won't feel crowded even at the height of summer.

Climate

As a general rule spring arrives later in coastal regions than inland, and nights are cool by the water, even in August. Autumn can last well into November, with warm clear days and crisp nights. Most of Atlantic Canada is blanketed by snow during winter. The ocean is at its warmest in August and early September.

The following are average daily maximum and minimum temperatures for Halifax, Nova Scotia.

Forecasts **Weather Channel Connection** (☎ *900/932–8437 95¢ per minute* ⊕ *www. weather.com*).

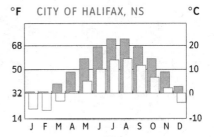

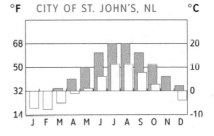

Nova Scotia

Peggy's Cove

WORD OF MOUTH

"Peggy's Cove is not really a town, it's a very small village. I think of it as an essential "scenic stop"—the tiny cove itself is ringed with wooden buildings and colourful fishing vessels, and the shoreline of the bordering open ocean is composed of exposed granite bedrock with the waves crashing against it. Very dramatic. But personally I would consider a lunch stop in another town along the coast, like Mahone Bay or Lunenburg, after (or before) an hour or so taking photos in Peggy's Cove."

—mat106

WELCOME TO NOVA SCOTIA

TOP REASONS TO GO

★ **Go Coastal:** The coastline is never more than 55 km (35 mi) away, with postcard-perfect fishing villages and sprawling sandy beaches.

★ **Step into the Past:** At the Fortress Louisbourg on Cape Breton Island, you can experience life in the 1740s as you walk the cobblestone streets of this faithfully reconstructed town.

★ **Music:** Traditional Celtic and Acadian music share the stage with rock, hip-hop, and jazz, giving Nova Scotia one of the hottest music scenes in Canada.

★ **Get Wet:** Five-thousand miles of seacoast and thousands of lakes, rivers, and brooks make a paradise for kayaking, canoeing, white-water rafting, sailing, swimming, whale-watching, and fishing.

★ **Seafood:** Nova Scotia is shaped liked a lobster claw, a happy coincidence since the lobster here is famously delicious; scallops, mussels, and salmon are also plentiful.

Dock street, Shelburne

1 Halifax/Dartmouth. Halifax is the province's biggest city, with a 250-year history as a center of military and trade, politics and culture. A walk downtown, or along the boardwalk by the sprawling harbor, showcases the mix of old and new, with lively restaurants, pubs, art galleries, heritage properties, and office towers.

2 South Shore & Annapolis Valley. The South Shore is on the Atlantic coast, the Annapolis Valley on the Bay of Fundy side. The South Shore is home to some of the province's most picturesque fishing villages, craggy coves, and white-sand beaches. The Annapolis Valley is the fertile heartland of the province, with orchards, vineyards, and farmers fields.

QUEBEC

1

Sheep, Fortress of Louisbourg, Cape Breton

PRINCE EDWARD ISLAND

NOVA SCOTIA

Ingonish

Margaree Harbour

4

19

Gulf of St. Lawrence

Port Hood 105

Iona

Glace Bay

Sydney

St George's Bay

Bras d'Or Lakes

Big Pond

Fortress Louisbourg

4

Antigonish

104

New Glasgow

Guysborough

Arichat

Canso

3

Sherbrooke Village

7

Tangier

O c e a n

A t l a n t i c

Clam digging on the Bay of Fundy

GETTING ORIENTED

Nova Scotia is all but surrounded by the Atlantic Ocean, save for the narrow stretch of land that connects it to New Brunswick and the rest of Canada. Secondary highways hug the coastline and meander through historic, smaller towns, while "100-series" arterial highways offer the fastest travel routes. Halifax, the capital, sits on the eastern coast, roughly the middle of the province's mainland. Southwest of Halifax, the South Shore runs all the way to Yarmouth, which has ferry service to and from Maine. The Annapolis Valley is the eastern spine of the province, beside the Bay of Fundy. The central and northern areas of the province lie beside the Northumberland Strait. Cape Breton Island is linked to the northeastern mainland by a causeway; the island is home to the Cabot Trail, a spectacular, soaring drive through the Cape Breton Highlands.

3 Eastern Shore & Northern Nova Scotia. The area east and north of Halifax has remarkable contrasts within a relatively short distance. The sparsely populated Eastern Shore is home to fishing villages, forests, and remote cranberry barrens. The Northumberland Strait has hiking trails and sandy beaches with the warmest ocean waters north of the Carolinas.

4 Cape Breton. The Island of Cape Breton is the Celtic heart of Nova Scotia. The gritty, industrial past of its towns and cities are in sharp contrast to the unspoiled natural beauty that defines the rural parts of the island.

NOVA SCOTIA PLANNER

Getting Here & Around

You can get to Nova Scotia by air, or there are car ferries that connect Nova Scotia with Maine, New Brunswick, Nova Scotia, PEI, and Newfoundland.

You'll appreciate having a car in Nova Scotia, with its lovely scenic drives; bus service is limited. The province has 11 designated "Scenic Travelways"—five in Cape Breton and six on the mainland—identified by roadside signs with icons that correspond with trail names. Routes are also shown on maps, available at gas stations and tourist info centers. Many roads in rural Nova Scotia require attentive driving, as they're narrow, not well signed, and don't always have a paved shoulder, but they are generally well surfaced and have exquisite scenery.

Moose!

Mainland Nova Scotia has very few moose but Parks Canada officials figure Cape Breton Island, where Alberta moose were reintroduced in the 1940s after a massive cull, is said to house five moose per km (roughly half-mile). Be on the look out—highway signs will remind you—especially around the Cabot Trail and other rural areas.

When to Go

With a spring that generally happens overnight Nova Scotia takes until mid-June to heat up. Many find July and August ideal months to visit. There's a saying in Nova Scotia: "If you don't like the weather—wait a minute," so come prepared—you may need a raincoat for the morning fog and showers, a sweater at night to keep the ocean breezes at bay, and your bathing suit for the blazing sun in between.

September has warm days and cool nights, not to mention Nova Scotia's Atlantic Film Festival and the Atlantic Fringe Festival. October heralds the arrival of the 10-day Celtic Colours International Festival. Most whale-watching, wildlife cruises, cycling tours, and sea-kayaking outfitters generally operate from mid-June to mid-September. Most golf courses stay open from May until late September, some into October. Ski season (downhill and cross-country) is mid-December to early April.

Will I See Whales?

The best whale-watching—for humpbacks, minke, pilot, fin, and right whales—is in the far east (like Pleasant Bay in Cape Breton) and extreme west (Brier Island) of the province. Most tour operators, whether through healthy competition or sheer self-confidence, guarantee sightings: if you don't see a whale, you get another tour for free!

You'll See Birds!

A healthy population of bald eagles nests in Cape Breton, where they reel above Bras d'Or Lake or perch in trees along riverbanks. The Bird Islands boat tour from Big Bras d'Or circles islands where Atlantic puffins, kittiwakes, and guillemots nest in rocky cliffs. In May and August, the Bay of Fundy teems with migrating shorebirds, and the tidal marshes near the end of the Bird Islands are home to great blue heron rookeries. *Where to Find the Birds in Nova Scotia*, published by the Nova Scotia Bird Society, is available locally in shops.

1

Local Food & Lodging

Famed for its seafood, fresh apples, blueberries, and corn, Nova Scotia cuisine's traditional ingredients are also, increasingly, part of something a bit more sophisticated, too. If you're serious about discovering Nova Scotian meals, try Hodge Podge—a summer staple of fresh beans, peas, carrots, and baby potatoes, cooked in cream. Seek out local favorites with curious names like Solomon Gundy (a pickled-herring pâté), *rappie* pie (a hearty chicken stew with dried, shredded potatoes), and blueberry grunt (a steamed pudding featuring Nova Scotia's finest berries). And of course, culled from the sea, savor fresh lobster and mussels, Digby scallops, and Atlantic salmon.

In terms of accommodation, Nova Scotia's strength lies in a sprinkling of first-class resorts that have retained a traditional feel, top country inns with a dedication to fine dining and high-level accommodation, a few superior corporate hotels, and some exceptional bed-and-breakfasts (particularly in smaller towns). Most resorts and many B&Bs are seasonal, closing after Thanksgiving. Expect to pay considerably more in Halifax and Dartmouth than elsewhere. Air-conditioning is the norm in most city hotels, but inns and B&Bs, especially along the vast coastline, rely more on the ocean breezes to cool you down. Nova Scotia's computerized system Check In (☎902/425–5781 or 800/565–0000 ⊕www.checkinnovascotia.com) provides information about and makes reservations with more than 700 hotels, motels, inns, campgrounds, and car-rental agencies.

What it Costs In Canadian Dollars

	¢	$	$$	$$$	$$$$
Restaurants	under C$8	C$8–C$12	C$13–C$20	C$21–C$30	over C$30
Hotels	under C$75	C$75–C$125	C$126–C$175	C$176–C$250	over C$250

Restaurant prices are per person for a main course at dinner. Hotel prices are for two people in a standard double room in high season.

Festival Fun

Nova Scotia is full of festivals. To celebrate the harvest there's the Apple Blossom Festival in Wolfville in May, celebrations run straight through delicacies and the season: June and July bring lobster festivals in Shelburne and Pictou, respectively, and a Seafest in Yarmouth in July celebrates all the fruits of the sea. August sees the blueberry festival in Oxford and scallop days in Digby.

There are also events all over the province highlighting the province's diversity of cultures: in June there's a three-day Greek fest in Halifax and a weekend-long multicultural festival on the Dartmouth waterfront. July has a celebration of all things Scottish at the Antigonish Highland Games. There's a two-week Acadian festival in Clare in August.

The sea inspires festivals like the Wooden Boat Festival in Mahone Bay in August; sailing race weeks are held every summer in Chester and Baddeck.

For music and arts lovers, Halifax hosts the Royal Nova Scotia International Tattoo (a military pageantry) in June, an Atlantic Jazz Fest in July, and a busker (street performers) festival in August. September brings a fringe theater festival and the Atlantic Film Fest while only Cape Breton can lay claim to the Celtic Colours International Festival every October.

Updated by
Amy Pugsley
Fraser

"INFINITE RICHES IN A LITTLE room," wrote Elizabethan playwright Christopher Marlowe. He might have been referring to Nova Scotia, Canada's second-smallest province, which packs an impossible variety of cultures and landscapes into an area half the size of Ohio. Fifty-six kilometers (35 mi) is the farthest you can get from the sea anywhere in the province.

Water, water everywhere, but that's not all. Within the convoluted coastline of Nova Scotia you'll find highlands that rival Scotland's; rugged fjords; rolling farmland; and networks of rivers, ponds, and lakes that call out to kayakers and canoers. Pounding waves in summer and the grinding ice of winter storms have sculpted the coastal rocks and reduced sandstone cliffs to stretches of sandy beach. Inland, the fertile fields of the Annapolis Valley yield peaches, corn, apples, and plums, which are sold at farm stands in summer and fall, and in spring and summer a succession of wildflowers cover the roadside with blankets of color: purple and blue lupines, yellow coltsfoot, pink fireweed. Thousands of years ago, scouring glaciers left scars on the land; the Halifax Citadel stands atop a drumlin, a round-top hill left by the retreating ice. Each of the resulting wild habitats—bogs, dry barrens, tidal wetlands, open fields, dense spruce woods, and hardwood forests—has its own distinctive plant life. Wildlife abounds: ospreys and bald eagles, moose and deer, whales in the waters off Cape Breton and Brier Island.

The original people of Nova Scotia, the Mi'Kmaqs, have been here for 10,000 years and in the early days of European exploration, French and English navigators found them settled on the shores and harvesting the sea. Later, waves of European immigrants filled the province: Germans in Lunenburg County; Highland Scots displaced by their landlords' preference for sheep; New England Loyalists escaping the American Revolution; blacks arriving as freemen or escaped slaves; Jews in Halifax, Sydney, and industrial Cape Breton; Ukranians, Poles, West Indians, Italians, and Lebanese drawn to the Sydney steel mill. As a result, there are Gaelic signs in Mabou and Iona, German sausage and sauerkraut in Lunenburg, and Greek-music festivals in Halifax. The Acadians fly their tricolor flag with pride and Scots step dance to antique fiddle airs. The fragrance of burning sweet grass mingles with the prayers of the Mi'Kmaqs' Catholic mass, the old blending with the new.

This is a small, buried nation with a capital city the same size as Marlowe's London. Before Canada was formed in 1867, Nova Scotians were prosperous shipwrights and merchants, trading with the world. Who created Cunard Lines? A Haligonian, Samuel Cunard. Those days brought democracy to the British colonies, left Victorian mansions in the salty little ports, and created a uniquely Nova Scotian outlook: worldly, approachable, and sturdily independent.

EXPLORING NOVA SCOTIA

Along the coast of Nova Scotia, the wild Atlantic Ocean crashes against rocky outcrops, eddies into sheltered coves, or flows placidly over expanses of white sand. In the Bay of Fundy, which has the highest tides in the world, the receding sea reveals stretches of red-mud flats; then it rushes back in a ferocious wall that should be treated with respect. Nova Scotia also has dense forests and rolling Annapolis Valley farms. In the province's most dramatic terrain, in Cape Breton, rugged mountains plunge to meet the waves.

If arriving in Nova Scotia from New Brunswick via the Trans-Canada Highway (Highway 104), there are three ways to proceed into the province. Amherst is the first community after the border and from here Highway 104 takes you toward Halifax, a two-hour drive away. You can opt for the northern drive, via Highway 6, which follows the shore of the Northumberland Strait; farther east is Cape Breton. Highway 2, to the south, is a less-traveled road and a favorite because of nearby fossil-studded shores. Branch roads lead to the Annapolis Valley and other points south. Drivers should be aware that the sharply curving rural roads warrant careful attention.

HALIFAX & DARTMOUTH

The cities of Halifax and Dartmouth gaze upon each other across Halifax Harbour, the second-largest natural harbor in the world. Once the point of entry to Canada for refugees and immigrants, the port remains a busy shipping center, with a flow of container ships and tugboats. Pleasure boats and yachts tie up alongside weathered schooners at the Historic Properties Wharf, and pubs, shops, museums, and parks welcome visitors and locals. In summer, jazz concerts and buskers, music festivals and sports events enliven the outdoor atmosphere. Art on exhibit, crafts sales, live theater, and fine food bring people here in all seasons. The film *Titanic* brought fresh attention to part of Halifax's history; some 150 victims of the disaster are buried in three cemeteries here, and the Maritime Museum of the Atlantic has a *Titanic* display.

HALIFAX

1,137 km (705 mi) northeast of Boston; 275 km (171 mi) southeast of Moncton, New Brunswick.

Halifax is an intimate city that's large enough to have the trappings of a capital city, yet small enough that many of its sights can be seen on a pleasant walk downtown.

SIGHTS TO SEE

❸ Anna Leonowens Gallery. The gallery is named for the Victorian woman who served as governess to the King of Siam, and whose memoirs served as inspiration for Rodgers and Hammerstein's *The King and I*. She also founded the Nova Scotia College of Art and Design. Three exhibition spaces serve as a showcase for the college faculty and students; the dis-

NOVA SCOTIA GREAT ITINERARIES

IF YOU HAVE 3 DAYS

Start in **Halifax**, a port city that combines old and new. Explore the South Shore and the Annapolis Valley, taking in the Lighthouse Route and Evangeline Trail, which loop back to Halifax. Head for **Peggy's Cove**, a fishing village perched on sea-washed granite and surrounded by coastal barrens. Explore the crafts shops of **Mahone Bay** and travel on to **Lunenburg** and the Fisheries Museum. Continue on Highway 3 or 103 to **Shelburne** on Day 2. Visit **Yarmouth** and travel on to **Digby** to try its famous scallops. **Annapolis Royal** is a lovely spot to spend an afternoon, or drive down Digby Neck to visit **Long Island and Brier Island** and catch a whale-watching cruise in season. Travel on to the elm-lined streets of **Wolfville**, home of Acadia University, and explore nearby Grand Pré National Historic Site. On Day 3, check tide times and drive to Minas Basin, where the tides are the highest in the world. A leisurely drive puts you back in Halifax by late afternoon.

IF YOU HAVE 5 DAYS

Spend a day or two in **Halifax** before exploring the Eastern Shore along Highway 7, which winds along a dramatic coastline. **Musquodoboit Harbour** is a haven for fishing enthusiasts. Nearby is Martinique Beach, one of Nova Scotia's best. Spend some time in **Sherbrooke Village**. Continue on Highway 7 toward **Antigonish** on the Sunrise Trail. Visit Hector Heritage Quay in **Pictou**, where the Scots landed in 1773. From Pictou, Highway 6 runs beside a string of beaches. Turn right to **Malagash** and Jost Vineyards. A half-hour drive takes you to **Amherst**. Continue on to **Joggins** and search for souvenirs in its sandstone cliffs. For more fossils, head to **Parrsboro**.

IF YOU HAVE 7 DAYS

Cape Breton Island is the perfect place for a leisurely 7-day tour. The coastal route takes you on a west-to-east loop from the Canso Strait Causeway. Overnight in **Mabou**, the heart of the island's rich musical tradition. From a base in **Margaree Harbour**, take a day or more to explore the Cabot Trail and Cape Breton Highlands National Park. Peruse crafts stores along St. Ann's Bay, but allow time to visit the Alexander Graham Bell National Historic Site in **Baddeck**. Spend the night in **Iona**. A day or two in **Sydney** positions you for an afternoon excursion to the Cape Breton Miners' Museum in **Glace Bay** and a daylong visit to Fortress of Louisbourg National Historic Park and the town of **Louisbourg**. Take Highway 4 back to Canso Causeway through **Big Pond**, and spend a day wandering the colorful Acadian villages of Isle Madame, such as **Arichat**.

An alternative 7-day tour, could be paring Cape Breton down to 2 or 3 days—a day in Louisbourg, one on the Cabot Trail, and one in Baddeck, for example—and combining this with a visit to the eastern shore/Sherbrooke and the Antigonish route.

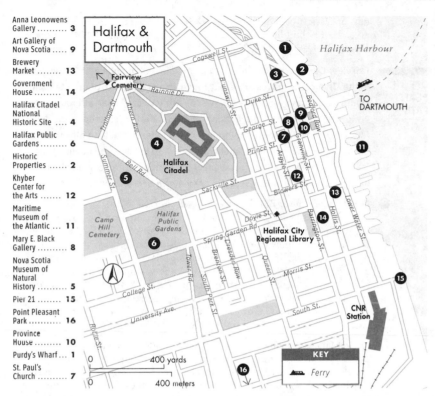

plays focus on contemporary studio and media art. ✉ *1891 Granville St.* ☎ *902/494–8223* ⊞ *Free* ⊘ *Tues.–Fri. 11–5, Sat. noon–4.*

❾ **Art Gallery of Nova Scotia.** Sheltered within this 1867 building, which saw service as a post office and RCMP headquarters, is an extensive permanent collection of more than 4,000 works, including an internationally recognized collection of Maritime and folk art by artists such as wood-carver Sydney Howard and painter Joe Norris. Also here is the actual home of the late folk painter Maude Lewis, whose bright, cheery paintings cover the tiny structure inside and out. The collection of contemporary art has major works by Christopher Pratt, Alex Colville, John Nesbitt, and Dawn McNutt. ✉ *1723 Hollis St.* ☎ *902/424–5280* ⊕ *www.agns.gov.ns.ca* ⊞ *$12* ⊘ *June–Aug., Mon.–Wed. and Fri.–Sun., 10–5, Thurs. 10–9; Sept.–May, Tues.–Fri. 10–5, weekends noon–5.*

⓭ **Brewery Market.** For the better part of two decades, this sprawling stone complex where Alexander Keith once brewed the beer that still bears his name has been better known as a Saturday farmers' market, but it also hosts several excellent eateries and a bakery (Cheelin, City Deli, Mary's Bread Basket) as well as gift shops, and a historic working brew house—complete with costumed interpreters to guide you through the process. At this writing, the market was scheduled to move to a seven-day operation called the Farmers' Seaport Market, in a brand new, green energy building at Pier 20, 1061 Marginal Road. ⊠*1496 Lower Water Sts.* ☎*902/423–2279* ☉*Sat. 7–1.*

OFF THE BEATEN PATH

Fairview Cemetery. This cemetery is the final resting place of 121 victims of the *Titanic.* The graves are easily found, in a graceful arc of granite tombstones. One grave—marked J. Dawson—attracts particular attention from visitors, though it's not the fictional Minnesota artist featured in the 1998 film, but James Dawson, a coal trimmer from Ireland. Nineteen other victims are buried in Mount Olivet Catholic Cemetery, 10 in the Baron de Hirsch Jewish Cemetery. The Maritime Museum of the Atlantic has an exhibit about the disaster. ⊠ *3720 Windsor St., 3 km (2 mi) north of downtown.*

⑭ Government House. Built between 1799 and 1805 for Sir John Wentworth, the Loyalist governor of New Hampshire, and his racy wife, Fannie (Thomas Raddall's novel *The Governor's Lady* tells their story), this house has since been the official residence of the province's lieutenant governor. It's North America's oldest consecutively occupied government residence, because the older President's House (the White House) was evacuated and burned during the War of 1812. Its construction, of Nova Scotian stone, was engineered by a Virginian Loyalist, Isaac Hildrith. The house, which has been restored to its original elegance, isn't open to the public. ⊠*1451 Barrington St.*

❹ Halifax Citadel National Historic Site. ★ The Citadel, erected between 1826 and 1856, was the heart of the city's fortifications and was linked to smaller forts and gun emplacements on the harbor islands and on the bluffs above the harbor entrance. Several other forts stood on the site before the present one. Kilted soldiers drill in front of the **Army Museum,** once the barracks, and a cannon is fired every day at noon—a tradition since 1749. Free tours with a costumed guide help bring the history of both the fort and the city to life. Before leaving, take in the view from the Citadel: the spiky downtown crowded between the hilltop and the harbor; the wooded islands at the harbor's mouth; and the naval dockyard under the Angus L. Macdonald Bridge, the nearer of the two bridges connecting Halifax with Dartmouth. The handsome, four-sided **Town Clock** on Citadel Hill was given to Halifax by Prince Edward, Duke of Kent, military commander from 1794 to 1800. ⊠*Citadel Hill* ☎*902/426–5080* ⊕*www.parkscanada.gc.ca* 🗓*June–mid-Sept. $10.90; May 7–31 and mid-Sept.–Oct. $7.15; rest of yr free* ☉*May 7–June 30, Sept., and Oct., daily 9–5; July and Aug., daily 9–6.*

❻ Halifax Public Gardens. One of the oldest formal Victorian gardens in ☾ North America, this city oasis had its start in 1753 as a private garden. Its layout was completed in 1875 by Richard Power, former gardener to the Duke of Devonshire in Ireland. Gravel paths wind among ponds, trees, and flower beds, revealing an astonishing variety of plants from all over the world. The centerpiece is a gazebo erected in 1887 for Queen Victoria's Golden Jubilee. The gardens are closed in winter but you can still take a pleasant walk along the cast-iron fence of

1

the perimeter. ⊠*Bounded by Sackville, Summer, and S. Park Sts. and Spring Garden Rd.*

❷ **Historic Properties.** These waterfront warehouses date from the early 19th century, when trade and war made Halifax prosperous. They were built by such raffish characters as Enos Collins, a privateer, smuggler, and shipper whose vessels defied Napoléon's blockade to bring American supplies to the Duke of Wellington. The buildings have since been taken over by high-quality shops, chic offices, and restaurants, including those in Privateer's Warehouse. ⊠*Lower Water and Hollis Sts.*

⓬ **Khyber Center for the Arts.** Primarily a gallery for young and emerging artists, the Khyber is home to works in numerous genres, including performance art. Its various galleries are in a turreted building built in the late 1800s by the Church of England. ⊠*1588 Barrington St.* ☎*902/422–9668* ⊠*Free* ⊙*Tues.–Sat. noon–5.*

⓫ **Maritime Museum of the Atlantic.** The exhibits in this restored chandlery and warehouse on the waterfront include small boats once used around the coast, as well as displays describing Nova Scotia's proud sailing heritage, from the days when the province, on its own, was one of the world's foremost shipbuilding and trading nations. Other exhibits explore the Halifax Explosion of 1917, shipwrecks, and lifesaving. Permanently moored outside, after a long life of charting the coasts of Labrador and the Arctic, is the hydrographic steamer *Acadia.* At the next wharf (summer only) is Canada's naval memorial, **HMCS** *Sackville,* the sole survivor of a fleet that escorted convoys of ships from Halifax to England during World War II.

The museum has a permanent exhibit about the *Titanic* disaster. With many victims buried in Halifax, the city was, in a sense, the ship's final destination. The display includes at least 20 artifacts and dozens of photographs. The centerpiece is the only surviving deck chair. Also on display are a section of wall paneling; a balustrade molding and part of a newel from the dual curving staircase; a cribbage board carved from *Titanic* oak by the carpenter of one of the rescue ships; and the log kept by a wireless operator at Cape Race, Newfoundland, on the fateful night. An extensive research library is open to the public by appointment only. ⊠*1675 Lower Water St.* ☎*902/424–7490 or 902/424–7491* ⊕*museum.gov.ns.ca/mma* ⊠*$8.50* ⊙*May–Oct., Mon. and Wed.–Sat. 9:30–5:30, Tues. 9:30–8; May and Oct., Sun. 1–5:30; June–Sept., Sun. 9:30–5:30; Nov.–Apr., Wed.–Sat. 9:30–5, Tues. 9:30–8, Sun. 1–5.*

❽ **Mary E. Black Gallery.** The exhibit space for the Nova Scotia Centre for Craft and Design presents rotating shows of high-quality crafts. ⊠*1061 Marginal Rd.* ☎*902/492–2522* ⊠*Free* ⊙*Mon.–Wed. and Fri. 11–5, Thurs. 11–8, Sat. 10–5, Sun. 1–5.*

❺ **Nova Scotia Museum of Natural History.** Most easily recognized by the huge fiberglass model of the tiny northern spring peeper (a frog) that "clings" to the side of the building May through October, the museum is the place to learn about whales, fossils, dinosaurs, birds, and mush-

A GOOD WALK

Begin on Upper Water Street at **Purdy's Wharf** ❶ for unobstructed views of Halifax Harbour. Continue south on Lower Water Street to the restored warehouses of the **Historic Properties** ❷, a cluster of boutiques and restaurants linked by cobblestone footpaths. Stroll south several blocks along the piers to the **Maritime Museum of the Atlantic** ⓫; the wharves outside often welcome transatlantic yachts and sail-training ships. Take the waterfront boardwalk behind the museum; ahead on your right is **Bishop's Landing,** a residential development with upscale shops that will tempt chocolate, wine, coffee, gelato, and cigar afficionados. Afterward, go through the main entrance and cross Lower Water Street to **Brewery Market** ⓭, a restored waterfront property with all sorts of shops and boutiques. The elevator at the office end of Brewery Market will take you to Hollis Street. Turn left, past several elegant Victorian town houses, notably Keith Hall, once the executive offices of the brewery.

Turn right onto Bishop Street and right again onto Barrington Street, Halifax's main downtown thoroughfare. The stone mansion on your right is **Government House** ⓮, the official residence of Nova Scotia's lieutenant governor. You can detour from Barrington Street onto Spring Garden Road and the attractive shops in the Park Lane and Spring Garden Place shopping centers; then walk west to the **Halifax Public Gardens** ❻, where you can rest on shaded benches amid flower beds and rare trees. A block north, on Summer Street, is the **Nova Scotia Museum of Natural History** ❺.

On your way back to Barrington Street on Bell Road and Sackville Street, you might notice the **Halifax Citadel National Historic Site** ❹, dominated by the fortress that once commanded the city. On a lot defined by Barrington, Argyle, and Prince streets lies **St. Paul's Church** ❼; one wall within its historic confines contains a fragment from the great Halifax Explosion of 1917. A block north and facing City Hall is the Grand Parade, where musicians perform at noon in summer. From here, the waterfront side of Citadel Hill, look uphill: the tall, stylish brick building is the World Trade and Convention Centre and is attached to the Halifax Metro Centre. Head down the hill on Prince Street, making a left on Hollis Street to **Province House** ❿, Canada's oldest legislative building. North of Province House, at Cheapside, is the **Art Gallery of Nova Scotia** ❾, which showcases a large collection of folk art. Walk a block west to Granville Street and two blocks north to the **Anna Leonowens Gallery** ❸. A final stop lies to the south: The new Port of Halifax seawall development, which houses a state-of-the-art satellite campus for the art college also plays host to the **Mary E. Black Gallery** ❽, and **Pier 21** ⓯, a former immigration center, which now houses a museum of immigration.

TIMING: The city of Halifax is fairly compact; depending on your tendency to stop and study, the above tour can take from a half to a full day. Pier 21 could take several hours in itself, so you may want to visit it separately from the walk.

rooms. The Nature Centre is home to live snakes, frogs, insects, and other creatures; the Butterfly Pavilion is filled with species from around the world. Nature talks, walks, and workshops are designed to appeal to all interests and ages. ✉ *1747 Summer St.* ☎ *902/424–7353* ⊕ *nature.museum.gov.ns.ca* ✑ *$8; free Wed. 5–8* ☺ *Mid-May–mid-Oct., Mon., Tues., and Thurs.–Sat 9:30–5:30, Wed. 9:30–8, Sun. 1–5; Nov.– mid-May, Tues. and Thurs.–Sat. 9:30–5, Wed. 9:30–8, Sun. 1–5.*

⑮ Pier 21. From 1928 until 1971, refugees, returning troop ships, war brides, and more than a million immigrants arrived on Canadian soil through Pier 21, the front door to Canada. It's now a museum where the immigrant experience is re-created through live performances, multimedia presentations, and displays of photographs, documents, and artifacts. ✉ *1055 Marginal Rd.* ☎ *902/425–7770* ⊕ *www.pier21.ca* ✑ *$8.50* ☺ *May–Nov., daily 9:30–5:30; Dec.–Mar., Tues.–Sat. 10–5; Apr., Mon.–Sat. 10–5.*

⑯ Point Pleasant Park. Most of the city's secondary fortifications have been turned into public parks. This one, which encompasses 186 wooded acres with walking trails and seafront paths, is popular with joggers and dog walkers and provides the perfect vantage point from which to watch ships entering and leaving the harbor. The park was leased from the British Crown by the city for 999 years, at a shilling a year. Its major military installation is a massive round martello tower dating from the late 18th century. In September 2003, Hurricane Juan tore through the park, uprooting or damaging 57,000 (about 70%) of the century-old trees in a matter of hours, leaving present-day park goers the same harbor views that must have inspired its use as a military command post in the first place. ✉ *About 12 blocks down S. Park St. from Spring Garden Rd.*

⑩ Province House. Charles Dickens proclaimed this structure, now a National Historic Site, "a gem of Georgian architecture." Erected in 1819 to house Britain's first overseas self-government, the sandstone building still serves as the meeting place for the provincial legislature. ✉ *1726 Hollis St.* ☎ *902/424–4661* ✑ *Free* ☺ *July and Aug., weekdays 9–5, weekends 10–4; Sept.–June, weekdays 9–4.*

❶ Purdy's Wharf. Named after a famous 19th-century shipping family, the wharf is composed of a pier and twin office towers that stand right in the harbor. The buildings actually use ocean water to generate air-conditioning. ✉ *Upper Water St.*

OFF THE
BEATEN
PATH

Deadman's Island. This tiny island is the final resting place of almost 200 American prisoners of war who died while imprisoned in Halifax during the War of 1812. A new US$10,000 memorial was unveiled by the U.S. Department of Veterans Affairs in 2005 to honor the men, who died of communicable diseases such as smallpox and were buried in mass graves. ✉ *Look for the Deadman's Island sign off Purcell's Cove Rd., 6 km (3.7 mi) northwest of downtown.*

❼ **St. Paul's Church.** Opened in 1750, this is Canada's oldest Protestant church and the burial site of many colonial notables. Inside, on the north end, a piece of metal is embedded in the wall. It is a fragment of the *Mont Blanc*, one of the two ships whose collision caused the Halifax Explosion of December 6, 1917, the greatest human-caused explosion before that at Hiroshima. ✉ *1749 Argyle St.* ☎ *902/429–2240* ⊙ *Sept.–May, weekdays 9–4:30; June–Aug., Mon.–Sat. 9–4:30.*

> ### WORD OF MOUTH
> "Halifax is a lovely city, urban with a small town feel . . . LOL, people actually still make eye contact there and will stop to offer assistance if they see you looking at a map." —Retired_teacher

WHERE TO STAY & EAT

$$$–$$$$ ✕ **Seven Wine Bar and Restaurant.** Forty-five wines by the glass will keep you busy while you enjoy the atmosphere at this moody, two-storey trendy spot. Downstairs, the interior is all dark brown–suede banquettes; upstairs boasts more traditional dining with white table cloths. There's an awning out front for all-weather meals in the summer months. ✉ *1579 Grafton St.* ☎ *902/444–4777* ▤ *AE, MC, V.*

$$$
Fodor'sChoice
★ ✕ **Da Maurizio Dining Room.** Subdued lighting, elegant decor, and fresh flowers on the tables make dining a lovely experience at this Italian restaurant. Chef Maurizio's creativity and attention to detail create meals that are both impressive and satisfying and make him a local legend. The excellent seared foie gras is always on the menu, as are the scampi, from the coast of Iceland, which are crowned with a heavenly garlic-and-cognac sauce. For dessert, the zabaglione is likely to leave you weak. The specialty wine list tops out at $325, but nice bottles can still be had for $35. ✉ *1496 Lower Water St.,* ☎ *902/423–0859* ▤ *AE, MC, V* ⊙ *Closed Sun. No lunch.*

$$$ ✕ **Fid.** A fid is a graceful nautical tool used to splice rope and at this small, minimalist restaurant, a two-minute walk from the main gates of the Halifax Public Gardens, the chef-owner splices together unusual flavors and textures. The halibut, when available, is the most popular dish on the menu and chocolate lovers should partake of the *moelleaux au chocolat*, molten chocolate-custard sauce within a shell of warm cake. ✉ *1569 Dresden Row* ☎ *902/422–9162* ▤ *AE, MC, V* ⊙ *Closed Mon. No lunch Tues. or weekends.*

$$$ ✕ **Press Gang.** Easily one of the hippest upscale establishments in Halifax, the Press Gang serves the freshest fish available. The Oyster bar offers the delicacy on the half-shell or Rockefeller-style, and for dinner, try the blackened-scallop chowder, citrus cumin–crab cakes, or the lavender-glazed rack of lamb. A muscadet from the well-stocked cellar is an excellent complement the seafood. The "Drill," four courses for two ($150), rarely disappoints and is an exceptional value. Thick, cold stone walls testify to the building's era—it was built in 1759—but the restaurant is warmed by comfortable seating and intimate lighting. ✉ *5218 Prince St.* ☎ *902/423–8816* ⚓ *Reservations recommended* ▤ *AE, DC, MC, V.*

$$$ ✕ **Salty's on the Waterfront.** Overlooking Privateer's Wharf and the entire
★ harbor, this restaurant gets the prize for best location in the city. Huge

bowls of steaming mussels and an excellent surf and turf crown a menu sure to satisfy any seafood lover. Request a table with a window view and save room for the famous dessert, Cadix (chocolate mousse over praline crust). The Bar & Grill ($$), on the ground level, is less expensive and serves lunch outside on the wharf in summer (be warned: it can be very windy). ✉*1869 Upper Water St.* ☎*902/423–6818* ⚓*Reservations recommended for upstairs* ▤*AE, D, DC, MC, V.*

$$–$$$ ✕**Bish World Cuisine.** Flavors from different parts of the world come
★ together at this airy yet intimate restaurant, bordered on three sides by large windows overlooking Halifax Harbor. Even though it's avant-garde food, you still feel like you're eating a real meal. Try the Madras lamb or the rare seared tuna with lemon grass and basmati rice. ✉*1475 Lower Water St.* ☎*902/425–7993* ▤*AE, MC, V* ⊗*Closed Sun. No lunch.*

$$–$$$ ✕**Chives Canadian Bistro.** The two chef-owners are wizards at defining
★ eclectic Canadian cuisine, with a few French, German, and Asian influences thrown in for good measure. The large, casual restaurant with planked-wood floors and cozy lighting also offers an intimate table for four in their wine "vault" (the restaurant used to be a bank). The menu adapts to what's fresh and seasonal at the fishmongers and the farmers' market but customers would have a fit if two key items—the Nova Scotia lamb shank and the bacon-wrapped port tenderloin—weren't available. Ditto for the crème brûlée. ✉*1537 Barrington St.* ☎*902/420–9626* ▤*AE, DC, MC, V.*

$$–$$$ ✕**Deco.** With its recycled building materials from the 1920s, this beautifully designed restaurant is truly an homage to Paris in the art-deco era. The food, however, is all modern—from the grilled mushroom appetizer to the bistro-style grilled sirloin, to the molten dark-chocolate cake with cabernet-raspberry sauce. ✉*5518 Spring Garden Rd.* ☎*902/423–9795* ▤*AE, MC, V.*

$$–$$$ ✕**The Wooden Monkey.** Located in the oldest residential building in Halifax (1749), this restaurant has a menu with a conscience and attracts diners with its locally grown macrobiotic and organic food, fair-trade organic coffee, and locally brewed beers and wines. Even if you don't enter for your health, stay for your taste buds: with starters such as julienne vegetable rolls and entrées like blackened haddock with homemade salsa, the Nova Scotia lamb burger, or scallops in a citrus-basil pesto, you'll soon be a convert. ✉*1685 Argyle St.* ☎*902/444–3844* ▤*AE, DC, MC, V.*

$–$$$ ✕**Dharma Sushi.** Tidy sushi, fresh sashimi, and feather-light tempura are artfully presented here and although the service is fast paced, the food doesn't suffer as a result. The daily lunch specials—including California rolls, vegetable tempura, and a popular chicken teriyaki—are a real deal and ready fast. ✉*1576 Argyle St.* ☎*902/425–7785* ▤*AE, MC, V* ⊗*Closed Sun. No lunch Sat.*

$–$$$ ✕**MacAskill's Restaurant.** Diners can experience Nova Scotian hospitality in this romantic dining room overlooking beautiful Halifax Harbour. On warm nights, try for one of the eight tables on the patio. The chefs create a variety of seafood dishes using the finest, freshest fish available. Specialties also include filet mignon with pepper sauce. Make sure to save some room for the dessert sampler—a trio of lemon mousse, German torte, and cheese cake. ⊠ *Dartmouth Ferry Terminal Bldg., 88 Alderney Dr.* ☎ *902/466–3100* ⊟ *AE, DC, MC, V* ⊗ *Closed Sun. Nov.–May. No lunch weekends.*

$–$$$ ✕ **Privateer's Warehouse.** History surrounds you in this centuries-old building, where three restaurants share early-18th-century stone walls and hewn beams. The Tap Room dining room, for private booked functions only, has a nautical theme and great views of the harbor. The Beer Market, on the middle level, specializes in seafood as well as traditional pub fare. The Lower Deck is a boisterous bar with long trestle tables and a patio, serving fish-and-chips and other pub food. ⊠ *Historic Properties, Lower Water St.* ☎ *902/422–1289* ⊟ *AE, DC, MC, V.*

$–$$ ✕ **Cheelin Restaurant.** Some of the freshest and most flavorful dishes in the region are prepared in the open kitchen at this small and informal Chinese restaurant. Each dish receives individual attention and care, and the chef-owner personally checks with diners to make sure they are satisfied. Noodle and dumpling dishes are very popular, but if you're looking for something different, try the amazing stuffed eggplant in Yu Xiang (dark Szechuan) sauce. ⊠ *Brewery Market, 1496 Lower Water St.* ☎ *902/422–2252* ⊟ *AE, MC, V* ⊗ *No dinner Mon. No lunch Sun.*

$–$$ ✕ **Economy Shoe Shop.** Variety rules at this chaotic, ever-popular establishment with a bar and three restaurants. Start with an imported beer in the Belgian bar, enjoy tapas in the Atrium, head to Backstage to dine among the fake trees and other theatrical decorations, and enjoy the private cave in the Diamond for after-dinner coffee or, in summer, sit on the deck, which is always packed with locals. Food at the Shoe Shop is adventurous—though not haute cuisine—and portions are generous. ⊠ *1663 Argyle St.* ☎ *902/423–7463* ⊟ *AE, D, DC, MC, V.*

$–$$ ✕ **Il Mercato Ristorante.** Enter this Italian eatery at your own risk: the gleaming display cases of antipasti and desserts—including the *zuccotto,* a dome of chocolate and cream, and the gelati and sorbetti—are sure to tempt. In the heart of the downtown shopping district, Il Mercato is an ideal lunch stop but come early for dinner, because this hopping place does not take reservations. ⊠ *5650 Spring Garden Rd.* ☎ *902/422–2866* ⚖ *Reservations not accepted* ⊟ *AE, MC, V.*

¢–$$ ✕ **The Harbourside Market.** This casual, market-inspired cluster of resta-
    ♺ raunt boutiques is perfect for families, and probably the most economical place to eat dinner on the Halifax waterfront. Located in the back of Historic Properties, there are six restaurants to choose from—kids can have pizza or burgers and there's seafood (including a full steamed lobster), deluxe wraps, or wonderful Greek dishes for the grown-ups. Seating is inside (with full windows overlooking neighboring Dartmouth) or outside. The Shipwreck Pub has beer on tap and wine, and to finish your meal, there are gourmet goodies from the on-site coffee shop or ice cream and gelato on the premises and nearby on the waterfront boardwalk. ⊠ *1869 Upper Water Street* ☎ *902/422–3077* ⊕ *www.historicproperties.ca/merch_1.htm* ⊟ *AE, MC, V.*

¢–$$ ✕ **Satisfaction Feast.** This small vegetarian restaurant is informal, friendly, and usually packed at lunchtime. The food is wholesome, with lots of ethnic influences—think fresh whole-wheat bread and curries. Sweet, sharp ginger beer is brewed on the premises and is wonderful cold, with soda water, or hot, as a tea. Enjoy an organic coffee with one of the fine cakes or desserts. ✉ *1581 Grafton St.* ☎ *902/422–3540* ☐ *MC, V.*

$$$–$$$$ ⚎ **Delta Halifax.** This business-class hotel has spacious, attractive rooms, most with a panoramic harbor view and an enclosed walkway provides easy access to the Historic Properties and Scotia Square mall. The Crown Bistro ($$–$$$) has more refined dishes as well as lighter fare. ✉ *1990 Barrington St., B3J 1P2* ☎ *902/425–6700 or 877/814–7706* ☐ *902/425–6214* ⊕ *www.deltahotels.com* ⟲ *279 rooms, 21 suites* ⟳ *In-room: high-speed. In-hotel: restaurant, bar, pool, gym, concierge, laundry service, parking (fee), no-smoking rooms, some pets allowed, minibar, refrigerators on request* ☐ *AE, DC, MC, V.*

$$$–$$$$ ⚎ **Prince George Hotel.** Contemporary mahogany furnishings fill the
★   rooms at this luxurious and understated business-oriented hotel, and quiet and calm prevail in the public areas. Expert staff, in starched uniforms, wait to fulfill your every wish. Gio Restaurant ($$) serves eclectic cuisine in a casual setting. The hotel is connected by underground tunnel to the World Trade and Convention Centre; walkways provide access to shops, offices, and entertainment, including the harborside casino. ✉ *1725 Market St., B3J 3N9* ☎ *902/425–1986, 800/565–1567 in Canada* ⊕ *www.princegeorgehotel.com* ⟲ *189 rooms, 14 suites* ⟳ *In-room: Wi-Fi. In-hotel: restaurant, bar, pool, gym, concierge, parking (fee)* ☐ *AE, DC, MC, V.*

$$–$$$$ ⚎ **Cambridge Suites.** Besides the obvious convenience of being able to prepare your own food and chill a bottle of wine, the best feature of this all-suites hotel is its location near downtown Halifax and Citadel Hill. It's four blocks (albeit up a steep hill) from the waterfront hub and one block from Spring Garden Road's fabulous shopping and people-watching. ✉ *1583 Brunswick St., B3J 3P5* ☎ *902/420–0555 or 800/565–1263* ☐ *902/420–9379* ⊕ *www.cambridgesuiteshalifax. com* ⟲ *200 suites* ⟳ *In-room: kitchen, Wi-Fi. In-hotel: restaurant, room service, bar, fitness center, hot tub, sauna* ☐ *AE, D, DC, MC, V* ⦿ *CP.*

$$–$$$$ ⚎ **Halifax Marriott Harbourfront** Built low to match the neighboring historic ironstone buildings, this waterfront hotel varies in appearance from others in the chain and its convenient location in the Historic Properties area contributes to its elegance. Rooms are fairly spacious; all have desks and sitting areas. A five-minute stroll through a walkway takes you to Halifax's only casino. ✉ *1919 Upper Water St., B3J 3J5* ☎ *902/421–1700* ☐ *902/422–5805* ⊕ *www.marriott.com* ⟲ *335 rooms, 19 suites* ⟳ *In-room: Wi-Fi. In-hotel: restaurant, coffee shop, room service, bar, pool, gym, hair salon, spa, concierge, laundry service, parking (fee), no-smoking rooms* ☐ *AE, DC, MC, V.*

$$–$$$$ ⚎ **The Halliburton.** Three 19th-century town houses were elegantly renovated to create this hotel and period antiques and goose-down duvets await you in the comfortable (but dark) rooms. Suites have fireplaces, and there's a lovely garden. The rates here vary, with some topping $300. Local game and Atlantic seafood are served in the small but elegant dining room Stories ($$–$$$$). ✉ *5184 Morris St., B3J 1B3*

☎902/420–0658 ᗡ902/423–2324 ⊕www.thehalliburton.com ⇆25 rooms, 4 suites ⌂ In-hotel: restaurant, parking (no fee), no elevator ⊟AE, DC, MC, V ⏀CP.

$$–$$$$ 🖵**Westin Nova Scotian.** An enormous brick building, this grand hotel sits solidly in downtown Halifax, next to the VIA Rail station, with the harbor behind it and Cornwallis Park in front. All rooms have the chain's signature "heavenly beds" with duvet and five pillows, and are outfitted with ergonomic chairs and a desk. The earthy room tones of a 2004 renovation are complemented by burgundy velvet drapes. The restaurant serves fresh fish and shellfish dishes as well as pastas and meatier fare. ⊠1181 Hollis St., B3H 2P6 ☎902/421–1000 or 877/993–7846 ᗡ902/422–9465 ⊕www.westin.ns.ca ⇆297 rooms, 13 suites ⌂In-room: dial-up. In-hotel: restaurant, bar, tennis court, pool, gym, laundry service, no-smoking rooms, minibar ⊟AE, DC, MC, V.

$$–$$$ 🖵**Inn on the Lake.** A great value in a quiet location, this small country club–style hotel sits on 5 acres of parkland on the edge of a Fall River lake, 30 minutes from Halifax and 10 minutes from the airport. Rooms are spacious and have balconies, and many have whirlpool tubs. ⊠3009 Highway 2, Fall River B2T 1J5 ☎902/861–3480 or 800/463–6465 ᗡ902/861–4883 ⊕www.innonthelake.com ⇆20 rooms, 20 suites ⌂In-room: Wi-Fi. In-hotel: restaurant, bar, tennis courts, pool, beachfront, airport shuttle, parking (no fee), no elevator ⊟AE, MC, V.

$$–$$$ 🖵**Marriott Residence Inn.** This all-suites hotel opened in 2004 and offers a variety of studio, one-bedroom, and two-bedroom options. Weekday guest receptions with appetizers, a hot breakfast buffet, and grocery-shopping service make this an attractive option for any traveler, especially for extended stays. There are a coffee shop and a seasonal tourism information center on the first floor. ⊠1599 Grafton St., B3J 2C3 ☎902/422–0493 or 800/331–3131 ⊕www.marriott.com ⇆92 suites ⌂In-room: kitchen, high-speed. In-hotel: gym, laundry facilities, laundry service, parking (fee), no-smoking rooms, some pets allowed ⊟AE, D, DC, MC, V ⏀CP.

$ 🖵**Garden View Bed & Breakfast.** This lovely Victorian home sits on a quiet residential street near the Halifax Commons and you can relax in the living room in front of the fire. The garden is especially charming. The living room has cable TV and DVD. Breakfast is served in the dining room. Only one room has a private bathroom. ⊠6052 Williams St., B3K 1E9 ☎902/423–2943 or 888/737–0778 ᗡ902/423–4355 ⊕www.interdesign.ca/gardenview ⇆3 rooms, 1 with bath ⌂In-room: no a/c, no phone (some), no TV (some). In-hotel: no-smoking rooms, no elevator ⊟MC, V ⏀BP.

¢ 🖵**Dalhousie University.** Dalhousie University rents their no-frills rooms from May through August: singles are $35 and two-bedroom apartments are $68. Most have shared baths and a buffet breakfast is available at a minimal charge. You'll have access to the Dalplex athletic facility nearby; ask for a schedule with pool times, court times, and classes. ⊠1233 LeMarchant St., B3H 3P6 ☎902/494–8840 ᗡ902/494–8455 ⊕www.dal.ca/confserv ⇆420 rooms without bath,

1

20 apartments ⚡ *In-room: no a/c, no phone, no TV. In-hotel: pool, gym* ▭*MC, V.*

NIGHTLIFE & THE ARTS

FESTIVALS Halifax has a burgeoning film industry, the product of which is presented at the **Atlantic Film Festival** (☎*902/422–3456* ⊕*www.atlanticfilm. com*), held the third week in September. The festival also showcases feature films, TV movies, and documentaries made outside of Halifax. Admission to films often includes admission to a party or gala event following the screening. During the first week of September the **Atlantic Fringe Festival** (☎*902/435–4837 or 800/565–0000* ⊕*www.funfringe. ca*) presents numerous theatrical shows in a variety of venues scattered throughout the downtown area. **The Halifax International Busker Festival** (✉ ☎*902/429–3910 or 866/773–0655* ⊕*www.buskers.ca*) has been bringing international street performers to the waterfront area and city streets for more than two decades. It takes place every August and includes several performers and events for children.

The Royal Nova Scotia International Tattoo (✉*Metro Centre, Brunswick Street* ☎*902/420–1114* ⊕*www.nstattoo.ca* ▭*$28–$55*) is a celebration of military instruments (brass and drums), and military-inspired music that runs the first week of July.

The internationally acclaimed **Scotia Festival of Music** (☎*902/429–9467* ⊕*www.scotiafestival.ns.ca*) presents classical musicians via concert and master classes each May and June. The **TD-Canada Trust Jazz Festival** (☎*902/492–2225* ⊕*www.jazzeast.com*), with an eclectic selection of jazz styles, takes place in mid-July. Some concerts are free.

THEATER **Grafton Street Dinner Theatre** (✉*1741 Grafton St.* ☎*902/425–1961* ⊕*www.graftonstdinnertheatre.com*) holds performances Tuesday through Sunday. The **Halifax Feast Company** (✉*Maritime Centre, 1505 Barrington St.* ☎*902/420–1840*) presents musical comedies Wednesday through Sunday. The **Neptune Theatre** (✉*1593 Argyle St.* ☎*902/429–7300, 800/565–7345 information, 902/429–7070 box office* ⊕*www.neptunetheatre.com*), Canada's oldest professional repertory playhouse, has a main stage and studio theater under one roof. It stages year-round performances ranging from classics to comedy and contemporary Canadian drama. In July and August, **Shakespeare by the Sea** (☎*902/422–0295* ⊕*www.shakespearebythesea.ca*) performs the Bard's works Thursday through Sunday evenings at 7 PM, and weekends at 1 PM in Point Pleasant Park, at the southern end of the Halifax peninsula. The natural setting—dark woods, rocky shore, and ruins of fortifications—is a dramatic backdrop. No tickets are required—just show up and contribute to the bucket ($10 is suggested).

NIGHTLIFE Haligonians love their pubs and their music; this city has more bars per capita than anywhere else in Canada. At **Bearly's House of Blues and Ribs** (✉*1269 Barrington St.* ☎*902/423–2526*), a dark, low-ceiling tavern with a couple of pool tables, you can dine on ribs, burgers, and fish-and-chips while listening to outstanding blues artists every evening except Monday and Wednesday. At **Bubbles Mansion** (✉*5287 Prince St.* ☎*902/405–4505*) your erstwhile host is the dweeby, cat-loving Bubbles from the Canadian mockumentary television show *Trailer Park Boys*. You'll know you've reached the right place by all the shopping carts hanging off the massive, bubbly-eyed street sign.

The trendiest spot in town, **Economy Shoe Shop Cafe and Bar, Backstage, and Diamond** (⊠*1663 Argyle St.* ☎*902/423–7463*), has a variety of options: choose a quiet booth, a table in the middle of the action, or the gardenlike rooftop patio in summer. The eclectic surroundings alone are worth a visit and food is served until 2 AM. Live jazz can be heard Monday; author readings are on Tuesday. The **Marquee Club** (⊠*2037 Gottigen St.* ☎*902/429–3020*), a cabaret-style venue with two stages and a seating capacity of 850, presents some of the hottest entertainment in town. The club buzzes until 3:30 AM with live rock, blues, and alternative bands. Downstairs there's jazz, blues, and acoustic evenings. The bar has a good selection of locally brewed beers on tap. The **Old Triangle** (⊠*5136 Prince St.* ☎*902/492–4900*), a comfortable Irish pub, has traditional Irish, Scottish, and local music nightly.

Reflections Cabaret (⊠*5184 Sackville St.* ☎*902/422–2957*), though considered a gay bar, is better described as an "anything goes" bar. Drag queens mingle with throngs of university students and strobe lights and pounding music inspire dancing and drinking until 3:30 AM. Funky folk art hangs on the walls at the laid-back **Soho Kitchen** (⊠*1667 Argyle St.* ☎*902/423–3049*). Jazz groups perform or jam Tuesday and Thursday through Saturday nights. Since 1948, patrons have been carving their initials and graffiti into the tables at the **Seahorse Tavern** (⊠*1659 Argyle St.* ☎*902/423–7200*), where cold draft beer washes down pub food. You can shoot a game of pool, contemplate the large aquarium, or sit at the bar and start a conversation with one of the regulars.

SPORTS & THE OUTDOORS

CANOEING Some beautiful century-old private homes dot the North West Arm, and the bench of a canoe is definitely the best seat from which to view them. **St. Mary's Boat Club** (⊠*1641 Fairfield Rd., off Jubilee Rd.* ☎*902/490–4688*) rents canoes, weekends only, by the hour for adults 18 years and older and to younger certified canoeists.

GOLF Within an easy drive of downtown Halifax is **Granite Springs Golf Club** (⊠*4441 Prospect Rd.* ☎*902/852–4653*), an 18-hole, par-72, semiprivate course open to green-fee play. **Glen Arbour** (⊠ *40 Clubhouse Lane, Hammonds Plains* ☎*902/835–4944*) has two courses (18 holes and 9 holes) in this residential/golf community that are open to transient players after 10 AM during the week and after 11 AM on the weekends—but if you book four days in advance, you can start earlier. Green fees vary with the months of the summer.

HOCKEY The **Halifax Mooseheads** (⊠*Halifax Metro Centre, 1800 Argyle St.* ☎*902/496–5993 information, 902/421–8000 Metro Centre, 902/451–1221 tickets*), a Junior A-division hockey team, play September through March.

☾ **Hatfield Farms Adventures** (⊠*1840 Hammonds Plains Rd.* ☎*902/835–5676 or 877/835–5676*) has a wide range of riding experiences for all levels, including overnight camping, trail rides, a petting pen, and pony rides.

SEA KAYAKING   **Coastal Adventures Sea Kayaking** (☎877/404–2774) has a wide range of ocean tours for the beginner or experienced kayaker from spring through autumn, weather permitting.

SHOPPING
There's no shortage of places to shop for local art and presents to take home.

The **Art Gallery of Nova Scotia Shop** (✉*1741 Hollis St.* ☎*902/424–7542*) carries a good selection of arts and crafts; it also has a wonderful café decorated with colorful regional art. **Attica** (✉*1566 Barrington St.* ☎*902/423–2557*) sells furniture, objets d'art, and housewares by Canadian and international designers. You can find fine crafts in the stores within the large **Barrington Inn Complex** (✉*1875 Barrington St.*).

The **Great Northern Knitters** (✉*1781 Lower Water St.* ☎*902/422–9209*) sells wool and cotton sweaters, plus souvenir caps and sweatshirts and a wide range of knitted items, all at reasonable prices. In addition to being a deli and bakery with great takeout, the **Italian Gourmet** (✉*5431 Doyle St.* ☎*902/423–7880*) stocks a selection of imported gift items, including ceramics, exotic foodstuffs, and cooking gadgets.

At **Nova Scotian Crystal Ltd.** (✉*George and Lower Water Sts.* ☎*902/492–0416*) is the place to watch Waterford master craftspeople blowing glass into graceful decanters and bowls, which can be purchased in the showroom. **Pete's Frootique** (✉*1515 Dresden Row*) is the brainchild of British greengrocer (and Canadian TV personality) Pete Luckett. Stop in at the vast gourmet food–and–produce store for a quick bite in the café or a ready-made gourmet sandwich for a picnic at the nearby Public Gardens. **Park Lane** (✉*5657 Spring Garden Rd.*) is a stylish indoor mall with everything from handcrafted clothing to Canadian books and bath salts. The **Plaid Place** (✉*1903 Barrington St.* ☎*902/429–6872 or 800/563–1749*) has an array of tartans and Highland accessories.

Spring Garden Road is the liveliest shopping street in town. On it you'll find **Mills** (✉*5486 Spring Garden Rd.* ☎*902/429–6111*), an upscale mini-department store with three floors of fashions, accessories, perfumes, cosmetics, and gifts. Busking musicians serenade shoppers flowing in and out of the mall at **Spring Garden Place** (✉*5640 Spring Garden Rd.*). **Jennifer's of Nova Scotia** (✉*5635 Spring Garden Rd.* ☎*902/425–3119*) sells traditional crafts from around the province, soaps, hooked mats, tartan clothing, ceramics, and pewter.

☺ **Woozles** (✉*1533 Birmingham St.* ☎*902/423–7226* ⊕*www.woozles.com*) is a lovely alternative to chain book and toy stores. Packed with books—many of them Canadian and local authors—the store somehow manages to shoe-horn a slew of popular kids' toys in as well as the books.

DARTMOUTH

Immediately north of Halifax via the A. Murray Mackay and Angus L. Macdonald bridges.

The 23 lakes within Dartmouth's boundaries, which have given Dartmouth the moniker "City of Lakes," provided the Mi'Kmaqs, the original people of Nova Scotia, with a canoe route to the province's interior and to the Bay of Fundy. A 19th-century canal system connected the lakes for a brief time, but today there are only ruins, which have been partially restored as historic sites. You can drive, or take the ferry from Halifax to Dartmouth—the two cities are closely connected, and only about a 20-minute ferry ride away. If you walk along the water behind the modern Law Courts in Halifax, near the Historic Properties, you soon reach the Dartmouth ferry terminal, jammed with commuters during rush hour. The terminal is home to the oldest operational saltwater ferry service in North America, which began in 1732. If you do take the ferry (its $2 fare is the cheapest Halifax Harbor cruise and it's only about a 20–minute ride), be sure to check out the sculptures by artist Dawn McNutt in the courtyard just outside the Dartmouth terminal. You may also want to head straight up the hill, along Pleasant Street, to explore funky secondhand stores, pawnbrokers, and antiques and curio shops.

If you'd rather walk to Dartmouth, try the Angus L. Macdonald Bridge, which has a walkway and a bicycle path—the bridge is 2 km (1 mi) long, so estimate a 20-minute walk from stem to stern. After you come off the bridge, keep right until you can follow the wooden boardwalk for a stroll along the water. Eventually you arrive at the Dartmouth ferry terminal, where you can return to downtown Halifax or continue along the boardwalk to see remnants of the Shubenacadie Canal.

The **Black Cultural Centre for Nova Scotia,** in Westphal (a neighborhood of Dartmouth), is in the heart of the oldest black community in the area. The museum, library, and educational complex are dedicated to the preservation of the history and culture of blacks in Nova Scotia, who first arrived here in the 1600s. The center holds an annual celebration of black culture, music, and food in October. ⊠ *Hwy. 7 and Cherrybrook Rd.* ☎ *902/434–6223* ⊠*$5* ⊙*June–Sept., weekdays 9–5, Sat. 10–5.*

WHERE TO STAY & EAT

$$–$$$ ✕ **La Perla.** The rich food at this northern Italian restaurant overlooking the harbor is consistently excellent, and there's a fine wine cellar. Servings are hearty. Calamari tossed with chilies and tomato has never been so tender; snails swim in a heady Gorgonzola cream sauce. For dessert, try the homemade ice cream or sorbettis. Each of the three dining rooms has a distinctive character. ⊠ *73 Alderney Dr.* ☎ *902/469–3241* ⊕ *www.laperla.ca* ⊟ *AE, MC, V.*

$–$$$$ ▦ **Sterns Mansion B&B.** This beautifully restored, century-old home is on a quiet residential street within walking distance of the Dartmouth ferry terminal. The tastefully decorated house has antique furnishings and hardwood floors. Several rooms have whirlpool tubs and gas fireplaces. Honeymoon packages—complete with breakfast in bed—are a specialty. ✉*17 Tulip St., B3A 2S5* ☎*902/465–7414 or 800/565–3885* 🖷*902/466–2152* ⊕*www.sterns-mansion.com* ⇆*4 rooms, 1 suite* ⚒*In-room: VCR, Wi-Fi. In-hotel: no elevator* ⊟*AE, MC, V* ⍾❘*BP.*

$–$$$ 🏨 **Park Place Ramada Renaissance.** In Dartmouth's Burnside Industrial Park, this luxury hotel caters to business travelers and families. There is a 108-foot indoor waterslide. ✉*240 Brownlow Ave., B3B 1X6* ☎*902/468–8888, 800/561–3733 in Canada* 🖷*902/468–8765* ⊕*www.ramadans.com* ⇆*178 rooms, 30 suites* ⚒*In-hotel: restaurant, room service, bar, pool, gym, parking (no fee), Wi-Fi* ⊟*AE, DC, MC, V.*

> ## THE ACADIANS
>
> The Acadians are the descendents of the French colonists who settled in this area in the 1600s. In 1755, after residing for a century and a half in Nova Scotia, chiefly in the Annapolis Valley, the Acadians were expelled by the British—an event that inspired Henry Wadsworth Longfellow's famous poem *Evangeline*. Some eluded capture and others slowly crept back; many settled in New Brunswick and along this shore of Nova Scotia.

THE ARTS

The **Alderney Theatre** (✉*2 Ochterloney St., Dartmouth* ☎*902/461–4698* ⊕*www.alderneylanding.com*) is home to the Eastern Front Theatre Company, which produces, presents, and hosts professional Canadian theater.

SPORTS

ROCK CLIMBING   **Ground Zero Climbing Gym** (✉*105 Akerley Blvd., Dartmouth* ☎*902/468–8788*) has challenging indoor-climbing equipment and supervision.

SOUTH SHORE & ANNAPOLIS VALLEY

The South Shore is on the Atlantic side of the narrow Nova Scotia peninsula, the Annapolis Valley is on the Bay of Fundy side, and although they're less than an hour apart by car, the two seem like different worlds. The South Shore is rocky coast, island-dotted bays, fishing villages, and shipyards; the Annapolis Valley is lumberyards, farms, vineyards, and orchards. The South Shore is German, French, and Yankee; the valley, British. The sea is everywhere on the South Shore; in the valley the sea is blocked from view by a ridge of mountains.

Highway 103, Highway 3, and various secondary roads form the province's designated Lighthouse Route, which leads southwest from Halifax down the South Shore. It ends in Yarmouth, where the Evangeline Trail begins, winding along the shore of St. Mary's Bay through a succession of Acadian villages collectively known as the French Shore. The villages blend into one another for about 32 km (20 mi), each one, it seems, with its own wharf, fish plant, and Catholic church.

The Annapolis Valley runs northeast, sheltered on both sides by the North and South mountains. Occasional roads over the South Mountain lead to the South Shore; short roads over the North Mountain lead to the Fundy shore. Like the South Shore, the valley is punctuated with pleasant small towns, each with a generous supply of extravagant Victorian homes and churches. The rich soil of the valley bottom supports dairy herds, hay, grain, root vegetables, tobacco, and fruit. Apple-blossom season (late May and early June) and the fall harvest are the loveliest times to visit.

PEGGY'S COVE

48 km (30 mi) southwest of Halifax.

Peggy's Cove, on Highway 333, marks the entrance to St. Margaret's Bay, which has been guarded for years by its famous octagonal lighthouse. The cove, with its houses huddled around the narrow slit in the boulders, is probably the most photographed village in Canada. Don't be tempted to venture too close to the lighthouse—many an unwary visitor has been swept away by the mighty surf that sometimes breaks here. You can drive almost to its base, but you'd do better to park in the spacious public lot below it and enjoy the village's shops and services during the three-minute walk up to the lighthouse.

A simple granite **memorial** (⊠ *Hwy. 333*) for 1998 Swissair Flight 111, which crashed into the waters off Peggy's Cove, commemorates "those who helped and those who died"—the 229 casualties and the courageous Nova Scotia fisherfolk for their recovery work and the unstinting comfort they offered to grieving families. Another memorial stands in the town of Blandford directly across the cove.

WHERE TO STAY & EAT

$$–$$$$ ✕**Candleriggs Dining Room.** Maritime fare—like seafood chowder or the lobster platter—abounds at this restaurant with its own gift shop. ⊠ *8545 Peggy's Cove Rd., 3 km (2 mi) west of Peggy's Cove, Indian Harbour* ☎ *902/823–2722* ═ *AE, MC, V* ⊘ *Closed Dec.–Apr. and Mon. and Tues. May, June, and Sept.–Nov.*

$–$$$ ✕**Sou'wester Restaurant.** Sou'wester, at the base of the Peggy's Cove lighthouse, serves home-style fare, including a wide range of Maritime specialties—try the *Solomon Gundy* (herring and onion with sour cream)—and fish-and-chips. There's also a large souvenir shop. ⊠ *178 Peggy's Point Rd., off Hwy. 333* ☎ *902/823–2561* ═ *AE, DC, MC, V.*

$–$$$ 🏠**Havenside B&B.** At this luxurious home, multilevel decks overlook a
★   delightful seascape near Peggy's Cove. Saltwater swimming, a serene gathering room with fireplace and library, a games room with a pool table, and a "breakfast that makes lunch redundant"—fresh homemade muffins, pancakes, French toast, eggs—enhance the package. ⊠ *225 Boutillier's Cove Rd., Hackett's Cove B3Z 3J6* ☎ *902/823–9322 or 800/641–8272* 🖷 *902/823–9322* ⊕ *www.havenside.com* ➴ *3 rooms, 1 suite* ⚲ *In-room: no a/c, no phone, no TV, Wi-Fi. In-hotel: no-smoking rooms, no elevator* ═ *MC, V* ¶⊘ *BP.*

SHOPPING

Beales' Bailiwick (⊠ *124 Peggy's Point Rd.* ☎ *902/823–2099*) carries outstanding crafts—Maritime-designed clothing, pewter, jewelry, and more. The adjoining coffee shop affords the best photo opportunity for

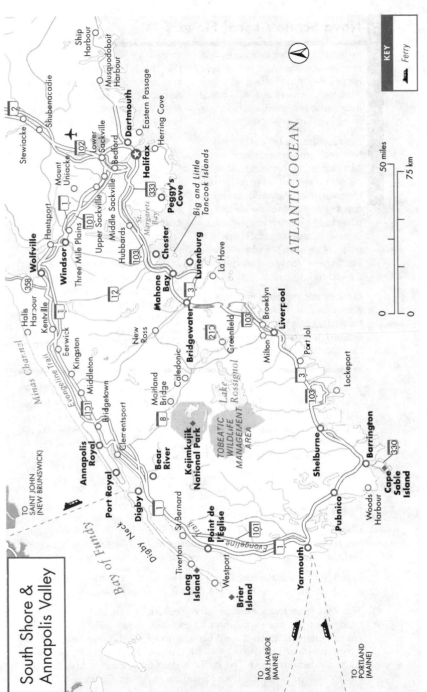

South Shore & Annapolis Valley

KEY

⛴ Ferry

ATLANTIC OCEAN

0 — 50 miles

0 — 75 km

TO SAINT JOHN (NEW BRUNSWICK)

TO BAR HARBOR (MAINE)

TO PORTLAND (MAINE)

Bay of Fundy

Minas Channel

Digby Neck

Ship Harbour
Musquodoboit Harbour
Shubenacadie
Stewiacke
Mount Uniacke
Lower Sackville
Bedford
Dartmouth
Eastern Passage
Herring Cove
Halifax
Peggy's Cove
Hantsport
Upper Sackville
Middle Sackville
Three Mile Plains
Hubbards
St. Margarets Bay
Chester
Mahone Bay
Lunenburg
Big and Little Tancook Islands
La Have
Wolfville
Windsor
Halls Harbour
Kentville
Berwick
Kingston
Middleton
New Ross
Bridgewater
Greenfield
Brooklyn
Liverpool
Port Jol
Milton
Lake Rossignol
TOBEATIC WILDLIFE MANAGEMENT AREA
Maitland Bridge
Caledonic
Lockeport
Bridgetown
Clarentsport
Keijimkujik National Park
Bear River
Annapolis Royal
Port Royal
Digby
St. Bernard
Shelburne
Barrington
Cape Sable Island
Woods Harbour
Pubnico
Tiverton
Westport
Point de l'Eglise
Long Island
Brier Island
Yarmouth

Evangeline Trail

2
102
101
1
358
12
103
333
3
210
101
8
330
103
3

Nova Scotia's Local Flavors

Nova Scotia's verdant landscapes and churning seas are a feast for the eyes. Happily, they also provide a feast for the table, with an extraordinary mix of fresh seafood and beef, and mouthwatering fruits and vegetables.

Nova Scotians will tell you that the best meals are often created in their own kitchens, recipes made with local ingredients and handed down through the generations. Many of those dishes now sit side by side at the dinner tables of all Nova Scotians, regardless of family lineage or cultural background. It's easy to see why a Nova Scotian party starts—and finishes—in the kitchen.

At restaurants, especially in Halifax, many local chefs have gone back to the future, fusing traditional ingredients and dishes with modern flair into inventive, delicious Canadian cuisine.

To wash it down, try a beer (or two) from the growing number of micro-breweries around the province. With names such as Propeller, Garrison, Keltic, and Rudder's, they draw on the history of the province and produce distinctive, tasty ale, lager, stout, and more. Local wines are growing in popularity and reputation as well. Try Jost from Malagash, Sainte Famille Winery from Falmouth, and Domaine de Grand Pré near Wolfville.

And what better way to cap a Nova Scotian feast than with a dram of the acclaimed Glen Breton, the only single-malt whiskey made in North America. (Nova Scotia may mean "New Scotland," but you still can't call it "Scotch" unless it's actually produced in Scotland.) In Gaelic, they call single malt *Uisge beatha* ("the water of life"). A dram of Glen Breton and you'll know why.

Peggy's Cove and the lighthouse, and the renovated red schoolhouse next door is a venue for summertime theater and concerts. **Train Station Gift Shop** (✉ *5401 St. Margaret's Bay Rd., head of St. Margaret's Bay, Upper Tantallon* ☎ *902/826–7532*), in a 1900 train station, is just the ticket for a selection of Maritime arts, Nova Scotia books and tartan, and heritage lace. The caboose is home to an array of children's toys.

CHESTER

64 km (40 mi) west of Peggy's Cove.

Chester, a charming little town on Mahone Bay, is a popular summer retreat for an established population of well-heeled Americans and Haligonians whose splendid homes and yachts rim the waterfront.

In fact, yachting is the town's principal summer occupation, culminating each August in **Chester Race Week,** Atlantic Canada's largest regatta.

The **Ross Farm Living Museum of Agriculture,** a restored 19th-century farm, illustrates the evolution of agriculture from 1600 to 1925. The animals here are those found on a farm of the 1800s—draft horses, oxen, and older breeds or types of animals. Blacksmithing and other crafts are demonstrated. The Pedlar's Shop sells items made in the community. ✉ *Hwy. 12, 29 km (18 mi) inland from Chester, New Ross*

☎*902/689–2210 or 877/689–2210* 🖅*$6* ⊙*May–Oct., daily 9:30–5:30; Nov.–Apr., Wed.–Sun. 9:30–4:30, hrs vary; call ahead.*

The scenic **Big and Little Tancook islands,** 8 km (5 mi) out in Mahone Bay, have a year-round **passenger-only ferry** (☎*902/275–3221*) that runs from the dock in Chester. Reflecting its part-German heritage, Big Tancook claims to make the best sauerkraut in Nova Scotia. Exploration of the island is made easy by walking trails. The boat runs four times daily Monday through Thursday, six times on Friday, and twice daily on weekends. The 45-minute ride costs $5 (round-trip).

WHERE TO STAY & EAT

¢–$ ✕**Fo'c'sle Tavern.** This rustic midtown pub has nautical touches, including a deliciously ugly ship's figurehead, maps, displays of seamen's knots, and a ship's wheel. The mood is jolly, the food is abundant and affordable, and the potbellied woodstove exudes warmth and goodwill on chilly nights. The hearty pub fare includes hefty servings of fish-and-chips, seafood chowders, and steaks, as well as a weekend breakfast buffet. ✉*42 Queen St.* ☎*902/275–1408* ▤*V.*

¢–$

Fodor'sChoice

★

✕**Julien's Pastry Shop & Bakery.** Grab a few delectable goodies to go along with the deluxe sandwiches from this fabulous French bakery and then take a picnic along Chester's scenic waterfront. Julien's is open from 8 AM to 5 PM. ✉*43 Queen St.* ☎*902/275–2324* ▤*MC, V* ⊙*Closed Mon. mid-Sept.–mid-June.*

$–$$$ ✕▣**Dauphinee Inn.** On the shore of Hubbards Cove, this charming country inn has first class accommodations and an excellent restaurant ($$–$$$), the Hot Rocks: it's a social-dining concept where you are invited to cook fresh vegetables, seafood, beef, or chicken on a hot slab of granite. Opportunities abound for bicycling, bird-watching, and deep-sea fishing, and six golf courses are within a half-hour drive. The spacious rooms have antique beds with old-fashioned quilts and newer touches such as whirlpool tubs and CD players. ✉*167 Shore Club Rd., Box 640, Exit 6 off Hwy. 103, 19 km (12 mi) east of Chester, Hubbards Cove B0J 1T0* ☎*902/857–1790 or 800/567–1790* 🖷*902/857–9555* ⊕*www.dauphineeinn.com* ⇝*6 rooms* ⚲*In-room: no a/c, no phone, Wi-Fi. In-hotel: restaurant, bar, no-smoking rooms, no elevator* ▤*AE, D, DC, MC, V* ⊙*Closed Nov.–Apr.* ⦵*BP.*

SHOPPING

Fiasco (✉*54 Queen St.* ☎*902/275–2173*) is an eclectic shop with everything from clothing and baby gear to ships' models and hooked rugs by local artisans. The earthenware pottery at **Jim Smith Fine Studio Pottery** (✉*Duke St.* ☎*902/275–3272*) is as cheerful as its bright yellow-and-green building on Chester's front harbor. **Warp & Woof** (✉*81 Water St.* ☎*902/275–4795*) is the place for locally made hooked rugs, children's sweaters, pewter ware, beach-inspired giftware, and kitchen items.

MAHONE BAY

24 km (15 mi) west of Chester.

This quiet town perched on the idyllic bay of the same name comes alive each summer, and many of Nova Scotia's finest artists and artisans are represented in the studios and galleries that line the narrow streets. Three impressive churches stand shoulder to shoulder near the waterfront, their bells vying for attention each Sunday morning. There are wonderful opportunities for sailing, kayaking, and walking.

In July the annual **Wooden Boat Festival** celebrates the town's heritage as a shipbuilding center.In October the hay-stuffed and pumpkin-laden street-side and storefront displays brighten up the **Scarecrow Festival.**

WHERE TO STAY & EAT

$–$$ ✕**Innlet Café.** This pleasant restaurant has a fine view of the town across the bay. The broad Canadian-style menu has poultry and meats, an understandable emphasis on chowders and seafood, and a few vegetarian options. The Heavenly Chicken has been a delicious mainstay at the café for years. ⊠*249 Edgewater St.* ☎*902/624–6363* ⊟*MC, V.*

¢–$ ✕**Mug & Anchor Pub.** Take in a view of the bay from inside this old British-style alehouse, or enjoy waterside dining on the deck. There is basic pub fare, such as fish-and-chips and hamburgers, but you can also get Lunenburg County favorites like fish cakes and beans. Lunenburg scallops are a specialty, as is the Mug & Anchor meat pie. In summer the pub swells with the sounds of live jazz, blues, and folk music every other Saturday night. ⊠*643 Main St.* ☎*902/624–6378* ⊟*AE, D, MC, V.*

$–$$ 🏠**Countryside B&B.** Lessons in alpaca etiquette are part of the service at this waterfront farm with a private dock—alpaca roam the meadows and barns. Inside, antiques and original art share space with naval memorabilia. A sumptuous candle-lit breakfast might include homemade treats such as wild-blueberry crepes or baked French toast. ⊠*28 Silver Point Rd.–R.R. 2, B0J 2E0* ☎*902/627–1112* ⊕*www. countrysidebb.com* 🛏*3 rooms* ♿*In-room: VCR. In-hotel: no elevator* ⊟*MC, V* ⍾*BP.*

$ 🏠**Amber Rose Inn.** All the creature comforts plus expert knowledge of this historic area are available at this 1875 inn. Each of the large suites has a whirlpool tub and handsome antiques. It's not unusual to hear your bilingual hosts chatting in Spanish around the table in the morning, where the lavish breakfast might include Sky-High Pie (spinach and cheese) or strata (asparagus and egg). ⊠*319 Main St., Box 450, B0J 2E0* ☎*902/624–1060* 🖷*902/624–0997* ⊕*www.amberroseinn. com* 🛏*3 suites* ♿*In-room: refrigerator. In-hotel: parking (no fee), no-smoking rooms, no elevator* ⊟*AE, MC, V* ⍾*BP.*

SHOPPING

Amos Pewter (⊠*589 Main St.* ☎*902/624–9547 or 800/565–3369*) has been using traditional methods to make pewter since 1974 and a studio in an 1888 seaside building offers interpretive displays and demonstrations. Jewelry, sculptures, ornaments, and sand dollars are among the items available, along with a new original-design Christmas ornament each year. **Candy Cravings** (✉*662 Main St.* ☎*902/624–0333*), with it's brightly colored porch and shingles, is a can't-miss building on Mahone Bay's main thoroughfare. Sugar-free diabetic products can be found here, along with 72 kinds of bulk candies and nostalgia eats.

★ The work of fine Atlantic Canada artists and artisans is for sale at **Moorings Gallery & Shop** (✉*575 Main St.* ☎*902/624–6208*). **Suttles and Seawinds** (✉*466 Main St.* ☎*902/624–6177*) has a worldwide reputation for their distinctively designed, high-quality quilts. An adjacent carriage house is a gallery for stunning quilts and fabrics.

LUNENBURG

9 km (6 mi) south of Mahone Bay.

A feast of Victorian-era architecture, wooden boats, steel draggers (a fishing boat that operates a trawl), historic inns, and good restaurants, Lunenburg delights all the senses. The center of town, known as Old Town, is a UNESCO World Heritage Site, and the fantastic old school on the hilltop is the region's finest remaining example of Second Empire architecture, an ornate style that began in 19th-century France.

In August, the annual **Folk Art Festival** draws gawkers and shoppers alike to view the equally vibrant and wacky folk art that put Nova Scotia on the artistic map.

★ Lunenburg is home port to the *Bluenose II* (☎*866/579–4909* ⊕*www. schoonerbluenose2.ca*), a tall-ship ambassador for Canada sailing out of Lunenburg, Halifax, and other ports. She's a replica of the first *Bluenose*, the great racing schooner depicted on the back of the Canadian dime that was the winner of four international races and the pride of Canada. When in port, the *Bluenose II* is open for tours through the Fisheries Museum of the Atlantic. Two-hour harbor sailings in summer cost $35.

☾ The **Fisheries Museum of the Atlantic,** on the Lunenburg waterfront, gives
Fodor's Choice a comprehensive overview of Nova Scotia fisheries with demonstra-
★ tions such as sail making, dory building, boat launching, and fish splitting. A touch tank with starfish, shellfish, and anemones; participatory demonstrations of rug hooking and quilting; and a daylong schedule of films at the theater make visiting here a busy but rich experience. Add to that the *Bluenose* exhibit, celebrating the tall ship that won acclaim for Canada, plus a gift shop and seafood restaurant, and your day is full. ✉*68 Bluenose Dr.* ☎*902/634–4794* ⊕*museum.gov.ns.ca/ fma* ▦*$9 May–Oct., free Nov.–Apr.* ⊙*July and Aug., 9:30–7; May, June, Sept., and Oct., daily 9:30–5:30; Nov.–Apr., weekdays 9–4 or by appointment.*

WHERE TO STAY & EAT

$–$$$ ✕**Grand Banker Seafood Bar & Grill.** A wide variety of seafood at modest prices is the mainstay at this bustling, big-menu establishment. You can dine on scallops, shrimp, or lobster in season, or, for those with hearty appetites, the seafood platter with a combination. ⊠*82 Montague St.* ☎*902/634–3300* ⊟*AE, D, DC, MC, V.*

$–$$$ ✕**Old Fish Factory Restaurant.** In the Fisheries Museum of the Atlantic, the Old Fish Factory overlooks Lunenburg Harbour. It specializes in seafood (try the excellent tortilla lobster pizza with Thai sauce—it's not as rich as it sounds), but you can also get steak and other dishes. ⊠*68 Bluenose Dr.* ☎*902/634–3333 or 800/533–9336* ⊟*AE, D, DC, MC, V* ⊗*Closed Nov.–early May.*

$–$$ ✕**Magnolia's Grill.** This happening, kitschy 1950s diner is as famous for
★ its key lime pie as for its creole peanut soup. Full of vintage collectibles, the popular and always-packed grill also serves local fare such as cod cheeks and pulled pork. ⊠*128 Montague St.* ☎*902/634–3287* ⊟*AE, MC, V* ⊗*Closed Dec. and Jan.*

$$ ⊡**Lunenburg Inn.** JFK's father, Joseph Kennedy, patronized this hostelry long before it became the gracious inn it is today: In those days it had 13 cell-size rooms sharing a single bathroom. Today, the two suites and five rooms with private baths are spacious and furnished with fine antiques. An elegant main-floor parlor filled with books adjoins the bright blue-and-white dining room; a computer with wireless Internet access in the sitting room adds a modern touch. Visitors receive the benefits of the owners' health-conscious baking, especially in the afternoon refreshments. The top-floor 775-square-foot suite has a tiny kitchenette. ⊠*26 Dufferin St., B0J 2C0* ☎*902/634–3963 or 800/565–3963* 🖷*902/634–9419* ⊕*www.lunenburginn.com* ⇆*5 rooms, 2 suites* ⅃*In-room: no a/c (some), kitchenette (some), VCRs and DVDs (some). In-hotel: no-smoking rooms, public Internet, no elevator* ⊟*DC, MC, V* ⦿*BP.*

$–$$ ⊡**Arbor View Inn.** Leaded and stained-glass windows, extravagant wood trim, and handsome antiques enhance every room of this grand, early-20th-century house and spacious grounds invite strolls. The top-floor suite has a queen-size canopy bed, a two-person whirlpool tub, and a deck. ⊠*216 Dufferin St., B0J 2C0* ☎*800/890–6650 or 902/634–3658* ⊕*www.arborview.ca* ⇆*2 rooms, 2 suites* ⅃*In-room: no a/c, no phone, no TV. In-hotel: no-smoking rooms, no elevator* ⊟*MC, V* ⦿*BP.*

$ ⊡**1826 Maple Bird House B&B.** Just steps from the Fisheries Museum and Lunenburg's fascinating waterfront, this B&B has a huge garden overlooking the harbor and a golf course. The piano in the drawing room sets the relaxing mood that characterizes this home and the hosts know a thing or two about breakfast—crepes, omelets, cereals, and fruits appear in ample amounts. ⊠*36 Pelham St., Box 278, B0J 2C0* ☎*902/634–3863 or 888/395–3863* ⊕*www.maplebirdhouse.ca* ⇆*4 rooms* ⅃*In-room: no a/c, no phone, no TV. In-hotel: pool, no-smoking rooms, no elevator* ⊟*MC, V* ⦿*BP.*

$ ⊡**Pelham House Bed & Breakfast.** Close to downtown, this sea captain's home, circa 1906 and decorated in the style of the era, has a friendly golden retriever and three cats who greet guests and then return to their own quarters next door. The veranda overlooks the harbor. The large, airy rooms are outfitted in a homey, country fashion, with lots of wicker, quilts, and pine furniture gracing the original wood floors.

✉*224 Pelham St., Box 358, B0J 2C0* ☎*902/634–7113 or 800/508–0446* 🖷*902/634–7114* ⊕*www.pelhamhouse.ca* ⤸*4 rooms* &*In-room: no a/c, no phone, no TV. In-hotel: laundry facilities, no-smoking rooms, no elevator* ⊟*AE, MC, V* ⎡◯⎤*BP.*

SPORTS & THE OUTDOORS

June through October **Lunenburg Whale-Watching** (☎*902/527–7175*) has three-hour trips daily at 8:30, 11:30, 2:30, and 5:30, seven days a week, from the Fisheries Museum Wharf for $45. You can also arrange for bird-watching excursions and tours of Lunenburg Harbour.

SHOPPING

Black Duck Gallery and Gifts (✉*8 Pelham St.* ☎*902/634–3190*) sells handmade kites, local art, books, and an imaginative selection of gifts. The **Houston North Gallery** (✉*110 Montague St.* ☎*902/634–8869*) represents both trained and self-taught Nova Scotian artists as well as Inuit soapstone carvers and printmakers. It's closed in January. The **Lunenburg Forge & Metalworks Gallery** (✉*146 Bluenose Dr.* ☎*902/634–7125*) is a traditional artist-blacksmith shop on the waterfront. One-of-a-kind handcrafted wrought-iron items and custom orders, including time-honored designs and whimsical creations, are available. Colorfully painted metal folk art fills the back courtyard of **Out of Hand** (✉*135 Montague St.* ☎*902/634–3499*), a gift shop and gallery. It's open seven days a week April to December. Right next door is **The Spotted Frog** (✉*125 Montague St.* ☎*902/634–1976*) a folk-art gallery that represents local artists.

BRIDGEWATER

18 km (11 mi) west of Lunenburg.

Known as the "Main Street of the South Shore," Bridgewater is home to the South Shore's biggest mall, as well as banks, a hospital, museums, recreational facilities, and a visitor information center. Straddling the LaHave River, the town has views of the countryside, with ox farms and eagle nesting areas; the ocean, with fishing villages; historic sites (LaHave was the first area settled by the French in 1632); and magnificent sand beaches famous for windsurfing, clam digging, or just relaxing.

The **DesBrisay Museum** explores the history and people of Lunenburg County and has changing exhibits on art, science, technology, and history. The gift shop carries books by local authors, local arts and crafts, and toys. ✉*130 Jubilee Rd.* ☎*902/543–4033* 🎟*$3 mid-May–Sept., free Oct.–mid-May* ◷*Mid-May–Sept., Mon.–Sat., 9–5, Sun., 1–5; Oct.–mid-May, Wed.–Sun. 1–5.*

The **Wile Carding Mill,** a water-powered mill with an overshot wheel, operated from 1860 to 1968. Docents tell the story of Dean Wile's woolen mill. ✉*242 Victoria Rd.* ☎*902/543–8233* 🎟*$3* ◷*June–Sept., Mon.–Sat. 9:30–5:30, Sun. 1–5:30.*

LIVERPOOL

46 km (29 mi) south of Bridgewater.

Nestled on the estuary of the Mersey River, Liverpool was settled around 1760 by New Englanders and is now a fishing and paper-milling town. During the American Revolution and the War of 1812, Liverpool was a privateering center; later, it became an important shipping and trading port.

In a renovated Canadian National railway station, the **Hank Snow Country Music Centre Museum** commemorates the great country singer whose childhood home is nearby. A country-music archive and library, and memorabilia of the singer's career are on view. A new memorabilia gallery highlights new Canadian country-music stars. ✉*148 Bristol Ave., off Hwy. 103* ☎*902/354–4675 or 888/450–5525* 🖃*$3* ⊙*Mid-May–mid-Oct., Mon.–Sat. 9–5, Sun. noon–5.*

The **Sherman Hines Museum of Photography** has vintage photos and cameras and the work of the noted photographer. Changing exhibits in the galleries feature top Canadian photographers, and the research center offers a good collection of photographic books and thousands of photographs. ✉*219 Main St.* ☎*902/354–2667* 🖃*$4* ⊙*Mid-May–June, Sept., and Oct., Mon.–Sat. 10–5:30; July and Aug., Mon.–Sat. 10–5:30, Sun. 12:30–5:30.*

★ **Rossignol Cultural Centre.** This refurbished high school is now home to an eclectic mix of two galleries and five museums, including a trapper's cabin, an early-20th-century drugstore, 50 stuffed-wildlife exhibits, an outhouse museum, and a complete oval wood-paneled drawing room brought over from an English manor house. ✉*205 Church St.* ☎*902/354–3067* ⊕*www.rossignolculturalcentre.com* 🖃*$4* ⊙*Mon.–Sat. 10–5:30; July and Aug., also Sun. noon–5:30.*

Fort Point Lighthouse Park, on the site where explorers Samuel de Champlain and Sieur de Monts landed in 1604, overlooks Liverpool Harbour. Interpretive displays and models in the 1855 lighthouse recall the area's privateering and shipbuilding heritage. Among the special events are Privateer Days, held the first weekend of July, which includes a legal marriage in 1780s style, an encampment of the King's Orange Rangers (a group that reenacts the exploits of a pro-British American Revolution brigade posted to Nova Scotia 1778–83), and opportunities to meet local artisans. ✉*End of Main St. off Hwy. 103* ☎*902/354–5260* 🖃*By donation* ⊙*May, June, Sept., and Oct., daily 10–6; July and Aug., daily 9–7.*

The **Simeon Perkins House,** built in 1766, is the historic home of privateer-turned-leading-citizen Simeon Perkins, who kept a detailed diary about colonial life in Liverpool from 1760 until his death in 1812. Built by ships' carpenters, the house gives the illusion of standing in the upside-down hull of a ship. ✉*105 Main St.* ☎*902/354–4058* 🖃*$2* ⊙*June–mid-Oct., Mon.–Sat. 9:30–5:30, Sun. 1–5:30.*

One of the last untouched tracts of coastline in Atlantic Canada, **Kejimkujik Seaside Adjunct** has isolated coves, broad white beaches, and imposing headlands and is protected by Kejimkujik National Park. A hike along the 6-km (4-mi) trail reveals a pristine coastline that is home to harbor seals, eider ducks, and many other species. To protect nesting areas of the endangered piping plover, parts of the St. Catherine's River beach (the main beach) are closed to the public from late April to early August. ⊠ *Off Hwy. 103, 25 km (16 mi) southwest of Liverpool, Port Joli* ☎ *902/682–2772* ⌧ *$4 May 15–Oct. 14* ⊙ *Daily 24 hrs.*

WHERE TO STAY & EAT

$–$$$ ✗ **Quarterdeck Grill.** The restaurant deck at this Summerville Centre restaurant is directly over the water at high tide, giving spectacular views of surf and sand. The landmark restaurant uses seasonal fresh ingredients and is well known for its steamed lobster and grilled-fish dishes, especially the trio of lobster: tails stuffed with scallops and shrimp. ⊠ *7499 Hwy. 3, 15 km (10 mi) west of Liverpool* ☎ *902/683–2998 or 800/565–1119* ⊟ *AE, DC, MC, V.*

$–$$$ ✗⊞ **Lane's Privateer Inn.** Famed buccaneer Captain Joseph Barss once occupied this 200-year-old inn overlooking the Mersey River, but today it has comfortable guest rooms, a restaurant serving Canadian fare ($–$$$), a pub, a bookstore-café, and a specialty-food shop. Most of the 27 inn rooms have a river or harbor view. Nearby, there's windsurfing, golfing, deep-sea fishing, and five spectacular beaches. Lane's is within walking distance of Liverpool's major attractions and within 15 km (9 mi) of the Kejimkujik Seaside Adjunct. ⊠ *27 Bristol Ave., B0T 1K0* ☎ *902/354–3456 or 800/794–3332* ⊜ *902/354–7220* ⊕ *www.lanesprivateerinn.com* ⌁ *27 with bath* ⌂ *In-room: Wi-Fi. In-hotel: bar, no-smoking rooms, no elevator* ⊟ *AE, MC, V* ⎮⊙⎮ *CP.*

$$–$$$$ ⊞ **Quarterdeck Beachside Villas & Grill.** Built just above the high-water mark, these quality villas make you feel like you're staying on a secluded houseboat. They're cozy—with propane fireplaces—and practical, too: some have full kitchens and rent by the week. The rolling lawns leading down to the water are perfect for badminton, and the beach plays host to volleyball, beach toys, sea kayaking, and body surfing. ⊠ *7499 Hwy. 3, 15 km (10 mi) west of Liverpool,* ☎ *902/683–2998 or 800/565–1119* ⊕ *www.quarterdeck.ns.ca* ⌁ *13 villas, 2 suites, 1 cottage* ⌂ *In-room: fireplaces, kitchens (some), kitchenettes (some), ceiling fans (some), Wi-Fi, DVD. In hotel: no-smoking rooms* ⊟ *AE, DC, MC, V* ⎮⊙⎮.

SPORTS & THE OUTDOORS

The **Mersey River** drains Lake Rossignol, Nova Scotia's largest freshwater lake, and has good trout and salmon fishing.

KEJIMKUJIK NATIONAL PARK

67 km (42 mi) northwest of Liverpool.

The gentle waterways of this 381-square-km (147-square-mi) park have been the canoe routes of the Mi'Kmaq for thousands of years. Today the routes and land trails are well marked and mapped, permitting canoeists, hikers, and campers to explore, swim in the warm lake, and glimpse white-tailed deer, beaver, owls, loons, and other wildlife. Canoes and camping equipment can be rented. Park staffers lead interpretive hikes and canoe trips, or you can explore on your own. In late September and early October, the park's deciduous forests blaze with color. ⊠ *Hwy. 8, between Liverpool and Annapolis Royal, Maitland Bridge* ☎ *902/682–2772* ⊕ *www.pc.gc.ca* ⊠ *$5.50* ☉ *Daily 24 hrs.*

WHERE TO STAY & EAT

¢–$ ✕▥ **Whitman Inn.** Wilderness, education, and luxurious dining are all part of the experience at this friendly inn next to Kejimkujik Park. Nature and canoeing packages are available, and weekend workshops range from quilting, photography, and writing to stress management or wine tasting. Antiques fill the rooms. A two-bedroom apartment has a full kitchen, a living room, and a private entrance. The small restaurant ($–$$) serves interesting full breakfasts and dinners that include seafood, poultry, and a vegetarian option. The chef whips up beautifully creative dishes with fresh herbs and seafood in season—a contrast to the simple pine tables and chairs. ⊠ *12389 Hwy. 8, Kempt B0T 1B0* ☎ *902/682–2226 or 800/830–3855* ☐ *902/682–3171* ⊕ *www. whitmaninn.com* ⋄ *8 rooms, 1 apartment* ⚲ *In-room: no a/c, no TV. In-hotel: restaurant, pool, no elevator* ⊟ *MC, V.*

$$–$$$$ ▥ **White Point Beach Resort.** Activities from kayaking and surfing to bird-
         ☾ ing and walking nature trails make for dynamic holidays at this resort.
         ★ Also on-site is a beachfront grill restaurant with outdoor buffets and barbecues. Choose a cozy room outfitted with pine furniture in one of the lodges or a one- to three-bedroom cottage with a living room and fireplace, along the beach or nestled amid mature trees. A full children's program daily enables parents to take advantage of golf and tennis or even just a private stroll on the beach. ⊠ *Exit 20A off Hwy. 103, White Point B0T 1G0* ☎ *902/354–2711 or 800/565–5068* ☐ *902/354–7278* ⊕ *www.whitepoint.com* ⋄ *77 rooms, 44 cottages* ⚲ *In-room: no a/ c (some), refrigerator. In-hotel: golf course, tennis courts, pool, spa, beachfront, bicycles, no-smoking rooms* ⊟ *AE, MC, V.*

$–$$ ▥ **Mersey River Chalets.** Barbecues, yoga, crafts instruction, swimming
    ★ in the lake, sing-alongs around the bonfire, and outdoor sports such as canoeing and kayaking fill the agenda at this 375-acre wilderness resort. Seven two-bedroom chalets are nestled in dense forest and you can see river and waterfall scenery from the nearly 2-km-long (1-mi-long) boardwalk. For even closer encounters with nature, there are tepees built on platforms on the shore of Lake Harry. ⊠ *Off Hwy. 8, General Delivery, Caledonia B0T 1B0* ☎ *902/682–2443* ☐ *902/682– 2332* ⊕ *www.merseyriverchalets.com* ⋄ *7 chalets, 5 tepees* ⚲ *In-*

room: no a/c, no TV. In-hotel: seasonal restaurant, tennis court, no elevator ⊟*MC, V.*

⚠️**Kejimkujik National Park Campground.** This huge national park in the middle of the province is a haven for canoeists and hikers. Campsites are unserviced. Winter camping is available with pit toilets. In season a canteen in the park has basic groceries, take-out food, and ice cream. There are some extra-large (up to 50 feet) RV sites. Reservations are essential on holiday weekends and recommended from July 1 through September 15. ♿*Flush toilets, pit toilets, showers, fire pits* ⏏*123 tent sites, 233 RV sites, 46 back-country sites* ⌧*Off Rte. 8, 65 km (40 mi) north of Liverpool, Maitland Bridge* ☎*902/682–2772 or 877/737–3783* ⊟*AE, MC, V.*

SPORTS & THE OUTDOORS
Jakes Landing (☎*902/682–5253*), within Kejimkujik Park, rents bicycles, boats, kayaks, and canoes, and the owner, Peter Rogers, is a veteran canoeist who offers summer canoe instruction and some recreational guiding in and around Kejimkujik Park.

SHELBURNE

69 km (43 mi) south of Liverpool.

Shelburne's high noon occurred right after the American Revolution, when 16,000 Loyalists briefly made it one of the largest communities in North America—bigger than either Halifax or Montréal at the time. Today it's a fishing and shipbuilding town at the mouth of the Roseway River.

Tours of some of Shelburne's historic homes are offered during periodic fund-raising endeavors; **Shelburne Visitor Information** (☎*902/875–4547*) has details.

Many of Shelburne's homes date to the late 1700s, including the **Ross-Thomson House,** now a provincial museum. Inside, the only surviving 18th-century store in Nova Scotia contains all the necessities of that period. ⌧*9 Charlotte La.* ☎*902/875–3141* ⌧*$3* ⊙*June–mid-Oct., daily 9:30–5:30; mid-Oct.–May, call ahead for hrs.*

WHERE TO STAY & EAT

$$–$$$
Fodor'sChoice
★

✕**Charlotte Lane Café.** Swiss specialties, along with seafood, meats, pastas, and salads are served in this beautifully restored building, which dates to the mid-1800s. The rack of lamb with port wine–orange sauce and sundried berries is a specialty. The café has a pleasant garden patio and a shop selling local crafts. ⌧*13 Charlotte La.,* ☎*902/875–3314* ⊟*MC, V* ⊙*Closed Sun. and Mon. and mid-Dec.–early May.*

$–$$$
🏨**Cooper's Inn.** One of the last cooperages in North America is also a unique inn on Shelburne's historic waterfront, which was the site of a major Loyalist landing in 1783. Across the street, you can purchase one of the namesake barrels or planters. Inside the elegant 1784 inn are antiques and fine art. ⌧*36 Dock St., B0T 1W0* ☎*902/875–4656 or 800/688–2011* 🖷*902/875–4447* ⊕*www.thecoopersinn.com* ⏏*7 rooms, 1 suite* ♿*In-room: Wi-Fi, no a/c. In-hotel: no elevator, off-street parking (no fee)* ⊟*AE, MC, V* ⊙*Closed Nov.–Mar.* ⧉*BP.*

BARRINGTON

40 km (25 mi) south of Shelburne.

Tiny Barrington has a long history reflected in a clutch of interesting museums.

The **Barrington Woolen Mill Museum** represents a thriving late-19th-century industry in which the mill produced durable wool for fishermen's clothing. Today it has demonstrations of hand spinning and details about sheep raising and wool processing. ⊠*2368 Hwy. 3* ☎*902/637–2185* ✉*$3* ⊘*June–Sept., Mon.–Sat. 9:30–5:30, Sun. 1–5:30.*

The **Old Meeting House Museum** served as a church, town hall, and election center for New England settlers in the late 1700s. It's the oldest nonconformist house of worship in Canada, with a graveyard next door where members of the original Cape Cod families who built it are buried. ⊠*2408 Hwy. 3* ☎*902/637–2185* ✉*$3* ⊘*June–Sept., Mon.–Sat. 9:30–5:30, Sun. 1–5:30.*

The reproduction **Seal Island Lighthouse** is a lighthouse interpretation center that houses the original light and affords a fine view of the coastline. ⊠*Hwy. 3* ☎*902/637–2185* ✉*$3* ⊘*June–Sept., Mon.–Sat. 9:30–5:30, Sun. 1–5:30.*

CAPE SABLE ISLAND

8 km (5 mi) south of Barrington over the causeway.

Nova Scotia's southernmost extremity is the 21-km (13-mi) road that encircles Cape Sable Island, a Yankee community with fine beaches and connected to the mainland by a bridge. On the island, the fishing village of Clark's Harbour sits on an appealing harbor sprinkled with colorful fishing boats. Hawk Point, just beyond the town, has excellent bird-watching and a fine view of the 1861 Cape Sable Island Lighthouse.

The **Archelaus Smith Museum,** named for an early New England settler, recaptures late-1700s life with household items such as quilts, toys, and cradles plus fishing gear and information about shipwrecks and sea captains. ⊠*Hwy. 330* ☎*902/745–3361* ⊕*www.museum.gov. ns.ca/musdir/archelaussmithmuseum.htm* ✉*By donation* ⊘*Mid-June–Sept., Mon.–Sat. 9:30–5:30, Sun. 1:30–5:30.*

PUBNICO

48 km (30 mi) northwest of Barrington.

Pubnico marks the beginning of the Acadian milieu; from here to Digby the communities are mostly French-speaking. No fewer than seven towns bear the name Pubnico: Lower West Pubnico, Middle West Pubnico, and West Pubnico are all on the west shore of Pubnico Harbour; three East Pubnicos are on the eastern shore; and then there's just plain Pubnico, at the top of none other than Pubnico Harbour. These towns were founded by Phillipe Muis D'Entremont, and they once constituted the only barony in French Acadia.

WHERE TO EAT

$–$$ ✗ **Red Cap Restaurant.** This venerable 1946 establishment, which seats 140, overlooks Pubnico Harbour and includes a six-unit motel and a café that serves an acclaimed version of rappie pie. The menu also

> **A LOCAL DELICACY**
>
> Favorite local fare around Pubnico and Digby includes *rappie* pie, made of meat or poultry with potatoes from which much of the starch has been removed. Most restaurants along the shore here serve some variation of it.

lists lobster and other seafood, chowder, and bread pudding. ⊠ *Exit 31 off Rte. 335 S, Middle West Pubnico B0W 2M0* ☎ *902/762–2112* 🖥 *902/762–2887* ⊕ *www.redcapmotel-rest.com* ▭ *AE, MC, V.*

YARMOUTH

41 km (25 mi) north of Pubnico.

Yarmouth has attracted visitors for nearly three centuries, and they're still pouring in, chiefly by car ferry from Bar Harbor, Maine, and cruise ferry from Portland, Maine. In fact, the town's status as a large port city and its proximity to New England accounted for its early prosperity, and its great shipping heritage is reflected in its fine harbor, two marinas, and museums. Handsome Victorian architecture, a pleasantly old-fashioned main street lined with friendly shops, and easy access to the Acadian villages to the north or the Lighthouse Trail to the south make Yarmouth much more than just a ferry dock.

The **Yarmouth County Museum & Archives** has one of the largest collections of ship paintings in Canada; artifacts associated with the *Titanic*; exhibits of household items displayed in period rooms; musical instruments, including rare mechanical pianos and music boxes; and items that richly evoke centuries past. The museum has a preservation wing and an archival research area, where local history and genealogy are documented. Next door is the **Pelton-Fuller House,** summer home of the original Fuller Brush Man; it's maintained and furnished much as the family left it. ⊠ *22 Collins St.* ☎ *902/742–5539* ⊕ *yarmouthcountymuseum.ednet.ns.ca* 🖥 *Museum $3, museum and Pelton-Fuller House $4, archives $5* ☉ *Museum June–mid-Oct., Mon.–Sat. 9–5, Sun. 2–5; mid-Oct.–May, Tues.–Sun. 2–5. Pelton-Fuller House June–mid-Oct., Mon.–Sat. 9–5.*

♻ The **Firefighters Museum of Nova Scotia** recounts Nova Scotia's fire-fighting history through photographs and artifacts, including vintage pumpers, hose wagons, ladder trucks, and an 1863 Amoskeag Steamer. Kids can don a fire helmet and take the wheel of a 1933 Bickle Pumper. ⊠ *451 Main St.* ☎ *902/742–5525* 🖥 *$3* ☉ *June and Sept., Mon.–Sat. 9–5; July and Aug., Mon.–Sat. 9–9, Sun. 10–5; Oct.–May, weekdays 9–4, Sat. 1–4.*

WHERE TO STAY & EAT

$$-$$$ ✗**Chez Bruno Cafe Bistro.** It might be surprising to find a Mediterannean bistro in Yarmouth, but don't be surprised by how good it is. They serve everything from fresh seafood to sandwich wraps to homemade Belgian waffles. ✉*278 Main St.* ☎*902/742–0031* ▭*AE, V* ⊗*Closed Sun.*

¢-$$ ✗**JoAnne's Quick 'n Tasty.** Laminated tables, vinyl banquettes, and bright lights greet you at this venerable, no-nonsense '50s-style diner. Dishes include fresh seafood and standbys like turkey burgers and club sandwiches. Haligonians are known to make the three-hour trek for the famed hot lobster sandwich. Best of all is the rappie pie, with crisply refried potatoes baked with chicken. ✉*Hwy. 1, 4 km (2 mi) northeast of Yarmouth, Dayton* ☎*902/742–6606* ▭*MC, V* ⊗*Closed Dec.–mid-March.*

$$-$$$
★   🏨**Charles C. Richards House Historic Bed & Breakfast.** One of Nova Scotia's most distinctive B&Bs, this grand old Queen Anne–style structure was built as a wealthy industrialist's residence in 1893, using the finest imported materials. It later served time as a Women's Army Corps barracks, the town library, and finally an apartment building. In 1999, it was lovingly restored by energetic young owners and the spacious rooms are well outfitted, with scrupulously polished antiques. A tropical conservatory opens onto a wide veranda and a patio. Breakfast is an elegant affair. ✉*17 Collins St., B5A 3C7* ☎*902/742–0042 or 866/798–0929* 🖷*902/742–0326* ⊕*www.charlesrichardshouse.ns.ca* ➥*3 rooms* ♿*In-room: no a/c. In-hotel: no-smoking rooms, no elevator* ▭*AE, MC, V* ⦿|*BP.*

$-$$ 🏨**Harbour's Edge Bed & Breakfast.** The large rooms in this serene 1864 home with a spectacular view of Yarmouth Harbour, are named for women who lived in the town. Ornate wrought-iron fireplaces dominate the parlor and dining room, which open onto a veranda overlooking the harbor. At high tide the water laps against the lawn; at low tide myriad birds pay frequent visits. Harbour's Edge was reclaimed by new owners after a fire in 1990, and they are landscaping the vast 2-acre garden, with its century-old rhododendrons, quince, laburnum, and Japanese cherry trees. ✉*12 Vancouver St., B5A 2N8* ☎*902/742–2387* ⊕*www.harboursedge.ns.ca* ➥*4 rooms* ♿*In-room: Wi-Fi, no a/c, no phone, no TV. In-hotel: no-smoking rooms, no elevator* ▭*MC, V* ⦿|*BP.*

$ 🏨**Murray Manor Bed & Breakfast.** The distinctive, pointed windows of this handsome 1825 Gothic-style house are reminiscent of a church. Century-old rhododendrons bloom in the garden and decorate the long dining room table, where guests share a hearty breakfast of fresh fruit, eggs, and maple sausages. The ferry terminal is a block away. The rooms share one bathroom. ✉*225 Main St., B5A 1C6* ☎*902/742–9625 or 877/742–9629* ⊕*www.murraymanor.com* ➥*3 rooms without bath* ♿*In-room: Wi-Fi, no a/c, no phone. In-hotel: no-smoking rooms, no elevator* ▭*MC, V* ⦿|*BP.*

SHOPPING

Professional potters Michael and Frances Morris, tired of crafts shows, opened a crafts shop called **At the Sign of the Whale** (✉*543 Hwy. 1, R.R. 1, Dayton* ☎*902/742–8895)* in their home on the outskirts of Yarmouth and the antique furniture forms a handsome backdrop for the work of 150 artisans and craftspeople. Wood, textiles, pewter, clothing, paintings, and the Morrises' own excellent stoneware are for sale.

POINT DE L'ÉGLISE

70 km (43 mi) north of Yarmouth.

Home to the province's only French university and known for its focus on the French language and culture, Point de l'Église (Church Point) also holds the oldest Acadian festival in the Atlantic Province, the **Festival Acadien de Clare,** each year during the second week of July. The municipality is mainly inhabited by Acadians and conducts its business in both official languages, unique in the province.

Université Ste-Anne (✉*1695 Hwy. 1* ☎*888/338–8337*) is the only French-language institution among Nova Scotia's 17 degree-granting colleges and universities. Founded in 1891, this small university off Highway 1 is a focus of Acadian studies and culture in the province. The university offers five-week immersion French courses in summer.

St. Mary's Church, along the main road that runs through Point de l'Église, is the tallest and largest wooden church in North America. Completed in 1905, it's 190 feet long and 185 feet high. The steeple, which requires 40 tons of rock ballast to keep it steady in the ocean winds, can be seen for miles on the approach. Inside the church is a small museum with an excellent collection of vestments, furnishings, and photographs. Tours are given by appointment. ✉*Main Rd.* ☎*902/769–2832* 💲*$2* ⊙*Mid-May–mid-Oct., daily 9–5.*

EN ROUTE

St. Bernard Church, a few miles north of Point de l'Église, marks the end of the French Shore. Because of the magnificent acoustics, internationally acclaimed choirs sometimes perform in the town's impressive granite Gothic church, which seats 1,000. ✉*Rte. 1, St. Bernard* ☎*902/837–5687* 💲*By donation* ⊙*Mid-June–mid-Sept., daily 8–5; mid-Sept.–mid-June, call ahead.*

DIGBY

35 km (22 mi) northeast of Point de l'Église.

Digby is an underappreciated town—people tend to race to or from the ferry connecting the town with Saint John, New Brunswick—but there's quite a bit to the town, including a rich history that dates to the arrival in 1783 of Loyalist refugees from New England; a famous scallop fleet that anchors in colorful profusion at the waterfront; and the plump, sweet scallops that are served everywhere. The waterfront begs for a leisurely stroll to view the Annapolis Basin and the boats; you can buy ultrafresh halibut, cod, scallops, and lobster—some merchants will even cook them up for you on the spot. You can also sample Digby chicks—salty smoked herring—in pubs or buy them from fish markets.

Digby Scallop Days is a four-day festival replete with parades, fireworks, and food in early August.

The **Admiral Digby Museum** relates the history of Digby through interesting collections of furnishings, artifacts, paintings, and maps. ⊠*95 Montague Row* ☎*902/245–6322* ✉*By donation* ⊗*June–Aug., Tues.–Sat., 9–5; Sun. 1–5.*

WHERE TO STAY & EAT

$$–$$$ ✕▦ **Digby Pines Golf Resort and Spa.** Complete with fireplaces, sitting
★   rooms, walking trails, and a view of the Annapolis Basin, this casually elegant property offers myriad comforts. It contains a Norman château–style hotel, 31 cottages, and lavish gardens. Local seafood with a French touch is served daily in the restaurant ($$$–$$$$), and the lounge is perfect for quiet relaxation. A 2,500-square-foot Aveda spa opened in 2005 and its poolside facility is a relaxing spot after a round of golf on the par-71, 18-hole course. ⊠*103 Shore Rd., Box 70, B0V 1A0* ☎*902/245–2511 or 800/667–4637* 🖷*902/245–6133* ⊕*www. digbypines.ca* ⇆*84 rooms, 6 suites, 31 cottages* ♿*In-hotel: restaurant, bar, golf course, tennis courts, pool, gym, no-smoking rooms* ▭*AE, D, DC, MC* ⊗*Closed mid-Oct.–May.*

$ ✕▦ **Coastal Inn Kingfisher.** This traditional strip motel is a handy budget hotel, near all of Digby's attractions. The big highlight, though, is the restaurant: the dining room has one of the widest arrays of scallops in Digby, including Scallops l'Acadie (with tomatoes, brandy, and black olives) and Southern Scallops (with peaches and peach schnapps). Try the creamed scallops on toast for breakfast. ⊠*111 Warwick St., Box 280, B0V 1A0* ☎*902/245–4747 or 800/401–1155* 🖷*902/245–4866* ⊕*www.coastalinns.com* ⇆*36 rooms* ♿*In-hotel: no elevator* ▭*AE, MC, V.*

$–$$ ▦ **Thistle Down Country Inn.** A flower-decorated haven overlooks the Annapolis Basin and Digby's fishing fleet at this 1904 home, furnished with antiques. A newer annex has larger rooms with more modern decor. Try the scallop omelet for breakfast. Fresh local seafood is served at the 6:30 dinner (reservations essential), followed by rich, homemade desserts. ⊠*98 Montague Row, Box 508, B0V 1A0* ☎*902/245–4490 or 800/565–8081* 🖷*902/245–6717* ⊕*www.thistledown.ns.ca* ⇆*12 rooms* ♿*In-room: a/c, DVDs (some), refrigerator (some). In-hotel: no-smoking rooms, public Internet, no elevator* ▭*AE, DC, MC, V* ⊗*Closed Nov.–Apr.* ✵*BP.*

BEAR RIVER

16 km (10 mi) southeast of Digby.

A thriving arts-and-crafts center in summer, and almost a ghost town in winter, Bear River is called the Switzerland of Nova Scotia because of the delightful vista of its deep valley, dissected by a tidal river. Some buildings have been built on stilts to stay above the tides. Crafts shops and coffee shops dot the main street.

The **Riverview Ethnographic Museum** houses a collection of folk costumes and artifacts from around the world. ⊠ *18 Chute Rd.* ☎ *902/467–4321* 🖾 *By donation* ☉ *By appointment.*

ANNAPOLIS ROYAL

29 km (18 mi) northeast of Digby.

Annapolis Royal's history spans nearly four centuries, and the town's pleasant and quiet appearance today belies its turbulent past. One of Canada's oldest settlements, it was founded as Port Royal by the French in 1605, destroyed by the British in 1613, rebuilt by the French as the main town of French Acadia, and fought over for a century. Finally, in 1710, New England colonists claimed the town and renamed it in honor of Queen Anne. There are approximately 150 historic sites and heritage buildings here, including the privately owned 1708 DeGannes-Cosby House, the oldest wooden house in Canada, on St. George Street, the oldest town street in Canada.

A lively **market** with fresh produce, home baking, local artists, and street musicians takes place every Saturday mid-May through mid-October on St. George Street, next to Ye Olde Town Pub.

From late-June through September, the Historical Association of Annapolis Royal offers **walking tours** of the town with charming guides dressed in typical early-18th-century clothing. This is an entertaining way to learn more about the historic significance and cultural heritage of the region. Tours depart from the lighthouse at the center of town at 2 PM every Monday, Wednesday, and Thursday, and cost $7.

★ **Fort Anne National Historic Site,** first fortified in 1629, holds the remains of the fourth fort to be erected here and garrisoned by the British as late as 1854. Earthwork fortifications, an early-18th-century gunpowder magazine, and officers' quarters have been preserved. Four hundred years of history are depicted on the Fort Anne Heritage Tapestry. A $7 guided **candlelight tour of the Garrison Graveyard** is a summer specialty Tuesday through Thursday and Sunday at 9:30 PM (meet in the parking lot at the Fort). ⊠ *323 St. George St.* ☎ *902/532–2397 or 902/532–2321* ⊕ *www.parkscanada.gc.ca* 🖾 *Grounds free, museum $4* ☉ *Mid-May–mid-Oct., daily 9–5:30; mid-Oct.–mid-May, by appointment.*

The **Annapolis Royal Historic Gardens** are 10 acres of magnificent, historically themed gardens, including a Victorian garden and a knot garden, a typical Acadian house with garden, and a 2,000-bush rose collection. ⊠ *441 Upper St. George St.* ☎ *902/532–7018* 🖾 *$8.50* ☉ *Mid-May–June and Sept.–mid-Oct., daily 9–5; July and Aug., daily 8–dusk.*

The **Annapolis Royal Tidal Power Project,** ½ km (¼ mi) from Annapolis Royal, was designed to test the feasibility of generating electricity from tidal energy. This pilot project is the only tidal generating station in North America and one of only three operational sites in the world. The interpretive center explains the process with guided tours. ⊠ *236 Prince Albert Rd., Annapolis River Causeway* ☎ *902/532–5454 or*

902/532–2306 ⌨ *$5* ⊘ *Mid-May–mid-June and Sept.–mid-Oct., daily 10–6; mid-June–Aug., daily 9–8.*

🖑 Apple orchards, green lawns, and beautiful trees of the Annapolis Valley cover **Upper Clements Park,** which has 26 rides and attractions. Brave the Tree Topper Roller Coaster, the highest ride in Atlantic Canada, or take a dip on the 302-foot Fundy Splash Water Slide. For a tamer time, there's also a train ride, old-fashioned carousel, and indoor-outdoor golf. Bring your lunch and eat at one of the picnic tables in the apple orchard. Admission includes entry to the 30-acre wildlife park, just across the street. The sanctuary features local wild animals—bear, moose, reindeer, and cougar among them—some rescued and rehabilitated from injury and released back into the park's natural setting. ⊠ *Exit 22 off Hwy. 101* ☎ *902/532–7557* ⌨ *$7.50* ⊘ *Mid-June–mid-Sept., daily 11–7. Animal park mid-May–mid-Sept., daily 10–7; mid-May–mid-June and mid-Sept.–mid-Oct., Sun. 10–5.*

WHERE TO STAY & EAT

$–$$ ✕ **Charlie's Place.** Fresh local seafood as well as meat and vegetarian fare are prepared in Cantonese style at this pleasant restaurant on the edge of town. ⊠ *38 Prince Albert Rd. (Hwy. 1)* ☎ *902/532–2111* ⊟ *AE, MC, V.*

¢–$$ ✕ **Ye Olde Town Pub.** Down-home lunches and dinners are served at this merry, low-key pub popular with locals who appreciate the good homemade fare, including the always excellent apple crisp. Diners sometimes spill out onto the patio, which is adjacent to a square where markets and music take place in summer. ⊠ *11 Church St.* ☎ *902/532–2244* ⊟ *MC, V.*

¢–$ ✕ **German Bakery and Garden Cafe.** As the name suggests, there are plenty of Germanic influences at this soup and sandwich café, including schnitzel, sauerkraut, and sausages. All are served in a garden that overlooks the Annapolis Royal Historic Gardens. ⊠ *441 St. George St.* ☎ *902/532–1990* ⊟ *MC, V* ⊘ *Closed Oct.–May. No dinner.*

¢–$$ ✕🖾 **Garrison House Inn.** Opened in 1854, when Annapolis Royal was the capital of Nova Scotia, this inn facing Fort Anne and its extensive parkland has been carefully restored with period furniture and Victorian-era touches. It comes complete with a friendly ghost, called Emily, whose playful presence is apparently made known only to women. Three intimate private dining rooms ($$$–$$$$) and a dining deck are the settings for dinners that favor fresh seafood, especially scallops and salmon. Breakfast is included in the room rate during summer. ⊠ *350 St. George St., B0S 1A0* ☎ *902/532–5750* 🖷 *902/532–5501* ⊕ *www. garrisonhouse.ca* ↘ *7 rooms, 1 suite* ♿ *In-hotel: restaurant, no elevator* ⊟ *AE, MC, V* ⊘ *Closed Jan.–Mar.*

$$–$$$ 🖾 **Queen Anne Inn.** This lovely old Victorian mansion is surrounded by a 5-acre garden. Large guest rooms are handsomely decorated with period furniture and Victorian accessories and have extra touches such as hand-

made soaps. The owners pride themselves on their three-course breakfast affair. ✉ *494 Upper St. George St., Box 218, B0S 1A0* ☎ *902/532–7850 or 877/536–0403* 🖷 *902/532–2078* ⊕ *www.queenanneinn.ns.ca* ⤵ *12 rooms* ♿ *In-room: Wi-Fi, CD players, DVDs. In-hotel: restaurant, no-smoking rooms, no elevator* ☰ *MC, V* ⦿ *BP.*

$$
★ 🏨 **The Bailey House.** This relative newcomer to Annapolis Royal (it opened in 2005) does everything right and is the only B&B in town located on the water. The Georgian-style house, dating to 1770, has been immaculately restored. Wood moldings, painted pine floors, and even the oddly shaped front door with its massive wrought-iron hinges are all original and accentuate the historic character and charm of the place. Each room has a fireplace, an en-suite bathroom, elegant period-style furniture, and views of the Annapolis Bay. Afternoon refreshments are included in the room rate, as is a large breakfast that includes freshly made scones or muffins, yogurt, fruit, and hot entrées such as vegetable egg frittata, or baked-apple pancake. ✉ *150 St. George St., B0S 1A0* ☎ *877/532–1285 or 902/532–1285* ⊕ *www.baileyhouse.ca* ⤵ *2 rooms* ☰ *MC, V* ⦿ *BP.*

$–$$
★ 🏨 **Bread and Roses Inn.** Rivalry between a doctor and a dentist gave Annapolis Royal this interesting hostelry. In 1880, the town doctor built a new house and the town dentist, in the spirit of competition, set out to build a better one. Today this Queen Anne–style inn is replete with exquisite architectural details and trim made from mahogany, black walnut, black cherry, and other woods. A traditional fountain is on the front lawn, and the garden invites sitting and strolling. Lavish breakfasts may include homemade scones or muffins, and the popular Three-Cheese Egg, a delectable quiche made with a variety of cheeses. ✉ *82 Victoria St., B0S 1A0* ☎ *902/532–5727 or 888/899–0551* ⊕ *www.breadandroses.ns.ca* ⤵ *9 rooms* ♿ *In-room: no a/c (some), some satellite TV, Wi-Fi. In-hotel: no-smoking rooms, no elevator* ☰ *AE, MC, V* ⦿ *BP.*

$–$$
🏨 **Hillsdale House Inn.** Princes, kings, and prime ministers have all visited this historic 1849 property, which is furnished with antiques and paintings and surrounded by 12 acres of lawns and gardens. The renovated coach house has added two bright and spacious rooms to the original 11 bedrooms. The large breakfast includes homemade breads and jams. ✉ *519 George St., Box 148, B0S 1A0* ☎ *902/532–2345 or 877/839–2821* 🖷 *905/532–2345* ⊕ *www.hillsdalehouseinn.ca* ⤵ *13 rooms* ☰ *MC, V* ⦿ *BP.*

PORT ROYAL

8 km (5 mi) west (downriver) from Annapolis Royal on the opposite bank.

One of the oldest settlements in Canada, Port Royal was Nova Scotia's first capital (for both French and English) until 1749, and the province's first military base.

The **Port Royal National Historic Site** is a reconstruction of a French fur-trading post originally built by Sieur de Monts and Samuel de Champlain in 1605. Here, amid the hardships of the New World, North America's first social club—the Order of Good Cheer—was founded, and Canada's first theatrical presentation was written and produced by Marc Lescarbot. Knowledgeable, costumed guides are on-site and can answer any questions about the original trading post and the men who lived here. ✉ *Hwy. 1 to Granville Ferry, then left 12 km (7 mi) on Port Royal Rd.* ☎ *902/532–2898 or 902/532–5589* ✆ *$3.95* ⊙ *June and July, daily 9–6; May 15–30, Sept.–mid–Oct., daily 9–5:30.*

LONG ISLAND & BRIER ISLAND

Tiverton, Long Island, is a 5-min ferry ride from East Ferry at the end of Digby Neck. Brier Island is an 8-min ferry ride from Freeport, Long Island.

Digby Neck is extended seaward by two narrow islands, Long Island and Brier Island, and because the surrounding waters are rich in plankton, the islands attract a variety of whales, including finbacks, humpbacks, minkes, and right whales, as well as harbor porpoises. Wild orchids and other wildflowers abound, and the islands are also an excellent spot for bird-watching.

Brier Island Ferry (☎ *902/839–2302*) links the islands. Ferries must scuttle sideways to fight the ferocious Fundy tidal streams coursing through the narrow gaps. They operate hourly, at a cost of $5 return for car and passengers.

WHERE TO STAY & EAT

¢–$$ ✕▣ **Brier Island Lodge and Restaurant.** Atop a bluff at Nova Scotia's most westerly point, this rustic lodge commands a panoramic view of the Bay of Fundy. Most rooms have ocean and lighthouse views. Whale- and bird-watching and coastal hiking are the most popular activities here; closer to home there are hens, a flock of sheep, a pig, and some friendly dogs to delight children. Fish chowder, fish cakes, and scallops are dinner specialties in the attractive restaurant ($$), which also serves breakfast and packs box lunches for day-trippers. ✉ *Water St., Brier Island, Westport, B0V 1H0* ☎ *902/839–2300 or 800/662–8355* ✆ *902/839–2006* ⊕ *www.brierisland.com* ⌦ *39 rooms* ⚮ *In-room: no a/c. In-hotel: restaurant, bar, no-smoking rooms* ▭ *AE, DC, MC, V* ⊙ *Closed Nov.–Apr.*

SPORTS & THE OUTDOORS

WHALE   **Brier Island Whale and Seabird Cruises** (☎ *902/839–2995 or 800/656–*
WATCHING   *3660* ⊕ *www.brierislandwhalewatch.com*) offers whale-watching and seabird tours May through October. Onboard researchers and naturalists collect data for international research organizations. The fare is $48, and a portion of the fee is used to fund the research. **Mariner Cruises Whale & Seabird Tours** (☎ *902/839–2346 or 800/239–2189* ⊕ *www. novascotiawhalewatching.ca*) provides whale and seabird tours with an onboard photographer and a naturalist. The 2½- to 5-hour cruises ($48) run from mid-June to mid-October and include a snack.

WOLFVILLE

60 km (37 mi) east of Annapolis Royal.

Settled in the 1760s by New Englanders, Wolfville is a charming college town with stately trees and ornate Victorian homes. Dikes, built by the Acadians in the early 1700s to reclaim fertile land from the unusually high tides, can still be viewed in Wolfville at the harbor and along many of the area's back roads.

Chimney swifts—aerobatic birds that fly in spectacular formation at dusk—are so abundant in the Wolfville area that an interpretive display is devoted to them at the **Robie Tufts Nature Centre** (⊠ *Front St.* ☎ *No phone* ⊕ *www.wolfville.com/centre.htm*).

The **Grand Pré National Historic Site** commemorates the expulsion of the Acadians by the British in 1755. This tragic story is retold in an innovative multimedia presentation featuring holograms and a film at the visitor center. A statue of the eponymous heroine of Longfellow's epic poem, *Evangeline*, stands outside a memorial stone church, which contains Acadian genealogical records. ⊠ *Hwy. 1, 5 km (3 mi) east of Wolfville, Grand Pré* ☎ *902/542–3631* ⊠ *$7.15* ⊗ *May–Oct., daily 9–6.*

Get spectacular views of the Bay of Fundy on the 45-minute tour of 10-acre **Domaine de Grand Pré** vineyard. Tours and tastings are offered three times daily from mid-May through mid-October, or try the wines at the restaurant (Le Caveau), open for lunch and dinner March through December. There is also an on-site shop. ⊠ *11611 Hwy. 1, 3 km (2 mi) east of Wolfville* ☎ *902/542–1753 or 866/479–4637* ⊕ *www.grand-prewines.com* ⊠ *$6* ⊗ *Mar.–Dec., Wed.–Sun. 11–5.*

OFF THE BEATEN PATH

Hall's Harbour. One of the best natural harbors on the upper Bay of Fundy can be reached via Highway 359. Go for a walk on a gravel beach bordered by cliffs, try sea kayaking or wilderness camping, or seek out the intaglio printmaking studio and other artists' studios, open during summer months.

> **WORD OF MOUTH**
>
> Hall's Harbour is where you can see the dramatic tides if there at the right time plus enjoy a lobster dinner outside on a picnic table!
>
> —Tanya

While you're here, be sure to sample the eponymous specialty at **Hall's Harbour Lobster Pound & Restaurant** (⊠ *16 km [10 mi] north of Kentville on Rte. 359* ☎ *902/679–5299* ⊗ *Closed Nov.–Apr.*): you can pick your own lobster or leave it to the friendly staff.

Cape Blomidon. At Greenwich, take Highway 358 to Cape Blomidon via Port Williams and Canning for a spectacular view of the valley and the Bay of Fundy from the 600-foot Lookoff.

WHERE TO EAT

$$–$$$$ ✕ **Tempest.** Authentically prepared ethnic food and world-fusion cuisine
★ fill the lunch and dinner menu at this trendy, upscale restaurant. The
seafood chowder is a perfect example with finnan haddie and chorizo
sausage assuming the roles of the usual haddock and bacon. There's
also a superb Nova Scotia arctic char accompanied by local Tancook
Island sauerkraut. Between courses, there's an intermezzo sorbet, and
if you still have room, the Chocolate Duet provides a smooth ending.
The patio is open when the weather's fine. ⊠ *117 Front St.* ☎ *902/542–*
0588 ☲ *AE, MC, V* ⊘ *No lunch Mon.*

$$–$$$ ✕ **Acton's Grill & Café.** Originally started by restaurateurs from Toronto,
this appealing dining establishment has an interesting and eclectic
menu. Consider Digby scallops in fresh herbed pasta, or Fundy lobster.
⊠ *406 Main St.* ☎ *902/542–7525* ☲ *AE, DC, MC, V.*

$–$$$$ ✕▦ **Blomidon Inn.** Ramble through this inn's 3-acre English country gar-
★ den, with its fish-stocked ponds, roses, cacti, azaleas, and rhododen-
drons, and a terraced vegetable garden that also serves as a restaurant
when the weather is fine. Built by a shipbuilder in 1887, the inn is
filled with teak and mahogany, marble fireplaces, and a painted ceiling
mural. A two-story gift shop is packed with Maritime crafts. Intimate
meals are expertly prepared in the main dining room ($$–$$$$; reservations essential), where fresh Atlantic salmon—grilled, steamed or
plank—is a specialty. It's a family affair at the inn: the owners' sons are
the chef and sommelier. ⊠ *195 Main St., B4P 1C3* ☎ *902/542–2291 or*
800/565–2291 📠 *902/542–7461* ⊕ *www.blomidon.ns.ca* 🛏 *28 rooms*
⚭ *In-hotel: restaurant, tennis court, no elevator* ☲ *MC, V* ⊙ *CP.*

$–$$$ ▦ **Victoria's Historic Inn & Carriage House.** An 8-foot-high stained-glass
★ window imported from Britain more than a century ago sets the deco-
rative mood of this fine Victorian home, and richly carved Nova Sco-
tian furniture adds to the ambience. Rooms are spacious and suites
have double whirlpool tubs. The lavish breakfast celebrates the bounty
of the Annapolis Valley: expect plenty of blueberries and a wide selec-
tion of breakfast staples. ⊠ *600 Main St., B4P 1E8* ☎ *902/542–5744*
or 800/556–5744 ⊕ *www.victoriashistoricinn.com* 🛏 *14 rooms, 2*
suites ⚭ *In-room: VCR, Wi-Fi. In-hotel: no elevator* ☲ *AE, DC, MC,*
V ⊙ *BP.*

$–$$ ▦ **Farmhouse Inn Bed and Breakfast.** This 1860 B&B has cozy accom-
Fodor's Choice modations, most with a two-person whirlpool tub and/or propane fire-
★ place. Afternoon tea is complimentary, as is the pre-breakfast room
service of coffee, tea, and muffins, and breakfast itself. The cheery owners may suggest day trips to nearby Blomidon Provincial Park and Cape
Split for hiking, or to the 600-foot Lookoff, which affords panoramic
views of five counties. Bird-watchers will likely enjoy the maneuvers
of the chimney swifts on summer evenings. ⊠ *9757 Main St., 15 km*
(10 mi) north of Wolfville ☎ *902/582–7900 or 800/928–4346* ⊕ *www.*
farmhouseinn.ns.ca 🛏 *2 rooms, 4 suites* ⚭ *In-room: VCR. In-hotel: no*
elevator ☲ *AE, MC, V* ⊙ *BP.*

NIGHTLIFE & THE ARTS

★ The **Atlantic Theatre Festival** (⊠*504 Main St.* ☎*902/542–4242 or 800/337–6661*) stages classical plays mid-June through September; single tickets are $29.50.

SPORTS & THE OUTDOORS

★ A popular series of **hiking trails** (⊠*25 km [16 mi]) north of Wolfville*) leads from the end of Highway 358 to the dramatic cliffs of Cape Split, a 13-km (8-mi) round-trip.

SHOPPING

Casa Bella Gifts (⊠*464 Main St.* ☎*902/542–4400*) sells giftware, home decor, and jewelry in a pleasant shop on Wolfville's main thoroughfare. The **Weave Shed Crafts** (⊠*360 Main St.* ☎*902/542–5504*) is a cooperative crafts shop selling high-quality work in stained glass, pottery, wood, metal, and textiles, by local artisans.

WINDSOR

25 km (16 mi) southeast of Wolfville.

Windsor claims to be the birthplace of modern hockey—the game was first played here around 1800 by students of King's-Edgehill School, the first independent school in the British Commonwealth, and Canada's oldest private residential school—but the town's history dates further back, to 1703, when it was settled as an Acadian community.

Fort Edward, an assembly point for the Acadian expulsion, is the only remaining colonial blockhouse in Nova Scotia. ⊠*Exit 6 off Hwy. 1; take the 1st left at King St., then another left up street facing fire station* ☎*No phone* ⊕*www.glinx.com/~whhs/ftedward.html* ☜*Free* ☉*Mid-June–early Sept., Tues.–Sat., 10–6.*

The **Windsor Hockey Heritage Centre** takes a fond look at Canada's favorite winter sport with photographs and antique equipment and skates. ⊠*128 Gerrish St.* ☎*902/798–1800* ☜*Free* ☉*Weekdays 9–4, Sat. 10–5, plus early evening hrs in summer.*

☾ The **Mermaid Theatre of Nova Scotia** uses puppets and performers to retell traditional and contemporary children's classics. The troupe performs all over the world, but you can see the props and puppets on display right here. ⊠*132 Gerrish St.* ☎*902/798–5841* ⊕*www.mermaidtheatre.ns.ca* ☜*By donation* ☉*Jan.–Nov., weekdays 9–4:30.*

The **Haliburton House Museum,** a provincial museum on a manicured 25-acre estate, was the home of Judge Thomas Chandler Haliburton (1796–1865), a lawyer, politician, historian, and humorist. His best-known work, *The Clockmaker,* pillories Nova Scotian follies from the viewpoint of a Yankee clock peddler, Sam Slick, whose witty sayings are still commonly used. ⊠*414 Clifton Ave.* ☎*902/798–2915* ☜*$3.25* ☉*June–mid-Oct., Mon.–Sat. 9:30–5:30, Sun. 1–5:30.*

Tours at the family-owned **Sainte Famille Winery** in Falmouth, 5 km (3 mi) west of Windsor, combine ecological history with the intricacies of growing grapes and aging wine. Tasting is done in the gift shop, where bottles are sold at a steal. ✉*Dyke Rd. and Dudley Park La.* ☎*902/798–8311 or 800/565–0993* ⌨*$3.50* ⊘*Apr.–Dec., Mon.–Sat. 9–5, Sun. noon–5; Jan.–Mar., Mon.–Sat. 9–5.*

OFF THE BEATEN PATH

Uniacke Museum Park. This country mansion was built around 1815 for Richard John Uniacke, attorney general and advocate general to the Admiralty court during the War of 1812. Now a provincial museum, the house is preserved in its original condition with authentic furnishings. The spacious lakeside grounds are surrounded by walking trails. ✉ *758 Main Rd., 30 km (19 mi) east of Windsor, off Hwy. 1, Mount Uniacke* ☎ *902/866–2560* ⌨*$3.25* ⊘ *June–mid-Oct., Mon.–Sat. 9:30–5:30, Sun. 11–5:30.*

WHERE TO EAT

$–$$$ ✗**Kingsway Gardens Restaurant.** From the Bavarian decor to the homemade sauerkraut to the Black Forest cheesecake, this establishment declares its owner's German origins. Lunch and dinner specialties include German and Canadian variations on seafood, turkey, and chicken. ✉*Wentworth Rd., Exit 5A off Hwy. 101* ☎*902/798–5075* ⊟*AE, D, DC, MC, V.*

¢–$ ✗**Rose Arbour Café.** True to its name, the Rose Arbour has a flowery,
Fodor'sChoice bright interior, with posy-covered plates, cups, and saucers hung on
★ the walls. Tasty food, a smiling staff, and reasonable prices make this a pleasant find. Try the fish-and-chips or fresh clams in season, and one of their homemade desserts, such as the popular rice pudding or cheesecake. ✉*109 Gerrish St.* ☎*902/798–2322* ⊟*AE, MC, V.*

THE EASTERN SHORE & NORTHERN NOVA SCOTIA

From the rugged coastline of the Atlantic to the formidable tides of the Bay of Fundy and the gentle shores of the Northumberland Strait, the area east and north of Halifax presents remarkable contrasts within a relatively small area. The road toward Cape Breton meanders past fishing villages, forests, and remote cranberry barrens, whereas the Northumberland Strait is bordered by sandy beaches and hiking trails, and is rich with the heritage of its early Scottish settlers. The Bay of Fundy has spectacular scenery—dense forests and steep cliffs that harbor prehistoric fossils and semiprecious stones. The mighty Fundy tides are swift and dangerous but when they recede, you can walk on the bottom of the sea.

There are two excellent driving tours you can follow here. The Sunrise Trail Heritage Tour leads to unusual and historic sights along the Northumberland Strait, from the Tantramar Marsh in Amherst to the Heritage Museum at Antigonish and on to the still-active St. Augustine Monastery. The Fundy Shore Ecotour traces 100 million years of geology, the arrival of Samuel de Champlain, the legends of the Mi'Kmaq,

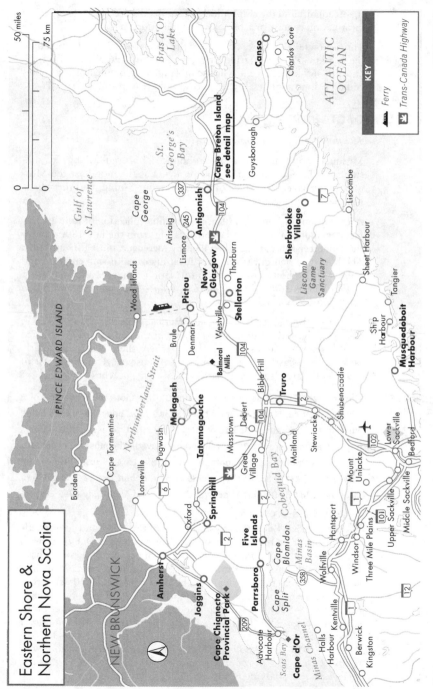

Eastern Shore & Northern Nova Scotia

ATLANTIC OCEAN

Canso

Charlos Core

Guysborough

Cape Breton Island see detail map

Bras d'Or Lake

St. George's Bay

Gulf of St. Lawrence

Liscombe

Sherbrooke Village

Liscomb Game Sanctuary

Sheet Harbour

Tangier

Ship Harbour

Musquedoboit Harbour

Cape George

Arisaig

Lismore

Antigonish

New Glasgow

Thorburn

Stellarton

Westville

Pictou

Brule

Denmark

Balmoral Mills

Bible Hill

Truro

Debert

Masstown

Great Village

Mainland

Stewiacke

Shubenacadie

Mount Uniacke

Lower Sackville

Bedford

Middle Sackville

Upper Sackville

PRINCE EDWARD ISLAND

Wood Islands

Northumberland Strait

Cape Tormentine

Borden

Lorneville

Pugwash

Malagash

Tatamagouche

Oxford

Springhill

Five Islands

Cape Blomidon

Minas Basin

Cobequid Bay

Hantsport

Windsor

Three Mile Plains

Wolfville

Kentville

Berwick

Kingston

NEW BRUNSWICK

Amherst

Joggins

Cape Chignecto Provincial Park

Parrsboro

Advocate Harbour

Cape d'Or

Scots Bay

Minas Channel

Halls Harbour

Cape Split

50 miles

75 km

the Acadians, and the shipbuilders. Tour details are available at visitor information centers or from Nova Scotia Tourism.

This region takes in parts of three of the official Scenic Trails, including the 315-km (195-mi) Marine Drive, the 316-km (196-mi) Sunrise Trail, and the 365-km (226-mi) Glooscap Trail. Any one leg of the routes could be done comfortably as an overnight trip from Halifax.

MUSQUODOBOIT HARBOUR

45 km (28 mi) east of Dartmouth.

Musquodoboit Harbour (locals pronounce it *must-*go-*dob-*bit) is a substantial village with about 2,500 residents at the mouth of the Musquodoboit River. The river offers good trout fishing, and the village has two lovely harbors.

A 1916 train station, five railcars, and a fine collection of railway artifacts, including a legion of lanterns dating from the late 1800s, make the volunteer-run **Musquodoboit Railway Museum** a must for rail buffs. The library is rich in railway and local historical documentation and photos. It also houses the visitor information center. ⊠ *Main St. (Hwy. 7)* ☎ *902/889–2689* ⊠ *By donation* ⊙ *June–Aug., daily 9–6; May and Sept., Thurs.–Sun. 10–6.*

One of the province's best beaches, **Martinique Beach,** is about 12 km (7 mi) south of Musquodoboit Harbour, at the end of East Petpeswick Road. Clam Bay and Clam Harbour (where there is a spectacularly popular sand-castle competition every August), several miles east of Martinique, are also fine, if occasionally foggy, beaches.

OFF THE BEATEN PATH

Moose River Gold Mines and Museum. On-the-spot radio coverage of a mine disaster put Moose River on the map in 1936. Today the town is quiet; a provincial park marks the site of the 12-day effort to rescue three miners trapped far underground (two of the men survived). The museum completes the story with displays, photographs, and artifacts. ⊠ *Moose River Rd. off Hwy. 224, 15 km (9 mi) east of Middle Musquodoboit* ☎ *902/384–2006 or 902/384–2484* ⊠ *Donations accepted* ⊙ *July and Aug., daily 10–5.*

WHERE TO STAY & EAT

$–$$ ✕⬚ **Salmon River House Country Inn.** Views of the water and countryside are glorious from the inn's guest rooms and cottages. One cottage on the ocean is intended for stays of a week or more. Some rooms have whirlpool tubs, and the cottage allows pets in the winter. At the inn, you can fish from the floating dock, hike the trails of the 30-acre property, or make use of the canoe, kayak, or rowboat. The Lobster Shack restaurant ($–$$$) serves lunch, dinner, and a breakfast buffet on its screened deck. ⊠ *9931 Hwy. 7, 10 km (6 mi) east of Musquodoboit Harbour, Salmon River Bridge, Jeddore B0J 1P0* ☎ *902/889–3353 or 800/565–3353* 🖷 *902/889–3653* ⊕ *www.salmonriverhouse.com* ➷*7 rooms, 1 cottage* ⊛ *In-room: no a/c, some DVDs. In-hotel: restaurant, no elevator, no-smoking rooms* ⊟ *AE, DC, MC, V.*

EN ROUTE As you travel through **Ship Harbour** on Highway 7, take note of the strings of colorful buoys, marking one of North America's largest cultivated mussel farms. Vistas of restless seas and wooded shorelines make for excellent photo opportunities. Inland, the area is a protected wilderness corridor with more than 50 undeveloped lakes, centuries-old pine and spruce trees, and some of the largest tracts of wild forest in Halifax.

SHERBROOKE VILLAGE

FodorsChoice
★
166 km (103 mi) northeast of Musquodoboit Harbour.

A living-history museum set within the contemporary town of Sherbrooke, Sherbrooke Village contains 30 restored 19th-century buildings that re-create life during the town's heyday, from 1860 to 1914. Back then, this was a prime shipbuilding, lumbering, and gold-rush center and artisans demonstrate weaving, wood turning, and pottery-, candle-, and soap making daily. A working water-powered sawmill is down the road. Special events, such as old-fashioned Christmas and courthouse concerts, are held throughout the year. ⊠ *Hwy. 7, Sherbrooke* ☎ *902/522–2400 or 888/743–7845* ⊕ *www.sherbrookevillage. ca* ☎ *$9* ☉ *June–mid-Oct., daily 9:30–5.*

OFF THE BEATEN PATH **Port Bickerton Lighthouse Beach Park.** Two lighthouses share a lofty bluff about 20 km (12 mi) east of Sherbrooke on Highway 211. One is still working; the other, built in 1910, houses the Nova Scotia Lighthouse Interpretive Centre, which recounts the history, lore, and vital importance of these lifesaving lights. Hiking trails and a boardwalk lead to a sandy beach. ⊠ *630 Lighthouse Rd., Port Bickerton* ☎ *902/364–2000* ☎ *$3* ☉ *June 15–Sept. 15, daily 9–5.*

WHERE TO STAY & EAT

$–$$ ✕⊞ **Black Duck Ocean View Inn.** From a third-floor picture window, equipped with binoculars and a telescope provided by the inn, you can observe birds, sea life, and maybe a star or two over Beaver Harbour. Expect lavish breakfasts of blueberry pancakes and fruit in the airy dining room ($–$$); for dinner, try the fisherman's lasagna (seafood and pasta in a cream sauce) or other seafood dishes. ⊠ *25245 Hwy. 7, 90 km (56 mi) west of Sherbrooke Village, Port Dufferin* ✑ *Box 227, Sheet Harbour B0J 3B0* ☎ *902/654–2237* ➴ *1 rooms, 2 suites* ♿ *In-room: no a/c, no TV, no phones. In-hotel: restaurant, no elevator* ☰ *MC, V* ⏍ *BP.*

$ ✕⊞ **Sherbrooke Village Inn & Cabins.** This comfy hostelry with rooms and woodsy cabins is a five-minute walk from St. Mary's River (open for trout and sometimes salmon fishing). Take part in nature walks and enjoy a spectacular view. The pleasant dining room ($$–$$$) serves homemade meals—full Canadian breakfasts, lunches, and dinners heavy on the seafood. The restaurant is closed from November to mid-April. ⊠ *7975 Hwy. 7, Box 40, Sherbrooke B0J 3C0* ☎ *902/522–2235* *or 866/522–3818 902/522–2716 www.sherbrookevillageinn.ca 15 rooms, 3 cabins In-room: no a/c, phones, Internet access. In-hotel: no-smoking rooms, no elevator AE, DC, MC, V.*

$ **St. Mary's River Lodge.** Sherbrooke Village is steps away from this lodge with immaculate rooms. The Swiss owners, in love with their adopted countryside, are helpful in planning day trips and tours. They also rent houses in nearby Port Hilford for weeklong stays. The views are notable, looking out onto the river and ocean bay frontage. *21 Main St., Sherbrooke B0J 3C0 902/522–2177 902/522–2626 www.riverlodge.ca 5 rooms, 1 suite, 2 houses In-room: no a/c (some), kitchen (some), VCR. In-hotel: no elevator MC, V BP.*

CANSO

123 km (76 mi) east of Sherbrooke Village.

Canso is one of Nova Scotia's oldest settlements, founded in 1605. Each July the town holds the **Stan Rogers Folk Festival** (*www.stanfest.com*), which commemorates the much-loved Canadian folk singer and composer.

The **Canso Island National Historic Site** details early struggles to control the lucrative fishing industry. A free boat ride takes you to the island for an interpretive tour of what remains of a once-thriving community, a 1744 casualty of the war between France and England. Graphics, models, and audiovisuals set the scene. *Canso Waterfront, off Union St. 902/295–2069 www.parkscanada.ca By donation June–mid-Sept., daily 10–6.*

WHERE TO STAY & EAT

$–$$ **Last Port Restaurant.** Fish-and-chips is a popular menu item at this fast-food restaurant with friendly service. Breakfast choices include eggs any way you like 'em with bacon, ham, sausage, or bologna. *10 Hwy. 16, B0H 1H0 902/366–2400 or 877/366–2400 AE, MC, V.*

$–$$ **SeaWind Landing Country Inn.** On a 20-acre coastal estate, this restored sea captain's home—with bird-watching, interpretive nature walks, and sandy beaches—is a luxurious escape. Short boat tours to offshore islands, where seals bask and bald eagles soar, include white-linen lunches served with fine wines. The inn is furnished with antiques, quilts, and fine art, and the comfortable rooms, close to the seaside, have ocean or garden views. Most rooms have whirlpool baths, balconies, and private entrances. *1 Wharf Rd., just south of Canso, Charlos Cove B0H 1T0 902/525–2108 www.seawindlanding.com 12 rooms In-room: DVDs, no a/c, dial-up. In-hotel: beachfront, bicycles, public Internet, no elevator AE, MC, V Closed mid-Oct.–mid-May.*

ANTIGONISH

85 km (53 mi) northwest of Canso.

Antigonish, on the main route to Cape Breton Island, is home to **St. Francis Xavier University** (✉ *West St., off Hwy. 104* ☎ *902/863–3300* ⊕ *www.stfx.ca*), a center for Gaelic studies and the first coeducational Catholic institution to graduate women. The university **art gallery** (☎ *902/867–2303*) has changing exhibits year-round. A drama program is presented all summer at the **Festival Antigonish** (☎ *902/867– 3333 or 800/563–7529* ⊕ *www.festivalantigonish.com*), with matinees for kids, evening performances for adults, and theater camps in the 226-seat theater.

The **Antigonish Heritage Museum** (✉ *20 E. Main St.* ☎ *902/863–6160* ☑ *Free* ☺ *July and Aug., Mon.–Sat. 10–5; Sept.–June, weekdays 10– noon and 1–5*), in a 1908 rail station, depicts the town's early history.

The biggest and oldest **Highland Games** (☎ *902/863–4275* ⊕ *www. antigonishhighlandgames.com*) outside of Scotland are held here each July, complete with caber tossing, Highland flinging, and pipe skirling.

WHERE TO STAY & EAT

$$–$$$$ ✗ **Gabrieau's Bistro.** Gabrieau's has earned a place in Antigonish hearts
FodorśChoice   with its pleasant interior and epicurean yet affordable menu of Conti-
★   nental cuisine. Seafood, gourmet pizzas, luscious desserts, and several vegetarian selections are available. ✉ *350 Main St.,* ☎ *902/863–1925* ⊕ *www.gabrieaus.com* ⊟ *AE, D, MC, V* ☺ *Closed Sun.*

$–$$$ ✗ **Lobster Treat Restaurant.** This cozily decorated brick, pine, and stained-glass restaurant was once a two-room schoolhouse. The varied menu includes fresh seafood, chicken, pastas, stir-fries, and bread and pies baked on the premises. It's a good choice for families, with a children's menu and a relaxed atmosphere. ✉ *241 Post Rd. (Trans-Canada Hwy.)* ☎ *902/863–5465* ⊟ *AE, MC, V* ☺ *Closed mid-Nov.–mid-Apr.*

$–$$ ✗ ⛉ **Maritime Inn.** The Main Street Café ($$–$$$) at this inn serves breakfast, lunch, and a tempting dinner menu with lots of seafood options. Try the tropical-glazed haddock and shrimp or the baby back ribs. One of five in a Maritime chain, this property has two sizes of rooms and one two-bedroom suite with a whirlpool bath. ✉ *158 Main St., B2G 2B7* ☎ *902/863–4001 or 888/662–7484* 🖷 *902/863–2672* ⊕ *www.maritimeinns.com* ⇜ *31 rooms, 1 suite* ৬ *In-room: VCR (some), Wi-Fi. In-hotel: restaurant, room service, no-smoking rooms, some small pets allowed, no elevator* ⊟ *AE, D, DC, MC, V.*

SPORTS & THE OUTDOORS

A 3-km (2-mi) **walking trail** along the shoreline of Antigonish Harbour borders a large tidal marsh teeming with ospreys, bald eagles, and other birds.

SHOPPING

Lyncharm Pottery (✉ *9 Pottery La.* ☎ *902/863–6970* ⊕ *www.lyncharm. com*) produces handsome functional stoneware that's sold in its own shop and exported worldwide. The **Lyghtesome Gallery** (✉ *166 Main*

St. ☎*902/863–5804* ⊕*www.lyghtesome.ns.ca*) has a good variety of Nova Scotian art at reasonable prices.

■ EN ROUTE

The **Sunrise Trail** (✉ *Hwy. 337 from Antigonish to Cape George, then Hwy. 245 to New Glasgow*) runs north from Antigonish for a glorious drive along St. George's Bay with its many good swimming beaches. After you've passed through this area, the road abruptly climbs 1,000 feet to Cape George. High above the sea, the road runs west along Northumberland Strait through farmlands and tiny villages such as Arisaig, where you can search for fossils on the shore. Lismore, just a few miles west of Arisaig, affirms the Scottish origin of its people with a stone cairn commemorating Bonnie Prince Charlie's Highland rebels, slaughtered by the English at Culloden in 1746. Lobster is landed and processed in shoreside factories, making the town a great place to buy fresh lobster.

STELLARTON

60 km (37 mi) west of Antigonish.

Ⓒ The **Nova Scotia Museum of Industry** brings industrial heritage to life. Like factory and mine workers of old, you punch in with a time card. Hands-on exhibits show how to hook a rag mat, print a bookmark, work a steam engine, or assemble a World War II artillery shell. Interactive computer exhibits explore multimedia as a tool of industry. Canada's oldest steam locomotives and a model railway layout are also displayed, and there's a restaurant, too. ✉ *147 N. Foord St., Exit 24 off Hwy. 104* ☎*902/755–5425* ⊕*www.industry.museum.gov.ns.ca* ✇*$7.50* ☉ *Year-round, weekdays 9–5; May and June, Sat. 9–5, Sun. 1–5; July–Oct., Sun. 10–5.*

PICTOU

20 km (12 mi) north of Stellarton.

First occupied by the Mi'Kmaqs, this town became a Scottish settlement in 1773 when the first boat of Scottish Highlanders landed: it had the distinction of being "the birthplace of New Scotland." Thirty-three families and 25 unmarried men arrived aboard the *Hector*, an aging cargo ship that was years later reproduced in minute detail and launched in the harbor.

The **Hector Heritage Quay,** where the new 110-foot fully rigged *Hector* can be toured, recounts the story of the hardy Scottish pioneers and the flood of Scots who followed them. There are working blacksmith and carpentry shops, along with an interpretive center. ✉ *33 Caladh Ave.* ☎*902/485–4371 or 877/574–2868* ✇*$5* ☉ *Mid-May–late Oct., Mon.–Sat. 9–5, Sun. 10–5.*

A lively **weekend crafts market** takes place on Saturday and Sunday at the waterfront, from June to September, showcases crafts and craftspeople from the area and across the province.

Melmerby Beach, one of the warmest beaches in the province, is about 23 km (14 mi) east of Pictou. To get here, follow the shore road from Highway 104.

WHERE TO STAY & EAT

¢–$$ ✕⊞**Braeside Country Inn.** Every nook and cranny has collectible treasures on display at this handsome 1938 inn perched on a 5-acre hillside. China, crystal, silver, statuary, inlaid lacquer, and gadgets invite hours of browsing. You can stroll to the historic waterfront or watch your ship come into Pictou Harbour from the picture window in the dining room ($$–$$$$), where prime rib and seafood are specialties. ⊠126 Front St., Box 1810, B0K 1H0 ☎902/485–5046 or 800/613–7701 ⊟902/485–1701 ⊕www.braesideinn.com ⊷18 rooms &In-room: refrigerator (some), VCR (some), Wi-Fi. In-hotel: restaurant, no-smoking rooms, no elevator ⊟AE, DC, MC, V ⏐◯⏐BP.

$–$$$ ⊞**Stonehame Lodge & Chalets.** Handmade quilts and welcoming jars of
Fodor'sChoice   homemade jam await, along with lots of peace and quiet at these log
★   chalets and lodge rooms atop Fitzpatrick Mountain. In season, you can swim in the heated outdoor pool, hike or ski nearby woodland trails, visit a neighboring dairy farm, take a sleigh ride, see crop harvesting, or just relax before the chalet's woodstove or in the outdoor hot tub. ⊠R.R. 3, 12 km (7½ mi) west of Pictou, Exit 19 or 21 off TCH 104, Scotsburn B0K 1R0 ☎902/485–3468 or 877/646–3468 ⊕www.stonehamechalets.com ⊷5 rooms, 10 chalets &In-room: no a/c (some), kitchen (some), kitchenette (some), VCR, DVD. In-hotel: some pets allowed, bicycles, no elevator ⊟AE, DC, MC, V.

$–$$ ⊞**Auberge Walker Inn.** A registered Heritage Property from 1865, this friendly inn is a block from the historic Pictou waterfront. Twelve-foot ceilings grace the inn's rooms. ⊠34 Coleraine St., B0K 1H0 ☎902/485–1433 or 800/370–5553 ⊟902/485–1222 ⊕www.walkerinn.com ⊷10 rooms, 1 suite &In-room: Wi-fi, no a/c, no phone. In-hotel: no-smoking rooms, no elevator ⊟AE, MC, V ⏐◯⏐CP.

$–$$ ⊞**Customs House Inn.** A former customs house on Pictou's waterfront is now a nifty inn, with spacious high-ceiling rooms overlooking the water. A basement pub, open June through September, occasionally has Celtic entertainment. ⊠38 Depot St., Box 1542, B0K 1H0 ☎902/485–4546 ⊟902/485–1657 ⊕www.customshouseinn.ca ⊷8 rooms &In-room: kitchen (some), Wi-Fi, DVD, no elevator ⊟AE, DC, MC, V ⏐◯⏐CP.

¢–$$ ⊞**Consulate Inn.** From 1810 to 1836 this was a private home but between 1836 and 1896 it was the U.S. Consulate. Today, the inn is a showplace for the innkeeper's creativity: she's a skilled quilter and painter and colorful quilted hangings and original art decorate the spacious rooms in the main house. Rooms in the next-door annex have private patios or balconies, and the two-bedroom cottage has a full kitchen and a deck overlooking Pictou Harbour. ⊠157 Water St., Box 1642, B0K 1H0 ☎902/485–4554 or 800/424–8283 ⊟902/485–1532 ⊕www.consulateinn.com ⊷10 rooms, 1 cottage &In-room: no a/c (some), refrigerator (some), VCR, Wi-Fi, no elevator ⊟AE, MC, V ⏐◯⏐BP.

NIGHTLIFE & THE ARTS

The **DeCoste Entertainment Centre** (⊠ *Water St.* ☎ *902/485–8848 or 800/353–5338* ⊕ *www.decostecentre.ca*) is a handsome theater that presents a summer-long program of concerts, pipe bands, Highland dancing, and *ceilidhs* (Gaelic music and dance).

SHOPPING

The artisans' cooperative **Water Street Studio** (⊠ *110 Water St.* ☎ *902/485–8398*) sells hand-dyed and natural yarns, felted woolen items, and knit items such as hats, socks, shawls, and scarves, plus weaving, blankets, pottery, stained glass, jewelry, and woodwork.

NEW GLASGOW

22 km (14 mi) southwest of Pictou.

The largest community along the Sunrise Trail has a rich Scottish heritage and from the 1820s to the 1920s, New Glasgow was a major shipbuilding center and port. The town's prosperity has always been linked to the East River, so the ongoing redevelopment of the riverfront seems appropriate.

New Glasgow is the setting in early August of the **Riverfront Music Jubilee** (☎ *902/752–6972* ⊕ *www.jubilee.ns.ca*), which attracts local and national performers.

In mid-July it's the site of the **Festival of the Tartans,** which includes Highland dancing, the Pictou County Pipes and Drums on Parade, a kilted golf tournament, concerts, beer gardens, and much more.

TATAMAGOUCHE

50 km (31 mi) west of Pictou.

Despite the size of its population—all of 700 souls—Tatamagouche is a force to be reckoned with: Canada's second-largest Oktoberfest and a major quilt show are held here each fall, and summer brings strawberry and blueberry festivals, lobster and chowder suppers, and a lively farmers' market on Saturday mornings. This charming town on Highway 6 on the North Shore is at the juncture of two rivers, and Tatamagouche is a Mi'Kmaq name meaning "meeting place of the waters." An old rail bed along the river's edge, part of the Trans-Canada Trail, is ideal for hiking, cycling, walking, and bird-watching.

The **Sunrise Trail Museum** traces the town's Mi'Kmaq, Acadian, French, and Scottish roots and its shipbuilding heritage. ⊠ *216 Main St.* ☎ *902/657–2689* ⊡ *$2* ⊙ *Late June–early Sept., daily 9–5.*

Local artists' work is shown at the **Fraser Cultural Centre,** which promotes arts, crafts, and cultural activities through demonstrations and exhibits. The building also houses the Tatamagouche visitor information center, North Shore archives, and a display about the giantess Anna Swan, who was born near Tatamagouche and earned fame in P.T. Barnum's American Museum in New York. ⊠ *362 Main St.* ☎ *902/657–3285* ⊡ *By donation* ⊙ *Mid-May–Aug., daily 10–4; Sept., daily 1–4.*

OFF THE BEATEN PATH

Balmoral Grist Mill Museum. A water-powered gristmill, built in 1874, serves as the centerpiece of this museum near Tatamagouche. It's one of the few operating mills in Nova Scotia and you can observe milling demonstrations, stroll the 1-km (½-mi) walking trail, and buy freshly ground flour in the shop. ⊠ *660 Matheson Brook Rd., Balmoral Mills* ☎ *902/657–3016* ⊕ *www.museum. gov.ns.ca/bgm* 🎫 *$3.25* ⊗ *June–mid-Oct., Mon.–Sat. 9:30–5:30, Sun. 1–5:30; demonstrations Mon.–Sat., 10–noon and 2–4, Sun. 2–4.*

> ### THE GIANT ANNA SWAN
>
> Anna Swan, born near Tatamagouche, in 1846, weighed 18 pounds and was 27 inches long when she was born, was 4 feet 6 inches when she was four years old, 5 foot 2 at the age of 6, and 6 feet 2 by the time she was 10. She joined P.T. Barnum's museum when she was 7 feet 2, but continued to grow for several more years until she reached her full height of 7 feet 5½ inches. She married another famously tall person: Martin Van Buren Bates, who is believed to have been at least 7 foot 9.

1

WHERE TO STAY & EAT

¢–$$ ✕ **Big Al's Acadian Restaurant and Lounge.** Local giantess Anna Swan and her husband are on display here in murals and wooden statues depicting the village's history. Overlooking Tatamagouche Bay, Big Al's serves steaks, seafood, and chicken wings, as well as pizza from Papa Al's Pizza, which is in the same building. ⊠ *9 Station Rd.* ☎ *902/657–0335* 🖷 *902/657–3341* ☰ *AE, V.*

$$$$ ✕🛏 **Fox Harb'r Golf Resort & Spa.** Manor-style houses have suites with views of the Northumberland Strait, plus luxuries such as heated-marble–bathroom floors, propane fireplaces, and terrace access at this 1,000-acre gated complex with a manicured garden. A sprawling, 18-hole traditional Scottish golf course on the jagged ocean coastline is the resort's crown jewel—a round of golf is $200. Trap and skeet shooting can be done on-site. The cuisine ($$$$) is classic French and European, and frequent options are halibut, lobster, rack of lamb, and filet mignon. Guests arrive by car, private plane, or boat. ⊠ *1337 Fox Harbour Rd., 22 km (13½ mi) west of Tatamagouche and 8 km (5 mi) north of Wallace, B0K 1Y0* ☎ *902/257–1801 or 866/257–1801* 🖷 *902/257–1852* ⊕ *www.foxharbr.com* ➥ *72 suites* ⌂ *In-room: kitchen, Wi-Fi. In-hotel: 2 restaurants, golf course, tennis courts, pool, spa, no-smoking rooms, minibars, no elevator* ☰ *AE, D, DC, MC, V* ⊗ *Closed late Oct.–May.*

$–$$ ✕🛏 **Train Station Inn.** Railway history lives on in Tatamagouche, where
★ this unique inn has B&B accommodations in a century-old station and in seven cabooses parked nearby. The stationmaster's quarters include three rooms, a guest parlor, and a kitchen and laundry for guest use. Downstairs, a main-floor café, where tasty breakfasts are served, is decorated with authentic railroad memorabilia. The caboose suites have all the creature comforts, plus touches of railroad life—signal switches and elevated conductors' cupolas with their revolving chairs. Land and sea dinners are served in the dining car ($$–$$$). ⊠ *21 Station Rd., B0K 1V0* ☎ *902/657–3222 or 888/724–5233* ⊕ *www.trainstation.ca*

⊅3 rooms, 7 suites △In-room: no TV (some), Wi-Fi. In-hotel: laundry facilities, no elevator ⊟AE, DC, MC, V ℍCP.

$ 🖳**Balmoral Motel.** This small motel overlooks Tatamagouche Bay and offers water views from all rooms. There is direct access to walking, cross-country skiing, and snowmobiling on the nearby Trans-Canada Trail. ⊠131 Main St., B0K 1V0 ☎902/657–2000 or 888/383–9357 🖷902/657–2205 ⊕www.balmoralmotel.ca ⊅18 rooms △In-room: no a/c, Wi-Fi, no elevator. In-hotel: public Internet, no-smoking rooms, some pets allowed ⊟AE, MC, V.

SHOPPING

At **Sara Bonnyman Pottery** (⊠Hwy. 246, 1½ km [1 mi] uphill from post office ☎902/657–3215 ⊕www.sarabonnymanpottery.com), watch the well-known potter at work each morning, producing handsome stoneware pieces bearing sunflower and blueberry motifs, and her one-of-a-kind plates and bowls. She also makes wool hand-hooked rugs in colorful primitive designs. The studio is open Monday through Saturday 10 to 4, June through mid-September, and by appointment off-season. Maritime crafts sold at the **Sunflower Crafts Shop** (⊠249 Main St. ☎902/657–3276) include pewter, wood, baskets, wrought iron, quilts, candles, Chéticamp hooking, the work of noted local potter Sara Bonnyman, and unusual framed pictures made of caribou tufting. The shop is open June 15 through December 24, Monday through Saturday 10 to 4:30.

MALAGASH

17 km (11 mi) west of Tatamagouche.

Malagash is best known for its winery, **Jöst Vineyards,** that flourishes in the warm climate moderated by the Northumberland Strait. A surprisingly wide range of wines is produced here, including a notable ice wine (a sweet wine made after frost has iced the grapes). There's also a well-stocked wine shop. ⊠Hwy. 6 off Hwy. 104 ☎902/257–2636 or 800/565–4567 ⊕www.jostwine.com ⊙Mid-June–mid-Sept., daily 9–6; mid-Sept.–mid-June, daily 10–5; tours mid-June–mid-Sept., daily noon and 3.

SPRINGHILL

40 km (25 mi) west of Malagash.

The coal-mining town of Springhill, on Highway 2, was the site of the famous mine disaster of the 1950s immortalized in the folk song "The Ballad of Springhill," by Peggy Seeger and Ewen McColl.

You can tour a real coal mine at the **Springhill Miners Museum.** Retired miners act as guides and recount firsthand memories of mining disasters. ⊠145 Black River Rd., off Hwy. 2 ☎902/597–3449 ⊠$5.25 ⊙June–Sept., daily 9–5.

Springhill is the hometown of internationally acclaimed singer Anne Murray, whose career is celebrated at the **Anne Murray Centre.** ⊠*36 Main St.* ☎*902/597–8614* ⊠*$6* ⊗*Mid-May–mid-Oct., daily 9–5.*

OFF THE BEATEN PATH

Wild Blueberry & Maple Centre. This center in Oxford, about 10 km (6 mi) outside of Springhill, details the history of two tasty industries—75% of Nova Scotia's blueberry and maple-syrup production occurs in surrounding Cumberland County. Self-guided tours, interactive displays, and a beehive tell the story. ⊠*105 Lower Main St., Oxford* ☎*902/447–2908* ⊕*www.town. oxford.ns.ca* ⊠*Free* ⊗*May 15–June and Sept.–Oct. 15, daily 10–4; July and Aug., daily 9–6.*

AMHERST

28 km (17 mi) northwest of Springhill.

Near the New Brunswick border, this now-quiet town was a bustling center of industry and influence from the mid-1800s to early 1900s. Four of Canada's Fathers of Confederation hailed from Amherst, including Sir Charles Tupper, who later became prime minister.

In contrast with tame Amherst is the **Tantramar Marsh**, alive with incredible birds and wildlife. It was originally called Tintamarre (literally "din," in French) because of the racket made by vast flocks of wildfowl. Said to be the world's largest marsh, the Tantramar is a migratory route for hundreds of thousands of birds, and a breeding ground for more than 100 species.

From Amherst, the Sunrise Trail heads toward the Northumberland Strait, and the Glooscap Trail runs west through fossil country. The **Fundy Shore Ecotour** (☎*902/893–8782, 800/895–1177 in Canada*), which mainly follows near the Glooscap Trail, has been developed by the local tourism authority to highlight the region's six distinct ecozones. Brochures are available at information centers; call for locations.

WHERE TO STAY & EAT

$-$$ ⨯☷**Amherst Shore Country Inn.** This seaside country inn, with a beautiful view of Northumberland Strait and acres of lawns and gardens, has rooms, suites, and a cottage fronting 600 feet of private beach. Relax in comfort surrounded by antique furnishings and handmade quilts. Some suites have double whirlpool baths, propane fireplaces, and small decks. The two-bedroom rustic seaside cottage has kitchen facilities. Well-prepared four-course, prix-fixe dinners incorporating homegrown produce are served at one daily seating ($$$$; reservations essential). Look for themed gourmet or romantic packages. ⊠*Hwy. 366, 32 km (20 mi) northeast of Amherst, Lorneville B4H 3X9* ☎*800/661–2724* ☎☎*902/661–4800* ⊕*www.ascinn.ns.ca* ⤴*4 rooms, 4 suites, 1 cottage* ♿*In-room: In-hotel: restaurant, beachfront, no-smoking rooms, no elevator* ⊟*AE, MC, V* ⊗*Closed weekdays Nov.–Apr.*

$$ ☷**Wandlyn Inn.** Just inside the Nova Scotia–New Brunswick border, this dependable inn offers a slew of extras, such as free newspapers,

magazines, and kids' meals. Rooms are comfortable and convenient, and the attached Cellar Lounge is a good place to unwind. ✉ *Victoria St.–Trans-Canada Hwy., Box 275, B4H 3Z2* ☎ *902/667–3331 or 800/561–0000* 🖷 *902/667–0475* ⊕ *www.wandlyninns.com* 💬 *88 rooms & In-hotel: restaurant, pool, laundry facilities, Wi-Fi, no elevator* ⊟ *AE, DC, MC, V.*

JOGGINS

35 km (22 mi) southwest of Amherst.

Joggins's main draw is the coal-age fossils embedded in its 150-foot sandstone cliffs.

☾ At the **Joggins Fossil Centre** you can view a large collection of 300-million-year-old fossils and learn about the region's geological and archaeological history. Admission includes a free fossil when you leave the center. Maps are issued for independent fossil hunters. ✉ *30 Main St.* ☎ *902/251–2727* 🖷 *By donation* ☾ *June–Sept., daily 10:30–6:30.*

CAPE CHIGNECTO & CAPE D'OR

70 km (43 mi) southwest of Joggins.

Two imposing promontories—Cape Chignecto and Cape d'Or—reach into the Bay of Fundy near Chignecto Bay.

Fodor'sChoice   Cape Chignecto is home to the newest provincial park, **Cape Chignecto**
★   **Provincial Park.** Opened officially in 1998, the park is an untouched wilderness with 10,000 acres of old-growth forest harboring deer, moose, and eagles. It's circumnavigated by a 51-km (31-mi) hiking trail along rugged cliffs that rise to 600 feet above the bay. Wilderness cabins and campsites are available. ✉ *1108 West Advocate Rd., off Hwy. 209, West Advocate* ☎ *902/392–2085* ⊕ *www.capechignecto.net* 🖷 *$3.20* ☾ *Early May–Mid-Nov., Mon.–Sat. 8–8, Sun. 8–5.*

Fodor'sChoice   South of Cape Chignecto is **Cape d'Or** *(Cape of Gold)*, named by Samuel
★   de Champlain for its glittering veins of copper. The region was actively mined a century ago, and at nearby Horseshoe Cove you may still find nuggets of almost pure copper on the beach as well as amethysts and other semiprecious stones. Cape d'Or's hiking trails border the cliff edge above the Dory Rips, a turbulent meeting of currents from the Minas Basin and the Bay of Fundy punctuated by a fine lighthouse.

A delightful beach walk at **Advocate Harbour,** named by Samuel de Champlain for a lawyer friend, follows the top of an Acadian dike that was built by settlers in the 1700s to reclaim farmland from the sea. Advocate Beach, noted for its tide-cast driftwood, stretches 5 km (3 mi) from Cape Chignecto to Cape d'Or.

The **Age of Sail Museum Heritage Centre** traces the history of the area's shipbuilding and lumbering industries. You can also see a restored 1857 Methodist church, a blacksmith shop, and a lighthouse. ✉ *Hwy. 209,*

Port Greville ☎902/348–2030 ☞$3 ⊘*July and Aug., daily 10–6; June and Sept., Thurs.–Mon. 10–6.*

WHERE TO STAY & EAT

¢–$ ✕**Fundy Tides Campground Restaurant.** This small restaurant is large on hospitality. In the campground's main building, the 20-seat restaurant serves diner-type food that ranges from hamburgers to seafood. Everything is made from scratch, from the fries to the fish batter. You can eat-in or take-out. ⊠*95 Mills Rd., Advocate Harbour* ☎902/392–2584 *or* 888/392–2584 ⊟*No credit cards* ⊘*Closed mid-Oct.–mid-May.*

$$ ▦**Driftwood Park Retreat.** Five mist-blue cottages face the Fundy shore and its powerful tides. Four of the two-story, two-bedroom units have pine floors, gas fireplaces, well-equipped kitchens, and upstairs living rooms with fine views of the bay. The fifth cottage is an open-plan ranch unit with living room, dining room, and kitchen area. The living room has a propane fireplace. The cottages are close to a driftwood beach, hiking trails, and clam-digging and mineral-hunting areas. ⊠*47 Driftwood La., West Advocate B0M 1A0* ☎902/392–2008 *or* 866/810–0110 ⊜902/392–2041 ⊕*www.driftwoodparkretreat.com* ⌨*5 cottages* ⚿*In-room: no a/c, kitchen, no TV. In-hotel: laundry service, no-smoking rooms, no elevator* ⊟*MC, V.*

¢ ▦**The Lighthouse on Cape d'Or.** Before automation, two light keepers manned the crucial light on the rocky Cape d'Or shore, and their cottages have been transformed—one to an excellent restaurant with full bar and the other to a small inn with a comfortable lounge and picture windows overlooking the Minas Basin. This wild and lovely place offers hiking, bird-watching, seal sightings, outdoor lobster boils and clambakes, and exceptional young hosts whose warmth and gourmet cooking make leaving difficult. A common area has a breakfast bar, books and games, and a small refrigerator. Getting here is a bit challenging: a 5½-km-long (3-mi-long) road off Highway 209 from Advocate, then a steep gravel path down to the shore. ⊠*Cape d'Or off Hwy. 209* ☏*Box 122, Advocate B0M 1A0* ☎902/670–0534 ⊕*www.capedor.ca* ⌨*4 rooms, 2 with bath* ⚿*In-room: no a/c, no TV. In-hotel: restaurant, no-smoking rooms, no elevator* ⊟*No credit cards* ⊘*Closed late Oct.–mid-May.*

> ## WORD OF MOUTH
>
> "A little known B&B in Nova Scotia and one of the highlights of our trip is the Cape D'Or Lighthouse B&B, overlooking the Bay of Fundy. It only has 4-rooms and some might think it rustic, but if you want a unique experience and a great view, this is the place."
>
> —mcmouse

¢ ▦**Reid's Tourist Home.** Nestled between Cape d'Or and Cape Chignecto, this cattle farm is a working operation where you can enjoy the bucolic pleasures of country life or take a short walk to the Fundy shore. The suites occupy a separate building near the picturesque farmhouse. Chignecto Park is just over 1 km (½ mi) away. ⊠*1391 W. Advocate Rd., West Advocate* ☏*R.R. 3, Parrsboro B0M 1S0* ☎902/392–2592 ⊜902/392–2523 ⌨*4 suites* ⚿*In-room: no a/c, refrigerator, no elevator* ⊟*No credit cards* ⊘*Closed Oct.–May.*

¢ ⚏ **Spencer's Island B&B.** Once home to Captain Bigelow, who built the *Mary Celeste*. The house today is a modest and friendly B&B with cozy rooms and an antiques-furnished parlor. Wood-burning fireplaces and a vintage woodstove are warmly welcoming. Blueberry waffles and cheese soufflé are breakfast favorites. The inn is just uphill from the Spencer's Island lighthouse and the Fundy shore, and it's a 10-minute drive from the wilderness of Cape Chignecto. ⊠ *Off Hwy. 209, Spencer's Island* ⌑ *R.R. 3, Parrsboro B0M 1S0* ☏ *902/392–2721* ⇆ *3 rooms* ⚭ *In-room: no a/c, no elevator* ⊟ *No credit cards* ⊘ *Closed Sept.–May* ⓘ *BP.*

> ### THE MYSTERY OF THE MARY CELESTE
>
> The *Mary Celeste*, originally christened the *Amazon*, was built on Spencer's Island, in 1861. Its first captain died on the ship's maiden voyage and the boat was renamed. Then, in 1872 the ship set sail for Europe carrying a cargo of wine and liquor. Less than a month later it was discovered abandoned at sea, all sails set, and undamaged, but without a trace of the crew and passengers.

▌ **EN ROUTE** A cairn at **Spencer's Island Beach** on Highway 209 commemorates the *Mary Celeste.*

PARRSBORO

55 km (34 mi) east of Cape d'Or.

A center for rock hounds and fossil hunters, Parrsboro is the main town on this shore and holds the **Nova Scotia Gem and Mineral Show** every third weekend of August.

The fossil-laden cliffs that rim the **Minas Basin** are washed by the world's highest tides twice daily. The result is a wealth of plant and animal fossils revealed in the rocks or washed down to the shore.

Semiprecious stones such as amethyst, quartz, and stilbite can be found at **Partridge Island,** 1 km (½ mi) offshore and connected to the mainland by an isthmus.

Ⓒ The **Fundy Geological Museum** isn't far from the Minas Basin area, where some of the oldest dinosaur fossils in Canada have been found. Two-hundred-million-year-old dinosaur fossils are showcased here alongside other mineral, plant, and animal relics. ⊠ *162 Two Island Rd.* ☏ *902/254–3814* ⊕ *www.fundygeo.museum.gov.ns.ca* ⚏ *$6.25* ⊘ *June–mid-Oct., daily 9:30–5:30; mid-Oct.–May, Tues.–Sat., hrs vary, call ahead.*

Ⓒ The world's smallest dinosaur footprints, along with rare minerals, rocks, and fossils, are displayed at Eldon George's **Parrsboro Rock and Mineral Shop and Museum.** Mr. George, a goldsmith, lapidary, and woodcarver, sells his work in his shop and has tours for fossil and mineral collectors. ⊠ *349 Whitehall Rd.* ☏ *902/254–2981* ⚏ *Donations accepted* ⊘ *May–Oct., daily 9–6.*

Although fossils have become Parrsboro's claim to fame, this harbor town was also a major shipping and shipbuilding port, and its history is described at the **Ottawa House Museum-by-the-Sea**. This house, which overlooks the Bay of Fundy, is the only surviving building from a 1700s settlement. It was later the summer home of Sir Charles Tupper (1821–1915), a former premier of Nova Scotia who was briefly prime minister of Canada. ✉ *1155 Whitehall Rd., 3 km (2 mi) east of downtown* ☎ *902/254-2376* 💲 *$2* ☉ *Mid-June–mid-Sept., daily 10–6.*

WHERE TO STAY & EAT

$–$$ ✗ **Harbour View Restaurant.** Fresh scallops and lobster, along with clams, flounder, and other seafood, are menu staples at this beachfront restaurant. The dining room, with windows overlooking the water and the lighthouse, displays paintings and photos of Parrsboro's past. Breakfast is also served all day. ✉ *476 Pier Rd.* ☎ *902/254-3507* ▤ *AE, MC, V* ☉ *Closed mid-Oct.–Apr.*

$–$$ ✗ **Stowaway Restaurant.** The menu is rich in seafood—thick chowder, fish-and-chips, and scallops—but includes chicken and meat dishes at this friendly and spacious place. In one wing a bakery ruins diets with its fresh apple pies, doughnuts, and bread. There's a take-out counter, too. Breakfast is served. ✉ *121 Main St.* ☎ *902/254-3371* ▤ *AE, DC, MC, V.*

$$$$ ⊡ **Beach House on Hatfield Road.** Fourteen picture windows provide panoramic views of the Bay of Fundy and a saltwater marsh. The two-story house can sleep six to eight, is on two beaches, and is close to all the attractions of the Glooscap Trail. Fully equipped, from beach towels to wireless Internet, fondue pots to a fireplace, it includes two bedrooms, two bathrooms, a sunroom, balconies, a dining room, and a sitting room with fireplace. The house is rented in one-week increments for summer and shorter breaks in winter. ✉ *19 km (12 mi) west of Parrsboro, Fox River* 🖭 *Reservations: 96 Sherwood Ave., Toronto, ON M4P 2A7* ☎ *116/181-4096* 🖷 *416/487-4048* ⊕ *www.novascotiabeachhouse. com* ⇌ *1 house* ⚬ *In-room: no a/c, kitchen. In-hotel: beachfront, laundry facilities, no-smoking rooms, some pets allowed, Wi-Fi, no elevator* ▤ *No credit cards.*

$–$$$$ ⊡ **Parrsboro Mansion Inn.** This 1880 home, set far back on a 4-acre lawn, presents an imposing face; inside it's brightly modern, with contemporary European art and furnishings. The owners invite guests to learn about regeneration and relaxation through magnetic-field therapy. The quiet ground-floor rooms are spacious with big windows and have sitting areas. Each room is decorated in an individual theme. ✉ *3196 Eastern Ave., Box 579, B0M 1S0* ☎ *866/354-2585* 🖷 *902/254-2585* ⊕ *www.parrsboromansion.com* ⇌ *3 rooms, 1 suite* ⚬ *In-room: no a/c (some), DVD, Wi-Fi. In-hotel: pool, laundry facilities, no-smoking rooms, no elevator* ▤ *AE, MC, V* ☉ *Closed Nov.–June* ⧈ *BP.*

$–$$ ⊡ **Maple Inn, Parrsboro.** Local residents often reserve Room 1 in this Italianate-style home built 1860–90, because many of them were born here when the building was a hospital and this was the delivery room. All the rooms, however, are dramatic, including one that's painted black with lush, flowery touches. Parrsboro's center and the Bay of Fundy are within walking distance. ✉ *2358 Western Ave., Box 457, B0M*

1S0 ☎877/627–5346 🖷902/254–3735 ⊕*www.mapleinn.ca* ⇍6 *rooms, 2 suites* ☆*In-room: DVD (some), Internet access (some), no a/c. In-hotel: no-smoking rooms, no elevator* ▤*AE, MC, V* ⑩|*BP.*

$ 🖭 **Gillespie House Inn.** Wild roses border the driveway leading up to this handsome home and a lavish vegetarian breakfast and tons of visitor information are part of the service. Antique furnishings, hardwood floors, and fireplaces take you back in time in this 1890s home. Theater and kayaking excursions can be arranged. ✉*358 Main St., B0M 1S0* ☎*902/254–3196 or 877/901–3196* ⊕*www.gillespiehouseinn.com* ⇍*7 rooms* ☆*In-room: no a/c, no TV. In-hotel: bicycles, Wi-Fi, no elevator* ▤*AE, MC, V* ⊘*Closed Nov.–Apr.* ⑩|*BP.*

NIGHTLIFE & THE ARTS

Ship's Company Theatre (✉*18 Lower Main St.* ☎*902/254–2003 or 800/565–7469* ⊕*www.shipscompany.com*) presents top-notch plays, comedy, and a concert series at its new facility, built in 2005. The *Kipawo,* a former Minas Basin ferry, has been integrated into the lobby and is the site of book and poetry readings. **Joy Laking Studio Gallery** (✉*6730 Hwy. 2, 5 km [3 mi] east of Bass River, Portaupique* ☎*902/647–2816 or 800/565–5899* ⊕*www.joylakinggallery.com*), midway between Truro and Parrsboro, is owned by one of Nova Scotia's best-known painters.

FIVE ISLANDS

24 km (15 mi) east of Parrsboro.

Among the most scenic areas along Highway 2 is Five Islands, which, according to Mi'Kmaq legend, was created when the god Glooscap threw handfuls of sod at Beaver, who had mocked and betrayed him.

Five Islands Provincial Park, on the shore of Minas Basin, has a campground ($19.22 a night), a beach, and hiking trails. Interpretive displays reveal the area's interesting geology: semiprecious stones, Jurassic-age dinosaur bones, and fossils. The Five Islands Lighthouse, at Sand Point Campground, has access to good swimming and clamming; you can "walk on the ocean floor" at low tide, when the water recedes nearly 1 mi, but beware the awesome return of the tides, which can outrun man or beast. ✉*Hwy. 2, 32 km (20 mi) east of Parrsboro and 57 km (35 mi) west of Truro* ☎*902/254–2980* ▧*Free* ⊘*Mid-May–Aug., daily dawn–dusk.*

Cobequid Interpretation Centre highlights the geology, history, and culture of the area with pictures, videos, and interpretive panels. Get a sweeping view of the countryside and the impressive tides from the World War II observation tower. The center is home base for **Kenomee Hiking and Walking Trails,** which allow you to explore the area's varied landscapes—the coast itself plus cliffs, waterfalls, and forested valleys. ✉*3246–3248 Hwy. 2, Central Economy* ☎*902/647–2600* ▧*By donation* ⊘*June and Sept.–mid-Oct., daily 9–5; July and Aug., daily 9–6.*

WHERE TO STAY

$ ⚇**Gemstow Bed and Breakfast.** Breakfast is served in an airy sun porch that overlooks flowery perennial beds and has a fine vista of Five Islands and beyond. Photographers nab their best shots of the wind-swept islands from the front deck. Inside, the rooms and the lounge are tastefully furnished. Your host—who has a cat and a dog on-site—leads hikes to a hidden waterfall or clamming on the shore. ✉*463 Hwy. 2, 20 km (12 mi) east of Parrsboro, Lower Five Islands B0M 1N0* ☎*902/254-2924* ⊕*www3.ns.sympatico.ca/gemstow* ⇄*2 rooms* ⌂*In-room: no a/c, no phone, no TV, no elevator* ☰*MC, V* ⦿*BP.*

TRURO

67 km (42 mi) east of Five Islands.

Throughout Truro, watch for the Truro Tree Sculptures—a creative tribute to trees killed by the dreaded Dutch Elm disease. Artists Albert Deveau, Ralph Bigney, and Bruce Wood have been transforming the dead trees into handsome sculptures of historical figures, wildlife, and cultural icons. An international tulip festival takes place in May. Truro's central location places it on many travelers' routes.

Truro's least-known asset is also its biggest—the 1,000-acre **Victoria Park,** where, smack in the middle of town, you can find hiking trails, a winding stream flowing through a deep gorge with a 200-step climb to the top, and two waterfalls. ✉*Park Rd.* ☎*902/893-6078* ⊠*Free* ⦿*Daily dawn–dusk.*

WHERE TO STAY & EAT

$–$$ ✗**Frank & Gino's Grill and Pasta House.** Each of this restaurant's corners is filled with memorabilia focusing on one of four themes: Marilyn Monroe, antique sports, local lore, or traveling ships. Enjoy the popular pasta or ribs, along with a full menu. Portions are generous—pasta includes salad and bread—so Frank & Gino's Teeny Weeny Cheesecake is just the right size for a taste-of-heaven dessert. ✉*286 Robie St.* ☎*902/895-2165* ⊕*www.frankandginos.com* ☰*AE, DC, MC, V.*

¢–$ ✗**Sugar Moon Farm Maple Products & Pancake House.** Nova Scotia's only
☺ year-round maple destination is this log sugar camp and pancake house
Fodor's Choice nestled in the Cobequid Mountains about 30 km (19 mi) north of
★ Truro. Enjoy whole-grain buttermilk pancakes and waffles, maple syrup, local sausage, fresh biscuits, maple baked beans, and organic coffee. One night each month, a guest chef prepares a gourmet meal ($69). From 9 to 5 daily in the summer and on weekends the rest of the year, you can tour the working maple farm and hike the sugar woods; in spring, you can also see demos. ✉*Alex MacDonald Rd., Earltown* ☎*902/657-3348 or 866/816-2753* ⊕*www.sugarmoon.ca* ☰*MC, V* ⦿*Closed weekdays Sept.–June.*

$$ ✗⚇**John Stanfield Inn.** Rescued from demolition and moved to this
★ site, the John Stanfield Inn has been beautifully restored to its original Queen Anne style, with delicate wood carvings, elaborate fireplaces, bow windows, and fine antique furniture. The restaurant ($$–$$$$) serves unusual seafood specialties and desserts such as berries

Romanoff. ✉*437 Prince St., B2N 1E6* ☎*902/895–1505, 902/895–1651, 800/561–7666* 🖶*902/893–4427* ⊕*www.johnstanfieldinn.com* ⇱*10 rooms* ♿*In-room: kitchen (some), Wi-Fi. In-hotel: restaurant, bar, laundry service, no-smoking rooms, no elevator* ▭*AE, D, DC, MC, V* ⦿*CP.*

$ 🛏**Suncatcher Bed and Breakfast.** Call this modest B&B 10 minutes outside of Truro a glass act: stained glass adorns every available window, wall, and cranny. On the nonglass front, the breakfast menu includes homemade breads, jams, muffins, fruits (in season), bacon or sausage, and eggs. The hosts know their province from stem to stern and cheerfully advise on itineraries and attractions. The four rooms share two bathrooms. ✉*25 Wile Crest Ave.–R.R. 6, B2N 5B4* ☎*877/203–6032* 🖶☎*902/893–7169* ⊕*www.bbcanada.com/1853.html* ⇱*2 rooms with ensuites* ♿*In-room: no a/c. In-hotel: no-smoking rooms, no elevator* ▭*AE, V* ⦿*BP.*

SPORTS & THE OUTDOORS

Riding the rushing tide aboard a 16-foot self-bailing Zodiac with **Shubenacadie River Runners** (✉*8681 Hwy. 215, Maitland* ☎*902/261–2770 or 800/856–5061* ⊕*www.tidalborerafting.com*) is an adventure you won't soon forget. Tide conditions and time of day let you choose a mildly turbulent ride or an ultrawild one. A 3½-hour excursion costs $75 (with a barbecue), and a two-hour trip is $55 (with a snack). Gear included in both. The **Truro Raceway** (✉*Main St.* ☎*902/893–8075*) holds year-round harness racing.

CAPE BRETON ISLAND

The highways and byways of the Island of Cape Breton, including those on the **Cabot Trail,** make up one of the most spectacular drives in North America. As you wind through the rugged coastal headlands of Cape Breton Highlands National Park, you can climb mountains and plunge back down to the sea in a matter of minutes. Every May the rugged but

Fodor's Choice   beautiful terrain plays host to **The Cabot Trail Relay Race,** a 17-stage run
★   over almost 300 km (185 mi).

The Margaree River is a cultural dividing line: south of the river the settlements are Scottish, up the river they are largely Irish, and north of the river they are Acadian French. Maritime cultural heritage is alive and vibrant and ancient dialects can still be heard in the villages. Wherever you go in Cape Breton you are sure to experience warmth and hospitality.

Bras d'Or Lake, a vast, warm, almost landlocked inlet of the sea, occupies the entire center of Cape Breton. The coastline of the lake is more than 967 km (600 mi) long, and people sail yachts from all over the world to cruise its serene, unspoiled coves and islands. Bald eagles have become so plentiful around the lake that they are exported to the United States to restock natural habitats. Four of the largest communities along the shore are native Mi'Kmaq communities.

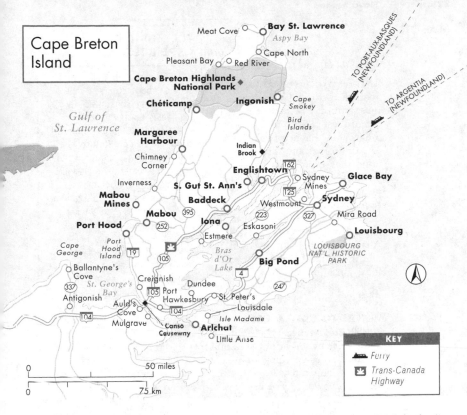

Cape Breton Island

Gulf of St. Lawrence

Bras d'Or Lake

St. George's Bay

LOUISBOURG NAT'L. HISTORIC PARK

KEY
Ferry
Trans-Canada Highway

0   50 miles

0   75 km

EN ROUTE

Allow five days for a meandering tour of approximately 710 km (440 mi) that begins by entering the island via the Canso Causeway on Highway 104. Turn left at the rotary and take Highway 19, the Ceilidh Trail, which winds for 129 km (80 mi) along the mountainside through glens and farms, with fine views across St. George's Bay to Cape George. This western shoreline of Cape Breton faces the Gulf of St. Lawrence and is famous for its sandy beaches and warm salt water.

PORT HOOD

45 km (28 mi) northwest of the Canso Causeway on Hwy. 19; 103 km (64 mi) northwest of Antigonish.

At this fishing village you can buy lobster and snow crab fresh off the wharf as the boats return in midafternoon. With a little persuasion, one of the fisherfolk might give you a lift to **Port Hood Island,** 2 km (1 mi) across the harbor. It's a 10-minute walk from the island's wharf to the pastel-color cliffs of wave-mottled alabaster on the seaward shore. Both the village and the island have sandy beaches ideal for swimming.

MABOU

13 km (8 mi) northeast of Port Hood on Hwy. 19.

The pretty village of Mabou is very Scottish, with its Gaelic signs and most Saturday nights offer a helping of local culture in the form of a dance or "kitchen party," which is an informal and intimate gathering that usually involves music and dance. Check bulletin boards at local businesses for information about these events. This is the hometown of national recording and performing artists such as John Allan Cameron, Jimmy Rankin, and the Rankin Family. Stop at a local gift shop and buy music to play as you drive down the long fjord of Mabou Harbour.

> ### THE MUSIC OF CAPE BRETON
>
> If Halifax is the heart of Nova Scotia, Cape Breton is its soul, complete with soul music—flying fiddles, boisterous rock, and velvet ballads. Cape Breton musicians—weaned on Scottish jigs and reels—are among the world's finest. In summer there are local festivals and concerts and most every community in the southern end of Inverness County takes a different night of the week to offer a square dance. Bulletin boards, newspapers, visitor information centers, and a toll-free events line June to October (☎888/562–9848) list square-dance times and locations.

WHERE TO STAY & EAT

$–$$$ ✕ **Mull Café & Deli.** It's doubtful you'll drive by this informal restaurant on Mabou's main thoroughfare without seeing a parking lot full of cars. One of the most popular establishments on western Cape Breton, the café draws diners for its pasta, seafood chowder, fish-and-chips, steaks, and homemade desserts. The restaurant has a deli counter and is fully licensed. Local artwork is on display. The café closes at 8 PM in summer and 7 PM in winter. ✉*11630 Rte. 19* ☎*902/945–2244* ⊕*www.duncreigan.ca* ⊟*AE, MC, V.*

$–$$$ ✕⌨ **Duncreigan Country Inn.** Though they were built in the 1990s, these buildings on the shore of Mabou Harbour suggest the early 1900s in design and furnishings. Several decks afford beautiful views and are ideal for relaxing, reading, and leaving your cares behind. The restaurant ($$$), open for dinner from July to mid-October, has an enviable reputation. A full breakfast buffet is included in the room rate in summer. ✉*11409–11411 Rte. 19, B0E 1X0* ☎*902/945–2207, 800/840–2207 for reservations* 🖷*902/945–2206* ⊕*www.duncreigan. ca* ⌨*7 rooms, 1 suite* ♿*In-room: satellite TV, whirlpool (some), Wi-Fi. In-hotel: restaurant, bicycles, no elevator* ⊟*MC, V.*

$–$$$ ⌨ **Glenora Inn & Distillery.** North America's first and Canada's only single-malt-whiskey distillery adjoins this friendly inn. Here you can sample a "wee dram" of the inn's own whiskey—Glen Breton Rare. Even if you don't stay overnight, you can take a tour of the distillery and museum, enjoy fine cuisine and traditional Cape Breton music, and tour the courtyard gardens. MacLellan's Brook runs through the property. Rooms in the inn overlook the courtyard; chalets have two-person whirlpool baths, woodstoves, and kitchens. ✉*Hwy. 19, Box 181, Glenville B0E 1X0* ☎*902/258–2662 or 800/839–0491* 🖷*902/258–3572* ⊕*www. glenoradistillery.com* ⌨*9 rooms, 6 chalets* ♿*In-room: no a/c (some),* *kitchen (some), satellite TV. In-hotel: restaurant, bar, gift shop, no elevator* ▭ *AE, D, MC, V* ⊙ *Closed Nov.–May.*

NIGHTLIFE

To sample Cape Breton's famous music scene and grab a quick bite or a cool ale, drop into the **Red Shoe Pub** (⊠ *Main St. [Rte. 19]* ☎ *902/945–2326 or 902/945-2996* ⊕ *www.redshoepub.com* ⊙ *Mid-Oct.–May*). Once home to dry goods and groceries, it's music and conversation you find now in this former general store. You might even see one of the owners take the stage—in 2005, four Rankin sisters became proprietors, adding an outdoor deck, a full bar, and innovative Nova Scotia cooking. Every night there's music: Monday to Wednesday, with supper (5 to 7 PM); Thursday through Saturday, late evening (10 to 1 AM), and on Sunday there's a ceilidh (4 to 7 PM).

MABOU MINES

10 km (6 mi) northwest of Mabou.

This quiet area is a place so hauntingly exquisite that you expect to meet the *sidhe*, the Scottish fairies, capering on the hillsides. Within the hills of Mabou Mines is some of the finest hiking in the province, and above the land fly bald eagles, plentiful in this region. Inquire locally or at the tourist office in Margaree Forks for information about trails.

OUTDOORS & SPORTS

★ Gaelic and English names on wooden signs mark the way for 15 **hiking trails** on more than 20 square km (8 square mi) of coastal wilderness in Cape Mabou. All are as natural as possible. Some follow old cart tracks that connected pioneer settlements. Gaelic-speaking immigrants from Scotland settled this region of plunging cliffs, isolated beaches, rising mountains, glens, meadows, and hardwood forests. Trail maps are available at local retailers or by mail from the **Cape Mabou Trail Club** (⊠ *Inverness, B0E 1N0*). Include $2 and a self-addressed, stamped envelope.

> **WORD OF MOUTH**
>
> "Hiking in Cape Breton is as good as it gets. Once you get to Cape Breton, you may nwot want to leave."　　　　—fewglow

MARGAREE HARBOUR

33 km (20 mi) north of Mabou.

The Ceilidh Trail joins the Cabot Trail at Margaree Harbour at the mouth of the Margaree River, a famous salmon-fishing and fly-fishing stream and a favorite canoe route.

Exhibits at the **Margaree Salmon Museum,** in a former schoolhouse, include fishing tackle, photographs, and other memorabilia related to salmon angling on the Margaree River. ⊠ *60 E. Big Intervale Rd., North East Margaree* ☎ *902/248-2848* 🖾 *$2* ⊙ *Mid-June–mid-Oct., daily 9–5.*

WHERE TO STAY & EAT

$–$$$ ✕⊡ **Normaway Inn & Cabins.** Nestled on 250 acres in the hills of the Margaree Valley at the beginning of the Cabot Trail, this secluded 1920s inn has distinctive rooms and cabins, most with woodstoves and screened porches. Nightly entertainment might be a film or traditional music, and there are weekly square dances in the Barn. The restaurant ($$$$) is known for its country cuisine, particularly the vegetable chowders and fresh seafood ragout. Cabins and the dining room are available off-season by arrangement. ✉ *691 Egypt Rd., Box 101, 3 km (2 mi) off Cabot Trail, B0E 2C0* ☎ *902/248–2987 or 800/565–9463* 🖷 *902/248–2600* ⊕ *www.normaway.com* ☛ *12 rooms, 17 cabins* ♿ *In-room: no a/c, no TV. In-hotel: restaurant, tennis court, no elevator* ▣ *MC, V* ⊘ *Closed mid-Oct.–mid-June.*

CHÉTICAMP

26 km (16 mi) north of Margaree Harbour.

This Acadian community has the best harbor and the largest settlement on this shore. Even after 200 years of history, Chéticamp's Acadian culture and traditions are still very much a way of life in the region. Nestled between the mountains and the sea, the community offers the pride, traditions, and warmth of Acadian hospitality. Its tall silver steeple towers over the village, which stands exposed on a wide lip of flat land below a range of bald green hills. Behind these hills lies the high plateau of the Cape Breton Highlands. The area is known for its *suêtes,* strong southeast winds of 120 km to 130 km (75 mi to 80 mi) per hour that may develop into a force of up to 200 km (125 mi) per hour: they've been known to blow the roofs off buildings.

Chéticamp is famous for its hooked rugs, available at many local gift shops.

The **Dr. Elizabeth LeFort Gallery and Museum: Les Trois Pignons** displays artifacts, fine hooked rugs, and tapestries. LeFort, born in 1914, created more than 300 tapestries, some of which have been hung in the Vatican, the White House, and Buckingham Palace. The museum is also an Acadian cultural and genealogical information center. ✉ *15584 Cabot Trail, Box 430, B0E 1H0* ☎ *902/224–2642* 🖷 *902/224–1579* ⊕ *www.lestroispignons.com* ▣ *$5* ⊘ *July and Aug., daily 9–7; May, June, Sept., and Oct., daily 9–5.*

La Pirogue Museum. This fascinating museum is set to reopen in 2008 but call to confirm before you go. The dazzling collection of Gilbert van Ryekevorsel's underwater photography, traditional rag rugs, an

1

Acadian homestead reproduction, fishery displays, and artifacts from the Charles Robin store, founded in the 18th century, are found in the Cheticamp Development Commission's three-level waterfront museum. This is an ideal place to learn about the community's ties to fishing. A geothermal heat pump extracts saltwater from the sea to heat and cool the building. ✉ *15359 Cabot Trail* ☎ *902/224–3349* 🖷 *902/224–2801* ⊕ *www.members.tripod.com/cbmuseums/id58.html* 🎫 *$5* 🕙 *Seasonal operation; call for hrs.*

WHERE TO STAY & EAT

$$–$$$ ✕ **Le Gabriel.** You can't miss Le Gabriel, with its large lighthouse entranceway—and you won't want to: the casual tavern offers simple but good fresh fish dinners and traditional Acadian dishes, such as meat pie, fish cakes, or *fricot* (a hearty stew with potatoes, pork bits, chives, and beef or chicken). Snow crab and lobster specials are available in season. ✉ *15424 Cabot Trail* ☎ *902/224–3685* ⊕ *www.legabriel.com* 🖃 *AE, MC, V* 🕙 *Dining room closed late Oct.–Apr.*

$$–$$$$ 🏨 **Cabot Trail Sea & Golf Chalets.** Next to Le Portage Golf Course and overlooking the ocean, these chalets are ideal for families and golfers. One- and two-bedroom units have covered decks with gas barbecues, and some have fireplaces. The three-bedroom country suite has a washer, dryer, and dishwasher. ✉ *71 Fraser Doucet La., Box 324, B0E 1H0* ☎ *902/224–1777 or 877/224–1777* 🖷 *902/224–1999* ⊕ *www. seagolfchalets.com* 🛏 *12 chalets, 1 suite* ♿ *In-room: no a/c, kitchen (some). In-hotel: golf course, no elevator* 🖃 *AE, D, MC, V* 🕙 *Closed mid-Oct.–mid-May.*

¢–$ 🏨 **Chéticamp Outfitters' Inn Bed & Breakfast.** The clean and cozy rooms at this homey inn overlook the ocean, mountains, and valley. The furniture includes homemade wooden pieces, paintings by the innkeeper, and quilts. Fantastic blueberry muffins are a highlight of the home cooked breakfast. ✉ *13938 Cabot Trail, B0E 1H0* ☎ *902/224–2776* ⊕ *www.cheticampns.com/cheticampoutfitters* 🛏 *6 rooms, 1 chalet* ♿ *In-room: no a/c, refrigerator (some), VCR (some), satellite TV (some), no elevator* 🖃 *AE, MC, V* 🕙 *Closed Dec.–Apr. 15* 🍽 *BP.*

SPORTS & THE OUTDOORS

WHALE WATCHING   Chéticamp is known for its whale-watching cruises, which depart from the government wharf twice daily in May, three times daily June through August. **Captain Zodiac Whale Cruise** (☎ *902/224–1088 or 877/232–2522* ⊕ *www.wesleyswhalewatch.com*) guarantees whale sightings on a two-hour Zodiac tour ($39). **Whale Cruisers Ltd.** (☎ *902/224–3376 or 800/813–3376*) is a reliable charter company, and was the first whale-watching company in Nova Scotia. Tours run two or three times daily, May 15 through October 15, and are $25. Expect to see minke, pilot, and finback whales in their natural environment; seabird and bald-eagle sightings are also common.

CAPE BRETON HIGHLANDS NATIONAL PARK

Fodor'sChoice *5 km (3 mi) north of Chéticamp; 108 km (67 mi) north of Ingonish.*
★ A 950-square-km (366-square-mi) wilderness of wooded valleys, plateau barrens, and steep cliffs, this park stretches across northern Cape Breton from the gulf shore to the Atlantic. The highway through the park (world-renowned Cabot Trail) is magnificent. It rises to the tops of the coastal mountains and descends through scenic switchbacks to the sea. In fact, the road has been compared to a 106-km (66-mi) roller-coaster ride, stretching from Chéticamp to Ingonish. Good brakes and attentive driving are advised. Pull-offs provide photo opportunities, and exhibits explain the land and history. For wildlife watchers there's much to see, including moose, eagles, deer, bears, foxes, and bobcats—your chances of seeing wildlife are better if you venture off the main road and hike one of the trails at dusk or dawn. Note that it is illegal to feed or approach any animal in the park. Always take care to observe the animals from a safe distance; in particular, you should exercise caution driving in the moose zones, marked by signs on the highway. Moose sometimes claim the road as their own and stand in the middle of it. Hitting one can be damaging to both you and the animal.

High-altitude bogs are home to delightful wild orchids and other unique flora and fauna. If you plan to hike or camp in the park, stop at the Chéticamp Information Centre for advice and necessary permits. A park permit or pass is required for sightseeing along sections of the Cabot Trail highway when within the National Park and for use of the facilities such as exhibits, hiking trails, and picnic areas; there are additional fees for camping, fishing, and golf. ⊠ *Entrances on Cabot Trail near Chéticamp and Ingonish* ☎ *902/224–2306, 902/224–3814 bookstore* ⊕ *www.pc.gc.ca* ⊠ *$6.90* ⊗ *Year-round, daily dawn–dusk.*

For those who prefer to stay on dry land to observe sea life, stop by the **Whale Interpretive Centre.** Using zoom scopes on the whale-spotting deck, you may catch a close-up glimpse of many different species of whales that are often frolicking just offshore from the center. Inside the modern structure, exhibits and models explain the unique world of whales. ⊠ *104 Harbour Rd., Pleasant Bay* ☎ *902/224–1411* 🖷 *902/224–1751* ⊕ *www.whalecentre.ca* ⊠ *$4.50* ⊗ *Mid-June–early Sept., 9–8; mid-May–mid-June and early Sept–Oct., 9–6.*

OFF THE BEATEN PATH

Gampo Abbey. The most northerly tip of the island is not part of the National Park; a spur road (take a left at Pleasant Bay) creeps along the cliffs to Red River, beyond which, on a broad flat bench of land high above the sea, is this Tibetan Buddhist monastery. It's possible to tour the abbey when it's not in retreat. The only way to know whether a tour is available is to drive to the abbey and check the sign at the gate. If the abbey is closed, you can continue down the road for about ½ km (¼ mi) to visit the Stupa, a large and elaborate shrine, dedicated to world peace.

SPORTS & THE OUTDOORS

WHALE
WATCHING

All whale-watching tours have a money-back guarantee if you don't see a whale.

You may see pilot, finback, humpback, or minke whales on **Captain Mark's Whale & Seal Cruise** (☎902/224–1316 or 888/754–5112 ⊕*www.whaleandsealcruise.com*). An underwater video camera adds to the experience. Cruises allow for exploration of sea caves, waterfalls, and rock and cliff formations along a remote stretch of unspoiled Cape Breton coastline. Tours are May 15 through October 15 and cost $25 to $44. **Fiddlin' Whale Tours** (☎902/224–2424 or 866/688–2424) throws a "kitchen party" on the water, so you can enjoy live traditional Cape Breton fiddling on the boat while cruising the seas. Tours ($30) are June 1 through October 1. **Wesley's Whale Watching** (☎902/224–1919 or 866/999–4253) leads two-hour trips in Cape Island boats May 15 through October 15 to see whales, dolphins, seals, and scenery. Tours are $25.

BAY ST. LAWRENCE

76 km (47 mi) north of Chéticamp.

The charming fishing village of Bay St. Lawrence is nestled in a bowl-shape valley around a harbor pond. You can hike along the shore to the east and the Money Point Lighthouse, or find a quiet corner of the shoreline for contemplation.

Cabot's Landing Provincial Park (⊠*Bay St. Lawrence Rd., 2 km [1 mi] north of Four Mile Beach Inn* ☎*No phone*) is a must-visit for views, walking, and a sandy beach enclosed by rugged mountains. It's a perfect spot for a picnic. Admission to the park is free, and it's open daily 9 to 9 mid-May through mid-October. A National Historic Site cairn of Italian explorer John Cabot is on-site.

OFF THE
BEATEN
PATH

Meat Cove. Named for the moose and (now absent) caribou that roamed the highlands and once supplied protein for passing sailing vessels, Meat Cove feels like the end of the earth. It lies at the end of a daunting 12-km (7-mi) mostly unpaved road along a precipitous cliff marked by sudden switchbacks. It's spectacular. To get here, leave the Cabot Trail at Cape North on the Bay St. Lawrence Road. At the foot of the hill leading into St. Margaret's, turn left and follow the sign to Capstick; that road leads to Meat Cove.

WHERE TO STAY

$–$$
Fodor'sChoice
★

🗹 **Four Mile Beach Inn.** The view of Aspy Bay and the ridge of the highland mountains is fantastic from this large white 19th-century house near Cabot's Landing. The hosts know the Cabot Trail and can provide personalized day planning. Canoeing and kayaking are possible from the small dock on the property, and bike rentals are available. Rooms are clean and have a country look. The suites have a private entrance and a deck. An old-fashioned general store sells ice cream and souvenirs. ⊠*R.R. 1, Aspy Bay, Cape North B0C 1G0* ☎*902/383–2282 or 888/503–5551* ⊕*www.fourmilebeachinn.com* ↪*3 rooms, 5 suites*

⚐ *In-room: a/c (some), kitchen (some), no TV. In-hotel: bicycles, public Internet, no elevator* ☲*AE, MC, V* ⊘*Closed mid-Oct.–June* ⦙⦿⦙*CP.*

SPORTS & THE OUTDOORS
Capt. Cox's Whale Watch (☎*902/383–2981 or 888/346–5556* ⊕*www. aco.ca/captcox*) gives several tours daily—weather permitting—July through August. The cost is $25. If you don't see a whale, you get another, free trip.

INGONISH

113 km (70 mi) northeast of Chéticamp; 37 km (23 mi) south of Bay St. Lawrence.

Ingonish, one of the leading vacation destinations on the island, is actually several villages—Ingonish Centre, Ingonish Beach, South Ingonish Harbour, and Ingonish Ferry—on two bays, divided by a long narrow peninsula called Middle Head. Each bay has a sandy beach.

> **WORD OF MOUTH**
>
> "You will love Ingonish! . . . Be sure and go all the way to Meat Cove via White Point when you have a clear day."   —smcgown

OFF THE BEATEN PATH

Bird Islands. The small islands just 2 km (1 mi) off the entrance to the Bras d'Or Lake are the Bird Islands, breeding grounds for Atlantic puffins, other seabirds, bald eagles, and gray seals. From Baddeck, take Highway 105 east 35 km (22 mi) to Exit 14, then left 6 km (4 mi) to Bird Island Boat Tour. Boat tours ($33) are offered several times daily mid-May to mid-September from Bird Island Boat Tour (⊠*1672 Old Rte. 5, Big Bras d'Or* ☎*902/674–2384 or 800/661–6680* ⊕*www.birdisland.net*). Landing by private boat is forbidden.

WHERE TO STAY & EAT

$$$$
Fodor'sChoice
★

╳⦙⦙ **Keltic Lodge.** Spread across cliffs overlooking the ocean, the provincially owned Keltic Lodge is on the Cabot Trail in Cape Breton Highlands National Park and has stunning views of Cape Smokey and the surrounding highlands. Kilted doormen greet guests at the lodge entrance. Rooms in the main lodge have charm and character; rooms at the Inn at Keltic are larger and air-conditioned. Cottages and suites are also available. Activities include golfing on the challenging Highlands Links and guided hikes. Freshwater and saltwater beaches are within walking distance and nightly entertainment is offered in the Highland Sitting Room, a perfect venue for a relaxing cocktail by the fire. Seafood stars in the Purple Thistle Dining Room ($$$$). The 5,000-square-foot Spa at Keltic opened on the property in 2005, taking full advantage of the cliffside view. ⊠*Middle Head Peninsula, Ingonish Beach* ☎*902/285–2880 or 800/565–0444* ⊕*www.signatureresorts. com* ⌑*72 rooms, 2 suites, 11 cottages* ⚐*In-room: no a/c (some). In-hotel: 2 restaurants, pool, beachfront, bicycles, laundry service* ☲*AE, D, DC, MC, V* ⊘*Closed late Oct.–mid-May* ⦙⦿⦙*MAP.*

1

$-$$$$ ⚏**Glenghorm Beach Resort.** You can swim in the ocean, and hike or bike from the motor inn, cottages, or beach-house suites. Locally made souvenirs and handicrafts are for sell at the gift shop. ✉*36743 Cabot Trail, Box 39, B0C 1K0* ☎*902/285–2049 or 800/565–5660* 🖨*902/285–2395* ⊕*www.capebretonresorts.com* ↪*54 rooms, 10 suites, 10 cottages* ♿*In-room: no a/c (some). In-hotel: restaurant, bar, pool, exercise room, beachfront, laundry facilities, no elevator* ▭*AE, D, DC, MC, V* ⊘*Closed Nov.–mid-May.*

$$-$$$ ⚏**Lantern Hill & Hollow.** Hearing the surf is no problem at this intimate property since the six cottages are just steps from a 3-km (2-mi) beach: perfect for lazy summer days, a quick dip, and nightly bonfires. Bonfire wood is supplied, as are beach toys. Five cottages have two bedrooms, and the sixth is a one-bedroom unit with a corner whirlpool tub. Each comes fully equipped, including patio furniture and barbecue, and have covered verandas. Guests in the main house have a large patio overlooking the beach. ✉*36845 Cabot Trail, B0C 1L0* ☎*902/285–2010 or 888/663–0225* 🖨*902/285–2001* ⊕*www.lanternhillandhollow.com* ↪*3 suites, 6 cottages* ♿*In-room: no a/c, kitchen (some), mini-fridge, no elevator* ▭*MC, V* ⊘*mid-Oct.–late May.*

$-$$ ⚏**Castle Rock Country Inn.** Surrounded by an idyllic setting of mountains and ocean, and offering the tranquility of a lounge area, the Castle Rock provides an excellent environment for contemplation and relaxation. The spacious guest rooms have queen beds, and most have an additional sofa bed; some have ocean views. The Georgian-style inn is right on the Cabot Trail in Ingonish Ferry. ✉*39339 Cabot Trail, B0C 1L0* ☎*902/285–2700 or 888/884–7625* 🖨*902/285–2525* ⊕*www. ingonish.com/castlerock* ↪*16 rooms* ♿*In-room: no a/c, satellite TV, no elevator* ▭*AE, MC, V.*

SPORTS & THE OUTDOORS
Perennially ranked as one of Canada's top courses, **Highlands Links** (✉*Cape Breton Highlands National Park* ☎*902/285–2600 or 800/441–1118* ⊕*www.highlandslinksgolf.com*) has abundant natural scenery in the form of mountains and sea, not to mention great golfing. It's open daily, from mid-May until the end of October, dawn until dusk, weather permitting. A round of 18 holes is $88.

ENGLISHTOWN

65 km (40 mi) south of Ingonish on Hwy. 312.

A short (five-minute) ferry ride heads from Jersey Cove across St. Ann's Bay to Englishtown, home of the celebrated Cape Breton Giant, Angus MacAskill. Ferries run 24 hours a day; the fare is $5 per car.

The **Giant MacAskill Museum** holds artifacts of the 7-foot 9-inch man who traveled with P. T. Barnum's troupe in the 1800s. His remains are buried in the local cemetery nearby. ✉*Hwy. 312* ☎*902/929–2875* 🎫*$1* ⊘*Mid-June–mid-Sept., daily 9–6.*

SOUTH GUT ST. ANN'S

10 km (6 mi) west of Englishtown.

Settled by the Highland Scots, South Gut St. Ann's is home to Gaelic College, North America's only Gaelic college. From the Gaelic College of Celtic Arts and Crafts, you can follow the Cabot Trail as it meanders along the hills that rim St. Ann's Bay. The 30-km (19-mi) stretch between St. Ann's and Indian Brook is home to a collection of fine crafts shops.

The **Great Hall of the Clans** depicts Scottish history and has an account of the Great Migration, the exodus of Scottish people for the new world in the late 18th and early 19th centuries. The college offers courses in Gaelic language and literature, Scottish music and dancing, weaving, and other Scottish arts. There's also a Scottish gift shop. ⊠ *Gaelic College, 51779 Cabot Trail, Exit 11 off Hwy. 105* ☎ *902/295–3411* ⊕ *www.gaeliccollege.edu* ⊡ *$7* ⊙ *Mid-June–mid-Sept., daily 9–5.*

WHERE TO STAY

$–$$ 🖫 **English Country Garden Bed & Breakfast.** A peaceful, lakefront setting greets you at this 1940 home, 12 km (7½ mi) from South Gut St. Ann's; there are three guest suites and a B&B cottage. The African Room, the Conservatory, the Russian Room, and the barrier-free Rose Cottage are richly decorated from the owners' travels and collections of antiques. The owners are adding walking trails through the birch trees to MacDonald's Pond. With advance notice, an evening meal ($80 per couple) is available for in-house guests; a full English breakfast is included. The B&B is ideally situated to explore the artisans of St. Ann's Bay along the Cabot Trail, and there's snowshoeing on the property in winter. TVs and DVDs are available on request. ⊠ *45478 Cabot Trail, Indian Brook, B0C 1H0* ☎ *866/929–2721* ⊕ *www.capebretongarden.com* ⟲ *3 suites, 1 cottage* ⟳ *In-room: no a/c, Internet, no phone. In-hotel: no elevator* ⊟ *MC, V* ⊙*l BP.*

BADDECK

20 km (12 mi) south of South Gut St. Ann's.

Baddeck, the most highly developed tourist center on Cape Breton, has more than 1,000 motel beds, a golf course, fine gift shops, and many restaurants. This was also the summer home of Alexander Graham Bell until he died here at the age of 75. The annual **regatta** of the Bras d'Or Yacht Club is held the first week of August. Sailing tours and charters are available, as are bus tours along the Cabot Trail.

On the waterfront, check out the **Water's Edge Gallery,** chock-full of original works from Cape Breton and Maritime artists.

The **Celtic Colours International Festival** (☎ *902/562–6700 or 877/285–2321* ⊕ *www.celtic-colours.com*) takes place during 10 days spanning the second and third weekends in October. It draws the world's best Celtic performers at the height of autumn splendor. International artists travel from Celtic countries around the world, and homegrown talent shines in 44-plus performances in more than 38 communities scattered around the island. The cost for each performance is $20 to $90. Workshops and seminars covering all aspects of Gaelic language, lore, history, crafts, and culture fill the festival days.

Ⓒ The **Alexander Graham Bell National Historic Site of Canada** explores Bell's ★ inventions. Experiments, kite making, and other hands-on activities are designed for children. From films, artifacts, and photographs, you learn what ideas led Bell to create man-carrying kites, airplanes, and a record-setting hydrofoil boat. The site has reduced services from the end of October through May. ⊠ *559 Chebucto St.* ☎ *902/295–2069* ⊕ *www.parkscanada.ca* ⊠ *$7.15* ⊙ *July–mid-Oct., daily 8:30–6; mid-Oct.–May, daily 9–5; June, daily 9–6.*

At the **Wagmatcook Culture & Heritage Centre** the ancient history and rich traditions of the native Mi'Kmaq are demonstrated on request. Mi'Kmaq guides provide interpretations and cultural entertainment. The on-site restaurant highlights traditional foods such as moose and eel dishes, as well as more contemporary choices. The crafts shop has products by local native people. ⊠ *Wagmatcook First Nation, Rte. 105, 16 km (10 mi) west of Baddeck* ☎ *902/295–2999* ⊕ *www.wagmatcook.com* ⊠ *Free* ⊙ *Year-round.*

WHERE TO STAY & EAT

$$–$$$ ✕ **Baddeck Lobster Suppers.** For super-fresh lobster, try this restaurant in a former legion hall. During busy times, you may have to wait for a table. Entrées come with mussels, chowder, dessert, beverage, and homemade buns and biscuits. At lunch, the menu is considerably cheaper and options include a lobster-roll platter, chowder, mussels, and homemade beef soup. There's a bar and a gift shop. ⊠ *17 Ross St.* ☎ *902/295–3307* ☎ *902/295–3424* ☐ *MC, V* ⊙ *Closed mid-Oct.–mid-June.*

$$–$$$$ ✕▣ **Inverary Resort.** On the shores of the magnificent Bras d'Or Lake, this resort has stunning views and lots of activities. You can choose from cottage suites, modern hotel units, or the elegant 100-year-old main lodge; some rooms have fireplaces. There's boating on the premises and swimming close to the village, but the resort remains tranquil. Dine at the elegant main dining room ($$–$$$) where a bounty of seafood—from smoked salmon and scallops to seafood chowder and lobster—is tempered by dishes like the New Zealand lamb and strip loin with mushroom oil. ⊠ *Hwy. 205 and Shore Rd., Box 190, B0E 1B0* ☎ *902/295–3500 or 800/565–5660* ☎ *902/295–3527* ⊕ *www.capebretonresorts.com/inverary.asp* ⊷ *129 rooms, 9 cottages* ⌂ *In-room: Wi-Fi. In-hotel: restaurant, bar, tennis courts, pool, gym, spa, water sports, bicycles, no elevator* ☐ *AE, D, DC, MC, V.*

$$–$$$$ ▣ **Auberge Gisele's Inn.** This inn and motel share lovely landscaped flower gardens and overlook the Bras d'Or Lake. The atmosphere is one of tasteful hospitality. Some rooms have fireplaces. The chef prepares breakfast and dinner. Deal a hand in the card-playing room or enjoy a cocktail on the outdoor patio. The executive suites have whirlpool tubs and gas fireplaces. Rooms are modern and deluxe. ⊠ *387 Shore Rd., B0E 1B0* ☎ *902/295–2849* ☎ *902/295–2033* ⊕ *www.giseles.com*

⮱*75 rooms, 3 suites* ⟐*In-room: dial-up. In-hotel: laundry facilities* ⊟*AE, D, MC, V* ⊘*Closed late Oct.–early May.*

¢–$ ⌧ **Bain's Heritage House B&B.** Built in the 1850s, this lovely heritage home is in the center of Baddeck. On cooler evenings you can relax in front of the fire in the sitting room. ✉*121 Twining St., B0E 1B0* ☎*902/295–1069* ⮱*3 rooms, 1 with bath* ⟐*In-room: no a/c, no elevator* ⊟*MC, V* ⦿❙*BP.*

IONA

56 km (35 mi) south of Baddeck.

Iona, where some residents still speak Gaelic, is the site of a living-history museum. To get here from Baddeck, take Trans-Canada Highway 105 to Exit 6, which leads to Little Narrows, where you can take a ferry to the Washabuck Peninsula.

Fodor'sChoice   The **Highland Village Museum** is set high on a mountainside, with a
★   spectacular view of Bras d'Or Lake and the narrow Barra Strait. The village's 11 historical buildings were assembled from all over Cape Breton to depict the Highland Scots' way of life from their origins in the Hebrides to the present day. Among the staff at this museum are a smith in the blacksmith shop and a clerk in the store. ✉*4119 Hwy. 223* ☎*902/725–2272* ⊕*www.highlandvillage.museum.gov.ns.ca* ✍*$9* ⊘*June–mid-Oct., daily 9:30–5:30.*

WHERE TO STAY & EAT

$–$$ ✕⌧ **Highland Heights Inn.** The rural surroundings, the Scottish home-style cooking served near the restaurant's huge stone fireplace, and the view of the lake substitute nicely for the Scottish Highlands. The inn is on a hillside beside the Nova Scotia Highland Village, overlooking Iona. The salmon (or any fish in season), fresh-baked oatcakes, and homemade desserts at the restaurant ($–$$$) are good choices. Staff at the inn can help plan adventures such as whale-watching, golf, and sailing. ✉*4115 Hwy. 223, B2C 1A3* ☎*902/725–2360 or 800/660–8122* 🖷*902/725–2800* ⊕*www.highlandheightsinn.ca* ⮱*32 rooms* ⟐*In-room: no a/c. In-hotel: restaurant, no-smoking rooms, no elevator* ⊟*D, MC, V* ⊘*Closed mid-Oct.–mid-May.*

▌ EN
ROUTE   **The Barra Strait Bridge joins Iona to Grand Narrows. The East Bay route runs through the Mi'Kmaq village of Eskasoni, the largest community of native people in the province. The First Nation community holds an annual pow-wow in June with traditional dancing, singing, and ceremonies, providing a great avenue to experience this culture.**

SYDNEY

60 km (37 mi) northeast of Iona.

The heart of Nova Scotia's second-largest urban cluster, this city encompasses villages, unorganized districts, and a half dozen towns. Most sprang up around the coal mines, which fed the steel plant at Sydney.

1

These are warmhearted, interesting communities with a diverse ethnic population that includes Ukrainians, Welsh, Poles, Lebanese, West Indians, and Italians. Most residents are descendants of the miners and steelworkers who arrived a century ago when the area was booming.

Sydney has the island's only real airport, its only university, and a lively entertainment scene that specializes in Cape Breton music. It is also a departure point—fast ferries leave from North Sydney for Newfoundland, and scheduled air service to Newfoundland and the French islands of St-Pierre and Miquelon departs from Sydney Airport. Cruise ships have been a familiar sight since 1962 and dock at the big violin scultpure on the waterfront.

WHERE TO STAY & EAT

$–$$$ ✕ **Governor's Pub and Eastery.** Sydney's first mayor, Walter Crowe, once lived in this Victorian home, built in the late 1800s. The restaurant, with hardwood floors, a fireplace, and high ceilings, is known for its seafood and steaks, though it has a full menu. Both the restaurant and the pub upstairs have two large patios that overlook Sydney Harbour. Desserts are homemade. ⌧ *233 Esplanade B1P 1A6* ☎ *902/562–7646* ▤ *AE, D, MC, V.*

$$–$$$$ ✕▦ **Gowrie House.** This unexpected find between North Sydney and
★ Sydney Mines, minutes from the Newfoundland ferry, is shaded by towering trees on grounds filled with gardens and flowering shrubs. Cherry trees supply the main ingredient for chilled black-cherry soup in the restaurant ($$$$). Antiques, fine art, and exquisite china add to the elegance. The main house has six rooms; the secluded garden house four more; and the caretaker's cottage provides deluxe private accommodation. Whether you stay overnight or are a guest for dinner only, dinner reservations are essential. ⌧ *840 Shore Rd., Sydney Mines B1V 1A6* ☎ *902/544–1050 or 800/372–1115* ⊕ *www.gowriehouse. com* ⇱ *10 rooms, 1 cottage* ₺ *In-hotel: restaurant, no elevator* ▤ *AE, MC, V* ▮◯▮ *BP.*

$$–$$$ ▦ **Cambridge Suites Hotel.** Put yourself in the center of the action on the Sydney waterfront by staying at this comfortable all-suites hotel. Some of the spacious rooms directly overlook the harbour. ⌧ *380 Esplanade, B1P 1B1* ☎ *902/562–6500 or 800/565–9466* ⊕ *www.cambridgesuitessydney.com* ⇱ *147 rooms* ₺ *In-room: kitchen, dial-up. In-hotel: restaurant, lounge, fitness center, no-smoking rooms* ▤ *AE, D, DC, MC, V* ◯ ▮◯▮ *CP.*

$$–$$$ ▦ **Delta Sydney.** This hotel is on the harbor, beside the yacht club and close to the center of town. Guest rooms are pleasant and have harbor views. The restaurant ($$) specializes in seafood and pasta. The 50-foot waterslide makes it fun for kids, too. ⌧ *300 Esplanade, B1P 1A7* ☎ *902/562–7500 or 800/565–1001* ◳ *902/562–3023* ⊕ *www.deltahotels.com* ⇱ *152 rooms* ₺ *In-hotel: restaurant, bar, hot tub, pool, gym, Wi-Fi* ▤ *AE, DC, MC, V.*

NIGHTLIFE & THE ARTS

Many fiddlers appear at the weeklong **Big Pond Festival** (⌧ *Rte. 4, 1 km [½ mi] east of Rita's Tea Room* ☎ *902/828–2667*) in mid-July. At the **Casino Nova Scotia** (⌧ *525 George St.* ☎ *902/563–7777*) you can try the slot machines, roulette, or gaming tables or enjoy live entertainment. **Smooth Herman's** (✉424 Charlotte St. ☎902/539–0408) is an upbeat spot with live music on weekends.

GLACE BAY

21 km (13 mi) east of Sydney.

A coal-mining town and fishing port, Glace Bay has a rich history of industrial struggle.

★ The **Cape Breton Miners' Museum** houses exhibits and artifacts illustrating the hard life of early miners in Cape Breton's undersea collieries. Former miners guide you down into the damp recesses of the mine and tell stories of working all day where the sun never shines. ✉42 Birkley St., Quarry Point ☎902/849–4522 ⊕www.minersmuseum.com ✉Museum $5, museum and mine tour $10 ⊘June 1–Sept. 1, daily 10–6, until 7 on Tues.; Sept. 2–Oct. 30, daily 9–4; Oct. 31–June 1, weekdays 9–4.

The **Marconi National Historic Site of Canada** commemorates the site at Table Head, where in 1902 Guglielmo Marconi built four tall wooden towers and beamed the first official wireless messages across the Atlantic Ocean. An interpretive trail leads to the foundations of the original towers and transmitter buildings. The visitor center has large models of the towers as well as artifacts and photographs chronicling the radio pioneer's life and work. ✉Timmerman St. (Hwy. 255) ☎902/842–2530 ⊕www.parkscanada.ca ✉Free ⊘June–mid-Sept., daily 10–6.

NIGHTLIFE & THE ARTS
Glace Bay's grand Victorian-style **Savoy Theatre** (✉116 Commercial St. ☎902/842–1577 ⊕www.savoytheatre.com), built in 1927, is home to a variety of live drama, comedy, and music performances.

LOUISBOURG

55 km (34 mi) south of Glace Bay.

Though best known as the home of the largest historical reconstruction in North America, Louisbourg is also an important fishing community with a lovely harbor front.

★ The **Fortress of Louisbourg National Historic Site of Canada** may be the most remarkable site in Cape Breton. After the French were forced out of mainland Nova Scotia in 1713, they established their headquarters here in a walled and fortified town on a low point of land at the mouth of Louisbourg Harbour. The fortress was twice captured, once by New Englanders and once by the British; after the second siege, in 1758, it was razed. Its capture was critical in ending the French empire in America. A quarter of the original town has been rebuilt on its foundations, just as it was in 1744, before the first siege. Costumed actors re-create the activities of the original inhabitants; you can watch a military drill, see nails and lace being made, and eat food prepared from 18th-century recipes in the town's three inns. Plan on spending at least a day. Louisbourg tends to be chilly, so pack a warm sweater or jacket. Walking tours are given in English and French from June to October. ⊠*259 Parks Service Rd.* ☎*902/733–2280 or 888/773–8888* ⊕*www. parkscanada.ca* ☑*$16.35* ⊗*June and Sept., daily 9:30–5; July and Aug., daily 9–5:30; Oct. 1–15, daily 9:30–5; Oct. 15–31, by guided tour only. English tours at 11 and 2, French tour at 1.*

Traditional Cape Breton music is played nightly at the **Louisbourg Playhouse,** a 17th-century-style theater that was originally constructed as part of a Disney movie set. ⊠*11 Aberdeen St.* ☎*902/733–2996 or 888/733–2787* ⊕*www.louisbourgplayhouse.com* ⊗*Mid-June–Oct.*

WHERE TO STAY & EAT

$–$$$　✗**Grubstake Restaurant.** Coquilles St. Jacques, chateaubriand, and stuffed sole are popular menu items at this 120-seat restaurant where elegant, family, and country cuisine are all wrapped into one. One part of the building is more than 100 years old. Desserts are made on-site. ⊠*7499 Main St., B1C IH8* ☎*902/733–2308* ⊕*www.c-level. com/grubstake* ☰*AE, MC, V* ⊗*Closed Nov.–mid-June.*

$–$$$$　✗🏠**Point of View Suites.** As the only Louisbourg property on the water, this deluxe beach house offers views of Fortress Louisbourg and the ocean. The owners grew up in Louisbourg and can provide insight on nearby activities. The suites have balconies, and most have cooking areas with utensils; the luxury apartments each have three queen-size beds, a full kitchen, and a hot tub. The casual beach-house restaurant ($$–$$$) specializes in lobster and crab boils, cooked nightly in season on their private beach and served in the dining room. ⊠*15 Commercial St. Ext., B1C 2J4* ☎*902/733–2080 or 888/374–8439* 🖷*902/733–2638* ⊕*www.louisbourgpointofview.com* ⇙*5 rooms, 15 suites* ⓔ*In-room: kitchen (some). In-hotel: restaurant, beachfront, laundry facilities, no-smoking rooms, no elevator* ☰*MC, V* ⊗*Closed Nov.–mid-May.*

$–$$$　🏠**Louisbourg Heritage House Bed & Breakfast.** Built in 1886, this former Victorian rectory also housed a museum–art gallery and then town offices before opening as a B&B in 2002. Original wood floors, high ceilings, and private balconies in each room add charm. In the town's center, the inn is nestled between two churches and is close to restaurants and the Louisbourg Playhouse. Some rooms have views of Fortress Louisbourg or the harbor. ⊠*7544 Main St., B1C 1J5* ☎*902/733–3222 or 888/888–8466* ⊕*www.louisbourgheritagehouse. com* ⇙*6 rooms* ⓔ*In-room: no a/c, refrigerator (some), no elevator* ☰*AE, MC, V* ⊗*Closed Nov.–June* ⍾*BP.*

$–$$　🏠**Cranberry Cove Inn.** This fully renovated home from the early 1900s is within walking distance of the Fortress of Louisbourg National Historic Park. Each room has a different theme, ranging from the captain's den to the secret garden. The inn has many antiques and Victorian decor. Rooms are available off-season by arrangement. High-end evening dining is available to guests and the public from mid-June through September ($$–$$$). ✉ *12 Wolfe St., B1C 2J2* ☎*902/733–2171 or 800/929–0222* 🖨*902/733–2171* ⊕*www.cranberrycoveinn.com* 🛏*7 rooms* ♨*In-room: no a/c, Wi-Fi. In-hotel: no-smoking rooms, no elevator* ⊟*AE, MC, V* ⚏*BP* ⊘*Open May–Oct.*

BIG POND

50 km (31 mi) west of Louisbourg.

This little town is made up of only a few houses, and one of them is the former home of singer-songwriter Rita MacNeil, who operates **Rita's Tea Room.** Originally a one-room schoolhouse, the building has been expanded to accommodate the multitude of visitors who come to sample Rita's Tea Room Blend Tea, which is served along with a fine selection of sandwiches and baked goods. You can visit a display room of Rita's awards and photographs and browse through her gift shop. ✉*Hwy. 4* ☎*902/828–2667* ⊕*www.ritamacneil.com* ⊘*Gift shop, June–Oct., daily 10–6; Tea room, July–mid-Oct.*

ARICHAT

62 km (38 mi) southwest of Big Pond.

The principal town of Isle Madame, Arichat is a 27-square-km (10-square-mi) island named for Madame de Maintenon, second wife of Louis XIV. Known today for its friendly Acadian culture and many secluded coves and inlets, the town was an important shipbuilding and trading center during the 19th century, and some fine old houses from that period still remain. The two cannons overlooking the harbor were installed after the town was sacked by John Paul Jones during the American Revolution.

To get here from Big Pond, take Route 4 to Highway 320, which leads through Poulamon and D'Escousse and overlooks Lennox Passage, with its spangle of islands. Highway 206 meanders through the low hills to a maze of land and water at West Arichat. Together, the two routes encircle the island, meeting at Arichat. The island lends itself to biking, as most roads glide gently along the shore. A good half-day hike leads to Gros Nez, the "large nose" that juts into the sea.

One of the best ways to experience Isle Madame is by foot. Try Cape Auguet Eco-Trail, an 8-km (5-mi) hiking trail that extends from Boudreauville to Mackerel Cove on Isle Madame and follows the rocky coastline overlooking Chedabucto Bay.

Arichat was once the seat of the local Catholic diocese. **Notre Dame de l'Assumption** church, built in 1837, still retains the grandeur of its former cathedral status. Its bishop's palace is now a law office. ✉*2316 Hwy. 206* ☎*902/226–2109* ⊠*Free* ⊘*Dawn–dusk. Mass, June–Sept., Sat. 7 PM and Sun. 9:30 AM.*

1

LeNoir Forge (✉ *Hwy. 206, off Hwy. 4 via Exit 46 to Isle Madame* ☎ *902/226–9364 or 902/226–0456*) is a restored French 18th-century stone blacksmith shop open June through August, daily 10 to 5.

■ OFF THE
BEATEN
PATH

Little Anse. With its red bluffs, cobbled shores, tiny harbor, and brightly painted houses, Little Anse can be particularly attractive for artists and photographers. The town is at the southeastern tip of Isle Madame.

NOVA SCOTIA ESSENTIALS

To research prices, get advice from other travelers, and book travel arrangements, visit www.fodors.com.

TRANSPORTATION

BY AIR

Westjet, Air Canada, and Air Canada Jazz provide service to Halifax and Sydney from various cities. Air travel within the area is very limited. Air Canada provides regional service to other provinces and to Sydney, Nova Scotia. Provincial Airlines, a regional Air Canada carrier, flies between Newfoundland, Labrador, and Halifax. Porter airlines provides service to Ottawa, Montréeal, and Toronto, whereas Sunwing flies daily to Toronto. United Airlines flies to Chicago from June through October, and offers daily nonstop service to Washington. American Eagle flies daily to New York (Laguardia and JFK). Halifax is also served by Continental (from Newark), and Northwest (from Detroit and Newark). Delta (through SkyWest) offers a weekly round-trip from Atlanta and Zoom Airlines now services four seasonal European gateways nonstop from Halifax (London, Glasgow, Belfast, and Paris). Icelandair travels three times a week to Reykjavíík.

The Halifax International Airport is 40 km (25 mi) northeast of downtown Halifax. Sydney Airport is 13 km (8 mi) east of Sydney.

Limousine and taxi services, as well as car rentals, are available at Halifax and Sydney airports. Airport bus service to Halifax and Dartmouth hotels from Halifax International Airport costs $36 round-trip, $18 one-way. Airbus has regular bus service from the Halifax airport to most major hotels in Halifax. Regular taxi and limo fares to Halifax from Halifax International are $53 each way. If you book ahead with Share-A-Cab, the fare is $28, but you must share your car with another passenger. The trip takes 30 to 40 minutes.

Contacts Airbus (☎ *902/873–2091*). **Halifax Robert L. Stanfield International Airport** (☎ *902/873–1223*). **Provincial Airlines** (☎ *709/576–1666, 800/563–2800 in Atlantic Canada* ⊕ *www.provair.com*). **Share-A-Cab** (☎ *902/429–5555*).**Sydney Airport** (☎ *902/564–7720*).**Zoom** (☎ *866/359–9666* ⊕ *www.flyzoom.com*).

BY BOAT & FERRY

Car ferries connect Nova Scotia with Maine and New Brunswick: Bay Ferries Ltd. sails from Bar Harbor and Portland Maine to Yarmouth, and from Saint John, New Brunswick, to Digby, Nova Scotia, between two and three times daily July through August and once daily May to June and September to October. Bay Ferries' Bar Harbor–Yarmouth and Portland–Yarmouth service uses a high-speed catamaran, which makes the crossings in 3 hours and 5½ hours, respectively. Known as *The Cat*, this catamaran is very popular for both its convenience and speed, so reserve ahead.

Weather permitting, from May through December, Northumberland Ferries operates between Caribou, Nova Scotia, and Wood Islands, Prince Edward Island, making the trip several times a day. Marine Atlantic operates regular, year-round between North Sydney and Port aux Basques, on the west coast of Newfoundland, and a three-times-a-week service between North Sydney and Argentia, on Newfoundland's east coast, runs from mid-June through September.

Metro Transit runs passenger ferries from the Halifax ferry terminal at Lower Water Street to Alderney Gate in downtown Dartmouth and to Woodside Terminal (near Dartmouth Hospital) on the hour and half hour from 6:30 AM to 11:45 PM. Ferries are more frequent during weekday rush hours; they also operate on Sunday in summer (10 to 6, June through September). Free transfers are available from the ferry to the bus system (and vice versa). A single crossing costs $2 and is worth it for the up-close view of both waterfronts.

Contacts Bay Ferries Ltd. (☎ *902/566–3838 or 888/249–7245* ⊕ *www.nfl-bay. com*). **Marine Atlantic** (☎ *902/794–5254 or 800/341–7981* ⊕ *www.marineatlantic. ca*). **Metro Transit** (☎ *902/490–6614 or 902/490–4000*). **Northumberland Ferries** (☎ *902/566–3838 or 800/565–0201*).

BY BUS

Because of conflicting schedules, getting to Nova Scotia by bus can be problematic. Greyhound Lines from New York and Montréal, connect with Acadian through New Brunswick. Acadian also provides service between urban centers within Nova Scotia. Airbus runs between the Halifax International Airport and major hotels in Halifax and Dartmouth. Shuttle van services with convenient transportation between Halifax and Sydney include Cape Shuttle Service and Scotia Shuttle Service.

There are a number of small, regional bus services; however, connections are not always convenient. Outside of Halifax there are no inner-city bus services. For information, call Nova Scotia Tourism.

Metro Transit provides bus service throughout Halifax and Dartmouth, the town of Bedford, and (to an increasingly broader extent) the outlying areas around Halifax. The fare is $2; only exact change is accepted.

Contacts Acadian (☎ *800/567–5151* ⊕ *www.smtbus.com*). **Airbus** (☎ *902/873–2091*). **Cape Shuttle Service** (☎ *800/349–1698*). **Metro Transit** (☎ *902/490–6614 or 902/490–4000* ⊕ *www.halifax.ca/metrotransit*). **Nova Scotia Tourism** (☎ *902/425–5781 or 800/565–0000* ⊕ *www.novascotia.com*). **Scotia Shuttle Service** (☎ *902/435–9686 or 800/898–5883* ⊕ *www.atyp.com/scotiashuttle*).

BY CAR

Halifax is the most convenient place from which to begin a driving tour of Nova Scotia or Atlantic Canada.

Most highways in the province lead to Halifax and Dartmouth. Highways 3/103, 7, 2/102, and 1/101 terminate in the twin cities. Many of the roads in rural Nova Scotia require attentive driving, as they are not well signed, are narrow, and do not always have a paved shoulder. But they are generally well surfaced and offer exquisite scenery.

Motorists can enter Nova Scotia through the narrow neck of land that connects the province to New Brunswick and the mainland. The Trans-Canada Highway (Highway 2 in New Brunswick) becomes Highway 104 on crossing the Nova Scotia border at Amherst. It is possible to drive over the Confederation Bridge from Prince Edward Island into New Brunswick near the Nova Scotia border. Otherwise, car ferries dock at Yarmouth (from Maine), Digby (from New Brunswick), Caribou (from Prince Edward Island), and North Sydney (from Newfoundland).

ROAD MAPS The province has 11 designated "Scenic Travelways," 5 in Cape Breton and 6 on the mainland, which are identified by roadside signs with icons that correspond with trail names. These lovely routes are also shown on tourist literature from Nova Scotia Tourism and on maps, which are available at gas stations and tourist information centers.

RULES OF THE ROAD Highways numbered from 100 to 199 are all-weather, limited-access roads, with 100-kph to 110-kph (62-mph to 68-mph) speed limits. The last two digits usually match the number of an older trunk highway along the same route, numbered from 1 to 99. Thus, Highway 102, between Halifax and Truro, matches the older Highway 2, between the same towns. Roads numbered from 200 to 399 are secondary roads that usually link villages. Unless otherwise posted, the speed limit on these and any roads other than the 100-series highways is 80 kph (50 mph).

BY TAXI

In Halifax, rates begin at about $3 and increase based on mileage and time. A crosstown trip should cost $7 or $8, depending on traffic. There are taxi stands at major hotels and shopping malls or you can usually hail a cab in the downtown area. Most Haligonians simply phone for taxi service.

Taxi Companies Casino Taxi (☎ *902/429–6666 or 902/425-6666*). **Yellow Cab** (☎ *902/420-0000 or 902/422-1551*).

CONTACTS & RESOURCES

EMERGENCIES
Emergency Services Ambulance, fire, or police (☎ *911*).

Hospitals Cape Breton Regional Hospital (✉ *1482 George St., Sydney* ☎ *902/567-8000*). **IWK Health Centre (for Women and Children)** (✉ *5850 University Ave., Halifax* ☎ *902/470-8888 switchboard*). **Queen Elizabeth II Health Sciences Centre** (✉ *1796 Summer St., Halifax* ☎ *902/473-2700 switchboard*). **South Shore Regional Hospital** (✉ *90 Glen Allan Dr., Bridgewater* ☎ *902/543-4603 switchboard*).

SPORTS & THE OUTDOORS

BICYCLING *Nova Scotia By Bicycle* ($13.95) is published by Bicycle Nova Scotia; it's available at Mountain Equipment Co-op, Cyclesmith, and The Book Room. Atlantic Canada Cycling can provide information on tours and rentals.

Contacts Atlantic Canada Cycling (☎ *902/423–2453 or 888/879–2453* ⊕ *www. atl-canadacycling.com*). **Bicycle Nova Scotia** (✉ *5516 Spring Garden Rd., Box 3010, Halifax B3J 3G6* ☎ *902/425–5450* ⊕ *www.bicycle.ns.ca*).**The Book Room** (✉ *1546 Barrinton St., Halifax* ☎ *902/423–8271*). **Cyclesmith** (✉ *6112 Quinpool Rd., Halifax* ☎ *902/425–1756*). **Mountain Equipment Co-op** (✉ *1550 Granville St., Halifax* ☎ *902/421–2667* ⊕ *www.mec.ca*).

BIRD-
WATCHING
Nova Scotia is on the Atlantic flyway and is an important staging point for migratory species. A fine illustrated book, *Birds of Nova Scotia,* by Robie Tufts is a must on every ornithologist's reading list. The Nova Scotia Museum of Natural History organizes walks and lectures for people interested in viewing local bird life in the Halifax area.

Contacts Nova Scotia Bird Society (☎ *902/445–2922* ⊕ *nsbs.chebucto.org*). **Halifax Field Naturalists** (⊕ *hfn.chebucto.org/fieldnat.html*). **Nova Scotia Museum of Natural History** (☎ *902/424–7353*).

CANOEING There are wonderful canoe routes in Kejimkujik National Park. Canoeing information is available from Canoe NS. The provincial department of Service Nova Scotia offers canoe route maps for sale online, by mail, or in person through the Nova Scotia Geomatics Centre in Amherst. The publication *Canoe Routes of Nova Scotia* has good information, and so does the Web site for Canoe/Kayak Nova Scotia, which lists a Waterway Index and locations to purchase local maps.

Contacts Canoe/Kayak Nova Scotia (☎ *902/425–5450 Ext. 316* ⊕ *ckns.home-stead.com*). **Nova Scotia Geomatics Centre** (☎ *902/667–7231 or 800/798–0706 [Nova Scotia only]*). **Service Nova Scotia** (⊕ *www.gov.ns.ca/snsmr/maps*).

FISHING You are required by law to have a valid Nova Scotia fishing license for inland lakes and rivers. A seven-day nonresident license costs $32.02; or by the day, $12.57. A guidebook, The Nova Scotia Anglers Handbook, is included in the price of the license and outlines where you can fish as well as opening and closing dates for the seasons. You do not need a licence to fish in tidal or saltwater in Nova Scotia. However, you must respect Canadian federal fishing seasons and bag limits. For information about obtaining licenses, contact Service Nova Scotia. For specific information on sport fishing in Nova Scotia, contact the Inland Fisheries Division of the Department of Fisheries.

Contacts Service Nova Scotia (☎ *902/424–4467 or 902/424–4821*). **Nova Scotia Department of Fisheries and Aquaculture, Inland Fisheries Division** (☎ *902/485–5056*).

GOLF The province offers golfers many well-manicured courses that are both panoramic and challenging. Contact Golf Nova Scotia for information on individual courses and tournaments. Tourism Nova Scotia also has information on golf packages.

Contacts **Golf Nova Scotia** (☎ *877/777–1117*).**Tourism Nova Scotia** (☎ *800/565–0000* ⊕ *www.golfnovascotia.com*).

HIKING Nova Scotia has a wide variety of trails along the rugged coastline and inland through forest glades, which enable you to experience otherwise inaccessible scenery, wildlife, and vegetation. *Hiking Trails of Nova Scotia,* published by Gooselane Editions, is available at most local bookstores. There are a number of Web sites that provide extensive information on routes and trails.

Contacts **Gooselane Editions** (✉ *469 King St., Fredericton, NBE3R 1E5* ☎ *506/450–4251*).**NovaTrails** (⊕ *www.novatrails.com*).**Trails Nova Scotia** (⊕ *www.trails.gov.ns.ca*).**Hiking in Nova Scotia** (⊕ *www.canadatrails.ca/ hiking/hike_ns.html*).

SKIING There are four alpine ski hills and hundreds of trails for cross-country skiing in Nova Scotia.

Contacts **Cross Country Ski Nova Scotia** (⊕ *www.crosscountryskins.homestead. com/crosscountryskins.html*). **Ski Ben Eoin** (☎ *902/828–2804* ⊕ *www.skibeneoin. com*). **Ski Martock** (☎ *902/798–9501* ⊕ *www.martock.com*). **Ski Wentworth** (☎ *902/548–2089* ⊕ *www.skiwentworth.ca*). **Ski Cape Smokey** (☎ *902/285–2760* ⊕ *www.skicapesmokey.com*).

TOURS

BOAT TOURS Boat tours have become very popular in all regions of the province. Murphy's on the Water sails various vessels: *Harbour Queen 1,* a paddle wheeler; *Haligonian III,* an enclosed motor launch; and *Mar,* a 75-foot sailing ketch. All operate from mid-May to late October from berths at 1751 Lower Water Street on Cable Wharf next to the Historic Properties in Halifax. Some tours include lunch, dinner, or entertainment. A cash bar may also be available. Costs vary, but a basic tour of the Halifax Harbour ranges from $17.99 to $44.99. Tours vary from one to four hours.

Harbour Hopper Tours offers a unique amphibious tour of historic downtown Halifax and the Halifax Harbour. Tours are approximately one-hour long (half on land, half on water) and run hourly from the early morning until late evening. The cost is $24.99 for adults or $70.99 for a family of four.

Contacts **Harbour Hopper Tours** (☎ *902/490–8687*). **Murphy's on the Water** (☎ *902/420–1015*).

BUS & RICKSHAW TOURS Ambassatours Gray Line Sightseeing and Cabana Tours run coach tours through Halifax, Dartmouth, and Peggy's Cove. Halifax Double Decker Tours offers two-hour tours on double-decker buses that leave daily from the Historic Properties in Halifax. Virtually every cab company in Halifax gives custom tours. Cab tours to locations such as Wolfville or Peggy's Cove are possible with prior arrangement. Prices vary, but be sure to set a fee with the tour guide before you begin. Rickshaw tours can be found on the waterfront.

Contacts **Cabana Tours** (☎ *902/455–8111*). **Ambassatours Gray Line Sightseeing** (☎ *902/423–6242*). **Halifax Double Decker Tours** (☎ *902/420–1155*).

Casino Cab (☎ *902/425-6666 or 902/429-6666*). **Yellow Cab** (☎ *902/420-0000 or 902/422-1551*).

WALKING
TOURS

Explore Halifax's rich tradition of stories of pirates, haunted houses, buried treasure, and ghosts with a ghoulish ghost walk. Tours begin at the Old Town Clock at 7:30 PM Wednesday through Sunday, May through October.

Contacts Ghost Walk of Historic Halifax (☎ *902/494-0525* ⊕ *www.tattletours. ca*). **Historical Walking Tour** (☎ *902/494-0525*).

VISITOR INFORMATION

Nova Scotia Tourism publishes a wide range of literature, including an annual (free) travel guide called the *Nova Scotia Doers and Dreamers Guide*. Call to have it mailed to you, or stop in at one of the visitor information centers for an in-person query.

Contacts Nova Scotia Tourism (☎ *902/425-5781 or 800/565-0000* ⊕ *www. novascotia.com*). **Nova Scotia Tourism** (☎ *902/424-4248*). **Tourism Cape Breton** (☎ *902/563-4636* ⊕ *www.cbisland.com*). **Tourism Halifax** (☎ *902/490-5946* ⊕ *www.halifaxinfo.com*).

New Brunswick

Kayaking on the bay of Fundy

WORD OF MOUTH

"The Fundy Tides are an extraordinary site at both Fundy National Park (or the adjacent village of Alma) and Hopewell Rocks, but are most dramatic if you are in one place long enough to witness the contrast between high and low tide. Staying somewhere like Moncton overnight would allow you to daytrip both spots."

—mat106

WELCOME TO NEW BRUNSWICK

TOP REASONS TO GO

★ **For a whale of a time—go whale watching:** There are licensed tour operators in St. Andrews, Blacks Harbour, Grand Manan, and Campobello Island.

★ **Acadian culture reigns in New Brunswick:** Must-do, must-see attractions include Le Pays de la Sagouine and Acadian Historical Village on the Acadian Coastal Drive.

★ **Salmon, Salmon, Salmon:** It's served at least two dozen ways in this province. Try casting your line and catching your own. You'll have no trouble finding professional outfitters in the Miramichi area.

★ **Take a hike:** The 13 provincial and national parks have amazing hiking trails. Sit on a mountain top and meditate. Watch birds from an ocean cliff.

★ **Go for a swim:** With 34 beaches you can choose from nippy to warm, fresh to salty, expansive spaces to intimate coves.

1 Saint John. The port city of Saint John is full of history, but is modern and fun. There are museums, old churches, and fine-dining choices galore. Don't miss the waterfront shops and activities.

2 The Fundy Coast. The Bay of Fundy is a diverse region with dramatic coastlines, tiny fishing villages, charming islands, and the highest tides in the world. Time seems to stand still here and life is laid-back and informal, yet rich in experiences like whale-watching.

Grand Manan Island

3 **The Acadian Coast & St. John River Valley.** Unlike the Bay of Fundy, the water on the Acadian coast is downright balmy and the selection of beaches can be mind-boggling. Another highlight of this region is the French Acadian culture with its distinct foods, music, and festivals. The St. John River—402 km (250 mi) of it—meanders through cities, townships, and charming villages. Pastoral farmland and the blue sweep of the water accompany you most of the way.

GETTING ORIENTED

New Brunswick has it all: a mighty river (with many other impressive waterways), coastal waters with the highest tides in the world, forests that sweep for miles, and mountain ranges that are perfect for activities like hiking and skiing. But most of all, this province has people who are hospitable and downright friendly. You'll find activities and attractions to suit every age and taste—and then some.

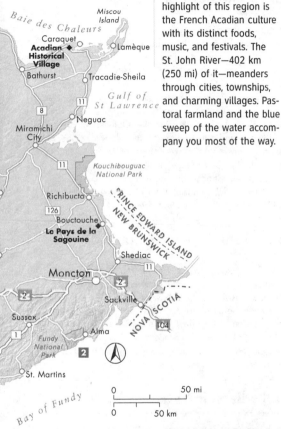

4 **Fredericton.** A gracious, small city situated on the gentle slope of the St. John River, Fredericton is the capital of New Brunswick and home to two fine universities. It's also a center of education, arts, and culture. Great shopping, too.

Acadian Village in Caraquet

NEW BRUNSWICK PLANNER

Getting Here and Around

With three major airports (Saint John, Fredericton, and Moncton) it's easy to arrange a flight to New Brunswick; each airport is about 10 to 15 minutes away from a major city center. There's also a ferry from Nova Scotia with daily service from Digby, Nova Scotia, to Saint John, New Brunswick.

Acadian Lines runs buses within the province and connects with most major bus lines.

New Brunswick is a large province. Unless you plan to fly into one of the hubs and stay there for your visit, you'd be wise to have a car. There's a good selection of car-rental agencies (book early for July and August). Cabs are relatively cheap and easily available for intercity travel, but the cities are small and quite easy to manage by foot.

Driving Tips

Watch out for moose—especially at night. Parts of the province are inhabited by the bulky creature, so pay attention to road signs (picture of a moose) and reduce speed at nighttime.

Making the Most of Your Time

If you have limited time, pick a region and leave to time explore: one of the big pleasures of Atlantic Canada is the slow pace, so relax and enjoy. The Fundy coast is a popular route and many prefer to spend less time in St. John, rather than more: Overnight in Alma, the town that services Fundy National Park, or in Moncton. One unforgettable New Brunswick experience is the sighting of a huge humpback, right whale, finback, or minke. Outfitters along the Bay of Fundy and a few on the eastern short take people to see a variety of whales. Most trips run from May through September. Then, if you have time, spend some time along the Acadian Coast absorbing some Acadian culture: the peninsula is so different from the rest of New Brunswick, you'll feel like you're in another country.

Take a Learning Vacation!

Sign up for cooking classes, learn to make silver jewelry, take horseback-riding lessons, monitor whales and sea life, or learn how to paint with watercolors. Throughout the province there are hot spots (for kids as well as adults) where you can learn a new skill or hone up on a hobby and have swell time in the process. New Brunswick leads the way in learning vacations. Call ☎800/561–0123 for information.

Off the Beaten Track

You'll be amazed at the things you'll find off the beaten track, including one-of-a-kind ecomuseums like the Olivier Soapery in Sainte-Anne-de-Kent, unusual islands like Ministers Island on the outskirts of St. Andrews, and hidden gems like the awe-inspiring walk along the gorge in Grand Falls. Attractions pop up in unexpected places like the Exhibit Hall at the Metepenagiag Heritage Park in Red Bank, inland from Miramichi. Don't hesitate to ask the locals what they would recommend. They'll also be thrilled to tell you about their favorite fishing hole, where to find rare birds, or how to locate the best cheese-maker in the region.

When to Go

With the exception of late March and April (which can be humdrum, cold, and wet) and possibly November (which can be unpredictable), New Brunswick is an attractive destination most of the year. New Brunswickers love winter sports, so from late December to mid-March options include skiing, snowshoeing, and snowmobiling. Ice fishing is gaining in popularity, too. In late spring the magic of casting a line for salmon is in the air. You can also bike, canoe, golf, kayak, and go birding. When the waters warm up (late June) swimming, scuba diving, garden touring, and kite-surfing kick in.

Fall colors are at their peak from late September through mid- or late October. The Autumn Colours Line (☎800/268-3255) provides daily information on where fall foliage is at its best. Many communities have special harvest-fest activities, especially around Canadian Thanksgiving (in October).

Tastes of New Brunswick

A spring delicacy are fiddleheads—emerging ostrich ferns that look like the curl at the end of a violin neck. These emerald gems are picked along riverbanks, then boiled and sprinkled with lemon juice or vinegar and butter, salt, and pepper. Seafood is plentiful all year (lobsters, oysters, crabs, mussels, clams, scallops, and salmon) and prepared in as many ways as there are chefs. Cast your line just about anywhere in New Brunswick and you'll find some kind of fish and chips. Try snacking on dulse, a dried purple seaweed, as salty as potato chips and as compelling as peanuts. The beer of choice is Moosehead, brewed in Saint John. The province has some fine food producers who do specialty items like maple syrup, cheeses, breads, smoked meats, and gourmet fare—often found at farmers' markets.

What It Costs In Canadian Dollars

	¢	$	$$	$$$	$$$$
Restaurants	under C$8	C$8–C$12	C$13–C$20	C$21–C$30	over C$30
Hotels	under C$75	C$75–C$125	C$126–C$175	C$176–C$250	over C$250

Restaurant prices are per person for a main course at dinner. Hotel prices are for two people in a standard double room in high season, excluding 14% harmonized sales tax (HST).

Festival Fun

With hundreds of festivals a year, New Brunswickers sure know how to celebrate! To find out what's going on, call (☎800/561-0123) or visit ⊕www.TourismNewBrunswick.ca and you'll have no trouble finding a shindig. Summer is the best time for festivals. In early July you can go to the Irish Festival (⊕www.canadasirishfest.com) in Miramichi or the Loyalist Heritage Festival (⊕www.loyalistheritagefestival.ca) in Saint John. The latter celebrates the founders of the city with reenactments of historical events and a variety of musical acts. Also in July is the New Brunswick Highland Games & Scottish Festival (⊕www.nbhighlandgames.com) in Fredericton and if you're a fan of lobster, time your visit to coincide with the Shediac Lobster Festival (⊕www.lobsterfestival.nb.ca).

In August you can attend the Acadian Festival (www.festivalacadiencaraquet.com) at Caraquet or the Atlantic Seafood Festival (⊕www.atlanticseafoodfestival.com) in Moncton, NB, in late August. The Chocolate Festival (⊕www.town.ststephen.nb.ca) in St. Stephen includes suppers, displays, and children's events. Saint John's Festival by the Sea (⊕www.festivalbythesea.com) draws hundreds of singers, dancers, and musicians. The New Brunswick Summer Music Festival (⊕www.unb.ca/FineArts/Music/festival), in Fredericton, features classical musicians.

Updated
by Sandra
Phinney

THE GREAT CANADIAN FOREST MEETS the sea in New Brunswick, where it is sliced by sweeping river valleys and modern highways. The province is an old place in new-world terms, and the remains of a turbulent past are still evident in some of its quiet nooks. Near Moncton, for instance, wild strawberries perfume the air of the grassy slopes of Fort Beauséjour, where, in 1755, one of the last battles for possession of Acadia took place—the English finally overcoming the French. The dual heritage of New Brunswick (33% of its population is Acadian French) provides added spice. Today New Brunswick is Canada's only officially bilingual province. Other areas of the province were settled by the British and by Loyalists, American colonists who chose to live under British rule after the American Revolution. If you stay in both Acadian and Loyalist regions, a trip to New Brunswick can seem like two vacations in one.

For every gesture as grand as the giant rock formations carved by the Bay of Fundy tides, there is one as subtle as the gifted touch of a sculptor in a studio. For every experience as colorful as salmon and fiddleheads served at a church supper, there is another as low-key as the gentle waves of the Baie des Chaleurs. New Brunswick is the luxury of an inn with five stars, or the tranquillity of camping under a million.

At the heart of New Brunswick is the forest, which covers 85% of the province's entire area—nearly all its interior. The forest drives the economy, defines the landscape, and delights hikers, anglers, campers, and bird-watchers—but New Brunswick's soul is the sea. The largest of Canada's three Maritime provinces, New Brunswick is largely surrounded by coastline. The warm waters of the Baie des Chaleurs, Gulf of St. Lawrence, and Northumberland Strait lure swimmers to their sandy beaches, and the chilly Bay of Fundy, with its monumental tides, draws breaching whales, whale-watchers, and kayakers.

EXPLORING NEW BRUNSWICK

Rivers and ocean are the original highways of New Brunswick, and the St. John River in the west and the Fundy and Acadian coasts in the south and east essentially encompass the province. A well-designed and marked system of provincial scenic drives takes you to most of the places you want to go. Begin in the south, on the phenomenal Fundy Coastal Drive (watch for the lighthouse-on-a-cliff logo). At the upper end of the bay it connects with the Acadian Coastal Drive (the logo is a setting sun and fishing boat), which hugs the gentle eastern shore. In the middle of the Acadian Drive is a bit of a detour for the Miramichi River Route (trees and a jumping salmon logo). The Acadian Drive eventually meets the Appalachian Range Route (mountains and cliffs logo). It takes you across the rugged northern part of the province, where the hardwood ridges ignite in a blaze of color in fall, and connects with the River Valley Scenic Drive (rolling green hills and wide blue river logo), which takes you down the entire western side of the province and back to Saint John, on the Fundy Coastal Drive, where the adventure began.

GREAT ITINERARIES

IF YOU HAVE 4 DAYS

If you have only a short time, concentrate on one region, such as the Fundy Coast. Art, history, nature, and seafood abound in the resort community of **St. Andrews by-the-Sea.** Whale-watching tours leave from the town wharf, there's an outstanding garden, and some of the province's finest crafts are found in its shops. Spend a day and a night. Just an hour's drive east of St. Andrews is the venerable city of **Saint John.** It's steeped in English and Irish traditions, rich in history and art. Spend a day and a night here, then take Route 1 past Sussex to Route 114 and **Fundy National Park.** Route 915 above the park hugs the coast. Watch for **Cape Enrage,** which is as dramatic as it sounds. There are lots of things to do around **Riverside-Albert** and **Hopewell Cape,** where the Fundy tides have sculpted gigantic flowerpot rocks that turn into islands at high tide. Finish the trip with **Moncton,** a microcosm of New Brunswick culture and less than an hour's drive from Riverside-Albert.

IF YOU HAVE 7 DAYS

Add an Acadian Coastal experience to the four-day tour above. Head north from **Moncton** and explore the area around **Shediac,** famous for its lobsters and Parlee Beach. **Bouctouche** is just beyond that, with its wonderful dunes and the make-believe land of La Sagouine. Another 50 km (31 mi) north is unspoiled **Kouchibouguac National Park,** which protects beaches, forests, and peat bogs. The coastal drive from Kouchibouguac Park to **Miramichi City,** about 75 km (47 mi), passes through several bustling fishing villages. Most of the communities are Acadian, but as you approach Miramichi City, English dominates again. A stopover here positions you perfectly to begin your exploration of the Acadian Peninsula. It's only about 120 km (74 mi) from Miramichi City to **Caraquet.** The entire peninsula is so different from the rest of the province, it's like a trip to a foreign country. The Acadian Historical Village is a careful re-creation of the traditional Acadian way of life.

IF YOU HAVE 10 DAYS

Follow the seven-day itinerary above. From **Caraquet** plan at least a half day to drive across the top of New Brunswick (Route 134 along the coast and Route 17 inland through the forest) to the St. John River valley. Begin your explorations among the flowers and the music of the New Brunswick Botanical Gardens in St-Jacques, just outside **Edmundston.** The drive from here to Fredericton is about 275 km (171 mi) of panoramic pastoral and river scenery, including a dramatic gorge and waterfall at **Grand Falls** and the longest covered bridge in the world at Hartland. **Kings Landing Historical Settlement,** near Fredericton, provides a faithful depiction of life on the river in the 19th century. With its Gothic cathedral, Victorian architecture, museums, and riverfront pathways, **Fredericton** is a beautiful, historic, and cultural stopping place. The drive from Fredericton to Saint John on Route 102 is just over 100 km (62 mi); about halfway between the two is the village of **Gagetown,** a must-see for art and history buffs.

2

SAINT JOHN

Like any seaport worth its salt, Saint John is a welcoming place. The natives welcomed Samuel de Champlain and Sieur de Monts when they landed here on St. John the Baptist Day in 1604. Nearly two centuries later, in May 1783, 3,000 British Loyalists—fleeing the aftermath of the American Revolutionary War—poured off a fleet of ships to make a home amid the rocks and forests. Two years later the city of Saint John became the first in Canada to be incorporated.

Although most of the Loyalists were English, there were some Irish among them. After the Napoleonic Wars in 1815, thousands more Irish workers found their way to Saint John. It was the potato famine that spawned the largest influx of Irish immigrants, though; a 20-foot Celtic cross on Partridge Island at the entrance to St. John Harbour stands as a reminder of the hardships and suffering they endured. Their descendants make Saint John Canada's most Irish city, a fact that's celebrated in grand style each March with a weeklong St. Patrick's celebration.

All the comings and goings over the centuries have exposed Saint Johners to a wide variety of cultures and ideas, and made it a sophisticated Maritime city with a vibrant artistic community. Major provincial artists such as Jack Humphrey, Miller Brittain, Fred Ross, and Herzl Kashetsky were born here, and Hollywood notables such as Louis B. Mayer, Donald Sutherland, and Walter Pidgeon grew up here. Visitors will discover rich and diverse cultural products in the city's urban core including a plethora of art galleries and antiques shops in uptown.

Industry and salt air have combined to give parts of this city a weather-beaten quality, but you also find lovingly restored 19th-century wooden and redbrick homes as well as modern office buildings, hotels, and shops. Harbour Passage, a redbrick walking and cycling path with benches and lots of interpretive information, begins at Market Square and winds along the waterfront all the way to the Reversing Falls. A shuttle boat between Market Square and the falls means you have to walk only one way (or both, of course).

DOWNTOWN SAINT JOHN

An ambitious urban-renewal program undertaken in the early 1980s spruced up the waterfront and converted old warehouses into trendy restaurants and shops. An underground and overhead walkway known as the "Inside Connection" links guest rooms, attractions, and shops.

SIGHTS TO SEE

❸ **Barbour's General Store.** This 19th-century shop, now a museum, is filled with the aromas of tobacco, smoked fish, peppermint sticks, and dulse, an edible seaweed. There's an old post office and a barbershop, too. ⊠ *Market Slip* ☎ *506/658–2939* ⛶ *Free* ☉ *Mid-June–mid-Sept., daily 9–6.*

❶ **King Street.** The steepest, shortest main street in Canada, lined with solid Victorian redbrick buildings, is filled with a variety of shops.

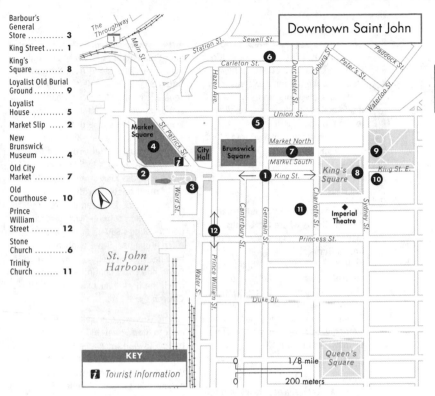

Downtown Saint John

2

KEY

🇮 Tourist information

0   1/8 mile

0   200 meters

St. John Harbour

❽ King's Square. Laid out in a Union Jack pattern, this green refuge has a two-story bandstand and a number of monuments. The mass of metal on the ground in its northeast corner is actually a great lump of melted stock from a neighboring hardware store that burned down in Saint John's Great Fire of 1877, in which hundreds of buildings were destroyed. ⊠*Between Charlotte and Sydney Sts.*

❺ Loyalist House. David Daniel Merritt, a wealthy Loyalist merchant, built this imposing Georgian structure in 1810. It is distinguished by its authentic period furniture and eight fireplaces. July through August the mayor sponsors a tea party here each Wednesday afternoon; admission to the house is free on these afternoons. ⊠*120 Union St.* ☎*506/652–3590* ☞*$3* ⊙*June, weekdays 10–5; July and Aug., daily 10–5; Sept.–May, by appointment.*

❷ Market Slip. The waterfront area at the foot of King Street is where the Loyalists landed in 1783. Today it's the site of Market Square, the Hilton Saint John Hotel, and restaurants, but it still conveys a sense of the city's Maritime heritage. A floating wharf accommodates boating visitors to the city and those waiting for the tides to be right to sail up the St. John River.

CLOSE UP

A Good Walk

Saint John is a city on hills, and **King Street ❶**, its main street, slopes steeply to the harbor. A system of escalators, elevators, and skywalks inside buildings allows you to climb to the top and take in some of the more memorable spots without effort, though you can also walk outside. A year-round information center is located about half way in the Shoppes of City Hall.

Start at the foot of King, at **Market Slip ❷**. This is where the Loyalists landed in 1783 and is the site of **Barbour's General Store ❸** and the Little Red Schoolhouse. At Market Square, restored waterfront buildings house historical exhibits, shops, restaurants, and cafés. Also here are the Saint John Regional Library, a year-round visitor information center, and the fine **New Brunswick Museum ❹**.

From the second level of Market Square a skywalk crosses St. Patrick Street, and an escalator takes you up into the City Hall shopping concourse. Here, you can branch off to Harbour Station, with its busy schedule of concerts, sporting events, and trade shows. Once you are through City Hall, another skywalk takes you across Chipman Hill and into the Brunswick Square Complex of shops, offices, and the city's largest hotel. To visit historic **Loyalist House ❺**, exit onto Germain Street and turn left; it's on the corner at the top of the hill. Continue on for a block to see the venerable **Stone Church ❻**. In the flavorful **Old City Market ❼**, across from Brunswick Square, make your way past fish- and cheesemongers, butchers, greengrocers, sandwich makers, and craftspeople. This is a great place to stop for lunch. When you leave by the door at the top of the market, you're

near the head of King Street and right across Charlotte Street from **King's Square ❽**. Take a walk through the square, past the statues and bandstand, to Sydney Street. Notice the walkways in the shape of the Union Jack Flag. Cross Sydney and you're in the **Loyalist Burial Ground ❾**. Make your way back to Sydney Street and then cross King Street East to the **Old Courthouse ❿** with its spiral staircase made from cantilevered stones. Head south on Sydney; turn right on King's Square South, and catch a glimpse of the handsome Imperial Theatre. Follow King's Square South and cross Charlotte Street to reach the back door of historic **Trinity Church ⓫**.

To end your walk, make your way back to King Street and walk down the hill toward the water. **Prince William Street ⓬** is at the foot of the hill, just steps from where you began at Market Slip. Turn left for antiques shops, galleries, and historic architecture.

TIMING: Allow the better part of a day for this walk if you include a few hours for the New Brunswick Museum and some time for shopping. If you don't stop, the route takes a couple of hours. On Sunday the indoor walkways are open but the City Market is closed.

4 **New Brunswick Museum.** Delilah, a
★ suspended, full-size young right-
☾ whale skeleton, is on display at
this fine museum. You can also hike
along a geologic trail and watch the
phenomenal Bay of Fundy tides rise
and fall in a glass tidal tube connected to the harborr. Creative
exhibits trace the province's industrial, social, and artistic history,
and outstanding artwork hangs in

> **WORD OF MOUTH**
>
> "Personally (and I live in Saint
> John), a trip to the City Market,
> and a walk through the Loyalist
> Burial Ground are a must (sounds
> morbid, but a very popular thing
> to do and a beautiful green space
> in the city)." —sar_gil

the galleries. The Family Discovery Gallery has fun and educational
games. ⊠ *Market Sq.* ☎ *506/643–2300* ⊕ *http://website.nbm-mnb.ca/
english/00aa.html* ⊿ *$6* ⊗ *Weekdays 9–5, Thurs. 9–9, Sat. 10–5, Sun.
noon–5; Closed Mon. mid-Nov.–mid-May.*

9 **Loyalist Burial Ground.** This Loyalist cemetery, now a landscaped park, is
like a history book published in stone. Brick walkways, gardens, and a
beaver-pond fountain make it a delightful spot. ⊠ *Sydney St., between
King and E. Union Sts.* ⊿ *Free* ⊗ *Daily 24 hrs.*

7 **Saint John City Market.** The 1876 inverted ship's-hull ceiling of this handsome market—Canada's oldest charter market—occupies a city block
between Germain and Charlotte streets. Its temptations include live
and fresh-cooked lobsters, great cheeses, dulse, and tasty, inexpensive
snacks, along with plenty of souvenir and crafts items. ⊠ *47 Charlotte
St.* ☎ *506/658–2820* ⊗ *Weekdays 7:30–6, Sat. 7:30–5.*

10 **Old Courthouse.** This 1829 neoclassical building has a three-story spiral staircase built of tons of unsupported stones. The staircase can be
seen year-round during business hours, except when court is in session.
Hours sometimes vary, so call ahead. ⊠ *King St. E and Sydney St.*
⊿ *Free* ⊗ *Weekdays 9–5.*

12 **Prince William Street.** South of King Street near Market Slip, this street
is full of historic bank and business buildings that now hold shops,
galleries, and restaurants. The lamp known as the Three Sisters, at the
foot of Prince William Street, was erected in 1848 to guide ships into
the harbor. Next to it is a replica of the Celtic cross on nearby Partridge
Island, where many immigrants landed and were quarantined.

6 **Stone Church.** The first stone church in the city was built for the garrison posted at nearby Fort Howe. The stone was brought from England
as ships' ballast. ⊠ *87 Carleton St.* ☎ *506/634–1474* ⊿ *By donation*
⊗ *July and Aug., Tues., Wed., and Fri. 8:30–3:30.*

11 **Trinity Church.** The present church dates from 1880, when it was rebuilt
after the Great Fire. Inside, over the west door, there's a coat of arms—a
symbol of the monarchy—rescued from the council chamber in Boston
by a British colonel during the American Revolution. It was deemed a
worthy refugee and given a place of honor in the church. ⊠ *115 Charlotte St.* ☎ *506/693–8558* ⊿ *Free* ⊗ *Hrs vary; call ahead.*

GREATER SAINT JOHN

Relax on a secluded beach, talk to the harbor seals, and listen to the birds, all within 10 minutes of downtown. The St. John River, its Reversing Falls, and St. John Harbour divide the city into eastern and western districts. The historic downtown area is on the east side. The venerable brick homes (like New York's and Boston's brownstones) near mercantile King Street enjoy the summer shade of mature trees. On the lower west side, painted-wood homes with flat roofs—characteristic of Atlantic Canadian seaports—slope to the harbor. Industrial activity is prominent on the west side, which has stately older homes on huge lots.

SIGHTS TO SEE

Carleton Martello Tower. The tower, a great place from which to survey the harbor and Partridge Island, was built during the War of 1812 as a precaution against an American attack. Guides tell you about the spartan life of a soldier living in the stone fort, and an audiovisual presentation outlines its role in the defense of Saint John during World War II. ⊠ *Whipple St. at Fundy Dr.* ☎ *506/636–4011* ⊒ *$3.95* ⊙ *June–early Oct., daily 10–5:30.*

Cherry Brook Zoo. Wildebeests and other exotic species are highlights of this small zoo with pleasant woodland trails. There's a monkey house and a trail with extinct-animal exhibits. ⊠ *901 Foster Thurston Dr.* ☎ *506/634–1440* ⊒ *$8* ⊙ *Daily, year-round 10. Closing varies from 4:30 to 7 depending on the season.*

Irving Nature Park. The ecosystems of the southern New Brunswick coast are preserved in this lovely 600-acre park on a peninsula close to downtown. Roads and eight walking trails (up to several miles long) make bird- and nature-watching easy. Many shorebirds breed here, and it's a staging site on the flight path of shorebirds migrating to and from the Arctic and South America. Stop at the information kiosk just inside the entrance for a naturalist's notebook, a guide to what you'll find in the park, season by season. Tours are available. ⊠ *Sand Cove Rd., from downtown take Rte. 1 west to Exit 119A (Catherwood Rd.) south; follow Sand Cove Rd. 4½ km (3 mi)* ☎ *506/632–7777* ⊒ *Free* ⊙ *May–mid-Nov., daily dawn–dusk; vehicles permitted 8–8.*

★ **Reversing Falls.** The strong Fundy tides rise higher than the water level of the river, so twice daily, at the Reversing Falls rapids, the tide water pushes the river water back upstream. When the tide ebbs, the river once again pours over the rock ledges and the rapids appear to reverse themselves. To learn more about the phenomenon, watch the film shown at the Reversing Falls Tourist Bureau. Jet-boat tours provide a wild ride as well as a closer

> **WORD OF MOUTH**
>
> "I went back to see the Reversing Falls at low tide. I agree that the falls are not that impressive, but it is kind of neat to go there twice and see the difference between high and low tides if the times are convenient and you are interested in that sort of thing."
>
> —just wandering

2

(and wetter) look. There are two restaurants here, too. A pulp mill on the bank is not so scenic, but multimillion dollar upgrades to pollution controls have eliminated any unpleasant odors. TIP: To appreciate fully the Reversing Falls takes time; you need to visit at high, slack, and low tides. Check with any visitor information office for these times to help you plan a visit. ⊠ *Rte. 100, Reversing Falls Bridge* ☎ *506/658–2937* ⌸ *Free* ☉ *Daily dawn–dusk; jet-boat tours June–mid-Oct., daily 10–dusk.*

🌳 **Rockwood Park.** Encompassing 2,200 acres, this is one of the largest in-city parks in Canada. There are hiking trails through the forest, 13 lakes, several sandy beaches, a campground, a golf course with an aquatic driving range, the Cherry Brook Zoo, horseback riding, and a unique play park for people of all ages. ⊠ *Main entrance off Crown St.* ☎ *506/658–2883* ⌸ *Free* ☉ *Daily 8–dusk.*

WHERE TO STAY & EAT

$$–$$$$ ✕ **Billy's Seafood Company.** It's a restaurant, it's an oyster bar, it's a fish market—and it's lots of fun, too, with jazzy background music and funny, fishy paintings. The fresh fish selection is impressive and everything is cooked to perfection. Huge pesto scallops are always a hit, as is the grilled halibut with blueberry balsamic vinegar. This is where "cedar planked salmon" originated. Dining outside is a treat, and you can also get live and cooked lobsters packed to go. ⊠ *Saint John City Market, Charlotte St. entrance* ☎ *506/672–3474 or 888/933–3474* ☐ *AE, DC, MC, V.*

¢–$$$$ ✕ **Steamer's Lobster Company.** Fishnets and lobster traps decorate this rustic spot, where a meal feels like part of a Maritime kitchen party. Fresh lobsters, mussels, and clams are steamed outside on the patio. A fun thing to do: sign up for The Water Street Dinner Theatre—the three-act comedy show that usually takes place on weekends at 6:30; for $40, you get a three-course meal, the show, and some lively entertainment. Check the playlist at www.waterstreetdinnertheatre.com. Cruise ships dock at Pugsley Terminal, across the street. ⊠ *110 Water St., just off Market Sq.* ☎ *506/648–2325* ☐ *AE, D, DC, MC, V.*

$$$ ✕ **Beatty and the Beastro.** This quirky (check out the specially made
★ plates) place next to the Imperial Theatre hops at lunchtime and during pretheater dinners. The frequently changing menu, with its distinctive European accent, takes advantage of local and seasonal meat, seafood, and produce. Breads and soups are specialties; there are times when Scotch broth is on the menu (it's the last stop for the local spring lamb). ⊠ *60 Charlotte St., at King's Sq.* ☎ *506/652–3888* ☐ *AE, DC, MC, V* ☉ *Closed Sun.*

$$–$$$ ✕ **Lemongrass Thai Fare.** Phad Yum, a traditional red curry with seafood and lime leaves, is the house specialty, but you could make a meal of appetizers such as *satay gai* (chicken, beef, or pork), *hoy op* (mussels), and *tod mun pla* (fish cakes). At this intimate restaurant in an old building with lots of character as well as a heated outdoor patio, you call the shots when it comes to the spices, so your meal is as hot (or not) as you like. There's even a limited "un-Thai'ed" menu. ⊠*42 Princess St.* ☎*506/657–8424* ▭*AE, MC, V* ⊗*No lunch weekends.*

$$ ✕**Opera Bistro.** Guests get celebrity treatment at this hip, savvy place that has exceptional service and truly great food. It's fun and unpretentious with a funky atmosphere, and the food features local ingredients with international flavor. The "Operetta-small plates" ($14–$18) are popular, and include Atlantic crab cakes served with apple and caper salsa. A bonus: homemade Gelato ice cream. ⊠*60 Prince William St.* ☎*506/642–2822* ▭*AE, MC, V.*

¢–$$ ✕**Taco Pica.** This modest place is a slice of home for the former Guatemalan refugees, now proud Canadian citizens, who run it as a worker's co-op. The atmosphere is colorful—ornamental parrots rule in the dining room—and the recipes are authentic: seasoned with garlic, mint, coriander seeds, and cilantro. A guitarist often entertains on Friday and Saturday evenings. ⊠*96 Germain St.* ☎*506/633–8492* ▭*AE, DC, MC, V* ⊗*Closed Sun.*

$$–$$$ ✕🏨**Delta Brunswick Hotel.** Part of Brunswick Square with its many shops and services, this hotel has the kind of courtly service once offered by the venerable department store it replaced on this site. Rooms are large, modern, and comfortable. Shucker's Restaurant ($$–$$$) specializes in New Brunswick's best, including dishes made with local seafood, fiddleheads, and blueberries. The property is connected by walkway to shopping and entertainment facilities. ⊠*39 King St., E2L 4W3* ☎*506/648–1981* 🖷*506/658–0914* ⊕*www.deltahotels.ca* ⇨*254 rooms* ♨*In-room: Wi-Fi. In-hotel: restaurant, bar, pool, gym, laundry facilities, parking (fee), some pets allowed, no-smoking rooms* ▭*AE, D, DC, MC, V.*

$$–$$$ ✕🏨**Dufferin Inn & Suites.** An elegant upscale four-room inn that's more than 100 years old, has been renovated with new-age comforts. You'll be delighted to find a keepsake of your stay to take home. It's the innkeepers way of saying "thank-you" for staying at the Dufferin Inn. Dinners are a special occasion in the San Martello Dining Room (have a drink in Library Bar beforehand). For a walk on the wild side, check out the cooking classes with the inn's chef—they include lunch or dinner. ⊠*357 Dufferin Row* ☎*506/642–2822* ⊕*www.dufferininn.com* ⇨*4 rooms* ♨*In-room: Wi-Fi, no a/c. In-hotel: restaurant, bar, laundry service, parking (fee), no-smoking rooms* ▭*AE, MC, V* ¶◎¶*BP.*

$–$$$ ✕🏨**Hilton Saint John.** In this Hilton, furnished in a traditional Loyalist manner, guest rooms overlook the harbor or the town. A pedestrian walkway system connects the 10-story property to uptown shops, restaurants, a library, a museum, an aquatic center, and a civic center. The large *Turn of the Tide* restaurant ($$$–$$$$) has terrific views of the harbor and an eclectic menu with local seafood, Alberta beef, and some Continental dishes. ⊠*1 Market Sq., E2L 4Z6* ☎*506/693–8484, 800/561–8282 in Canada* 🖷*506/657–6610* ⊕*www.hilton.com* ⇨*197 rooms* ♨*In-room: ethernet. In-hotel: restaurant, bar, pool, gym, laundry service, parking (fee), some pets allowed, no-smoking rooms* ▭*AE, D, DC, MC, V.*

$–$$$ ★ ✕🏨**Shadow Lawn Inn.** In an affluent suburb with tree-lined streets, palatial homes, tennis, golf, and a yacht club, this inn fits right in with its clapboards, columns, and antiques. Some bedrooms have fireplaces; one suite has a whirlpool bath. The chefs honed their skills in some of the finest upper-Canadian kitchens and their creative ideas are reflected in the dining room's ($$–$$$$) Continental and seafood dishes. ✉*3180 Rothesay Rd., 12 km (7 mi) northeast of Saint John, Rothesay E2E 5V7* ☎*506/847–7539 or 800/561–4166* 🖷*506/849–9238* ⊕*www. shadowlawninn.com* ⇢*9 rooms, 2 suites* ♿*In-room: Wi-Fi. In-hotel: restaurant, laundry service, parking (no fee), no-smoking rooms, some pets allowed no elevator* ⊟*AE, DC, MC, V* ⏱*CP.*

$$–$$$ 🖬**Inn on the Cove & Spa.** With its back lawn terraced down to the ocean, this inn near Irving Nature Park has as much character as its owners, who used to tape their delightful cooking show in the kitchen. Bedrooms are furnished with local antiques, and several have balconies overlooking the ocean. A four-course dinner (reservations essential) is served in a dining room with a view of the Bay of Fundy. Guests and nonguests can, with reservations, get treatments at the spa. ✉*1371 Sand Cove Rd., E2M 4Z9* ☎*506/672–7799 or 877/257–8080* ⊕*www. innonthecove.com* ⇢*8 rooms, 1 apartment* ♿*In-room DVD, Wi-Fi. In-hotel: spa, parking (no fee), no-smoking rooms, some pets allowed, no elevator* ⊟*AE, MC, V* ⏱*BP.*

$–$$ 🖬**Homeport Historic Bed & Breakfast Inn.** Graceful arches, fine antiques, Italian marble fireplaces, Oriental carpets, and a Maritime theme are at home in these 19th-century twin mansions built by a prominent Saint John shipbuilding family. The two buildings make a large inn that commands stunning harbor views and is close to downtown and to the Reversing Falls. Each oversize room is elegant, unique, and equipped with modern amenities, and one is rumored to have a ghost named Beatrice. Harbor breezes usually make air-conditioning unnecessary, but it is available if needed. Breakfasts are hearty. ✉*60–80 Douglas Ave., E2K 1E4* ☎*506/672–7255 or 888/678–7678* 🖷*506/672–7250* ⊕*www.homeport.nb.ca* ⇢*6 rooms, 4 suites* ♿*In-room: refrigerator (some), VCR, Wi-Fi. In-hotel: parking (no fee), no-smoking rooms, some pets allowed, no elevator* ⊟*AE, MC, V* ⏱*BP.*

NIGHTLIFE & THE ARTS

THE ARTS
★ **Saint John Arts Centre** (✉*20 Hazen Ave.* ☎*506/633–4870*), in a former Carnegie library, has several galleries displaying the work of local artists and artisans. Performance-art pieces are occasionally presented here. Saint John's theater, opera, ballet, and symphony productions take place at the **Imperial Theatre** (✉*King's Sq.* ☎*506/674–4100*), a beautifully restored 1913 vaudeville arena. Tours ($2) are available in July and August.

NIGHTLIFE
★ Top musical groups and other performers appear at **Harbour Station** (✉*99 Station St.* ☎*506/657–1234 or 800/267–2800* ⊕*www. harbourstation.nb.ca*). **O'Leary's Pub** (✉*46 Princess St.* ☎*506/634–7135*), in the middle of the Trinity Royal Preservation Area, specializes in old-time Irish fun complete with Celtic performers; on Wednesday,

Brent Mason, a well-known neofolk artist, starts the evening and then turns the mike over to the audience. **Tapps Brew Pub and Steak House** (⊠*78 King St.* ☎*506/634–1957*) pleases the over-30 crowd. Watch the action in the microbrewery, play cards at a big wooden table, or hide out in a secluded booth.

SPORTS & THE OUTDOORS

The **Reversing Falls Jet Boat** (⊠*Fallsview Park off Fallsview Dr.* ☎*506/634–8987 or 888/634–8987* ⊕*www.jetboatrides.com* ☉*June–mid-Oct.*) has 20-minute thrill rides in the heart of the Reversing Falls ($30). Be prepared for a wild ride and don't think for a second that the yellow slickers they supply will keep you dry—having a change of clothes in your car is an excellent idea. There is also the even more extreme option of bouncing down the river in a "bubble" contraption ($95). Age and size restrictions apply to the jet boat and bubble, and times depend on the tides. The company also offers more sedate sightseeing tours ($30) along the falls and up the river departing from Market Square June to mid-October, 10 AM to dusk. The **Rockwood Park Golf Course** (⊠*1255 Sandy Point Rd.* ☎*506/634–0090*) is an 18-hole course with an aquatic driving range as well. The course is 300 yards past Saint John Regional Hospital entrance; follow the signs to the hospital off Route 1 in Saint John.

SHOPPING

★ **Brunswick Square** (⊠*King and Germain Sts.* ☎*506/658–1000*), a vertical mall, has many top-quality boutiques. **Handworks Gallery** (⊠*12 King St.* ☎*506/652–9787*) carries the best professional crafts and fine art made in New Brunswick. **House of Tara** (⊠*72 Prince William St.* ☎*506/634–8272*) is wonderful for fine Irish linens and woolens. **Peter Buckland Gallery** (⊠*80 Prince William St.* ☎*506/693–9721*), open Tuesday through Saturday or by appointment, is an exceptionally fine gallery that carries prints, photos, paintings, drawings, and sculpture by Canadian artists, including Saint John native Jack Humphrey. **Tim Isaac Antiques** (⊠*97 Prince William St.* ☎*506/652–3222*) has fine furniture, glass, china, Oriental rugs, and a well-informed staff. Unique sales are often advertised in local papers. **Trinity Galleries** (⊠*128 Germain St.* ☎*506/634–1611*) represents fine Maritime and Canadian artists.

EN ROUTE

Unlike most Bay of Fundy beaches, New River Beach (⊠ *Off Hwy. 1, 50 km [30 mi] west of Saint John*) is sandy and great for swimming, especially if you wait until the tide is coming in. The sun warms the sand at low tide, and the sand warms the water as it comes in. It's part of a provincial park ($7 vehicle entrance fee) that offers interpretive programs. There are hiking trails and kayak rentals, too.

THE FUNDY COAST

Bordering the chilly and powerful tidal Bay of Fundy is some of New Brunswick's most dramatic coastline. This area extends from the border town of St. Stephen and the lovely resort village of St. Andrews, past tiny fishing villages and rocky coves, through Saint John, and on to Fundy National Park, where the world's most extreme tides rise and fall twice daily. The Fundy Isles—Grand Manan Island, Deer Island, and Campobello—are havens of peace that have lured harried mainlanders for generations. Some of the impressive 50-km (31-mi) stretch of coastline between St. Martins and Fundy National Park is accessible.

The **Fundy Trail Parkway** (⊕ *www.fundytrailparkway.com*) is 11 km (7 mi) of coastal roadway with a 16-km (10-mi) network of walking, hiking, and biking trails that lead to an interpretive center and suspension bridge at Big Salmon River. On the other side of the bridge is the Fundy Footpath for serious hikers. ☎ *506/833–2019* ✍*$3* ☉*Mid-May–mid-Oct.*

ST. STEPHEN

107 km (66 mi) west of Saint John.

The chocolate bar was invented in St. Stephen, across the St. Croix River from Calais, Maine, and the small town is a mecca for chocoholics. An elegant factory-outlet chocolate-candy store dominates the main street and in early August "Choctails," chocolate puddings, cakes, and even complete chocolate meals, are served during the Chocolate Festival. The provincial **visitor information center** (⊠*5 King St.* ☎*506/466–7390*) has details.

Ganong's famed, hand-dipped chocolates and other candies are available at the factory store, **Ganong Chocolatier** ⊠*73 Milltown Blvd.* ☎*506/465–5611* ☉*June–Aug., weekdays 8–7, Sat. 9–5, Sun. 10–5; Sept.–May, Mon.–Sat. 9–5).* There are factory tours ($3) during the first full week of August.

℃ The **Chocolate Museum,** behind Ganong Chocolatier, explores the sweet history of candy making with hand-dipping videos and hands-on exhibits. ⊠*73 Milltown Blvd.* ☎*506/466–7848* ⊕*www.chocolatemuseum.ca* ✍*$5* ☉*Mar.–Nov.; call for hours.*

EN ROUTE
St. Croix Island, an International Historic Site, can be seen from an interpretive park on Route 127, between St. Stephen and St. Andrews. This is where explorers Samuel de Champlain and Sieur de Monts spent their first harsh winter in North America in 1604.

ST. ANDREWS BY-THE-SEA

29 km (18 mi) southeast of St. Stephen.

St. Andrews by-the-Sea, a designated National Historic District on Passamaquoddy Bay, is one of North America's prettiest resort towns.

The Fundy Coast

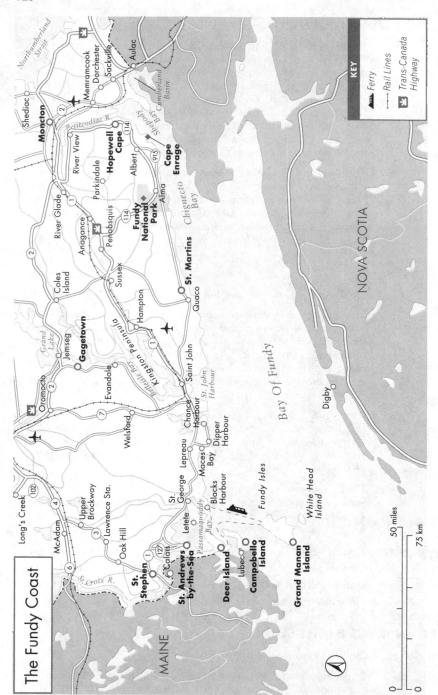

KEY

⚓ *Ferry*
┼┼ *Rail Lines*
▣ *Trans-Canada Highway*

NOVA SCOTIA

Bay Of Fundy

MAINE

Northumberland Strait

Cumberland Basin

Shepody Bay

Chignecto Bay

Grand Lake

Belleisle Bay

Kingston Peninsula

St. John Harbour

Passamaquoddy Bay

Fundy Isles

St. Croix R.

Petitcodiac R.

White Head Island

Aulac
Sackville
Dorchester
Memramcook
Shediac
Moncton
River View
Hopewell Cape
Albert
Cape Enrage
Alma
Parkindale
River Glade
Penobsquis
Fundy National Park
Anagance
Coles Island
Sussex
St. Martins
Hampton
Quaco
Jemseg
Gagetown
Evandale
Saint John
Oromocto
Welsford
Chance Harbour
Dipper Harbour
Maces Bay
Lepreau
St. George
Blacks Harbour
Letete
Upper Brockway
Lawrence Sta.
Oak Hill
McAdam
Long's Creek
St. Stephen
Calais
St. Andrews by-the-Sea
Deer Island
Lubec
Campobello Island
Grand Manan Island
Digby

114
915
1
2
7
4
6
3
1
127
102

50 miles
75 km

It has long been a summer retreat of the affluent (mansions ring the town). Of the town's 550 buildings, 280 were erected before 1880, and 14 of those have survived from the 1700s. Some Loyalists even brought their homes with them piece by piece from Castine, Maine, across the bay, when the American Revolution didn't go their way. For a self-guided tour, pick up a walking-tour map at the visitor information center at 46 Reed Avenue (next to the arena) and follow it through the pleasant streets. Water Street, by the harbor, has eateries, gift and crafts shops, and artists' studios.

A particular gem is the **Charlotte County Courthouse** (⊠ *123 Frederick St.*), which has been active since 1840. It was declared a National Historic Site in 1983. Tours are available during summer; check-in at the *Old Gaol.*

Directly adjacent to the courthouse is the stone-walled **Old Gaol,** which functioned as the town jail from 1834 to 1979. Today it houses the Charlotte County archives. Tours are given May through August. ⊠ *123 Frederick St.* ☎ *506/529–4248* ☜ *Free* ☉ *May–Aug. weekdays 9–5.*

Greenock Church (⊠ *Montague and Edward Sts.* ☎ *No phone*) owes its existence to a remark someone made at an 1822 dinner party about the "poor" Presbyterians not having a church of their own. Captain Christopher Scott, who took exception to the slur, spared no expense on the building, which is decorated with a carving of a green oak tree in honor of Scott's birthplace, Greenock, Scotland.

The **Ross Memorial Museum** was established by an American couple who had a summer home in St. Andrews for 40 years. The Rosses donated the trappings of that home—and an extensive collection of 19th century New Brunswick furniture and decorative artwork—to the town and purchased this 1824 Georgian mansion to house them. ⊠ *188 Montague St.* ☎ *506/529–5124* ☜ *Donations accepted* ☉ *Early June mid-Oct., Mon.–Sat. 10–4:30.*

ⓒ FodorsChoice ★ Nearly 2,500 varieties of trees, shrubs, and plants cover the 27 acres of woodland trails and many theme gardens at the **Kingsbrae Horticultural Garden,** one of Canada's most spectacular public gardens. One of the gardens is specially designed for touch and smell; other themed gardens are a rose garden, a bird and butterfly garden, and a gravel garden, just to name a few. A children's fantasy garden offers child-centered activities and there are daily kids programs from 1:30 to 2:30. Check out the new installation titled "Pericles," Canada's first Wollemi Pine. There are opportunities to take a ladybug to lunch, or to buy unusual plants. Kingsbrae also has an art gallery and a café. ⊠ *220 King St.* ☎ *506/529–3335* ⊕ *www.kingsbraegarden.com* ☜ *$9* ☉ *Mid-May–mid-Oct., daily 9–6.*

ⓒ The Huntsman Marine Science Centre provides educational displays at its **Huntsman Aquarium and Museum.** Marine life includes a teeming touch tank and some very entertaining seals that are fed at 11 and 4 daily. There is a new live-shark and giant-sturgeon exhibit, as well as free movies and slide shows. ⊠*1 Lower Campus Rd.* ☎*506/529–1202* ⊕*www.huntsmanmarine.ca* ⊠*$7.50* ⊙*May–Sept., daily 10–5.*

Ministers Island. This huge island estate, once completely self-sufficient, was the summer home of Sir William Van Horne, chairman of the Canadian Pacific Railway from 1899 to 1915. Touring the island can be done by car or you can access the island by boat. Check the tide schedule in the paper or call Minister's Island. On the island are the Covenhoven Mansion, where just a few artifacts are on display; a tidal swimming pool; a livestock barn; a cottage; an old windmill; and the 1790 Minister's House, from which the island takes its name. ■ TIP➜ If you drive over, be sure to leave the island before the tide comes in or you will be stuck for another 12 hours. ⊠*Bar Rd. off Rte. 127, 5 km (3 mi) north of St. Andrews* ☎*506/529–5081 for tour information* ⊠*$12, includes boat and guided tours* ⊙*June–Oct.*

WHERE TO STAY & EAT

$$–$$$$ ✕**The Gables.** You won't be disappointed by the steaks, salmon, or lobster dinners at this casual harborside eatery, but keep in mind that spanakopita is a specialty, as are a hugely popular lobster clubhouse sandwich and hearty seafood chowder. Handmade desserts top off a great meal in this casual harborside eatery. The owner's art decorates the walls, and there's a deck for alfresco dining in summer. ⊠*143 Water St.* ☎*506/529–3440* ☐*AE, MC, V.*

¢–$$ ✕**Ossie's Seafood Take-Out.** The gaudy billboard outside this unassuming take-out joint reads THE BEST SEAFOOD IN NORTH AMERICA, and those who have tried it tend to agree. A local institution since 1957, Ossie's seafood is deep-fried and served with a famous house tartar sauce. Other than the fried seafood, though, Ossie's also turns out fish chowder, turkey soup, rolls, and pies and other desserts. There is no dining room, but there are lots of picnic tables. ⊠*3222 Hwy. 1, Bethel* ☎*506/755–2758* ☐*No credit cards* ⊙*Closed late Oct.–early Apr.*

¢–$ ✕**Sweet Harvest Market.** Known for its natural products and made-on-site breads, cookies, cakes, cheesecakes, and preserves, this casual bakery-deli-restaurant is always experimenting. Try the salmon mouse or the house-made roast beef. ⊠*182 Water St.* ☎*506/529–6249* ☐*V.*

$–$$ ✕🏠**Rossmount Inn Hotel Restaurant & Bar.** "Hospitality plus" easily defines this inn, set on 87 acres at the base of Chamcook Mountain, and its charming owners. The rooms are understated and airy and the handsome dining room features crystal chandeliers and dark mahagony furniture, which sets the scene for fine dining ($$–$$$) at its best. Local seafood and organic produce (much of it plucked from the inn's organic garden minutes before a meal) are featured daily. The vanilla poached "naked" lobster with sweet-pea reduction is a masterpiece. The wine list is impressive, too. ⊠ *4599 Rte. 127, St. Andrews by-the-Sea* ☎*506/529–3351* ⌖*Reservations essential for dining room* ⊕ *www. rossmountinn.com* 🛏*18 rooms* ⚿ *In-room: Wi-Fi, no phone, no TV, no a/c. In-hotel: restaurant, bar, pool, no-smoking rooms* ☐*AE, MC, V* ⊙*Closed Jan.–Easter.*

2

$$$$ ⚷**Fairmont Algonquin.** This grand old resort, where the bellhops wear
★ kilts and dinner is served on the wraparound veranda in fine weather,
presides on a hill above town like an elegant dowager. The rooms have
an air of relaxed refinement; those in the newer Prince of Wales wing
are especially comfortable. The Passamaquoddy Dining Room, open
for breakfast and dinner (summer only), is noted for its seafood and
regional dishes. Other options are the casual Right Whale Pub and the
cozy Library Lounge and Bistro. Sign up for a beachfront lobster boil
in summer. Concierge service and children's programs are available in
summer. ✉*184 Adolphus St., E5B 1T7* ☎*506/529–8823* 🖷*506/529–
7162* ⊕*www.fairmont.com/algonquin* 🛏*234 rooms* ⚸*In-room:
refrigerator (some), WiFi. In-hotel: 3 restaurants, room service, bars,
golf course, tennis courts, pool, gym, spa, beachfront, bicycles, laundry
service, some pets allowed, no-smoking rooms* ▤*AE, DC, MC, V.*

$$$$ ⚷**Kingsbrae Arms.** This restored 1897 estate is an experience. Eclectic
Fodor'sChoice antiques fill the rooms, and pampering touches are plentiful—roses,
★ Belgian chocolates, plush robes, a pantry stocked with biscotti, and
daily afternoon tea. Expect excellent service from the gregarious owners and staff. The two-story carriage house has a private entrance,
patio, and balcony, plus a kitchen (minus stove). Fine dining here
reaches new heights with a "menuless" approach. The chef prepares a
daily degustation using the finest and freshest ingredients—perhaps a
fresh catch from the fishmonger or a last minute delivery of wild boar.
✉*219 King St., E5B 1Y1* ☎*506/529–4558* 🖷*506/529–1197* ⊕*www.
kingsbrae.com* 🛏*6 suites, 2 rooms* ⚸*In-room: DVD, VCR, dial-up.
In-hotel: pool, laundry service, no-smoking rooms, some pets allowed,
minibar (some), no elevator* ▤*AE, MC, V* ⑂*MAP.*

$$$–$$$$ ⚷**Pansy Patch.** A visit to this bed-and-breakfast, a 1912 Normandy-
★ style farmhouse with an art gallery, is a bit like a close encounter with
landed gentry who are patrons of the arts and who like their gardens
as rich and formal as their meals. Four rooms are in the Corey Cot-
tage next door. All rooms have period furniture and are individually
decorated. Afternoon tea and cookies are served wherever you like—in
the breakfast room, in your room, in the garden, or on the deck over-
looking the water. ✉*59 Carleton St., E5B 1M8* ☎*506/529–3834 or
888/726–7972* 🖷*506/529–9042* ⊕*www.pansypatch.com* 🛏*9 rooms*
⚸*In-room: no TV (some), In-hotel: ethernet, no elevator, no-smoking
rooms* ▤*AE, MC, V* ⊘*Closed mid-Oct.–mid-May* ⑂*BP.*

$$$ ⚷**Treadwell Inn.** Gardens, a huge deck, and balconies all overlook the
ocean at this gracious old inn. Built by a ships' chandler in about 1820,
the inn has been faithfully restored and furnished to reflect the era. All
the rooms are lovely, though the less expensive ones overlook the street.
The Snug & Oyster Bar serves breakfast, lunch, and dinner. ✉*129
Water St., E5B 1A7* ☎*506/529–1011 or 888/529–1011* 🖷*506/529–
4826* ⊕*www.treadwellinn.com* 🛏*6 rooms* ⚸*In-room: no a/c (some),
kitchen (some), dial-up. In-hotel: laundry service, no-smoking rooms,
no elevator* ▤*AE, MC, V* ⑂*BP.*

$–$$$ ⚷**Seaside Beach Resort.** If the click of a closing screen door sounds
like summer at the beach to you, this waterfront cluster of cottages is
your kind of place. At one end of the town's main street, the cabins,

cottages, and apartments are close to all the action and a beach. Units are simple but comfortable and well equipped, right down to big pots for boiling lobsters. It's a terrific, casual choice if you have kids and/or dogs. ⊠*339 Water St., E5B 2R2* ☎*506/529–3846 or 800/506–8677* 🖶*506/529–4479* ⊕*www.seaside.nb.ca* ⤳*24 cottages* ⌕*In-room: no a/c, kitchen (some). In-hotel: laundry facilities, no-smoking rooms, some pets allowed, no elevator* ⊟*AE, MC, V.*

SPORTS & THE OUTDOORS

ⓒ **St. Andrews Creative Playground** (⊠*168 Frederick St.*) is an amazing wooden structure for climbing, swinging, performing, making music, and playing games. The **Sunbury Shores Arts & Nature Centre** (⊠*139 Water St.* ☎*506/529–3386*) offers art workshops in drawing, etching, painting, pottery, and many other media, in conjunction with environmental excursions.

GOLF   The **Algonquin Golf Club** (⊠*Off Rte. 127* ☎*506/529–8165* ⊕*www. algonquingolf.com*) has a beautifully landscaped 18-hole, par-71 signature course, designed by Thomas McBroom. The holes on the back 9—especially the 12th—have beautiful views of Passamaquoddy Bay, as does the Clubhouse Grill.

WATER Whale and nature cruises and kayak tours all begin at the **Day Adven-**
SPORTS **ture Centre** at the town wharf. **Eastern Outdoors** (☎*506/529–8858 or 800/565–2925* ⊕*www.easternoutdoors.com*) has single and double kayaks, as well as lessons, tours, and white-water kayaking. **Fundy Tide Runners** (☎*506/529–4481* ⊕*www.fundytiderunners.com*) uses a 24-foot Zodiac to search for whales, seals, and marine birds. **Tall Ship Whale Adventures** (☎*506/529–8116*) operates the *Cory*, an elegant vessel for whale-watching. **Quoddy Link Marine** (☎*506/529–2600* ⊕*www.townsearch.com/quoddylink*) offers whale and wildlife tours for up to 47 passengers on a powered catamaran. **Seascape Kayak Tours** (☎*506/529–4866* ⊕*www.seascapekayaktours.com*) provides instruction as well as trips around the area from a half day to a week.

SHOPPING

Cottage Craft (⊠*Town Sq.* ☎*506/529–3190*) employs knitters year-round to make mittens, sweaters, blankets, and woolen crafts from its specially dyed wool. The **Crocker Hill Store/Steven Smith Designs** (⊠*45 King St.* ☎*506/529–4303*) has art and other items for those who love gardens and birds. **Garden by the Sea (NB)** (⊠*217 Water St.* ☎*506/529–8905*) is an aromatic shop with fabulous flowers, soaps, and teas. They specialize in all-natural body products including Bay of Fundy sea salts and ecoflowers.**Jon Sawyer Glass** (⊠*719 Mowat Dr.* ☎*506/529–3012*) is a glass studio where you can watch the artist blow exquisite goblets and other items most days between 9 and 5 (call first to be sure he is there). His pieces are also sold at Garden by the Sea on Water Street. Observe the smoking process of some of New Brunswick's best salmon at **Oven Head Salmon Smokers** (⊠*101 Oven Head Rd., off Hwy. 1, Bethel* ☎*506/755–2507 or 877/955–2507*). Buy the smoked salmon at the on-site store or in local grocery stores—or try it off the menu at many of the region's restaurants.

★ The **Seacoast Gallery** (✉174 *Water St.* ☎*506/529–0005*) carries fine arts and crafts by eminent New Brunswick artists. **Serendipin′ Art** (✉*168 Water St.* ☎*506/529–3327*) sells handblown glass, hand-painted silks, jewelry, and other crafts by New Brunswick artists.

GRAND MANAN ISLAND

35 km (22 mi) east of St. Andrews by-the-Sea to Black′s Harbour, 1½ hrs by car ferry from Black′s Harbour.

Grand Manan, the largest of the three Fundy Islands, is also the farthest from the mainland. You might see whales, seals, or a rare puffin on the way over. Circular herring weirs dot the island′s coastal waters, and fish sheds and smokehouses lie beside long wharfs that reach out to bobbing fishing boats. Place-names are evocative: Swallowtail, Southern Head, Seven Days Work, and Dark Harbour. It′s easy to get around; only about 32 km (20 mi) of road lead from the lighthouse at Southern Head to the one at North Head. John James Audubon, that human encyclopedia of birds, visited the island in 1831, attracted by the more than 240 species of seabirds that nest here. The puffin may be the island′s symbol, but whales are the stars. Giant finbacks, right whales, minkes, and humpbacks feed in the rich waters. With only 2,700 residents on the island, it may seem remote and quiet, but there is actually a lot going on and plenty to do including birding, kayaking, whale-watching, and beachcombing. There are lighthouses to visit, or you can hike a heritage trail, visit the Whale and Seabird Research station, or just hang around the busy wharves and chat with the fishermen. A day trip is possible, but you′ll wish you had planned to stay at least one night. Plan to be at the ferry early as it operates on a first-come, first-served basis.

Ferry service is provided by **Coastal Transport** (☎*506/662–3724* ⛴*Cars are $30 payable on return passage from Grand Manan; adults are $10.35; and children 5 to 12 years old are $5.50, under 5 free*), which leaves the mainland from Black′s Harbour, off Route 1, and docks at North Head on Grand Manan Island.

WHERE TO STAY & EAT

$–$$ ✕⛺ **Inn at Whale Cove.** Step back in time at this secluded waterfront compound where rustic surroundings join with elegant furnishings. Full breakfast is included for guests staying at the inn (not in the cottages). The dining room ($$–$$$) features fresh seasonal choices. Cottages are available by the week only. ✉*26 Whale Cove Cottage Rd., E5G 2B5* ☎*506/662–3181* ⊕*www.holidayjunction.com/whalecove* ➥*3 rooms, 3 cottages* ⚫*In-room: no a/c (some), no phone, no TV. In-hotel: beachfront, no-smoking rooms, some pets allowed, no elevator* ⊟*MC, V* ⊗*Closed Nov.–Apr.*

$–$$ ⛺ **Compass Rose.** Two charming small homes on the water combine to give this lovely English-style country inn a cottage atmosphere. The floral-themed guest rooms are bright and comfortable, and afternoon tea has evolved to include cappuccino, café au lait, and scones. A wall of windows in the dining room overlooks the busy fishing wharf. Bordering Stanley Beach, this area is one of the few places to find sand dollars and beachglass. A full breakfast is served each day, and all rooms overlook the water. ⊠ *65 Rte. 776, E5G 1A2* 🖃🖃*506/662–8570* ⊕*www.compassroseinn.com* ⇔*6 rooms* ᗕ*In-room: no a/c, no phone, no TV. In-hotel: restaurant, no kids under 12, no-smoking rooms* ⊟*MC, V* ⦿⎮*BP.*

$ 🖃**Marathon Inn.** This mansion built by a sea captain sits on a hill overlooking the harbor. It has been an inn since 1871, and many of its original furnishings can still be found in the guest rooms. Large black-and-white photos grace the living room. Seafood is featured in the dining room; lunch is not served, but guests can request packed lunches. ⊠ *19 Marathon La., Grand Manan E5G 3A4* 🖃*506/662–8488* ⊕*www.marathoninn.com* ⇔*24 rooms* ᗕ*In-room: no a/c, no TV (some). In-hotel: restaurant, bar, some pets allowed, no-smoking rooms, no elevator* ⊟*MC, V.*

SPORTS & THE OUTDOORS

WHALE WATCHING A whale-watching cruise from Grand Manan takes you well out into the bay. Dress warmly; some boats have winter jackets, hats, and mittens on board for those who don't heed this advice. Most operators give refunds if no whales are sighted. Interpreters on **Sea Watch Tours** (🖃*877/662–8552* ⊕*www.seawatchtours.com*) are very knowledgeable about the birds you might encounter on your cruise, as well as the whales. Trips ($55) are four to five hours, July through September. **Whales-n-Sails Adventures** (🖃*506/662–1999 or 888/994–4044* ⊕*www.whales-n-sails.com*) uses a 60-foot sailboat to visit the whales. Trips ($65, including tax, fish chowder, and hot drinks) are four to five hours, mid-June through mid-September.

For complete information on bird-watching, nature photography, hiking, cycling, horseback riding, sea kayaking, and whale-watching, contact **Tourism New Brunswick** (⊡*Box 12345, Fredericton E3B 5C3* 🖃*800/561–0123* ⊕*www.tourismnbcanada.com*).

Seascape Kayak Tours (🖃*506/747–1884* ⊕*www.seascapekayaktours.com/default1.htm*) in St. Andrews, provides visitors with high quality sea-kayaking experiences and responsible adventure tourism. Seascape has received international recognition for its sustainable tourism practices.

DEER ISLAND

50 km (31 mi) east of St. Andrews by-the-Sea to Letete, 40 mins by free ferry from Letete.

One of the pleasures of Deer Island is walking around the fishing wharves like those at Chocolate Cove. Exploring the island takes only a few hours; it's 12 km (7 mi) long, varying in width from almost 5 km (3 mi) to a few hundred feet at some points.

At **Deer Point,** walk through a small nature park while waiting for the ferry to Campobello Island. If you listen carefully, you may be able to hear the sighing and snorting of the **Old Sow,** the second-largest whirlpool in the world. If you can't hear it, you'll be able to see it, just a few feet offshore in the Western Passage off Point Park.

WHERE TO STAY & EAT

¢–$$$ ✕**45th Parallel Restaurant.** Seafood is an integral part of home cooking on the island, and especially at this restaurant. Their lobster roll is renowned but other popular menu items include fresh panfried haddock or scallops. Old-fashioned chicken dinners—baked chicken, stuffing, real gravy, mashed potatoes, veggies, and cranberry sauce—still exist here, too. Flowers surround this casual and friendly place and a newly enlarged dining terrace overlooks Passamaquoddy Bay. ⊠*941 Hwy. 772, Fairhaven* ☎*506/747–2222 year-round, 506/747–2231 May–Oct.* ▤*AE, MC, V* ☉*Closed weekdays Nov.–Mar.*

¢–$ ⊡**Sunset Beach Cottage & Suites.** A modern property surrounded by natural beauty, this complex is right on a secluded cove. Watch the porpoises and bald eagles during the day, and in the evening enjoy a rare east-coast treat—an ocean sunset in the newly installed hot tub. ⊠*21 Cedar Grove Rd., Fairhaven E5V 1N3* ☎*506/747–2972 or 888/576–9990* ⊕*www.cottageandsuites.com* ⇆*5 suites, 1 cottage* ⚒*In-room: no a/c (some), VCR. In-hotel: pool, no-smoking rooms, no elevator* ▤*V.*

SPORTS & THE OUTDOORS

Lumber's Outer Island Tours (⊠*Lord's Cove Wharf* ☎*506/747–2426 or 866/694–2537* ⊕*www.outerislandtours.com*) offers whale-watching and eco-tours ($50 tax, included). The captain is a ninth-generation Deer Islander.

CAMPOBELLO ISLAND

★ *40 mins by ferry (June to September) Campobello to Deer Island departs on the hour, every hour; 90 km (56 mi) southeast of St. Stephen via bridge from Lubec, Maine.*

Neatly manicured, preening itself in the bay, Campobello Island has always had a special appeal to the wealthy and the famous.

The 34-room rustic summer cottage of the family of President Franklin Delano Roosevelt is now part of a nature preserve, **Roosevelt Campobello International Park,** a joint project of the Canadian and U.S. governments. The miles of trails here make for pleasant strolling. President Roosevelt's boyhood summer home was also the setting for the movie *Sunrise at Campobello.* To drive here from St. Stephen (a trip of about 80 km [50 mi]), cross the border into Maine, drive down Route 1, and take Route 189 to Lubec, Maine; then cross a bridge to the island. ⊠*Roosevelt Park Rd.* ☎*506/752–2922* ⊡*Free* ☉*House late May–mid-Oct., daily 10–5:45 grounds daily year-round.*

The island's **Herring Cove Provincial Park** (⊠*Welshpool* ☎*506/752–7010*) has camping facilities, a restaurant, a 9-hole, par-36 Geoffrey Cornish golf course, a sandy beach, and miles of hiking trails.

WHERE TO STAY & EAT

¢–$$$$ ✕🏠 **Lupine Lodge.** Originally a vacation home built by the Adams family (friends of the Roosevelts) in the early 1900s, these three attractive log cabins on a bluff overlooking the Bay of Fundy are now a modern guest lodge. Nature trails connect Lupine Lodge to Herring Cove Provincial Park. Two of the cabins contain the guest rooms, which are rustic, with modern furniture and homemade quilts. The third cabin houses the dining room ($–$$), which specializes in simple but well-prepared local seafood. A deck overlooking the bay connects the three buildings. ✉ *610 Rte. 774, Welshpool E5E 1A5* ☎ *506/752–2555 or 888/912–8880* ⊕ *www.lupinelodge.com* ➴ *11 rooms* ☌ *In-room: no a/c, no phone, no TV. In-hotel: restaurant, bar, no-smoking rooms, no elevator* ▭ *MC, V.*

$ 🏠 **Water's Edge Villas.** Watch the sun set over the water from the deck of a modern, two-bedroom cottage with all the comforts of home, including a lobster pot and a barbecue. There's a kitchen, and the living room couch is a pullout so six can sleep comfortably. The water is just across the road, and the rocky beach is great for explorers. ✉ *37 Hutchins Rd., Welshpool E5E 1H1* ☎ *506/752–2359 or 800/836–7648* ⊕ ➴ *3 cottages* ☌ *In-room: VCR, no phone, no a/c. In-hotel: laundry service, no pets, no-smoking rooms* ▭ *MC, V.*

ST. MARTINS

45 km (28 mi) east of Saint John.

The fishing village of St. Martins has a rich shipbuilding heritage, whispering caves, miles of lovely beaches, spectacular tides, and a cluster of covered bridges, as well as several Heritage Inns and a couple of restaurants right on the beach. It's also the gateway to the Fundy Trail Parkway.

The scenic drive portion of the linear **Fundy Trail Parkway** extends to an interpretive center at Salmon River. The road closely parallels the cycling-walking Fundy Trail along the shore. There are lots of places to park and many accessible scenic lookouts. The Fundy Footpath for expert hikers continues through to Fundy National Park. The parkway portion operates mid-May through mid-October. ☎ *506/833–2019* ⊕ *www.fundytrailparkway.com* ✉ *$3.*

WORD OF MOUTH

"From Saint John to Alma, the secondary road which will take you through St. Martins is a nice drive. St. Martins is a lovely spot but you don't need to spend a lot of time. Good picture opportunity with covered bridges, etc. Not at all like Hopewell Rocks. Your other option would be to stop at Fundy (Alma) for the night giving you time to explore the National Park and the next day visit Cape Enrage (in my opinion, more spectacular than Hopewell Rocks) and then the Rocks on your way to PEI." —Tanya

WHERE TO STAY & EAT

$$-$$$ ✕ **Broadway Café.** On a quiet and colorful street in "downtown" Sussex, this charming café sits across from a defunct but well-maintained train station, now an ice-cream parlor and tourist center. Dine at a street-side table or in the shaded garden. Inside, the café is a jumble of Christmas lights, wooden booths, and artwork. Sandwiches, pizzas, and salads fill the lunch menu; eclectic dinner choices include curries, chicken paprika, quiches, rack of lamb, and plenty of seafood. There is often live music on dinner nights. ✉ *73 Broad St., 60 km (37 mi) northeast of St. Martins, Sussex* ☎ *506/433–5414* ▭*MC, V* ⊘*Closed Sun. No dinner Mon. and Tues.*

$-$$ ✕▥ **St. Martins Country Inn.** High on a hill overlooking the Bay of Fundy, this restored sea captain's home is furnished with Victorian antiques. The adjacent sea carriage house has four rooms. Formal dinners ($$–$$$) in the Candlelight Dining Room are excellent. Coquille St. Martins, a rich medley of lobster, scallops, shrimp, and crab in a creamy wine sauce, is the house specialty. Children are welcome to stay in the carriage house, though not in the main inn. ✉*303 Main St., E5R 1C1* ☎*506/833–4534 or 800/565–5257* 🖷*506/833–4725* ⊕*www.stmartinscountryinn.com* 🛏*16 rooms* ♿*In-room: VCR. In-hotel: restaurant, bar, laundry service, no-smoking rooms, no elevator* ▭*MC, V.*

$ ✕▥ **Weslan Inn.** Fireplaces, antiques, and lots of floral prints give the rooms in this Heritage Inn an English country feel. Breakfast is served in your room. The relaxed dining room (¢–$; reservations essential) specializes in seafood. ✉*45 Main St., E5R 1B4* ☎*506/833–2351* ⊕*www.weslaninn.com* 🛏*4 rooms* ♿*In-room: DVD, VCR. In-hotel: restaurant, laundry service, Wi-Fi, no elevator* ▭*MC, V* ¶◎*BP.*

$-$$ ▥ **Quaco Inn.** This luxurious property is situated just where the highest tides in the world sweep in and out each day, almost at your doorstep—a mere 150 feet away! The elegant guest rooms are furnished with antiques but have contemporary luxuries like whirlpool spa baths. The dining room serves delectable land and sea dishes ($$$): try the Quaco Duck, a breast of duck with a poached pear and a Port reduction. ✉*16 Beach St., E5R 1C7* ☎*506/833–4772* ⊕ *www.quacoinn.com/index.htm* 🛏 *12 rooms* ♿*In-room: Wi-Fi. In-hotel: restaurant, laundry service, free parking, no smoking, no pets* ▭*MC, V.*

$ ▥ **The Waterfront Bed & Breakfast.** A restored Victorian sea captain's home (c. 1841), this waterfront property is situated on the beautiful St Martins Beach, only minutes from sea caves and the heart of historic St. Martins. All three rooms are large, sunny, and comfortable with private balconies overlooking the bay. Walk the 5-km (3-mi) beach and collect shells and stones. A full breakfast is provided. ✉*296 Main St., E5R 1C2* ☎*506/833–9010* ⊕*www.bbcanada.com/thewaterfront* 🛏*3* ♿*In-hotel: free parking, no pets, no-smoking rooms* ▭*AE, DC, MC, V* ¶◎*BP.*

SPORTS & THE OUTDOORS

SKIING **Poley Mountain Resort** (✉ *Waterford Rd., 10 km [6 mi] southeast of Sussex* ☎*506/433–7653* ⊕*www.poleymountain.com*) has 23 trails, a snowboard park, a 660-foot vertical drop, night skiing, and half-pipe snowboarding.

FUNDY NATIONAL PARK

Fodor'sChoice *135 km (84 mi) northeast of Saint John.*
★

Fundy National Park is an awesome 206-square-km (80-square-mi) microcosm of New Brunswick's inland and coastal climates. Park naturalists offer several programs each day, including beach walks and hikes to explore the park's unique climatic conditions and the fascinating biological evolution evident in the forests. The park has 100 km (60 mi) of varied hiking and mountain-biking trails, year-round camping, golf, tennis, a heated Bay of Fundy saltwater pool, a playground, and a restaurant. In the evening there are interactive programs in the amphitheater and campfires. Its more than 600 campsites range from full service to wilderness. ⊠*Rte. 114, Alma E4H 1B4* ☎*506/887–6000* ⊕*www.pc.gc.ca* ⊠*$6.90.*

The small seaside town of **Alma** services Fundy National Park with motels, restaurants that serve good lobster, and a bakery that sells sublime sticky buns. Around this area, much of it in Albert County, there's plenty to do outdoors—from bird-watching to spelunking.

Salem & Hillsborough Railroad Inc. This is a leading railway museum and houses an extensive collection of railway artifacts. A gift shop and museum on-site are open daily 10 to 6 during July and August, otherwise by chance or appointment. ⊠*2847 Main St., Hillsborough E4H 2X7* ☎*506/734–3195 seasonal* ⊕*www.shrr.ca* ⊠*$5,* sr. *$4,* youth *$3,* family *$10* ⊗*Mid-June–early Sept., Tues., Wed., and weekends.*

WHERE TO STAY

$ 🏨**Falcon Ridge Inn.** Perched high above the village and the ocean, every window (and there are many) in this modern property affords a spectacular view, and eliminates any need for air-conditioning. A four-course dinner ($$$) is available with advance notice; seafood is a specialty. ⊠*24 Falcon Ridge Dr., E4H 4Z3* ☎*506/887–8110 or 888/321–9090* 🖶*506/887–2376* ⊕*www.falconridgeinn.nb.ca* ➹*4 rooms* &⌂*In-room: refrigerator, DVD, VCR, dial-up Internet. In-hotel: laundry service, no-smoking rooms, no elevator* ☰*AE, MC, V* ⑩*BP.*

$–$$ 🏨**Parkland Village Inn.** Right on the water and in the heart of the bustling village, this rambling inn with an original section and a modern addition has a large dining room ($–$$$) where the hummingbird feeders in the windows are frequently visited. Lobster and scallops are popular menu selections. ⊠*8601 Main St., E4H 1N6* ☎*506/887–2313* 🖶*506/887–2315* ⊕*www.parklandvillageinn.com* ➹*10 rooms, 5 suites* &⌂*In-room: refrigerator (some), Wi-Fi, no a/c. In-hotel: restaurant, bar, beachfront, laundry service, no-smoking rooms, no elevator* ☰*MC, V* ⊗*Closed Nov.–Apr.* ⑩*BP.*

SPORTS & THE OUTDOORS

BIRD-   The bit of shoreline at **Marys Point** (⊠*Follow signs off Rte. 915*) draws
WATCHING   tens of thousands of migrating birds, including semipalmated sandpipers and other shorebirds, each summer. The area, now a bird sanctuary and interpretive center, is near Riverside-Albert.

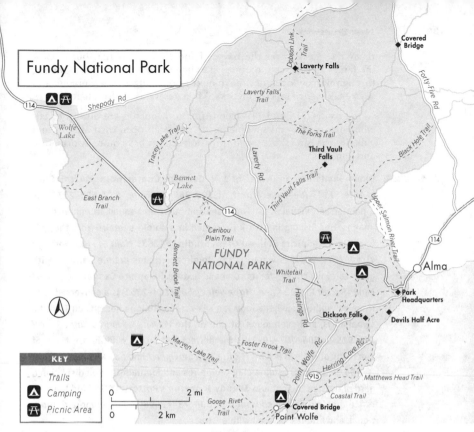

Fundy National Park

KEY
- - - *Trails*
▲ *Camping*
🎪 *Picnic Area*

0 ———— 2 mi
0 ———— 2 km

GOLF   The Fundy National Park Golf Club (✉ *Fundy National Park near the Alma entrance* ☎ 506/887–2970) is near cliffs overlooking the restless Bay of Fundy; it's one of the province's most beautiful and challenging 9-hole courses.

HORSEBACK RIDING   **Broadleaf Guest Ranch** (✉ *5526 Rte. 114, Hopewell Hill* ☎ 506/882–2349 *or* 800/226-5405 ⊕ *www.broadleafranch.com*) can provide an overnight adventure in the forest or a short trail ride through lowland marshes or along a beach. The Ranch Restaurant has themed evenings—for example, line dancing or roping instruction; reservations are required. Stay a while in a two-bedroom log cottage with all the comforts of home for $150 a night (5 people or less); $200 (6 people or more).

SEA KAYAKING   **Baymount Outdoor Adventures** (✉ *Hillsborough* ☎ 506/734–2660) offers sea kayaking around the Hopewell Rocks, as well as hiking, biking, and spelunking. **FreshAir Adventure** (✉ *16 Fundy View Dr., Alma* ☎ 506/887–2249 *or* 800/545–0020 ⊕ *www.freshairadventure.com*) conducts Bay of Fundy sea-kayaking excursions that last from two hours to three days. Guides, instruction, and equipment are provided.

SPELUNKING   **Baymount Outdoor Adventures** (✉ *Hillsborough* ☎ 506/734–2660 ⊕ *www.baymountadventures.com*) has interpreters who lead expeditions into the White Caves near the Bay of Fundy. Caving is fun, but not for the faint of heart, as it requires crawling on cave floors and slithering through narrow openings. Baymount also arranges hikes, biking, and sea kayaking at Hopewell Rocks. Make reservations for all activities.

Along routes 915 and 114 from Alma to Moncton are dozens of talented artists and craftspeople, many of whom open their studios and galleries to visitors. Visitor information centers have more information and a map.

EN ROUTE Lynne Saintonge, an owner of **Joie de Vivre Contemporary Art & Craft** (⊠ *Rte. 114, Riverside-Albert* ☎ *506/882-2276 or 877/595-2276*), is a painter and visual artist who uses computer and sound to enhance her images. Her fascinating work is created in a studio upstairs from the gallery. **Kindred Spirits Stained Glass Studio** (⊠ *2831 Main St., Hillsborough* ☎ *506/734-2342*) is where Diana Boudreau creates unique patterns with glass carefully chosen for its color and texture. **Samphire Casuals** (⊠ *Albert Mines Rd. off Rte. 114 near Hopewell* ☎ *506/734-2851*) is a converted one-room schoolhouse where Judy Tait silk-screens unique designs on T-shirts, sweatshirts, and even mugs. **Studio on the Marsh** (⊠ *Marys Point Rd. off Rte. 915* ☎ *506/882-2917*) is the perfect setting for wildlife art. Many of **Tim Isaac and Karin Bach's** (⊠ *Rte. 915 between Alma and Riverside-Albert* ☎ *506/882-2166*) wildlife clay sculptures and fountains are on display in a garden outside their studio. **Wendy Johnston's Pottery** (⊠ *Behind the post office on Main St., Hillsborough* ☎ *506/734-2046*) is contemporary, functional, and brightly colored with abstract designs.

CAPE ENRAGE

15 km (9 mi) east of Alma.

Route 915 takes you to the wild driftwood-cluttered beach at Cape Enrage, which juts out into the bay. A lighthouse, restaurant, gift shop, and some spectacular views can be found here.

SPORTS & THE OUTDOORS

Cape Enrage Adventures (⊠ *Off Rte. 915* ☎ *506/887-2273* ⊕ *www.capenrage.com*) has rappelling and rock-climbing ($48.50 for 2½ hours), kayaking ($59.50 half-day; $78 full day), an obstacle course ($13; 2 hours), beach hiking, and more! The five-day coastal hike is particularly challenging. Make reservations in advance. A restaurant, a gift shop, and rugged accommodations are on-site.

HOPEWELL CAPE

40 km (25 mi) northeast of Alma.

The coastal road (Route 114) from Alma to Moncton winds through covered bridges and along rocky coasts.

Fodor'sChoice ★ **Hopewell Rocks** is home to the famous Giant Flowerpots—rock formations carved by the Bay of Fundy tides. They're topped with vegetation and are uncovered only at low tide, when you can climb down for a closer study. There are also trails, an interactive visitor center, two restaurants, a gift shop, and a children's play area. Be careful, though—there are big cliffs at low tide, and you must exit the beach quickly when the tide comes in. *✉131 Discovery Rd. ☎877/734–3429 ⊕www.thehopewellrocks.ca $8 ⊙Late May–June, Sept., and Oct., daily 9–5; July and Aug., daily 8–8; closing hrs vary slightly, so call ahead.*

WORD OF MOUTH

"The Hopewell Rocks are amazing to see—you can watch the tide go in and out, and there is a good visitor center explaining the phenomenon. I don't think you need a whole day or night there, however. Look up the tides before you go and you can get some idea of when to arrive. Definitely try to arrive so you can walk down on the 'ocean floor.'" —nkh

2

WHERE TO STAY

$–$$ **Florentine Manor Heritage Inn.** With silver candlesticks on the dining-room table and handmade quilts on the beds, this restored old shipbuilder's house is a haven for honeymooners and romantics. All the rooms have at least two windows, the better to hear the birds in the trees outside. Two rooms have fireplaces and two have whirlpool baths. Picnic lunches and candlelight dinners are prepared by request. *✉356 Rte. 915, Harvey on the Bay E4H 2M2 ☎506/882–2271 or 800/665–2271 ⊕www.florentinemanor.com 9 rooms In-room: no a/c, no phone, no TV. In-hotel: bicycles, laundry service, no kids under 8, no-smoking rooms, no elevator MC, V BP.*

$–$$ **Innisfree Bed and Breakfast.** Everything about this B&B, an 1847 sea captain's home minutes from Hopewell Rocks, is Irish, from its name to the soda bread served at breakfast. The rooms are decorated with antiques and quilts, handmade by the owner, who also makes quilts and Irish knit sweaters to sell. A large family room with a surround-sound entertainment center has a great VHS/DVD library. Dinners are prepared on request, and you're welcome to use the kitchen refrigerator to store your barbecue fixings, and to use the outside grill. The house is surrounded by flower gardens, and there are a brook, a fountain, and lots of woodland and meadow trails. *✉4277 Highway 114, Hopewell Cape E4H 3P4 ☎506/734–3510 506/734–2559 ⊕www.innisfreebandb.com 4 rooms In-room: no a/c, VCR, dial-up. In-hotel: no kids under 12, no-smoking rooms, no elevator AE, MC, V ⊙Closed Dec.–Apr. BP.*

MONCTON

80 km (50 mi) northeast of Alma.

Moncton is Canada's first officially bilingual city. A friendly place, it is often called the Gateway to Acadia because of its mix of English and French and its proximity to the Acadian shore. Moncton has a renovated downtown with unique shops and restaurants. The greater Moncton area is considered the shopping mecca of Atlantic Canada with Moncton's Trinity Power Centre and its large warehouse stores. A water-theme park and nearby beaches make Moncton a cool summer spot, and the World Wine Festival in November and HubCap Comedy Festival in February warm up winter. A walking-tour brochure, available at the tourist information centers at Magnetic Hill on Route 126, downtown in Bore Park on Main Street and at the Greater Moncton International Airport, indicates the city's historic highlights.

This city has long touted two natural attractions: the Tidal Bore and the Magnetic Hill. You may be disappointed if you've read too much tourist hype, though.

In days gone by, before the harbor mouth filled with silt, the **Tidal Bore** was an incredible sight, a high wall of water that surged in through the narrow opening of the river to fill red mud banks to the brim. It still moves up the river, and is worth seeing, but it's no longer a raging torrent. Bore Park on Main Street is the best vantage point; viewing times are posted. Note the rapid and dramatic change in the river itself; at low tide the muddy river bottom is often visible, but within an hour of the arrival of the Bore, the water level rises about 25 feet (roughly 7½ meters) and fills the river to its banks.

☾ **Magnetic Hill** creates a bizarre optical illusion. If you park your car in neutral at the designated spot, you seem to be coasting uphill without power. Shops, a restaurant, the largest water park in Atlantic Canada, an award-winning zoo, a golf course, and a small railroad are part of the larger complex here; there are extra charges for the attractions. ⊠*North of Moncton off Trans-Canada Hwy. Exit 450 from Trans Canada Highway; watch for signs* ⌨*$5* ☉*May–early Sept., daily 8–8.*

☾ An excellent water-theme park, **Magic Mountain** is adjacent to Magnetic Hill. ⊠*Off Trans-Canada Hwy. Exit 450 on the outskirts of Moncton* ☎*506/857–9283, 800/331–9283 in Canada* ⌨*$22.50* ☉*Mid–late June and mid-Aug.–early Sept., daily 10–6; July–mid-Aug., daily 10–8.*

☾ The **Magnetic Hill Zoo,** the largest zoo in Atlantic Canada, has no shortage of exotic species, including lemurs, lions, and muntjacs (a type of small deer). A tropical house has reptiles, amphibians, birds, and primates, and at Old MacDonald's Barnyard, children can pet domestic animals or ride a pony in summer. ⊠*Off Trans-Canada Hwy. Exit 450 on the outskirts of Moncton* ☎*506/384–0303* ⌨*$8.50* ☉*Apr.–Oct.; hours vary.*

★ A restored 1920s vaudeville stage, the opulent **Capitol Theatre** is a beautiful attraction in itself as well as a venue for plays, musicals, ballets, and concerts. Free tours are given when guides are available. ⊠*811 Main St.* ☎*506/856–4379, 800/567–1922 in Canada* ☉*Tour times vary according to performances and availability; call ahead.*

2

The Atlantic Ballet Theatre of Canada is a professional touring company of high artistic standard. It just moved into the old Moncton YMCA building, a community landmark since 1870. Complete with roof garden and glass atrium, the building is undergoing an architectural renaissance which reflects the growing and vibrant cultural scene in the city. The company features a number of classically trained, soloist ballet dancers from around the world. ⊠*68 Highfield St., 2nd fl.* ☎*506/ 383–5951.*

The 1821 **Free Meeting House,** a simple and austere National Historic Site operated by the Moncton Museum, is one of the city's oldest standing buildings. It was built as a gathering place for all religious denominations without their own places of worship. ⊠*100 Steadman St.* ☎*506/856–4383* 🗒*Donations accepted* ☉*Mon.–Sat. 9– 4:30, Sun. 1–5.*

Comprehensive exhibits trace the city's history from the days of the Mi'Kmaq people to the present at the **Moncton Museum.** ⊠*20 Mountain Rd.* ☎*506/856–4383* 🗒*By donation* ☉*Mon.–Sat. 9–4:30, Sun. 1–5.*

The halls of the **Aberdeen Cultural Centre,** a converted schoolhouse, ring with music and chatter. This is home to theater and dance companies, a framing shop, and several galleries. **Galerie 12** represents leading contemporary Acadian artists. **Galerie Sans Nom** is an artist-run co-op supporting avant-garde artists from throughout Canada. The artist-run **IMAGO Inc.** is the only print-production shop in the province. Guided tours are available by appointment. ⊠*140 Botsford St.* ☎*506/857– 9597* 🗒*Free* ☉*Weekdays 10–4.*

At **Lutz Mountain Heritage Museum,** find genealogical records of the area's non-Acadian pioneer settlers from as far back as 1766. With over 3,000 artifacts, there's plenty to see. It's also a hands-on museum. ⊠*3143 Mountain Rd.* ☎*506/384–7719* ⊕*www.lutzmtnheritage.ca* 🗒*Donations accepted* ☉*July and Aug., Mon.–Sat. 10–6; Sept.–June by appointment.*

The **Acadian Museum,** at the University of Moncton, has a remarkable collection of artifacts reflecting 300 years of Acadian life in the Maritimes. There's also a fine gallery showcasing contemporary art by local and Canadian artists. ⊠*Clement Cormier Bldg., Université Ave* ☎*506/858–4088* ⊕*www.umoncton.ca/maum* 🗒*$4* ☉*June–Sept., weekdays 10–7, weekends 1–5; Oct.–May, Tues.–Fri. 1–4:30, weekends 1–4* ☉ *Closed Mon.*

WHERE TO STAY & EAT

$$$–$$$$ ✕**Little Louis's Oyster Bar.** "Intimate" and "interesting" are good words
★ to describe this second-floor restaurant where you can make a meal of oysters, though a great wine list, steaks, and other specialties such as osso buco steal some of the limelight from the excellent seafood. Live music plays Thursday through Saturday nights, with most Saturdays reserved for quiet jazz. ⊠*245 Collishaw St.* ☎*506/855–2022* ▭*AE, DC, MC, V* ☉*No lunch July and Aug.*

$$-$$$ ✕Pisces by Gaston. It didn't take long for this new kid on the block to develop a reputation for good food: the menu is creative, locally inspired, and ranges from inspired shellfish dishes to tender steaks. The decor is impressive and elegant, but the atmosphere is casual. Lunch is a particularly good option, with a spectacular seafood buffet. ⊠*300 Main St.* ☎*506/854–0444* ▤*AE, MC, V. JUN 2007*

$-$$ ✕Pastalli's. Seafood, steaks, lamb, and veal share the menu with pasta and pizzas at this upbeat Italian resto where old-world Italian flavors are showcased in a friendly new-world setting. The bread bar is almost as popular as the World Wine Cellar, where wine is sold by weight so you can try different kinds with different courses. ⊠*611 Main St.* ☎*506/383–1050* ▤*AE, D, DC, MC, V.*

¢-$$ ✕Pump House Brewery. The fare here goes above and beyond standard
★ pub grub, with wood-fired pizzas—the veggie version is particularly hearty—and vegetable quesadillas sharing the menu with burgers, steaks, club sandwiches, and snack food. Beer is brewed on site, and there's even a beer bread, made with grains left over from the brewing process. The root beer and cream soda, made in-house, are also delish. With metal fermentation tanks and bags of hops as part of the decor, this place is anything but formal. ⊠*5 Orange La.* ☎*506/855–2337* ▤*AE, MC, V.*

$$-$$$ ✕▣Delta Beauséjour. Moncton's finest hotel had a face-lift and is now
★ full of wonderful surprises. It is conveniently located downtown and has friendly service. L'Auberge, the main hotel restaurant ($-$$$$), has a distinct Acadian flavor, while the more formal Windjammer dining room ($$$$, reservations essential) is modeled after the opulent luxury liners of the early 1900s, with a sea-inspired menu featuring local lobsters and oysters. Try the chateaubriand buffalo for a tableside treat. ⊠*750 Main St. E1C 1E6* ☎*506/854–4344* 🖷*506/858–0957* ⊕*www.deltahotels.com* ➲*290 rooms, 6 suites* ♿*In-room: ethernet. In-hotel: 2 restaurants, pool, gym, laundry service, parking (no fee), no-smoking rooms, some pets allowed* ▤*AE, D, DC, MC, V.*

$$-$$$ ▣Ramada Plaza Crystal Palace. Part of an amusement complex, this hotel keeps the fun coming with theme rooms devoted to rock and roll, the Victorian era, and more. The hotel also has movie theaters, a giant bookstore, an indoor pool, and an indoor amusement park. Champlain Mall is just across the parking lot. Note that the hotel is technically in Dieppe, but the two cities are seamless and it is right on the border with Moncton. ⊠*499 Paul St., Dieppe E1A 6S5* ☎*506/858–8584 or 800/561–7108* 🖷*506/858–5486* ⊕*www.crystalpalacehotel.com* ➲*92 rooms, 23 suites* ♿*In-room: Wi-Fi, In-hotel: restaurant, pool, gym, room service, laundry services, no-smoking rooms* ▤*AE, D, DC, MC, V.*

$$ ▣Château Moncton Hotel & Suites. This modern châteaulike hotel stretches along the Petitcodiac River. The decor is European with custom-made cherrywood furniture. It's close to downtown businesses, large shopping malls, restaurants, theaters, and an amusement park. There is no restaurant on-site, but many are in easy walking distance. ⊠*100 Main St., E1C 1B9* ☎*506/870–4444 or 800/576–4040* 🖷*506/870–4445* ⊕*www.chateau-moncton.nb.ca* ➲*106 rooms, 12 suites* ♿*In-room:*

dial-up, minibar. In-hotel: bar, gym, no-smoking rooms ⊟*AE, DC, MC, V* ⚇*CP.*

NIGHTLIFE & THE ARTS

Fodor's Choice
★
Top musicians and other big acts appear at the **Coliseum Arena Complex** (⊠*377 Killam Dr.* ☎*506/857–4100* ⊕*www.monctoncoliseum.com*). **Studio 700** (⊠*700 Main St.* ☎*506/857–9117*) is open Wednesday through Sunday for rock, jazz, or blues, and dancing. There's live jazz on Friday; other live bands play Sunday. Upstairs from Club Cosmopolitan is the dinner theater at **McSweeney Company** (☎*506/857–9114*). Fermentation tanks are in plain view at the **Pump House Brewery** (⊠*5 Orange La.* ☎*506/855–2337*), where seasonal ales, such as pumpkin for Halloween, are served, along with house brews like blueberry ale—complete with floating blueberries. There's live Celtic music Saturday nights, and the pub is a venue for the HubCap Comedy Festival in February. **Rockin Rodeo** (⊠*415 Elmwood Dr.* ☎*506/384–4324*) is the biggest country-and-western bar in the province, with occasional live bands. **The Old Triangle Irish Alehouse** (⊠*751 Main St.* ☎*506/384–7474* ⊕*www.oldtriangle.com*), a creation of three Irishmen, has three lively rooms: the Snug, the Pourhouse, and Tigh An Cheoil (house of music)—they symbolize food for the body, drink for the spirit, and music for the soul.. **Voodoo** (⊠*938 Mountain Rd.* ☎*506/858–8844*) has lots of room for dancing and caters to the 25-plus crowd.

SPORTS & THE OUTDOORS

The Moncton area is home to two of New Brunswick's four signature golf courses.

Fox Creek Golf Club, inaugurated in 2005, offers an exceptional 6,900 yard course, 9,000 square foot clubhouse. It's fast becoming famous for the architectural and natural beauty of the course ⊠*200 Golf St.* ☎*506/859–4653* ⊕*www.foxcreekgolfclub.ca.* **Royal Oaks Golf Club** (⊠*1746 Elmwood Dr.* ☎*506/388–6257, 866/769–6257 in Canada* ⊕*www.royaloaks.ca*) is an 18-hole, par-72 PGA Championship course, the first Canadian course designed by Rees Jones.

☾ The **All World Super Play Park** (⊠*Cleveland Ave., Riverview*), across the river from Moncton, is a giant wooden structure with plenty of room for children to exercise their bodies and imaginations. **Supersplash Water Park** (⊠*City Centre, St. George Blvd.*) is a state-of-the-art outdoor water playground located in the rear of Moncton at Centennial Park. The big perk is that admission is free.

SHOPPING

Several spacious malls, a burgeoning business-park sector with huge warehouse-type stores that sell consumer goods (everything from office supplies to food, gardening, and home-building supplies), and unique boutiques downtown make Moncton one of New Brunswick's major shopping destinations. There's also quite a network of secondhand clothing stores—the Frenchy's chain is outstanding—with some amazing designer bargains. Farmers' markets and home-decorating shops are also gaining in popularity.

The **Dieppe Market** (⊠*333 Acadie Ave.* ☎*506/382–5750*) brims with fresh produce, baked goods, ethnic cuisine, and crafts every Saturday from 7 to 1. There's also a buzzing scene at **Moncton Market** (⊠*120 Westmorland St.* ☎*506/389–5969*), also open 7 to 1 on Saturday. Ethnic vendors serve delicious lunches Wednesday through Saturday. **Wheaton's** (⊠*1866 Mountain Rd.* ☎*506/855–7300*) is one link in a family-owned Maritime chain of country-style home-decor stores. Most of the wooden furniture is produced by the family. If you get caught up in this kind of shopping, plan on lunch at the in-house Cider Café.

THE ACADIAN COAST & ST. JOHN RIVER VALLEY

History and nature meet on the Tantramar salt marshes east of Moncton. Bounded by the upper reaches of the Bay of Fundy, the province of Nova Scotia, and the Northumberland Strait, the region is rich in history and culture and is teeming with birds. The marshes provide a highly productive wetland habitat, and this region is along one of North America's major migratory bird routes.

The white sands and gentle tides of the Northumberland Strait and Baie des Chaleurs are as different from the rocky cliffs and powerful tides of the Bay of Fundy as the Acadians are from the Loyalists. Along the Acadian Coast the water is warm, the sand is fine, and the accent is French—except in the middle. Where the Miramichi River meets the sea, there is an island of First Nations, English, Irish, and Scottish tradition that is unto itself, rich in folklore and legend. Many people here find their livelihood in the forests, in the mines, and on the sea. In the Acadian Peninsula, fishing boats and churches define the land where a French-language culture survives. You're not likely to run into any language barriers in stores, restaurants, and attractions along the beaten path, but down the side roads it's a different story altogether.

DORCHESTER & MEMRAMCOOK

Memramcook is 20 km (12 mi) southeast of Moncton. Dorchester is 10 km (6 mi) south of Memramcook.

Memramcook and Dorchester are located on opposite sides of a marsh. Acadian roots run deep in Memramcook: Dorchester was a center of British culture and industry long before the Loyalists landed and is home to some of the province's oldest buildings.

The **Bell Inn Restaurant** (⊠*3515 Cape Rd., off Rte. 106* ☎*506/379–2580*), on the village square in Dorchester, was built in 1811 as a stagecoach stop. It is reputed to be the oldest stone structure in New Brunswick. Wander through the three dining rooms while you wait for an old-fashioned, delicious roast turkey dinner. It's closed Monday.

Keillor House, Coach House Museum, and Saint James Church are three house museums. The Keilor House is an early Regency stone house contain-

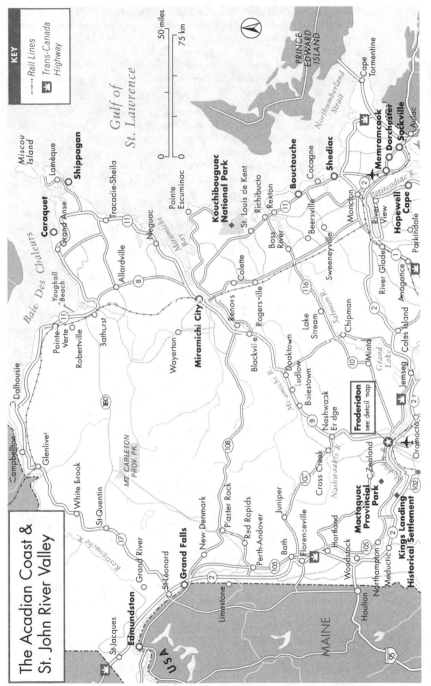

The Acadian Coast & St. John River Valley

50 miles
75 km

Gulf of
St. Lawrence

Miscou Island

PRINCE EDWARD ISLAND

Lamèque

Shippagan

Northumberland Strait

Cape Tormentine

Caraquet

Grand-Anse

Tracadie-Sheila

Neguac

Memramcook

Dorchester

Sackville

Aulac

Pointe Escuminac

Shediac

Petitcodiac R.

Bouctouche

Cocagne

Kouchibouguac National Park

St. Louis de Kent

Richibucto

Rexton

River View

Hopewell Cape

Hillsborough

Parkindale

Baie Des Chaleurs

Youghall Beach

Pointe Verte

Bathurst

Robertville

Allardville

Colette

Bass River

Beersville

Sweeneyville

Moncton

River Glade

Anagance

Colès Island

Miramichi City

Wayerton

Reno's

Rogersville

Lake Stream

Chipman

Minto

Grand Lake

Jemseg

Dalhousie

Campbellton

Glenlivet

White Brook

St-Quentin

MT. CARLETON PROV. PK.

Blackville

Doaktown

Ludlow

Boiestown

Nashwaak Bridge

Frederickton
see detail map

Oromocto

St-Jacques

Edmundston

Restigouche R.

Grand River

St-Léonard

Grand Falls

New Denmark

Plaster Rock

Red Rapids

Perth-Andover

Juniper

Bath

Florenceville

Hartland

Cross Creek

Zealand

Mactaquac Provincial Park

Kings Landing Historical Settlement

Nashwaaksis R.

Woodstock

Northampton

Meductic

Houlton

Limestone

MAINE

USA

95

Miramichi R.

Salmon R.

8

11

11

17

108

105

105

105

107

102

2

2

2

2

2

1

1

10

116

8

130

ing thousands of artifacts relating to mid-18th-century life; guides are in costume. St. James is also known as St. James Textile Museum and is just a minute's walk from Keilor house. The Coach House contains a fascinating penitentiary collection. ⊠*4974 Main St., Dorchester* ☎*506/379–6633 mid-June–mid-Sept.* ⊕*www.keillorhousemuseum. com* ⊠*$3 Keillor House, $2 Saint James Church* ⊙*June–mid-Sept., Mon.–Sat. 10–5, Sun. 1–5.*

The **Monument Lefebvre National Historic Site** explores the turbulent history of the Acadian people in passionate detail. It is housed in the original home of St. Joseph's College, the first degree-granting French-language institution in Atlantic Canada, instituted by Camille Lefebvre in 1864. ⊠*480 Central St., Memramcook* ☎*506/758–9808* ⊠*$3.95* ⊙*June–mid-Oct., daily 9–5; mid-Oct.–May, by appointment.*

SPORTS & THE OUTDOORS

Along the beaches at **Johnson's Mills** (⊠*Rte. 935, about 8 km [5 mi] south of Dorchester*) is part of the internationally recognized staging area for migratory shorebirds such as semipalmated sandpipers. The numbers are most impressive in July and August.

SACKVILLE

22 km (14 mi) southeast of Dorchester and Memramcook.

Sackville is an idyllic university town complete with a swan-filled pond. Its stately homes and ivy-clad university buildings are all shaded by venerable trees, and there's a waterfowl park right in town. It all makes for a rich blend of history, culture, and nature.

The **Sackville Waterfowl Park,** in the heart of the town, has more than 3 km (2 mi) of boardwalk and trails through 55 acres of wetlands. Throughout the marsh, viewing areas and interpretive signs reveal the rare waterfowl species that nest here. There's an interpretive center, and guided tours ($5) are available in French and English mid-June through mid-September. ⊠*Main St.* ☎*506/364–4967 (June–Aug.)* ⊕*www. sackville.com/visit/waterfowl* ⊠*Free* ⊙*Daily dawn–dusk.*

The sophisticated **Owens Art Gallery** is on the Mt. Allison University campus. One of the oldest and largest university art galleries in the country, it houses 19th- and 20th-century European, American, and Canadian artwork. ⊠*61 York St.* ☎*506/364–2574* ⊕*www.mta.ca/ owens* ⊠*Free* ⊙*Weekdays 10–5, weekends 1–5.*

Near the Nova Scotia border in Aulac and 12 km (7 mi) east of Sackville, the **Fort Beauséjour National Historic Site** holds the ruins of a star-shape fort that played a part in the 18th-century struggle between the French and English. Deportations of the Acadians began here. The fort has indoor and outdoor exhibits as well as fine views of the marshes at the head of the Bay of Fundy. ⊠*Rte. 106* ☎*506/364–5080 June–mid-Oct., 506/876–2443 mid-Oct.–May* ⊠*$3.95* ⊙*June–mid-Oct., daily 9–5.*

WHERE TO STAY & EAT

$ ✕⊡ **Marshlands Inn.** In this white clapboard inn with a carriage-house
★ annex, a welcoming double parlor with fireplace sets the comfortable
country atmosphere. Bedrooms are furnished with sleigh beds or four-
posters. The chefs offer traditional and modern dishes; seafood, pork,
and lamb are specialties ($$–$$$). In summer some of the herbs, veg-
etables, and flowers used in the kitchen and dining room come from the
property's own lovely gardens. ⊠ *55 Bridge St., E4L 3N8* ☎ *506/536–
0170 or 800/561–1266* 🖷 *506/536–0721* ⊕ *www.marshlands.nb.ca*
↪ *20 rooms* 🔧 *In-room: no a/c (some), no TV (some), Wi-Fi (some).
In-hotel: restaurant, no-smoking rooms, some pets allowed, no elevator* ▭ *MC, V* 🍴 *EP.*

SPORTS & THE OUTDOORS

Without a doubt, bird-watching is the pastime of choice in this region.
For information, contact the **Canadian Wildlife Service** (⊠ *17 Waterfowl La.* ☎ *506/364–5044*). **Cape Jourimain Nature Centre** (⊠ *Exit 51
off Rte. 16 at the foot of Confederation Bridge, Bayfield* ☎ *866/538–
2220 or 506/538–2220* ⊕ *www.capejourimain.ca*), at the Cape Jourimain National Wildlife Area, covers 1,800 acres of salt and brackish
marshes. Large numbers of waterfowl, shorebirds, and other species
can be seen here. The outstanding interpretive center includes a restaurant specializing in local fare and a boutique with nature art and
fine crafts. You will also find a viewing tower, 13 km (8 mi) of trails,
and daily programs. **Goodwin's Pond** (⊠ *Off Rte. 970*), near the Red-
Wing Blackbird Trail in Baie Verte, allows for easy viewing of wetland
birds and has more birds per acre than anywhere else in the province.
The **Port Elgin Rotary Pond and Fort Gaspereaux Trail** (⊠ *30 km [19 mi]
northeast of Sackville via Rte. 16*) have diverse coastal landscapes that
attract migrating waterfowl, bald eagles, and osprey. At the **Tantramar
Marshes** (⊠ *High Marsh Rd. between Sackville and Point de Bute*) you
may be able to spot marsh hawks. The **Tintamarre National Wildlife Area**
(⊠ *Goose Lake Rd. off High Marsh Rd.* ☎ *506/364–5044*) consists of
5,000 acres of protected land ideal for sighting several species of ducks,
rails, pied-billed grebes, and American bittern.

SHOPPING

Fog Forest Gallery (⊠ *14 Bridge St.* ☎ *506/536–9000* ⊕ *www.fogforest-
gallery.ca*) is a small, friendly, and reputable commercial gallery rep-
resenting Atlantic Canadian artists. The **Sackville Harness Shop** (⊠ *39
Main St.* ☎ *506/536–0642*) still makes harnesses for horses and is the
only place in North America that makes horse collars by hand. They
also make fine leather belts, wallets, bags, and jewelry.

SHEDIAC

25 km (16 mi) northeast of Moncton.

Shediac is the self-proclaimed Lobster Capital of the World and it has a
giant lobster sculpture to prove it. Beautiful Parlee Beach is what draws
people to this fishing village–resort town, though.

Acadian Culture

Culture is often defined by geographical boundaries. Acadian culture, however, defines Acadia, because it isn't so much a place as it is an enduring French society. In New Brunswick it abides (although not exclusively) above an imaginary line drawn from Edmundston to Moncton. In the heartland you hear remnants of Norman-French. Around Moncton you're just as apt to hear a melodious Acadian dialect called Chiac, a tweedy kind of French with flecks of English.

French settlers arrived in the early 1600s and brought with them an efficient system of dikes called *aboiteaux* that allowed them to farm the salt marshes around the head of the Bay of Fundy. In the 1700s they were joined by Jesuit missionaries who brought the music of Bach, Vivaldi, and Scarlatti along with their zeal. In 1713 England took possession of the region, and authorities demanded that Acadians swear an oath to the English crown. Some did, others didn't. By 1755 it didn't seem to matter. Only those who fled into the forests escaped Le Grand Dérangement—The Expulsion of the Acadians—which dispersed them to Québec, the eastern seaboard, Louisiana (where they became known as Cajuns), France, and even as far as the Falkland Islands. It was a devastating event that probably should have eradicated French language and culture in the Maritimes. It didn't.

Whether they were hiding deep in Maritime forests or living in exile, Acadians clung tenaciously to their language and traditions. Within 10 years of their deportation, Acadians began to return. They built new communities along coasts and waterways in the northeastern part of the province, remote from English settlement. By 1884 there was an Acadian national anthem and a flag.

The Acadian national holiday on August 15 provides an official reason to celebrate Acadian culture. Le Festival Acadien de Caraquet stretches the celebration out for two weeks. Caraquet is also home to Théâtre Populaire d'Acadie, which mounts original productions for French communities throughout the Maritimes and encourages contemporary Acadian playwrights. Books by Acadian authors, including internationally renowned Antonine Maillet, circulate in Québec, France, and Belgium. Conceptual artist Herménégilde Chiasson pushes the envelope with his poetry and painting, and Paulette Foulem Lanteigne's palette contains the bright colors that have traditionally defined the Acadian spirit.

The earliest Acadian settlers made elegant pine furniture. Modern Acadian artisans continue to make pottery and baskets. Handmade wooden spoons are doubly beautiful—in pairs they keep time to the music at kitchen parties, where Acadian families have traditionally sung their history around the kitchen fire. But it isn't necessary to have a party to enjoy "music de cuisine." Today, folk singer Edith Butler of Paquetville takes some of that history back to her French cousins in Paris. A lively pop band called Méchants Maquereaux (roughly translated that's "Naughty Mackerel") carries the same messages with a modern spin.

Clearly, the love of music endures here: it rings clear in churches; the cotillion and quadrille are danced at Saturday-night soirees; Acadian sopranos and jazz artists enjoy international renown; and a world-class Baroque-music festival in Lamèque still celebrates Bach, Vivaldi, and Scarlatti.

—Ana Watts

★ A 3-km (2-mi) stretch of glistening sand, **Parlee Beach** has been named the best beach in Canada by several surveys. It is a popular vacation spot for families and plays host to beach-volleyball and touch-football tournaments; an annual sand-sculpture contest and a triathlon are held here as well. Services include canteens and a restaurant. ⊠*Exit 37 off Rte. 133* ☏*506/533–3363* 🖃*$9 per vehicle* ⊙*Mid-May–mid-Sept., Daily 7 AM–9 PM.*

Parc de l'Aboiteau, on the western end of Cap-Pelé, has a fine, sandy beach as well as a boardwalk that runs through salt marshes where waterfowl nest. The beach complex includes a restaurant and lounge with live music in the evening. Cottages are available for rent year-round. ⊠*Exit 53 off Rte. 15* ☏*506/577–2080, for cottage information, 506/577–2005* 🖃*$4 per vehicle* ⊙*Beach June–Sept., daily dawn–dusk.*

WHERE TO STAY & EAT

$$$–$$$$ ✕**Paturel Shorehouse Restaurant.** This big "cottage" on the beach is quite cozy, and because it's right next door to a fish-processing plant, you can get nearly anything you want—even a 5-pound lobster. The chef has a way with salmon and sole. ⊠*46 Cap Bimet, at Legere St.* ☏*506/532–4774* ▤*AE, DC, MC, V* ⊙*Closed Oct.–May. No lunch.*

$$–$$$$ ✕**The Green House on Main Restaurant.** Loaded with charm, artwork, and antiques, this upbeat restaurant is trendy despite the building from the 19th century. You can eat outside on the heated patio or upstairs in the intimate dining room. The tiger prawns and Thai shrimp are faultless. ⊠*406 Main St.* ☏*506/533-7097* ▤ 🖃⊠ *MC, V.*

$–$$ ✕🏠 **Little Shemogue Country Inn.** The unusual name (pronounced shim-
Fodor's Choice o-*gwee*) is Mi'Kmaq for "good feed for geese." More surprising than
★ the name is the inn itself, a jewel hidden along a rough country road. The main inn is a beautifully restored country home. A three-story wall of windows in the common area of the modern Log Point annex over-looks the ocean; the rooms here are large and have ocean views and whirlpool tubs. The 200-acre property has its own white-sand beach, canoes, and trails along a salt marsh. The candlelight breakfast is served to strains of classical music, and there is an exquisite five-course, prix-fixe dinner ($$$$) served in four intimate dining rooms. Everything here is pure delight and exceptional value. ⊠*2361 Rte. 955, 40 km (25 mi) east of Shediac, Little Shemogue E4M 3K4* ☏*506/538-2320* 🖃*506/538-7494* ⊕*www.little-inn.nb.ca* 🛏*9 rooms* ⚹*In-room: Wi-Fi, no a/c (some). In-hotel: spa, beachfront, bicycles, no kids under 10, no-smoking rooms, no elevator* ▤*AE, MC, V.*

$$$–$$$$ 🏠 **Tait House.** This elegant and stately historic mansion smack in the middle of town was built back in 1911. The rooms have fireplaces, canopy beds, and Jacuzzis, and the on-site restaurant features contemporary cuisine as well as another menu that specializes in fondues—cheese, meat, fish, and dessert fondues—and seafood. ⊠*293 Main St.* ☏*506/532-4233* ⊕*www.maisontaithouse.com* 🛏*9 rooms* ⚹*In-room: Wi-Fi. In-hotel: restaurant, no-smoking rooms* ▤*AE, MC, V.*

$ 🏠 **Auberge Belcourt Inn.** This elegant Heritage Inn was built around 1910 and has been carefully restored and furnished with lovely period furniture. Five rooms have private baths en suite; two have bath opposite rooms. In summer the front veranda is an ideal spot for a drink before dinner at the Lobster Deck restaurant next door. ⊠*310 Main St., E4P 2E3* ☎*506/532–6098* ⧫*506/533–9398* ⊕*www.sn2000.nb.ca/comp/ auberge-belcourt* ⌁*7 rooms* &*In-room: no phone, no TV. In-hotel: laundry service, no-smoking rooms, no elevator* ⊟*AE, DC, MC, V* ⊙*Closed Dec. and Jan.* ⦿|*BP.*

BOUCTOUCHE

35 km (22 mi) north of Shediac.

This idyllic and bustling town on the sandy shores of Bouctouche Bay is famous as the home of K. C. Irving, patriarch of the New Brunswick Irving industrial dynasty; Le Pays de la Sagouine, a theme park built around an Acadian novel; and the area's pristine beauty. Its great dune is one of the few remaining on this coast of North America.

☺ **Le Pays de la Sagouine** is a theme park with a make-believe island community that comes to life in French in daylong musical and theatrical performances and dinner theater–musical evenings ($$$$) July through September. There are some English-language tours, and the Friday-night jam sessions are accessible for English-speaking visitors, too. La Sagouine is an old charwoman-philosopher created by celebrated Acadian author Antonine Maillet. ⊠*Exit 32 off Hwy. 11* ☎*506/743–1400 or 800/561–9188* ⊕*www.sagouine.com* 🎫*$15* ⊙*June–Sept., daily 9:30–5:30.*

★ ☺ **Irving Eco-Centre: La Dune de Bouctouche** is a superb example of a coastal ecosystem that protects the exceptionally fertile oyster beds in Bouctouche Bay. Hiking trails and boardwalks to the beach make it possible to explore sensitive areas without disrupting the environment of one of the few remaining great dunes on the northwest coast of the Atlantic Ocean. An outstanding interpretive center puts the ecosystem in perspective. The staff regularly conducts educational programs for adults and children. Swimming is allowed. ⊠*1932 Rte. 475* ☎*888/640–3300 or 506/743–2600* ⊕*www.irvingecocentre.com* 🎫*Free* ⊙*Hiking trails and boardwalk daily dawn–dusk. Visitor center July and Aug., daily 10–8; call ahead for reduced hrs in May, June, Sept., and Oct.*

☺ About 10 km (6 mi) up the coast from Bouctouche in Sainte-Anne-de-Kent is **The Olivier Soapery.** There's a skin-care art gallery, featuring paintings commissioned for soap labels throughout the years, and, naturally, plenty of soap for sale. By far the best attraction, however, is the soap-making demonstration, five times a day. ⊠*831 Rte. 505* ☎*506/743–8938 or 800/775–5550* ⊕*www.oliviersoaps.com* 🎫*Free* ⊙*June–early Sept., Sun.–Fri. 9–5; Closed Mon., Sept.–May, by appointment.*

WHERE TO STAY & EAT

$$$ ✕🏨**Auberge le Vieux Presbytère de Bouctouche.** This inn, formerly a rectory and then a retreat house complete with chapel (now a conference room), has a friendly staff and is brimming with atmosphere. The

restaurant, "Le Tire Bouchon" ($$–$$$), serves seafood and Acadian fare. The terraced café is lovely for lunch. ✉*157 chemin du Couvent, E4S 3B8* ☎*506/743–5568* 🖷*506/743–5566* 🌐*www.vieuxpresbytere. nb.ca* 🛏*17 rooms, 2 suites* ⚅*In-room: no a/c (some). In-hotel: restaurant, bicycles, no-smoking rooms* ☐*AE, MC, V* ⊗*Closed Oct.–May* ⼗◎*BP.*

KOUCHIBOUGUAC NATIONAL PARK

★ *40 km (25 mi) north of Bouctouche, 100 km (62 mi) north of Moncton.*

The park's white, dune-edged beaches, some of the finest on the continent, are preserved here. Kellys Beach is supervised and has facilities. The cycling is great, with more than 35 km (22 mi) of virtually flat biking trails. In winter the trails are ideal for cross-country skiing, snowshoeing, snow walking, and kick sledding. The park also protects forests and peat bogs, which can be explored along its 10 nature trails. There are lots of nature-interpretation programs, and you can canoe, kayak, and picnic, too. Bikes and boats can be rented. Reserve ahead for one of the 311 campsites. ✉*186 Rte. 117, Kouchibouguac* ☎*506/876–2443* 🌐*www.pc.gc.ca* 🎟*$6.90 late May–mid-Sept.; free mid Sept.–late May.*

MIRAMICHI

40 km (25 mi) north of Kouchibouguac, 150 km (93 mi) north of Moncton.

Celebrated for salmon rivers that reach into some of the province's richest forests, and the ebullient nature of its residents (Scottish, English, Irish, and a smattering of First Nations and French), this is a land of lumber kings, ghost stories, folklore, and festivals—celebrating the Irish in July and folk songs in August. Sturdy wood homes dot the banks of Miramichi Bay. The city of Miramichi incorporates the former towns of Chatham and Newcastle and several small villages. This is also where the politician and British media mogul Lord Beaverbrook grew up and is buried.

The **Atlantic Salmon Museum** provides a look at the endangered Atlantic salmon and at life in noted fishing camps along the rivers. ✉*263 Main St., 80 km (50 mi) southwest of Miramichi City, Doaktown* ☎*506/365–7787* 🌐*www.atlanticsalmonmuseum.com* 🎟*$5* ⊗*June–early Oct., daily 9–5.*

🜊 **Ritchie Wharf Park** has a nautical-theme playground complete with a "Splash Pad" that sprays water from below and dumps it from buckets above. Shops sell local crafts, and there are several restaurants and docking facilities. An amphitheater showcases local entertainers on Sunday afternoons in summer. ✉*Norton's La., Newcastle waterfront off King George Hwy.* 🎟*Free* ⊗*Park daily dawn–dusk. Shops June–early Sept., daily 9–9.*

Dare the Dark for the Headless Nun! is a tragic tale told in the dark while being led to the city's most infamous haunts by costumed guides. ⊠*French Fort Cove; watch for signs along the King George Hwy. through the city* 🕾*800/459–3131* ⚏*$10* ☽*July and Aug., Mon., Wed., and Fri. at dark.*

The **Central New Brunswick Woodmen's Museum** has a 100-year-old trapper's cabin, blacksmith shop, wheelwright shop, cookhouse-bunkhouse-dingle, and other exhibits pertaining to the woodman's way of life at this fabulous historic site. A popular 10-passenger amusement train ($2) is a 1½-km (1-mi) woodland adventure. ⊠*6342 Rte. 8, 110 km (68 mi) southwest of Miramichi City, Boiestown* 🕾*506/369–7214* ⊕*www.woodsmenmuseum.com* ⚏*$5* ☽*May–mid-Oct., daily 9:30–5.*

Beaubears Island. This national historic site, formerly a thriving shipbuilding center, is one of Miramichi interesting outdoor spots. A short boat trip will take you to see historic characters who love to share their colorful island stories and adventures. Admission includes the boat ride, a visit to the interpretive center, and a guided tour. 🕾*506/622–8526* ⊕ *www.beaubearsisland.ca* ⚏ *$10.*

WHERE TO STAY & EAT

$–$$ ✕**Cunard Restaurant.** With its Irish accent and lumberjack history, Miramichi is an unlikely place to find a great Chinese restaurant. The Cunard, however, has what it takes to make it anywhere. It is renowned for its Szechuan chicken and hot orange beef. Steaks and seafood are on the menu, too. ⊠*32 Cunard St.* 🕾*506/773–7107* ▭*AE, DC, MC, V.*

$$ ✕⌕**Rodd Miramichi River.** This grand riverside hotel, with warm natural wood and earth-tone interior, manages to feel like a fishing lodge. The rooms are comfortable, with lots of outdoorsy prints on the walls. The Angler's Reel Restaurant ($$–$$$) features 20 different fresh salmon dishes. ⊠*1809 Water St., E1N 1B2* 🕾*506/773–3111* 📠*506/773–3110* ⊕*www.rodd-hotels.ca* ⚏*76 rooms, 4 suites* ⚒*In-room: dial-up. In-hotel: restaurant, bar, pool, gym, pets allowed* ▭*AE, DC, MC, V.*

$$$ ⌕**Pond's Resort.** This property offers a traditional fishing-camp experience with a few added luxuries. The lodge and cabins are surrounded by trees and overlook the world-famous salmon river. There's a golf course nearby, too. ⊠*91 Porter Cove Rd., 100 km (62 mi) southwest of Miramichi City; follow signs on Rte. 8, Ludlow E9C 2J3* 🕾*506/369–2612* 📠*506/369–2293* ⊕*www.pondsresort.com* ⚏*1 5-bedroom lodge, 14 cabins* ⚒*In-room: no a/c (some), refrigerator. In-hotel: bar, tennis court, bicycles, laundry service, some pets allowed, no-smoking rooms, no elevator* ☽*Closed mid-Oct.–mid-Apr.* ▭*AE, DC, MC, V.*

OFF THE BEATEN PATH ★ **Metepenagiag Heritage Park.** Since 1975, over 100 archaeological sites have been discovered in the Red Bank area, and the park and new exhibit hall, adjacent to Metepenagiag Lodge, on the banks of the river, are a great way to learn about the ancient world. Don't miss the movie, *Metepenagiag, Where Spirits Live* in the intimate theater. The park and center celebrates and preserves the national significance of Augustine Mound and Oxbow National

Historic Sites of Canada, two of the most outstanding Aboriginal heritage archaeological sites in Eastern Canada. The center houses many interactive exhibits and is a top-notch attraction. ☎ *506/836–6118* 🖨 *506/836–6186* 🎫 *$8* ⊙ *May–Oct., daily 9–6; Nov.–Apr., daily 10–3.*

$ ⊡**Metepenagiag Lodge.** About a 20-minute drive from Miramichi on Route 420 West, in a community called Red Bank, the Metepenagiag Lodge is on the Little Southwest Miramichi River and specializes in outdoor and cultural adventures. The service is friendly, rooms are comfortable, and much of the food served incorporates items that have sustained the Mi'kmaq people for centuries—it's always delicious. Lumberjack-sized breakfasts are $6, lunches $10, and three-course dinners are $15. Fully air-conditioned, all 10 rooms have exits to a screened-in porch. ✉ *2202 MicMac Rd., Red Bank E9E 2P3* ☎ *506/836–6128* 🖨 *506/836–6188* ⊕ *www.metepenagiaglodge.com* ⊷ *10 rooms* ♿ *In-room: no TV (some). In-hotel: Wi-Fi, restaurant, no-smoking rooms* ▭ *DC, MC, V.*

SHIPPAGAN

37 km (23 mi) north of Tracadie-Sheila.

Shippagan is an important commercial fishing and marine education center as well as a bustling, modern town with lots of amenities. It's also the gateway to the idyllic islands of Lamèque and Miscou.

☾ The wonderful **Aquarium and Marine Centre** has a serious side and a fun side. The labs here are the backbone of marine research in the province, and the marine museum houses more than 3,000 specimens. A family of seals in the aquarium puts on a great show in the pool at feeding time. There's a wheelhouse where you can check all the electronic fish-finding devices, then steer the boat right to them, and a touch tank for making the acquaintance of various sea creatures. ✉ *100 rue de l'Aquarium* ☎ *506/336–3013* ⊕ *www.gnb.ca/aquarium* 🎫 *$8* ⊙ *May–Sept., daily 10–6.*

Across a causeway from Shippagan is Île Lamèque and the **Sainte-Cécile church** (✉ *Rte. 113 at Petite-Rivière-de-l'Île*). Although the church is plain on the outside, every inch of it is decorated on the inside. Each July, the **International Festival of Baroque Music** (☎ *506/344–5846 or 800/320–2276*) takes place here.

Île Miscou, accessible by bridge from Île Lamèque, has white sandy beaches.

CARAQUET

40 km (25 mi) west of Shippagan.

Perched along the Baie des Chaleurs, with Québec's Gaspé Peninsula beckoning across the inlet, Caraquet is rich in French flavor and is the acknowledged Acadian capital. Beaches are another draw.

The two-week **Acadian Festival** (☎506/727–2787), held here in August, includes the Tintamarre, in which costumed participants noisily parade through the streets, and the Blessing of the Fleet, a colorful and moving ceremony that eloquently expresses the importance of fishing to the Acadian economy and way of life.

★ ☉ A highlight of the Acadian Peninsula is **Acadian Historical Village.** The more than 40 restored buildings re-create Acadian communities between 1770 and 1939. There are modest homes, a church, a school, and a village shop, as well as an industrial area that includes a working hotel, a bar and restaurant, a lobster hatchery, a cooper, and tinsmith shops. The staff are bilingual and have fascinating stories to tell. The demonstrations are great fun, and visitors are invited to take part. ⊠*Rte. 11, 10 km (6 mi) west of Caraquet* ☎*506/726–2600 or 877/721–2200* ⊕*www.villagehistoriqueacadien.com* ☜*$15* ☉*June– early Sept., daily 10–6; mid-Sept., daily 10–5 with only 6 homes open; late Sept.–mid-Oct., daily 10–5.*

The **Pope's Museum,** 7 km (4 mi) outside of Caraquet, is the only museum in North America dedicated to papal history. It celebrates the church's artistic and spiritual heritage with models of buildings such as St. Peter's Basilica and the cathedral in Florence. ⊠*184 Acadie St., Grand-Anse* ☎*506/732–3003* ☜*$9* ☉*Mid-June–Aug., daily Wed.– Sun. 10–6 (last tour at 5).*

WHERE TO STAY & EAT

$$–$$$$ ✕ **La Fine Grobe-Sur-Mer.** North of Bathurst in Nigadoo, about 80 km (50 mi) outside of Caraquet, is one of New Brunswick's finest restaurants. The French cuisine, seafood, and wine are outstanding because the chef-owner never compromises. He grows his own herbs and greens, and bakes his baguettes in an outside oven. Lobster, lamb, and *lapin* (domestic rabbit) are all on the menu. The dining room is small but has a cozy fireplace and three walls of windows overlooking the ocean. Dinner is served each evening; lunch can be arranged. ⊠*289 rue Principal, Nigadoo* ☎*506/783–3138* ⊕*www.finegrobe.com* ▤*AE, DC, MC, V* ☉*Lunch by special arrangement only.*

$$$–$$$$ ✕▤ **Hotel Paulin.** Caraquet is famous not only for lobsters, oysters, arti-
★ sans, and festivals—but also for Hotel Paulin. A classic Victorian hotel built in 1891, it is now a historical boutique-style hotel on the Bay of Chaleur. Still owned and operated by the Paulin family, it offers more than a place to stay and dine. The owners are intimate with the area and can make off-the-beaten-path recommendations. Here, the meaning of excellence oozes out of every room, every meal, and every encounter. The nightly three- or four-course meals depend on guest preferences and what is fresh (local foods like a superb goat cheese are used, and seafood comes straight from the bay). ⊠*143 blvd. St-Pierre W, E1W 1B6* ☎*506/727–9981 or 866/727–9981* ▤*506/727–4808* ⊕*www.hotelpaulin.com* ▚*6 rooms, 6 suites* ♨*In-room: DVD, VCR, Wi-Fi. In-hotel: restaurant, room service, beachfront, bicycles, laundry service, no-smoking rooms, some pets allowed, no elevator* ▤*MC, V* ¶◎*BP.*

SPORTS & THE OUTDOORS

The eight trails on the 507-foot drop at **Sugarloaf Provincial Park** (⊠ *596 Val d'Amour Rd., 180 km [112 mi] north of Caraquet, Atholville E3N 4C9* ☎ *506/789–2366*) accommodate skiers of all levels. There are also 25 km (16 mi) of cross-country ski trails. Instruction and equipment rentals are available, and the lodge operates a lounge and cafeteria in winter. In summer an alpine slide offers fun on the ski hill, and there's lots of space for camping and hiking. You can also rent paddleboats.

ST. JOHN RIVER VALLEY

The St. John River valley scenery is panoramic—gently rolling hills and sweeping forests, with just enough rocky gorges to keep it interesting. The native peoples—French, English, Scots, and Danes who live along the river—ensure that its culture is equally intriguing. The St. John River forms 120 km (74 mi) of the border with Maine, then swings inland. Eventually it cuts through the heart of Fredericton and rolls down to Saint John. Gentle hills of rich farmland and the blue sweep of the water make this a lovely area in which to drive. In the early 1800s the narrow wedge of land at the northern end of the valley was coveted by Québec and New Brunswick; the United States claimed it as well. To settle the issue, New Brunswick governor Sir Thomas Carleton rolled dice with the governor of British North America at Québec. Sir Thomas won—by one point. Settling the border with the Americans was more difficult; even the lumberjacks engaged in combat. Finally, in 1842, the British flag was hoisted over Madawaska County. One old-timer, tired of being asked to which country he belonged, replied, "I am a citizen of the Republic of Madawaska." So began the mythical republic, which exists today with its own flag (an eagle on a field of white) and a coat of arms.

EDMUNDSTON

275 km (171 mi) northwest of Fredericton.

Edmundston, the unofficial capital of Madawaska, has always depended on the wealth of the deep forest around it—the legend of Paul Bunyan was born in these woods. Even today the town looks to the Fraser Papers pulp mills as the major source of employment.

St-Jacques, a suburb 5 km (3 mi) north of Edmundston, has Les Jardins de la République Provincial Park, plus recreational facilities, the Antique Auto Museum, and a botanical garden.

The annual **Foire Brayonne** (☎ *506/739–6608*), held in Edmundston over the long weekend surrounding New Brunswick Day (starts on Wednesday before the first Monday in August), is one of the largest Francophone festivals outside of Québec. It's also one of the liveliest and most vibrant cultural events in New Brunswick, with concerts by acclaimed artists as well as local musicians and entertainers.

At the **New Brunswick Botanical Garden** roses, rhododendrons, alpine flowers, and dozens of other annuals and perennials bloom in eight gardens. The music of Mozart, Handel, Bach, or Vivaldi often plays in the background. Two arboretums have coniferous and deciduous trees and shrubs. Mosaiculture plantings on metal frames placed throughout the gardens illustrate legends and cultural themes. Children enjoy the insectarium and candle-making workshops. ✉ *Main St., St-Jacques* ☎ *506/737–5383* ⊕ *www.umce.ca/jardin* 💲 *$14* ⊙ *June and Sept., daily 9–6; July and Aug., daily 9–8.*

WHERE TO STAY & EAT

$-$$ ✕🍽 **Auberge les Jardins Inn.** Fine French cuisine ($$–$$$$) is the major attraction at this modern inn whose rooms are decorated on woodland themes with maple, cedar, aspen, oak, and pine. Some rooms have whirlpool baths and others have fireplaces. There's lovely terrace dining in summer, a walking trail runs past the front door, and the New Brunswick Botanical Garden is nearby. The restaurant serves breakfast and dinner. ✉ *60 rue Principal, St-Jacques E7V 1B7* ☎ *506/739–5514 or 800/630–8011* ⊕ *www.auberge-lesjardins-inn.com* 📞 *30 rooms, 10 cottages* 🔑 *In-room: VCR, ethernet. In-hotel: restaurant, pool, bicycle rentals, laundry facilities, laundry service, no-smoking rooms, no elevator* 💳 *AE, DC, MC, V.*

SPORTS & THE OUTDOORS

Mont Farlagne (✉ *360 Mont Farlagne Rd., St-Jacques* ☎ *506/739–7669* ⊕ *www.montfarlagne.com*) has 19 trails for downhill skiing on a vertical drop of 600 feet. Its four lifts can handle 4,000 skiers per hour, and there's night skiing on eight trails. Snowboarding and tube sliding add to the fun. Equipment rentals are available, and there are a cafeteria and a bar.

GRAND FALLS

50 km (31 mi) southeast of Edmundston.

The St. John River rushes over a high cliff, squeezes through a narrow rocky gorge, and emerges as a wider river at the town of Grand Falls. The result is a magnificent cascade, whose force has worn strange round wells in the rocky bed, some as large as 16 feet in circumference and 30 feet deep.

A **pontoon boat** operates from the end of June through September at the lower end of the gorge and offers an entirely new perspective of the cliffs and wells. Boat tickets are available at the **La Rochelle Tourist Information Centre** (✉ *1 Chapel St.* ☎ *877/475–7769 or 506/475–7766* ⊕ *www.grandfalls.com*). ✉ *2 Chapel St.* ☎ *506/475–7760* 💲 *$10* ⊙ *Boat trips June–early Sept., daily 10–7 on the hr.*

The Gorge Walk, which starts at the **Malabeam Tourist Information Center** and covers the full length of the gorge, is dotted with interpretive panels and monuments. There's no charge for the walk, unless you descend to the wells ($3), which are holes worn in the rocks by the swirling water. Guided walking tours ($6) are also available. According to native legend, a young maiden named Malabeam led her Iroquois captors to their deaths over the foaming cataract rather than guide them to her village. The view overlooking the gorge (in and out) from the center is breathtaking. ✉*24 Madawaska Rd.* ☎*506/475–7788* 🔳*Free* ⊙*Daily dawn–dusk.*

The **Grand Falls Historical Museum** has pioneer and early Victorian artifacts as well as the balance beam used by a daredevil who crossed the falls on a tightrope. ✉*68 Madawaska Rd., Suite 100* ☎*506/473–5265* 🔳*$2* ⊙*July and Aug., weekdays 9–5.*

EN
ROUTE

About 75 km (47 mi) south of Grand Falls, stop in Florenceville for a look at the small but reputable **Andrew and Laura McCain Gallery** (✉*McCain St., Florenceville* ☎*506/392–6769*), which has launched the career of many New Brunswick artists. There are occasional children's programs.

If you're looking for less-crowded highways and typical small communities, cross the river to Route 105 at Hartland—about 20 km (12 mi) south of Florenceville— via the longest **covered bridge** in the world: it's 1,282 feet in length.

KINGS LANDING HISTORICAL SETTLEMENT

🄲 *210 km (130 mi) south of Grand Falls, 30 km (19 mi) west of*
Fodor's Choice *Fredericton.*
★

The Kings Landing Historical Settlement was built by moving period buildings to a new shore. To best appreciate the museum, plan to spend at least a half day. Route 102 passes through some spectacular river and hill scenery on the way, including the Mactaquac Dam—turn off here if you want to visit Mactaquac Provincial Park.

This excellent outdoor living-history museum on the St. John River evokes the sights, sounds, and society of rural New Brunswick between 1790 and 1900. The winding country lanes and meticulously restored homes pull you back a century or more, and programs are available to let you "process" wool "from sheep to shawl" and prepare herbal remedies from the plants in the lanes and gardens. There are daily dramas in the theater, barn dances, and strolling minstrels. See how the wealthy owner of the sawmill lived and just how different things were for the immigrant farmer. Hearty meals are served at the Kings Head Inn. Each week throughout the summer, children aged 9 to 14 can take part in the "Visiting Cousins" program where they dress in period costume, attend the one-room schoolhouse, and learn the chores, games, and mannerisms of 19th century youth. Never a dull moment! ✉*Exit 253 off Trans-Canada Hwy., near Prince William* ☎*506/363–4999* 🌐*www.kingslanding.nb.ca* 🔳*$15* ⊙*June–mid-Oct., daily 10–5.*

MACTAQUAC PROVINCIAL PARK

🕓 *12 km (7 mi) north of Mactaquac Park. 25 km (16 mi) west of Fredericton.*

Surrounding the giant pond created by the Mactaquac Hydroelectric Dam on the St. John River is Mactaquac Provincial Park. Its facilities include an 18-hole championship golf course, two beaches with lifeguards, two marinas (one for powerboats and the other for sailboats), supervised crafts activities, myriad nature and hiking trails, and a restaurant. Reservations are advised for the 300 campsites in summer but winter is fun, too: there are lots of trails for cross-country skiing, and snowshoeing. Sleigh rides are available by appointment. The toboggan hills and skating–ice hockey ponds are even lighted in the evening. ✉*Rte. 105 at Mactaquac Dam* ☎*506/363–4747* 💲*$7 per vehicle, mid-May–mid-Oct.; open for winter activities, weather permitting. (No entrance fee in winter)* 🕓*Daily dawn–dusk; overnight camping mid-May–mid-Oct.*

EN ROUTE   Oromocto, along Route 102 from Mactaquac Provincial Park, is the site of the Canadian Armed Forces Base, **Camp Gagetown**, the largest military base in Canada (not to be confused with the pretty village of Gagetown farther downriver). Prince Charles completed his helicopter training here. The base has an interesting military museum. ✉*Museum: Bldg. A5 off Tilley St.* ☎*506/422–1304* 💲*Museum free* 🕓*Weekdays 8–4.*

FREDERICTON

The small inland city of Fredericton spreads itself on a broad point of land jutting into the St. John River. Its predecessor, the early French settlement of St. Anne's Point, was established in 1642 during the reign of the French governor Villebon, who made his headquarters at the junction of the Nashwaak and St. John rivers. Settled by Loyalists and named for Frederick, second son of George III, the city serves as the seat of government for New Brunswick's 753,000 residents. Wealthy and scholarly Loyalists set out to create a gracious and beautiful place, and thus even before the establishment of the University of New Brunswick, in 1785, the town served as a center for liberal arts and sciences. It remains a gracious and beautiful place as well as a center of education, arts, and culture. St. John River, once the only highway to Fredericton, is now a focus of recreation. Fredericton is also the first city in Canada to offer free Wi-Fi. Called Fred-eZone, it allows free access to the Internet with Wi-Fi–enabled laptops or PDAs in many Fredericton public areas. To learn more check out 🌐*www.fred-ezone.ca.*

Lighthouse Adventure Centre. The downtown Lighthouse on the St. John River is a great place to get information or tickets for day adventures, craft workshops, cultural tours, and ghost walks. Bike rentals are available (and bike tours on Wednesday night for $10 person, including wheels). It's open June to September, but hours vary, so call first (☎*506/460–2939*).

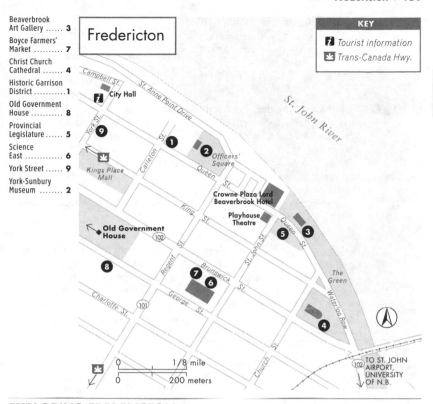

EXPLORING FREDERICTON

Downtown Queen Street runs parallel with the river, and has several historic sights and attractions. Most major sights are within walking distance of one another. An excursion to Kings Landing Historical Settlement, a reconstructed village, can bring alive the province's history.

Dressed in 18th-century costume, actors from the **Calithumpians Theater Company** (☎ *506/457–1975*) bring Fredericton history to life from Canada Day (July 1) to Labor Day. They conduct free historical walks several times a day. In the evening they offer Time Travellers Tours ($8) during which you meet famous characters from Fredericton's past, including Benedict Arnold, J.J. Audubon, Lord Beaverbrook, and Bliss Carmen. After dark, actors lead a Haunted Hike ($13) through historic neighborhoods and ghostly graveyards. The Haunted Hikes continue into the fall on weekends. Check at the **City Hall Visitor Information Centre** (⊠ *397 Queen St.* ☎ *506/460–2020*) for details.

SIGHTS TO SEE

❸ Beaverbrook Art Gallery. A lasting gift of the late Lord Beaverbrook,
★ this gallery could hold its head high in the company of some smaller European galleries. Salvador Dalí's gigantic *Santiago el Grande* has always been the star, but a rotation of avant-garde Canadian paint-

ings now shares pride of place. The McCain "gallery-within-a-gallery" is devoted to the finest Atlantic Canadian artists. ⊠*703 Queen St.* ☎*506/458–8545* ⊠*$5* ⊙*Fri.–Wed. 9–5:30, Thurs. 9–9.*

❼ **Boyce Farmers' Market.** It's hard to miss this Saturday-morning market because of the crowds. There are lots of local meat and produce, cheeses, baked goods, crafts, and seasonal items such as wreaths and maple syrup. The market sells good ready-to-eat food, from German sausages to tasty samosas. ⊠*Bounded by Regent, Brunswick, and George Sts.*

> ### FREDERICTON ARTS
>
> The **Downtown Fredericton Culture Crawl** takes place the last Thursday of every month, from May to September. During the festival, you can visit the art galleries, craft studios, and shops in the downtown area, all within walking distance of each other. It's free, and maps are available at City Hall Visitor Information Centre.

❹ ★ **Christ Church Cathedral.** One of Fredericton's prides, this gray stone building, completed in 1853, is an excellent example of decorated neo-Gothic architecture. The cathedral's design was based on an actual medieval prototype in England, and it became a model for many American churches. Inside is a clock known as "Big Ben's little brother," the test run for London's famous timepiece, designed by Lord Grimthorpe. ⊠*Church St.* ☎*506/450–8500* ⊠*Free* ⊙*Self-guided tours daily 9–4, except during services. Guided tours July and Aug., weekdays 9–6, Sat. 10–5, Sun. 1–5.*

OFF THE BEATEN PATH

Marysville. A National Historic District, Marysville is one of Canada's best-preserved examples of a 19th-century mill town. Its architecture and social history are amazing and can be appreciated with the help of a self-guided walking-tour booklet available at the York-Sunbury Museum and at Westminster Books on King Street. Marysville itself is on the north side of the St. John River, about 10 km (6 mi) from downtown Fredericton via Route 8.

❶ ☾ **Historic Garrison District.** The restored buildings of this British and Canadian post, which extends two blocks along Queen Street, include soldiers' barracks, a guardhouse, and a cell block. This is a National Historic Site and one of New Brunswick's top attractions. Local artisans operate studios in the casemates below the soldiers' barracks in Barracks Square. In July and August free guided tours run throughout the day, and there are outdoor concerts in Officers' Square Tuesday and Thursday evenings. Redcoat soldiers have long stood guard in Officers' Square, and a formal changing-of-the-guard ceremony takes place July and August at 11 AM and 4 PM with a third ceremony daily on Tuesday and Thursday at 4 PM. It's even possible for children of all ages to live a soldier's life for a while: each summer afternoon at 1:30, would-be redcoats get their own uniforms and practice drilling ($8 per person). At 4:30 PM the Caliathumpians offer songs and stories of the guardhouse. Sunday evenings in July and August, free classic movies are shown under the stars in Barracks Square at dusk. ⊠*Queen St. at Carleton St.* ☎*506/460–2129* ⊠*Free* ⊙*Daily 24 hrs.*

8 Old Government House. This imposing 1828 Palladian mansion has been restored as the official seat of office for the province's lieutenant governor. A hands-on interpretive center spans 12,000 years of history. Guided tours take in elegantly restored state rooms and art galleries. The 11-acre grounds include a 17th-century Acadian settlement and border an early Maliseet burial ground. ⊠ *51 Woodstock Rd.* ☎ *506/453-2505* ⊠ *Free* ⊙ *Mon.–Sat., 10 AM to 5 PM; Sun. noon–5.*

WORD OF MOUTH

"St. Andrew's is a lovely little town, fairly touristy.and your drive along the coast is probably around the same.Fredericton, on the otherhand is really beautiful, the downtown area is on a river, and I just love it.I am a little biased, as I am from F'ton, but I think it is more worth a visit then Saint John or Moncton." —LissaJ

5 Provincial Legislature. The interior chamber of the legislature, where the premier and elected members govern the province, reflects the taste of the late Victorians. The chandeliers are brass, and some of the prisms are Waterford. Replicas of portraits by Sir Joshua Reynolds of King George III and Queen Charlotte hang here. There's a freestanding circular staircase, and a volume of Audubon's *Birds of America* is on display. Call ahead to arrange a tour. ⊠ *Queen St.* ☎ *506/453-2527* ⊠ *Free* ⊙ *Legislature tours late May to late Aug., daily 9–7 (last tour at 6.30), Sept.–late May, weekdays 9–4. Library weekdays 8:15–5.*

6 Science East. This hands-on science center, in the former York County Jail, has family fun locked up with over 130 hands-on exhibits. Walk into a giant kaleidoscope, see a pattern-making laser beam, create a minitornado, explore the museum in the dungeon. There's a giant pirate ship in the outdoor playground. ⊠ *668 Brunswick St.* ☎ *506/457-2340* ⊕ *www.scienceeast.nb.ca* ⊠ *$5* ⊙ *June–Sept., Mon.–Sat. 10–5, Sun. 1–4; Oct.–May, Tues.–Fri. noon–5, Sat. 10–5.*

9 York Street. This is the city's high-fashion block, with designer shops, an incense boutique, a general store with an eclectic assortment of gifts and housewares, and a newsstand–cigar store. At the middle of the upriver side of the block is Mazucca's Alley, the gateway to more shops and the pubs and restaurants in Piper's Lane. King and Queen streets, at either end of the block, have some fun shops, too.

2 York-Sunbury Museum. The Officers' Quarters in the Historic Garrison District houses a museum that offers a living picture of the community from the time when only First Nations peoples inhabited the area, through the Acadian and Loyalist days, to the immediate past. Its World War I trench puts you in the thick of battle, and the shellacked remains of the giant Coleman Frog, a Fredericton legend, still inspire controversy. ⊠ *Officers' Sq., Queen St.* ☎ *506/455-6041* ⊠ *$3* ⊙ *June–Labor Day, Mon.–Sat. 10–5, Sun. 1–5; off-season by appointment.*

WHERE TO STAY & EAT

$-$$$$ ✕**Brewbaker's.** With an old-world Italian atmosphere, California and eclectic cuisine, and a rooftop garden patio, Brewbaker's is downtown's most popular casual lunch and dinner spot. Dishes include fabulous salads, authentic pastas, and thin-crust pizzas. Steak and seafood are also hot menu items. The duck and goat cheese pizza is superb. ⊠*546 King St.* ☎*506/459–0067* ☐*AE, DC, MC, V.*

$$-$$$ ✕**Amici.** This new restaurant has developed a fabulous reputation in no time flat, with its authentic Italian dishes that are mouthwatering and delicious. You can match your favorite pasta with your favorite sauce, or order from "land-and-sea" fare that includes osso buco and a shrimp-stuffed sole. For a walk on the wild side, try the white-chocolate cheesecake ravioli. ⊠*426 Queen St.* ☎*506/455–0300* ☐*AE, MC, V.*

$$-$$$ ✕**The Blue Door.** The idea here is upscale global cuisine with a particularly Asian (Thai) bent, and the food is inventive and consistently excellent, served in an intimate setting with superior service. Blue doors in unlikely places, colorful bar stools, and an extensive martini menu do the trick. There's seafood with a twist, too, such as maple-chili salmon and Athenian haddock. Lots of local fine art adds a nice touch—and it's for sale, too. ⊠*100 Regent St., at King St.* ☎*506/455–2583* ☐*AE, MC, V.*

$$-$$$ ✕**The Palate Restaurant & Café.** The kitchen is open, the atmosphere is
   ★   intimate, and the art is local (and available for sale). The chef leans toward Mediterranean and Western European dishes, but isn't afraid to experiment. Even lunches, which are a real bargain, are creative. There are Canadian dishes, too, including lots of seafood. ⊠*462 Queen St.* ☎*506/450–7911* ☐*AE, MC, V* ☉*Closed Sun.*

$-$$$ ✕**El Burrito Loco.** This ever-popular restaurant had a face-lift and expanded to a second floor. The recipes are authentic Mexican, as is the owner/cook. Everything is made on the spot, including the huevos rancheros for breakfast, and the burritos, tacos, and guacamole. Steak and lobster are on the menu, too, and there's a large patio and outdoor margarita bar in summer. ⊠*304 King St.* ☎*506/459–5626* ☐*AE, DC, MC, V.*

¢-$$ ✕**Trinitea's Cup.** Superb lunches, light dinners of hearty soups and sandwiches, and an astonishing array of tea—over 70 varieties, including bubble tea—are available and there's live music on Saturday night in the winter. High tea (by reservation) includes finger sandwiches, savories, assorted fruit, fancy squares and scones. ⊠*87 Regent St.* ☎*506/458–8327* ☐*AE, MC, V.*

$$$ ▥**Delta Fredericton Hotel.** This stately riverside property is a pleasant walk to the downtown core. The elegant country decor is almost as delightful as the sunset views over the river from the patio restaurant and many of the modern rooms. The gift shop carries top-notch crafts and the restaurant, Bruno's, serves legendary Sunday brunch buffets. ⊠*225 Woodstock Rd., E3B 2H8* ☎*506/457–7000* ☎*506/457–4000* ⊕*www.deltahotels.com* ⇨*208 rooms, 14 suites* ⚬*In-room: ethernet. In-hotel: 3 restaurants, bar, pools, gym, spa, laundry service, some pets allowed, no smoking rooms* ☐*AE, DC, MC, V.*

$$$ ▣**Holiday Inn Hotel and Resort Fredericton.** Overlooking the Mactaquac
⟳ Headpond, this modern hotel has a luxurious look, but a relaxed,
country atmosphere. There's a fireplace in the lobby, and the suites
have electric fireplaces. Some of the rooms with water views have
cathedral ceilings. The Verandah dining room overlooks the St. John
River and the cottages are ideal for boating and skiing families. ⊠*35
Mactaquac Rd., off Rte. 102, 20 km (12 mi) west of Fredericton, E3E
1L2* ☎*506/363–5111 or 800/561–5111* ☐*506/363–3000* ⊕*www.
holidayinnfredericton.com* ⟿*82 rooms, 4 suites, 6 cottages* ⟁*In-
room: dial-up In-hotel: Wi-Fi, bar, tennis court, pool, gym, laundry
facilities, laundry service, pets allowed, no-smoking rooms* ▤*AE, D,
DC, MC, V.*

$$–$$$ ▣**Crowne Plaza Lord Beaverbrook Hotel.** This venerable downtown
waterfront property in the midst of the city's most important land-
marks and historic sites is now part of the Crowne Plaza chain. It has
a pool and spa facilities. ⊠*659 Queen St., E3B 5A6* ☎*506/455–3371
or 866/444–1946* ☐*506/455–1441* ⊕*www.crowneplaza.com* ⟿*155
rooms, 13 suites* ⟁*In-room: Wi-Fi. In-hotel: 3 restaurants, bar, pool,
gym, laundry service, no-smoking rooms, some pets allowed* ▤*AE,
DC, MC, V.*

$–$$ ▣**The Very Best: A Victorian B&B.** This elegant home, with its fine antiques
and original artwork, is in the downtown Heritage Preservation Area.
Some rooms have fireplaces. ⊠*806 George St., E3B 1K7* ☎*506/451–
1499* ☐*506/454–1454* ⊕*www.bbcanada.com/2330.html* ⟿*5 rooms*
⟁*In-room: DVD, Wi-Fi. In-hotel: pool, bicycles, laundry facilities,
no-smoking rooms, A/C, no elevator* ▤*AE, MC, V* ⦿*BP.*

$ ▣**Carriage House Inn.** The lovely bedrooms in this venerable mansion
are furnished with Victorian antiques. Breakfasts, served in the ball-
room, are legendary. ⊠*230 University Ave., E3B 4H7* ☎*506/452–
9924 or 800/267–6068* ☐*506/452–2770* ⊕*www.carriagehouse-inn.
net* ⟿*10 rooms* ⟁*In-room: Wi-Fi. In-hotel: no-smoking rooms, no
elevator* ▤*AE, DC, MC, V* ⦿*BP.*

NIGHTLIFE & THE ARTS

THE ARTS

The **Calithumpians Theatre Company** (☎*506/457–1975*) has free outdoor
performances daily in summer (12:15 weekdays, 2 weekends) in Officers' Square, and an evening Haunted Hike ($13) ambles through a
historical haunted neighborhood and ghostly graveyards. The annual
Harvest Jazz and Blues Festival (⊠*65 York St.* ☎*506/455–4523 or
888/622–5837* ⊕*www.harvestjazzandblues.com*) takes place in early
fall. The **Playhouse** (⊠*686 Queen St.* ☎*506/458–8344*) is the venue
for theater and most other cultural performances, including Symphony
New Brunswick, Theatre New Brunswick, and traveling ballet and
dance companies.

NIGHTLIFE

★ Fredericton has a lively nightlife, with lots of live music in downtown
pubs, especially on weekends. King Street and Piper's Lane, off the
300 block of King Street, have a number of spots. **Gordie's Pub** (⊠*422*

Queen St. ☎*506/453–0582*) features R&B and blues. An eclectic collection of live bands—especially jazz and blues—plays at **The Capital** (✉*362 Queen St.* ☎*506/459–3558*). **Dolan's Pub** (✉*349 King St.* ☎*506/454–7474*) has live music on Thursday, Friday, and Saturday night. **Isaac's Way** (✉*73 Carleton St.* ☎*506/472–7937*) goes for cozy and romantic with leather booths and soft lights. **Jester's Court** (✉*426 Queen St.* ☎*506/450–9385*)is a pub with good atmosphere and a good selection of beer. The **Lunar Rogue** (✉*625 King St.* ☎*506/450–2065*) has an old-world pub atmosphere. There's live music Saturday night except in summer. **The Taproom** (✉*366 Queen St.* ☎*506/455–3647*)is also a good choice.

SPORTS & THE OUTDOORS

CANOEING & KAYAKING
Shells, canoes, and kayaks can be rented by the hour or day at the **Small Craft Aquatic Center** (✉*Behind Victoria Health Centre where Brunswick St. becomes Woodstock Rd.* ☎*506/460–2260*), which also arranges guided tours and instruction.

GOLF
The **Kingswood** (✉*31 Kingswood Park* ☎*506/443–3333 or 800/423–5969*) features an 18-hole, par-72 championship course and a 9-hole executive course designed by Cooke-Huxham International.

SKIING
Many of Fredericton's 70 km (44 mi) of walking trails, especially those along the river and in Odell and Wilmot parks, are groomed for cross-country skiing. Other trails are broken and useful for skate skiing, which doesn't require set tracks.

Ski Crabbe Mountain (✉*50 Crabbe Mountain Rd., 55 km [34 mi] west of Fredericton, Central Hainesville* ☎*506/463–8311* ⊕*www.crabbemountain.com*) has 18 trails, a vertical drop of 853 feet, snowboard and ski rentals, a ski shop, instruction, a skating pond, cross-country skiing, babysitting, and a lounge and restaurant.

WALKING
Fredericton has a fine network of walking trails, one of which follows the river from the Green, past the Victorian mansions on Waterloo Row, behind the Beaverbrook Art Gallery, and along the riverbank to the Sheraton. The **visitor information center** (✉*City Hall, Queen St. at York St.* ☎*506/460–2129*) has a trail map.

SHOPPING

Indoor mammoth crafts markets are held in the fall and a Labor Day-weekend outdoor crafts fair (the New Brunswick Fine Crafts Festival) is held in Officers' Square. Just the things for pottery, blown glass, pressed flowers, turned wood, leather, and other items, all made by members of the New Brunswick Craft Council.

★ **Aitkens Pewter** (⌂408 Queen St. ☎506/453–9474) makes its own pewter goblets, belt buckles, candlesticks, and jewelry. **Bejewel** (⌂540 Queen St. ☎506/450–7305) sparkles with wearable works of art. You can often see the jewelers working in the studio. **Botinicals** (⌂610 Queen St. ☎506/454–6101) sells crafts by juried Maritime artisans only. **Carrington & Co.** (⌂225 Woodstock Rd. ☎506/450–8415) in the Delta is a gem for crafts and clothes, especially Tilley Endurables. **Eloise** (⌂83 York St. ☎506/453–7715) carries women's fashions with flowing lines, made with natural fibers. **Gallery 78** (⌂976 Queen St. ☎506/454–5192) has original works by Atlantic Canadian artists. At **River Valley Crafts and Artist Studios** (⌂Soldiers' Barracks in the Historic Garrison District, Barracks Sq. off Queen St. ☎506/460–2878) you'll find pottery, jewelry, paintings, and native crafts. **String Fever Textiles** (⌂Queen St., at the York Sunbury Museum in the Historic Garrison District ☎506/443–9119) is a unique retail gallery featuring works by top textile artists from throughout the province. **Think Play** (⌂59 York St. ☎506/472–7529) has funky toys and games that appeal to all ages. The **Urban Almanac General Store** (⌂75 York St. ☎506/450–4334) has an eclectic collection of household gifts, gadgets, and gizmos of exemplary design.

GAGETOWN

50 km (31 mi) southeast of Fredericton. Rte. 2 is fast and direct; Rte. 102 from Fredericton is scenic.

Historic Gagetown bustles in summer, when artists welcome visitors, many of whom arrive by boat and tie up at the marina, to their studios and galleries. There are also several small restaurants with interesting menus.

The **Queens County Museum** is growing by leaps and bounds. Its original building, **Tilley House** (a National Historic Site) was the birthplace of Sir Leonard Tilley, one of the Fathers of Confederation. It displays Loyalist and First Nations artifacts, early-20th-century medical equipment, Victorian glassware, and more. The nearby old **Queens County Courthouse** (⌂Courthouse Rd. ☎506/488–2483) is part of the museum and has archival material and courthouse furniture, as well as changing exhibits. ⌂Front St. ☎506/488–2483 ⌐$2 for one building, $3 for both buildings ☉Mid-June–mid-Sept., daily 10–5.

WHERE TO STAY

¢–$ ⌂ **Step-Aside B&B.** This waterfront heritage B&B in the heart of the village overlooks the marina. There are some lovely antiques, and the rooms are bright and cheerful. Two of them are in the original house, and two more are in a modern addition. ⌂58 Front St., E5M 1A1 ☎506/488–1808 ⊕www.bbcanada.com/6860.html ⌐4 rooms ⌂In-room: no a/c, no TV. In-hotel: no-smoking rooms, no elevator ☐V ☉Closed Jan.–Apr. ⌐BP.

SHOPPING

Grimross Crafts (⊠*17 Mill Rd.* ☎*506/488–2832*) represents 25 area craftspeople. **Flo Grieg's** (⊠*36 Front St.* ☎*506/488–2074*) carries superior pottery made on the premises. **Juggler's Cove** (⊠*27 Front St.* ☎*506/488–2574*) is a studio-gallery featuring pottery, paintings, and woodwork. **Loomcrofters** (⊠*23 Loomcroft La., an extension of Tilly Rd.* ☎*506/488–2400*) is a good choice for handwoven items.

NEW BRUNSWICK ESSENTIALS

To research prices, get advice from other travelers, and book travel arrangements, visit www.fodors.com.

TRANSPORTATION

BY AIR

Airports in Saint John, Moncton, and Fredericton are served by Air Canada and Air Canada's Jazz. Moncton is also served by WestJet and Lufthansa; Fredericton also has Delta service to and from Boston.

New Brunswick has three major airports. Saint John Airport is about 15 minutes east of downtown. Moncton Airport is about 10 minutes east of downtown. Fredericton Airport is 10 minutes east of downtown.

Contacts Fredericton Airport (⊠*Lincoln Rd., Lincoln* ☎*506/460–0920* ⊕ *www.frederictonairport.ca*). **Moncton Airport** (⊠*Champlain Rd., Dieppe* ☎ *506/856–5444* ⊕ *www.gma.ca*). **Saint John Airport** (⊠*Loch Lomond Rd.* ☎ *506/638–5555* ⊕ *www.saintjohnairport.com*).

BY BOAT & FERRY

Bay Ferries Ltd. runs from Saint John, New Brunswick, to Digby, Nova Scotia, return, once or twice a day, depending on the season. The ferry, *Princess of Acadia* has been tastefully refurbished with a library, the cozy Sea Breeze lounge, and the "Little Mates Quarters" play station for kids. Passenger fares are $30 for an adult; it's $80 for a car, plus $20 fuel surcharge for the three-hour, one-way trip July through September. Off season rates are cheaper.

Deer Island Ferries run from Deer Island, New Brunswick, to Campobello, New Brunswick, and Eastport, Maine.

Coastal Transport has up to seven crossings per day from Black's Harbour to Grand Manan in July and August. Round-trip fares, payable on the Grand Manan side, are $31.40 for a car and $10.50 for an adult. A one-way crossing takes about 1½ hours. The half-hour ferry crossing from Letete to Deer Island is free. The July and August crossing from Deer Island to Campobello takes about 40 minutes. The car and driver fare is $13; passenger fares are $2.

Contacts Bay Ferries Ltd. (☎*902/245–2116 or 888/249–7245* ⊕ *www.nfl-bay. com*). **Deer Island Ferries** (☎*506/747–2159 or 877/747–2159* ⊕ *www.deer island.nb.ca/ferries.htm*). **Coastal Transport** (☎*506/662–3724 Ext. 1* ⊕ *www. coastaltransport.ca*).

2

BY BUS

Acadian Lines runs buses within the province and connects with most major bus lines.

Contacts **Acadian Lines** (☎ *506/870–4852 or 800/567–5151* ⊕ *www.acadian bus.com*).

BY CAR

Several car-rental agencies serve New Brunswick; call or visit the Web sites to search for pick-up and drop-off locations throughout the province.

From Québec, the Trans-Canada Highway (Route 2) enters New Brunswick at St-Jacques and follows the St. John River through Fredericton and on to Moncton and the Nova Scotia border. From Maine, Interstate 95 crosses at Houlton to Woodstock, New Brunswick, where it connects with the Trans-Canada Highway. Those traveling up the coast of Maine on Route 1 cross at Calais to St. Stephen, New Brunswick. New Brunswick's Route 1 extends through Saint John and Sussex to join the Trans-Canada Highway near Moncton.

New Brunswick has an excellent highway system with numerous facilities. The Trans-Canada Highway, marked by a maple leaf, is the same as Route 2. Route 7 joins Saint John and Fredericton. Fredericton is connected to Miramichi City by Route 8. Route 15 links Moncton to the eastern coast and to Route 11, which follows the coast to Miramichi City, around the Acadian Peninsula, and up to Campbellton. Get a good map at a visitor information center. Tourism New Brunswick has mapped five scenic routes: the Fundy Coastal Drive, the River Valley Scenic Drive, the Acadian Coastal Drive, the Miramichi River Route, and the Appalachian Range.

BY TRAIN

VIA Rail offers passenger service every day but Tuesday from Campbellton, Newcastle, and Moncton to Montréal and Halifax.

CONTACTS & RESOURCES

EMERGENCIES

Emergency Services **Ambulance, fire, police** (☎ *911*).

Hospitals **Campbellton Regional Hospital** (✉ *189 Lilly Lake Rd., Campbellton* ☎ *506/789–5000*). **Chaleur Regional Hospital** (✉ *1750 Sunset Dr., Bathurst* ☎ *506/548–8961*). **Dr. Everett Chalmers Hospital** (✉ *Priestman St., Fredericton* ☎ *506/452–5400*). **Dr. Georges Dumont Hospital** (✉ *330 Archibald St., Moncton* ☎ *506/862–4000*). **Edmundston Regional Hospital** (✉ *275 Hébert Blvd., Edmundston* ☎ *506/739–2200*). **Miramichi Regional Hospital** (✉ *500 Water St., Miramichi City* ☎ *506/623–3000*). **Moncton City Hospital** (✉ *135 MacBeath Ave., Moncton* ☎ *506/857–5111*). **Saint John Regional Hospital** (✉ *Tucker Park Rd., Saint John* ☎ *506/648–6000*).

SPORTS & OUTDOORS

Whale-watching, sea kayaking, bird-watching, scuba diving, garden touring, river cruising, and fishing are just a few of the province's great experiences. Contact Tourism New Brunswick for details.

Information Tourism New Brunswick (☎ 800/561–0123 ⊕ www.tourismnew-brunswick.ca).

BICYCLING   B&Bs frequently have bicycles for rent. Tourism New Brunswick has listings and free cycling maps. Baymount Outdoor Adventures operates bicycle tours for large groups along the Fundy shore near Hopewell Cape.

Contacts Baymount Outdoor Adventures (✉ 17 Elwin Jay Dr., Hillsborough ☎ 506/734–2660). **Tourism New Brunswick** (☎ 800/561–0123 ⊕ www.tourism newbrunswick.ca).

FISHING   New Brunswick Fish and Wildlife has information on sporting licenses and can tell you where the fish are.

Contact New Brunswick Fish and Wildlife (☎ 506/453–2440).

GOLF   The most up-to-date information about new courses and upgrades to existing courses is available at the New Brunswick Golf Association.

Contact New Brunswick Golf Association (☎ 506/451–1349 or 877/833–4662 ⊕ www.golfnb.com).

HIKING   The New Brunswick Trails Council has complete information on the province's burgeoning trail system.

Contact New Brunswick Trails Council (☎ 506/459–1931 or 800/526–7070 ⊕ www.sentiernbtrail.com).

TOURS

City of Saint John visitor information centers have brochures for three good self-guided walking tours. Rockwood Park Stables in Saint John has 4-passenger horse-drawn carriages ($65/hour) and 14-passenger trollies ($184/hour) for rent, and offers rides anywhere in the city.

Contacts City of St. John (☎ 506/658–2855). **Rockwood Park Stables** (☎ 506/633–7659).

VISITOR INFORMATION

Tourism New Brunswick can provide information on day adventures, scenic driving routes, accommodations, and the seven provincial tourist bureaus. Also helpful are the information services in large centers like Bathurst, Edmundston, St-Jacques, Fredericton, Grand Falls, Moncton, St. Andrews, Saint John, and St. Stephen.

Contacts City of Bathurst (☎ 506/548–0400 ⊕ www.bathurst.ca). **Edmundston–St-Jacques Tourism** (☎ 506/735–2747). **Fredericton Tourism** (☎ 506/460–2041, 506/460–2129, or 888/888–4768). **Go Moncton** (☎ 800/363–4558 ⊕ www.gomoncton. com). **St. Andrews Chamber of Commerce** (✉ 46 Reed Ave., St. Andrews ☎ 506/529–3555, 506/529–3556, or 800/563–7397). **Tourism New Brunswick** (✉ Box 12345, Fredericton E3B 5C3 ☎ 800/561–0123 ⊕ www.tourismnbcanada.com). **Tourism Saint John** (☎ 506/658–2990 or 866/463–8639 ⊕ www.tourismsaintjohn.com). **Town of Grand Falls** (⊕ www.grandfalls.com). **Town of St. Stephen** (✉ 34 Milltown Blvd., St. Stephen ☎ 506/466–7700 ⊕ www.town.ststephen.nb.ca).

Prince Edward Island

Jenna MacMillan as Anne of Green Gables

WORD OF MOUTH

"You must see the Anne of Green Gables 'home' [Green Gables, in Cavendish] . . . I believe it is illegal to go to PEI and NOT visit."

—LJ

WELCOME TO PRINCE EDWARD ISLAND

Yeo House, Green Park Provincial Park

TOP REASONS TO GO

★ **Beach, ocean, peace:** There are endless sandy beaches and private bathing spots; walk, wade, or bodysurf in the ocean, then settle in under the sun.

★ **Green grass, red clay, blue sky:** Admire the colorful fields, or gaze up at a sky that looks like it was painted just for you.

★ **Seafood that still tastes like the sea:** fresh from the nets, this is nothing like the frozen fish sticks of your childhood.

★ **Anne of Green Gables:** The orphan that nobody wanted has been adopted by the world; she's everywhere, at conferences, festivals, and in musicals.

★ **Get physical:** there's water to kayak, paths to hike, and trails to bike; Prince Edward Island is the place to reconnect with Mother Nature, or your travel companions.

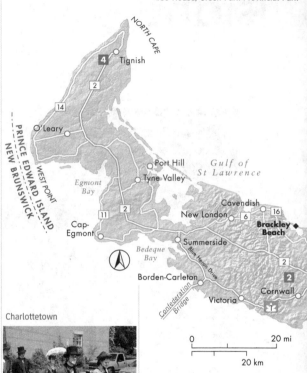

Charlottetown

1 Charlottetown. In summer, the downtown streets are dotted with people dressed as personages from the past, regaling you with tales about the Confederation debate.

2 Blue Heron Drive. Named after the bird that returns home in the spring, this route weaves through Prince Edward Island National Park and Anne of Green Gables country in a circuit of 190 km (118 mi).

Cavendish

GETTING ORIENTED

3

New erosion and time have chewed Prince Edward Island into a ragged crescent with deep inlets and tidal streams that divide the province into three nearly equal parts, known locally by their county names of Kings, Queens, and Prince (east to west). The Island is 195 km (121 mi) long, and ranges in width from 6 km (3 mi) to 61¼ km (38 mi). Despite the gentle hills in the eastern and central regions of Prince Edward Island, the land never rises to a height of more than 500 feet above sea level. To the west, from Summerside to North Cape, the terrain is flatter.

3 Points East Coastal Drive. Lighthouses, fishing ports, hidden coves, singing sands, golf courses, festivals, and campgrounds are numerous on this gentle eastern route.

4 North Cape Coastal Drive. First Nations, Acadians, the Celts, and the Scots all have a place in the history of this area, and the mix is stimulating.

PRINCE EDWARD ISLAND PLANNER

Getting Here & Around

A car, motorcycle, or moped is essential, as there is little public transport across the Island, though there is now municipal bus service in Charlottetown. If your plan is to set up camp in Charlottetown, renting a car after flying in is a good option. In the summer, bicyclists can enjoy the scenery, and it can be quite enjoyable to tour the Island that way. If you are touring Atlantic Canada, you can bring your car with you, you can cross by ferry from Caribou, Nova Scotia, to Wood Islands in Kings County, or by the Confederation Bridge, from Cape Jourimain in New Brunswick, to Borden-Carleton in Queens County.

It's Official

The Lady's Slipper is the provincial flower, and until recently that was the name for what's now called the North Cape Coastal Drive. Along that drive, and throughout the Island, you'll hear and see blue jays, the official bird, as they flit among hedges and trees, including red oaks, the official tree.

Making the Most of Your Time

On Prince Edward Island, making the most of your time might mean relaxing and slowing your pace. It might mean a leisurely lunch of mouthwatering Malpeque oysters, Island Blue mussels and lobster on a deck overlooking a harbor. Start your visit in Charlottetown, perhaps planning your visit to coincide with one of the province's many festivals. Then take a leisurely road trip around the Island. Kings, Queens, and Prince counties are each encircled by a scenic coastal road. Even if you venture inland, you are never more than 15 minutes by car from a beach or waterway.

When to Go?

The Island is generally considered a summer destination—July and August—when the ocean beaches have the warmest water north of the Carolinas, but don't overlook the "shoulder seasons." May, June, September, and October usually have fine weather and few visitors, although more travelers are discovering the joys of a fall visit. Some sights and restaurants outside the capital city close in September, but you can find food and lodging, especially in Charlottetown and Summerside. Fall is spectacularly colorful, a perfect time to hike and explore the 350-km-long (217-mi-long) Confederation Trail, which crosses the Island. Migratory birds arrive in vast numbers toward the end of summer, many staying until the snow falls. Winters are winters (this is Canada), but offer some of the Island's most overlooked activities: cross-country skiing, snowmobiling, and ice-skating.

You, Unplugged

On the Gentle Island, it's you and the elements. This is the place to escape information overload. Step outside wherever you are and you'll notice that there aren't any high-rise buildings blocking the blue sky. A traffic jam often means a few cars have slowed down so their drivers can greet each other. In the country, instead of pavement you see green and gold land. White noise and fluorescents have been replaced by birdsong and sunshine playing on sparkling water. A diet of hasty, prepackaged meals never looks the same after you bite into fresh-made food, its ingredients supplied by a farmer or fisherman who lives down the road. Many hotels don't have TVs, but they do offer canoes, bicycles, or access to the Confederation Trail. There are also spas and whirlpools with luxury products to work out the kinks after exerting yourself by jogging on a beach or boardwalk.

Local Dining & Lodging

Full-service resorts, luxury hotels, family-run farms, and moderately priced motels, cottages, and lodges are just some of your choices in Prince Edward Island. Due to the sandy composition of the land, it's too expensive to put in foundations for elevators, so few places have them, but the staff are always ready to help lift luggage. Book camp and hotel accommodations three to six months in advance for July and August.

Dining in Prince Edward Island has become much more pleasurable in the last few years as new and exciting restaurants have opened up, primarily in Charlottetown. You can eat Indian, Italian, French, Lebanese, or Canadian with a contemporary twist. There are traditional English pubs and Asian teahouses. Yet it's still a casual, relaxed experience for diners, even in the finest places. All restaurants, cafées, and pubs are nonsmoking. Water views are not hard to come by.

What It Costs In Canadian Dollars

	¢	$	$$	$$$	$$$$
Restaurants	under C$8	C$8– C$12	C$13– C$20	C$21– C$30	over C$30
Hotels	under C$75	C$75– C$125	C$126– C$175	C$176– C$250	over C$250

Restaurant prices are per person for a main course at dinner. Hotel prices are for two people in a standard double room in high season.

Festivals & Fun

Oysters. Lobsters. Blueberries. All things Irish. Sand sculptures. Summer: On Prince Edward Island, these are all reasons to celebrate, and there are festivals on the calendar to do just that. From May to December, the Charlottetown Festival turns Anne of Green Gables into a musical; Canada Day is marked with the Festival of Lights in July. If you can't get enough lobster, then Summerside is the place to be for a weeklong lobster carnival in July. For a taste of Acadian culture, take in the Festival Acadien de la Région Evangeline at Abram-Village in August. Kids will love the parade at Prince Edward Island's Old Home Week in Charlottetown, also in August. Both Charlottetown and the Tyne Valley host summer oyster-shucking championships, and around the Island you can enjoy Ceilidhs, live traditional Scottish or Irish entertainment, combining dancing, fiddling, and storytelling. At the Tour de PEI—Women's International Cycling Event (⊕ *www.tourdepei.com*), in early to mid-June, amateur cyclists can join professionals in this cross-bridge, cross-island event.

3

Updated by
Jeff Bursey

AN ENCHANTING MEDLEY OF RICH color, Prince Edward Island is a unique landmass with verdant patchwork fields that stretch out beneath an endless cobalt sky to meet the surrounding sea. At just 195 km (121 mi) long and 61¼ km (38 mi) wide, the accessible size is part of the Island's appeal. Warm hospitality welcomes you, and the laid-back, slow-paced Island lifestyle entices visitors back year after year. Almost every attraction and property is family-owned and -operated.

Originally settled by the French in 1603, Prince Edward Island was handed over to the British under the Treaty of Paris in 1763. Tensions grew as absentee British governors and proprietors failed to take an active interest in the development of the land, and the resulting parliamentary government proved ineffective for similar reasons. Yet the development of fisheries and agriculture at the beginning of the 19th century strengthened the économy. Soon settlement increased, and those who were willing to take a chance on the Island prospered.

Around the middle of the 19th century, a modern cabinet government was created, and relations between tenants and proprietors worsened. At the same time, talk of creating a union with other North American colonies began. In 1864, Charlottetown, the Island's capital city, was host of one of the most important meetings in Canadian history, which eventually led to the creation of the Dominion of Canada in 1867. Initially, Prince Edward Island was reluctant to join, having spent years fighting for the right to an autonomous government. After much deliberation, and although political upheaval had begun to subside, delegates decided that it was in the Island's best economic interest to join the Canadian Confederation.

The Confederation Bridge, linking Prince Edward Island's Borden-Carleton with New Brunswick's Cape Jourimain, physically seals the Island's connection with the mainland. To create this engineering marvel, massive concrete pillars—65 feet across and 180 feet high—were sunk into waters more than 110 feet deep to cope with traffic that now brings more than 1 million visitors annually. When the bridge first opened in 1997, some residents feared the loss of the Island's tranquility, and as you explore the villages and fishing ports, it's not hard to understand why. Outside the tourist mecca of Cavendish, otherwise known as Anne's Land, the Island seems like an oasis of peace in an increasingly busy world. Fears have diminished a lot over the years, and the bridge has moved into its second decade, still an engineering marvel and a great boon to travel, commerce, and culture. An influx of visitors, and the greater ability for islanders to visit other places, has increased the cross-pollination of ideas and made Prince Edward Island more easily accessible.

CHARLOTTETOWN

Prince Edward Island's oldest city, on an arm of the Northumberland Strait, is named for the stylish consort of King George III. This small city, peppered with gingerbread-clad Victorian houses and tree-shaded

PEI GREAT ITINERARIES

IF YOU HAVE 1 DAY

Leaving **Charlottetown** on Route 2 west, take Route 15 north to **Brackley Beach**. This puts you onto a 137-km-long (85-mi-long) scenic drive, marked with signs depicting a blue heron. Route 6 west takes you to **Cavendish**, an entryway to **Prince Edward Island National Park**. This area has enough attractions for a full day, in particular the beach and Green Gables. If you prefer to keep exploring, continue west on Route 6, with its fishing wharfs and scenic vistas. Blue Heron Drive (Route 20) takes you to the Anne of Green Gables Museum in Park Corner. Continue west, then south on Route 20 to Route 2 south (at Kensington) and turn onto Route 1A east (at Travellers Rest). Just north of the Confederation Bridge, follow the Trans-Canada Highway (Route 1) east back to Charlottetown. At seaside **Victoria**, stroll along the dock, with its restaurants and crafts shops.

IF YOU HAVE 3 DAYS

From **Charlottetown**, explore the historic sites of **Summerside** before heading for its bustling waterfront. Enjoy views of the harbor in a quieter setting on the new beach and boardwalk in the west end. Follow North Cape Coastal Drive through Acadian country to the Acadian Museum of Prince Edward Island in Miscouche. Leave midafternoon and take Route 12 to the scenic and peaceful **Tyne Valley**. From here, visit the Mi'Kmaq community at Lennox Island, where some fine traditional crafts are sold. The Mi'Kmaq Cultural Centre and Lennox Island Nature Trail are not to be missed. Stop by the historic Green Park in nearby **Port Hill** to stroll through a former shipyard or visit the museum.

On Day 3, make your way up to **North Cape** and explore its reef and the Atlantic Wind Test Site and Interpretive Centre. Plan to arrive early in the afternoon at **West Point**, where you can enjoy the beach and walking trails and visit the lighthouse.

IF YOU HAVE 7 DAYS

After a morning of shopping in **Charlottetown**, travel along Route 10 to **Victoria**. Enjoy lunch at one of this tiny village's three restaurants, then visit the crafts stores and the chocolate shop. Continue to the **Northwest Corner** to the restored stone train station at Kensington. The next day, drive north to the Woodleigh Replicas in Burlington. Then head east for lunch and fun in **Cavendish**. Start Day 3 at Green Gables and end at **Prince Edward Island National Park**, where you can relax on the beach. On Day 4, visit the Anne of Green Gables Museum in Park Corner. Then follow Blue Heron Drive to **Summerside** for shopping and a performance at the Jubilee Theatre. The next day, follow North Cape Coastal Drive (Route 11) to Cap-Egmont to view the bottle houses. Continue on to Route 178 and the pastoral hamlet of **Tyne Valley**. In nearby **Port Hill**, wander through the Shipbuilding Museum. Don't miss the Mi'Kmaq handicrafts on Lennox Island, off Route 12 on Route 163. End the day at **North Cape**, overlooking one of the world's longest natural rock reefs. On Day 6, hike or bike along the Confederation Trail, which begins at Mile 0 in Tignish. Complete your tour at **West Point**, whose lighthouse-museum has guest rooms.

3

squares, is the largest community (population 33,000) on the Island. It's often called the Cradle of Confederation, a reference to the 1864 conference that led to the union of Nova Scotia, New Brunswick, Ontario, and Québec in 1867, a country later joined by other British colonies to become the Canada we know today.

While suburbs were springing up around it, the core of Charlottetown remained unchanged, and the waterfront has been restored to recapture the flavor of earlier eras. Today the waterfront includes an area known as Peake's Wharf and Confederation Landing Park, with informal restaurants and handicraft and retail shops, as well as a walking path painted as a blue line on the sidewalk leading visitors through some of the most interesting historical areas of the Old City. Irene Rogers's *Charlottetown: The Life in Its Buildings,* available locally, gives much detail about the architecture and history of downtown Charlottetown.

EXPLORING CHARLOTTETOWN

You can see Charlottetown's historic homes, churches, parks, and waterfront on foot. The city center is compact, so walking is the best way to explore the area. Walk & Sea Charlottetown ⊕ *www.walk andseacharlottetown.com* has developed activity packages, ranging from two to eight hours in length, that include theater, oyster shucking, bicycling, seal-watching, and dining, among other activities. Pick up their *Take a Jaunt* brochure at your hotel, bed-and-breakfast, or any visitor center.

SIGHTS TO SEE

❾ **Beaconsfield Historic House.** Designed by the architect W. C. Harris and built in 1877 for wealthy shipbuilder James Peake Jr., this gracious Victorian home near the entrance to Victoria Park is one of the Island's finest historic homes, with 11 furnished rooms. Fine architectural details, such as plaster moldings and colored glass, make the house very grand. The story of James Peake, whose bankruptcy came soon after this house was built, is worth hearing. You can tour the first and second floors and enjoy views of the garden and Charlottetown Harbour. An on-site bookstore has museum publications as well as community histories. Special events such as musical performances and history-based lectures are held year-round. A carriage house on the grounds has a children's festival on weekday mornings during July and August **Beaconsfield Children's Festival** in July and August (call for exact times and price). ⊠ *2 Kent St.* ☎ *902/368–6603* ⊕ *www.peimuseum.com* 🎟 *$4.25* ⊙ *Sept.–June, call for hours; July and Aug., daily 10–5.*

❿ **Charlottetown Driving Park Entertainment Centre.** Since 1880 this track at the eastern end of the city has been the home of a sport dear to islanders—harness racing. Standardbred horses are raised around the Island, and harness racing on the ice and on country tracks has been popular for generations. In fact there are more horses per capita on the Island than in any other Canadian province. The Centre is a state-of-the-art entertainment facility featuring harness racing, slot machines, Texas

CLOSE UP

A Good Walk

Start your walk at the **Confederation Centre of the Arts** ❶ on Richmond Street, in the heart of downtown. It holds the provincial art gallery, the public library, and is home to the **Charlottetown Festival.** Next door, the **Province House National Historic Site** ❷ is the site of the first meeting to discuss federal union. Turn left off Richmond Street onto Prince Street to see **St. Paul's Anglican Church** ❸. Backtrack on Richmond two blocks and turn left onto Great George Street, home to **St. Dunstan's Basilica** ❹, with its towering twin Gothic spires. Great George Street ends at the waterfront, where the boardwalks of **Confederation Landing Park** ❺ lead past small eateries, shops, and **Founders' Hall** ❻. Break for lunch at the Merchantman Pub. The few blocks of Queen Street north of here, and the streets to the east, are rich in pubs and restaurants.

Back on the city's west end, the work of Robert Harris, Canada's foremost portrait artist, adorns the walls of **St. Peter's Cathedral** ❼ in Rochford Square, bordered by Rochford and Pownal streets. It's a bit of a walk (¾ km, or ½ mi) to get there, but **Victoria Park** ❽ provides a grassy respite edging the harbor front. Next, visit one of the finest residential buildings in the city, 19th-century **Beaconsfield Historic House** ❾, whose original owner went bankrupt shortly after it was finished. Leave time to observe a favorite Prince Edward Island pastime—harness racing—at **Charlottetown Driving Park Entertainment Centre** ❿, which is a 15-minute walk from downtown.

TIMING: The downtown area can be explored on foot in a few hours, but the wealth of historic sites and harbor views warrants a full day.

Hold'em Poker, and a simulcast theater bringing in racing from other tracks. There's delectable dining at the Top of the Park Dining Room. August features **Old Home Week,** when eastern Canada's best converge for 15 races in eight days. Old Home Week also brings the provincial agricultural exhibition and an entertainment midway to the Park. ⊠ *21 Exhibition Dr.* ☎ *902/620–4222* ⊕ *www.cdpec.ca* ⊠ *Free* ⊙ *Races Apr.–Jan., schedule varies. Old Home Week, mid-Aug., Mon.–Sat. twice daily.*

❶ **Confederation Centre of the Arts.** In historic Charlottetown, the Confederation Centre of the Arts houses a 1,102-seat main-stage theater, a 1,000-seat outdoor amphitheater, and a 190-seat second-stage theater off-site. The Centre is most famous for the **Charlottetown Festival,** which runs from mid-June to September, with concerts, comedy performances, art exhibitions, and musical-theater productions, including *Anne of Green Gables—The Musical*™. Weather permitting, the festival offers free lunchtime theater performances and concerts in the amphitheater and on the plaza. During fall and winter, the Centre presents a dynamic mix of touring and local productions, choral-music concerts, and special events. The art gallery has a varied year-round exhibition program showcasing contemporary and historical Canadian art, with special reference to Confederation. The public library is also here. The Centre's café and bar, Mavor's, with its outdoor courtyard,

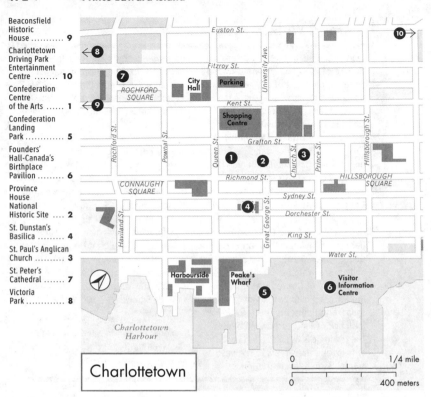

Charlottetown

is a cool place for lunch on a hot summer day. ⊠ *145 Richmond St.* ☎ *902/566–1267 or 800/565–0278* ⊕ *www.confederationcentre. com* ☉ *Oct.–May, daily 8–10; hrs extended June–Sept.*

⑤ **Confederation Landing Park.** This waterfront recreation area at the bottom of Great George Street marks the site of the historic landing of the Fathers of Confederation

in 1864. Walkways and park benches offer plenty of opportunities to survey the activity of the harbor, with the added attraction of banks and banks of wild rose bushes. During summer, performers in period costume stroll about the area re-creating historical events leading up to Canadian Confederation. **Peake's Wharf,** right next to the park, has casual restaurants and bars, souvenir and crafts shops, and a marina where boat tours may be arranged. ⊠ *Water St. between Queen and Hillsborough Sts.* ☒ *Free* ☉ *Daily dawn–dusk.*

6 **Founders' Hall—Canada's Birthplace Pavilion.** State-of-the-art displays and modern media at this 21,000-square-foot interpretive center, adjacent to Historic Charlottetown Waterfront, merge high-tech with history in the "Time Travel Tunnel" that transports visitors back to the Charlottetown Conference of 1864, eventually returning them to the present day with a greater understanding of how Canada came together as a country. Walk & Sea Charlottetown Boutique is a neat gift shop, the Island Grind Café will tend to your appetite—best to call for hours—and the Charlottetown Visitor Information Centre dispenses maps, brochures, and advice; you can also purchase dinner reservations, theater tickets, and much more while there. ✉ *Historic Charlottetown Waterfront, 6 Price St.* ☎ *902/368–1864 or 800/955–1864* ⊕ *www.foundershall.ca* ⊠ *$7* ☉ *Feb.–Apr., weekdays 10–3; early–mid-May, Tues.–Sat. 9–3:30; mid-May—mid-Oct., daily 8:30–4 or later in summer; mid-Oct.–Nov., Tues.–Fri. 9–3* ☉ *Closed Dec. and Jan.*

NEED A BREAK? **Cows Ice Cream (** ✉ *Queen St.* ☎ *902/892-6969* ⊕ *www.cows.ca* ✉ *Peake's Wharf* ☎ *902/566-4886***) is the most famous ice cream on the Island. Fresh milk from Prince Edward Island cows is carefully combined with other natural ingredients to create over 30 flavors of premium ice cream that should be slowly savored. While there, buy some of their humorously captioned cartoon cow-embellished T-shirts. Cows Ice Cream can also be found at Cavendish (on Rte. 6), in Summerside (Water St., across from Spinaker's Landing), in PEI Factory Shops in North River, in Gateway Village at the approach to the Confederation Bridge, and on board the PEI-Nova Scotia passenger ferry, The Confederation.**

❼ **Province House National Historic Site** This three-story sandstone building, completed in 1847 to house the colonial government and now the seat of the Provincial Legislature, has been restored to its mid-19th-century Victorian appearance. The many restored rooms include the historic Confederation Chamber, where representatives of the 19th-century British colonies met. The short historic film explains the significance of the meeting, and in summer, there are historical programs daily. Visitors to the public gallery of the Legislature are always welcome, and you might even see local politicians in debate. ✉ *Richmond St.* ☎ *902/566-7626* ⊠ *By donation* ☉ *Mid-Oct.–May, weekdays 9–5; June–mid-Oct., daily 8:30–5.*

❹ **St. Dunstan's Basilica.** One of Canada's largest churches, St. Dunstan's, is the seat of the Roman Catholic diocese on the Island. The church is known for its fine Italian carvings and twin Gothic spires. ✉ *Great George St.* ☎ *902/894-3486* ⊕ *www.stdunstans.pe.ca.*

❸ **St. Paul's Anglican Church.** Erected in 1896, this is actually the third church building on this site. The first was built in 1769, making this the Island's oldest parish. Large sandstone blocks give it a heavy exterior, but the interior soars, largely because of the vaulted ceilings, a common architectural feature of W. C. "Willy" Harris churches. It seats only 450, but appears much larger. Harris is reputed to be the

Island's finest architect, and St. Paul's will give you an idea why. Some of the stained glass dates back to the 19th century. ✉ *101 Prince St.* ☎ *902/892–1691* ⊕ *www.stpaulschurch.ca* ⊙ *Weekdays 9–5.*

❼ St. Peter's Cathedral. The murals by artist Robert Harris are found in **All Souls' Chapel,** designed in 1888 by his brother W. C. "Willy" Harris, the most celebrated of the Island's architects and the designer of many historic homes and buildings. This small chapel, a true gem, which is attached to the side of the cathedral, may be open for viewing by chance; if not, you should inquire inside the cathedral. ✉ *Rochford St.* ☎ *902/566–2102* ⊙ *Weekdays 9–5.*

❽ Victoria Park. At the southern tip of the city and overlooking Charlotte-
Ⓒ town Harbour are 40 beautiful acres that provide the perfect place to stroll, picnic, or watch a baseball game. Next to the park, on a hill between groves of white birches, is the white colonial **Government House.** Built in 1832 as the official residence for the province's lieuten-ant governors, it's open weekdays 10 to 4, with entry by donation. The collection of antique cannons that still "guard" the city's waterfront provides a play area for children. There is also a real playground, a pool, and a water-play area at the northwest entrance to the park. Runners or walkers can take advantage of the boardwalk that edges the harbor. ✉ *Lower Kent St.* ⊙ *Daily sunrise–sunset.*

WHERE TO STAY & EAT

¢–$$ ✕Interlude Cafe. This cosy restaurant has a devoted clientele who love the inexpensive meals that combine Asian spiced meat, seafood, chicken, and tofu with fruit and island potatoes. They're all homemade by Ally in her kitchen, and served with black, green, and bubble teas direct from Taiwan. Fruit chillers and yogurt drinks are better than most places' desserts. Take note of the unique decor, including 150-year-old windows, or enjoy the food while resting on an 800-year-old bench, which was once the root system of a tree. The staff is friendly, and it's no surprise that customers become friends with them, and each other. ✉ 223 University Ave ☎ 902/367-3055 ⊟ No credit cards ⊙ Closed weekends.

$$$ ✕The Pilot House. In the 19th-century Roger's Hardware building, this restaurant has fine dining and light pub fare. Original wood beams, brick columns, and a unique bar top made of black granite inlaid with bird's-eye maple wood make the place cozy. Certified Black Angus beef and fresh seasonal seafood are popular items on the creative dinner menu. ✉ *70 Grafton St.* ☎ *902/894–4800* ⊟ *AE, DC, MC, V.*

$$–$$$ ✕Claddagh Oyster House. Urban meets rural in this lively, upscale res-
★ taurant. Seafood is one of the many specialities here—the mussels, oys-ters, and whitefish are particularly good—but there's plenty to choose for beef, chicken, and pork lovers. Upstairs, the Olde Dublin Pub show-cases live musical entertainment seven nights a week from mid-June to mid-September. They have a large selection of draft and local beer. ✉ *131 Sydney St.* ☎ *902/892–6992* ⊟ *AE, DC, MC, V.*

$$–$$$ ✕ **Culinary Institute of Canada.** Students at this internationally acclaimed school cook under the supervision of their master-chef instructors as part of their training. Here's an opportunity to enjoy excellent food and top service at reasonable prices. At the very end of Sydney Street, next to Charlottetown Harbour, the institute has an elegant dining room with large windows that provide lovely water vistas. Many local residents come to this tastefully decorated dining room for a special culinary experience. ✉4 Sydney St. ☎902/894–6868 ☝Reservations essential ▤AE, MC, V ☉Closed last wk of July and 1st wk of Aug. Closed Sun. and Mon.

$$–$$$ ✕ **Piece a Cake Restaurant.** Head chef Aaron Gautreau brings a new sense of style and taste to this well-regarded restaurant. International cuisine and Asian-influenced appetizers and entrées are complemented by decadent, sumptuous desserts, like tortes and cheesecakes. There are gluten-free choices, too. Gautreau works in an open kitchen, making food preparation almost a performance. The menu is flexible and accommodating, and the staff is cheerful and efficient. Don't forget to ask for a window table. ✉119 Grafton St. ☎902/894–4585 ▤AE, MC, V ☉Closed Sun.

$$–$$$ ✕ **Sims Corner Steakhouse and Wine Bar.** This new addition to the capital city's dinner-hour restaurant scene offers a wide selection of choice Canadian AAA beef, aged 35 days for richer taste, as well as the impressive all-island oyster bar. They use fresh local produce, and like a few other restaurants, the menu contains celiac-friendly items. The warmth of the interior's earthy colors encourages you to linger in a comfortable plush booth. Or you might want to wander into the wine bar to select a nightcap from perhaps the biggest selection on the Island of Old and New World wines. ✉86 Queen St. ☎902/894–7467 ▬AE, DC, MC, V ☉No lunch.

$–$$$ ✕ **Flex Mussels.** Chef Garner Quain's creativity is behind every meal on this mussel and oyster-rich menu, as he tweaks traditional recipes to make food fun again, such as his lobster roll in tempura. If you're looking for new ways to taste mussels, choose among the 23 variations. Quain uses Island and Atlantic seafood, beef, and produce to ensure a fresh taste. The kitchen is open-concept, so the cooks prepare your mussels or oysters in front of you. Seat yourself in the restaurant with its casual, airy ambience, or enjoy the view of Peake's Wharf from the patio. ✉2 Lower Water St. ☎902/569–0200 ▤AE, MC, V.

$–$$$ ✕ **The Maple Grille.** This downtown nouveau cuisine/classic French restaurant features elegant dining in a casual atmosphere. They use island produce and seafood, with everything made fresh. For lunch, have the steak sandwich. Supper offers a choice of pastas, Angus-certified AAA beef, or the popular phyllo chicken, with Maple Avalanche for dessert. Their menu allows for some substitutions to suit dietary requirements. There are local brews, the staff is friendly, and you can talk in the booths without being overheard. ✉67 University Ave. ☎902/892–4411 ▤AE, MC, V ☉Closed Sun. mid-Sept.–mid-June.

$–$$$ ✕ **Merchantman Pub.** Located in a 19th-century building with original brick and open-beam ceilings, this friendly and popular pub has a traditional menu, with all the local favorites. The dinner menu is contemporary and features island products from land and sea, including fresh seafood and beef. Local and imported draft beer is on tap. The waterfront walking path near Confederation Landing Park is only steps away, great for whetting an appetite or working off a hearty meal. ⊠ *Queen and Water Sts.* ☎ *902/892–9150* ⊟ *AE, MC, V.*

$–$$$ ✕ **Off Broadway.** Nestled in the heart of historic downtown Charlottetown, Off Broadway (and the upstairs 42nd Street Lounge) has often been referred to as a gem. The intimate atmosphere, filled with cozy corners and private nooks, is tastefully done in exposed brick, original wood beams and artfully crafted wrought iron. The professional staff provides attentive service, while chef Ryan MacIsaac's creativity and attention to detail appears in a menu that is contemporary Canadian with a French influence. ⊠ *125 Sydney St.* ☎ *902/566–4620* ⊟ *AE, DC, MC, V.*

$–$$$ ✕ **Sirenella Ristorante.** Specializing in northern Italian cuisine, this res-
★ taurant has no equal in the city. It's almost tucked away, the front door set back from the street, and inside there's Italian music and quiet decor. The menu changes twice a year, and there's something for everyone. Owner Italo Marzari is behind each delightful dish—using island vegetables, beef, pork, and seafood extensively—and he handpicks the Italian wines. A private dining room seats up to 30 guests, and there's an outdoor patio for summer dining. The service is smart and courteous. ⊠ *83 Water St.* ☎ *902/628–2271* ⊟ *AE, DC, MC, V* ⊙ *Closed Jan.*

¢ ✕ **Beanz Espresso Bar.** This hip café with an outside patio is an excellent spot for hearty sandwiches, soups, salads, and coffee. The desserts are right out of an *Anne of Green Gables* church social—bakers who prepare these old-fashioned treats are a dying breed. The pies, squares, and cakes are mouthwatering, huge, and cheap. Beanz serves breakfast and lunch and closes at 6 PM Monday to Saturday, 5 PM Sunday. ⊠ *38 University Ave.* ☎ *902/892–8797* ⊟ *MC, V* ⊙ *No dinner.*

¢ ✕ **Formosa Tea House.** Perhaps the favorite lunch spot for Charlottetown's arts community, this teahouse serves traditional Taiwanese snacks and some of the best Asian teas on the Island. The restaurant is comfortably decorated in dark wood. ⊠ *186 Prince St.* ☎ *902/566–4991* ⊟ *No credit cards* ⊙ *Closed Sun.*

$$–$$$ ✕⊡ **Rodd Charlottetown—A Rodd Signature Hotel.** This five-story, red-brick hotel with white pillars and a circular driveway is just one block from the center of Charlottetown. The rooms have the latest amenities but retain the hotel's old-fashioned flavor (it was built in 1931) with reproductions of antique furnishings. The grandeur and charm of Chambers Restaurant and Lounge ($$–$$$) capture the elegance of an earlier era. ⊠ *Kent and Pownal Sts., Box 159, C1A 7K4* ☎ *902/894–7371 or 800/565–7633* ⊟ *902/368–2178* ⊕ *www.roddvacations.com* ⊅ *108 rooms, 7 suites* ⚬ *In-room: ethernet. In-hotel: restaurant, bar, pool, sauna, gym, public Wi-Fi, some pets allowed, no-smoking rooms* ⊟ *AE, DC, MC, V.*

$–$$$ ✕⊡ **Dundee Arms Inn.** Depending on your mood, you can choose to stay in either a 1960s motel or a 1903 Queen Anne–style inn. The motel is simple, modern, and neat; the inn is homey and furnished with brass and antiques. All suites have double Jacuzzis; two have working fire-

Enjoying Shellfish

Prince Edward Island shellfish enjoy a reputation of being among the world's best. The harvesting of these precious molluscs is apparent all along the shore: fishermen in small boats raking up oysters, rows of buoys holding up lines of mussels in bays and estuaries. Sometimes you can see the oyster beds at low tide. Sharp-edged, the oysters reach upwards, waiting for the water to return so they can open and feed. If the sun is low on the horizon, it will shine through those sharp edges, creating a jewel-like glow on the tidal flat.

You will also find them on almost every menu on the Island. The key is to get them fresh, and that means still alive. You want those oysters shucked after you order them. Shucking them and setting them on ice just doesn't cut it. If you want to be sure they're

fresh, shuck them yourself. Many places that sell oysters also sell the specialized knives for shucking. Ask the seller for pointers on how to shuck.

Mussels are slightly more complicated—you'll need a source of heat—but if you have a camp stove or housekeeping unit, mussels are an inexpensive treat. The ones that aren't closed or don't close when you run water over them should be thrown out. A great Island chef once said you can cook mussels in anything but water—wine, tomato juice, beer. Be creative! Put a little liquid in the bottom of a pot, throw the mussels on top, and turn up the heat. When they open four or five minutes later (if they don't open, don't eat them), they're ready to eat.

A little melted butter and lemon or garlic, and you're in heaven.

---

places. The Dundee Arms is only minutes from downtown. The Griffon Dining Room ($$–$$$$), filled with antiques, copper, and brass, serves French Continental cuisine such as fresh Atlantic salmon, beef tenderloin, and sea scallops. The Hearth and Cricket Pub ($–$$) serves hearty British fare and a good selection of local and imported beers. Enjoy the deck in the summer months. ✉200 Pownal St., C1A 3W8 ☎902/892–2496 or 877/638–6333 ☎902/368–8532 ⊕www.dundeearms.com ➾18 rooms, 34 suites ♿In-room: dial-up, Wi-Fi. In-hotel: 2 restaurants, bar, no-smoking rooms ☰AE, MC, V.

$$–$$$$ 🖫 **Delta Prince Edward Hotel.** Next to Peake's Wharf, the Delta Prince Edward has an ideal location from which to explore both the waterfront and historic downtown areas on foot. The hotel has the comforts and luxuries of its first-rate Delta counterparts, including a grand ballroom, a golf simulator, and a restaurant with an expansive international menu. Recreation facilities include a large indoor pool, indoor and outdoor hot tubs, aerobic classes, and a tanning booth. Its lobby and the main floor generally would benefit with an refurbishment as the decor is looking tired. Two-thirds of the guest rooms in the 10-story hotel have waterfront views. ✉18 Queen St., Box 2170, C1A 8B9 ☎902/566–2222 or 866/894–1203 ☎902/566–1745 ⊕www.deltaprinceedward.pe.ca ➾211 rooms, 33 suites ♿In-room: dial-up. In-hotel: restaurant, room service, bar, pool, gym, spa, laundry facili-

ties, laundry service, concierge, public Wi-Fi, parking (fee), no-smoking rooms, some pets allowed (fee) ☰*AE, DC, MC, V.*

$$–$$$$ 🖫 **Fairholm National Historic Inn.** Originally built in 1838 for Thomas
Fodor'sChoice   Heath Haviland, a noteworthy man in the early development of Prince
★   Edward Island, Fairholm is the finest Maritime example of the British architectural "Picturesque" movement. The seven spaciously elegant rooms include fireplaces; some rooms have whirlpool tubs. Enhanced with inlaid-hardwood floors, antiques, Island art, and wallpaper imported from England, this inn is a perfect alliance of British roots and Island hospitality. A hearty breakfast is included. It's close to the waterfront, shopping, restaurants, and theater. ⊠*230 Prince St., C1A 4S1* 🕾*902/892–5022 or 888/573–5022* 🖷*902/892–5060* ⊕*www. fairholm.pe.ca* 🖙*7 rooms* ♿*In room: DVDs, Wi-Fi.' In hotel: no-smoking rooms* ☰*AE, MC, V* ☲*BP.*

$$–$$$$ 🖫 **The Great George.** Closely linked with the founding of Canada as a
★   nation (the Fathers of Confederation stayed in these buildings during the 1864 Charlottetown Conference), this complex includes several historic 1800s structures: the 24-room Pavilion, the 5-room Wellington/Carriage House, and a couple of romantic hideaway suites. A continental breakfast buffet of homemade muffins, dessert breads, scones, mini-quiche, and cookies—along with fruit and yogurt—is presented in the Pavilion reception area each morning; there's complimentary tea and cookies in the afternoon and bar service in the evening. Wing chairs, sofas, private corners, and a working fireplace make the Pavilion reception area very welcoming. The town houses can accommodate families or groups; the Charlotte Club is a floor dedicated to women business travelers. The breadth of room choice and room locations in Victorian and modern designs make this attractive, centrally located complex a luxurious, must-stay destination. ⊠*58 Great George St., C1A 4K3* 🕾*902/892–0606 or 800/361–1118* 🖷*902/628–2079* ⊕*www.thegreatgeorge.com* 🖙*25 rooms, 20 suites, 10 houses* ♿*In-room: Dial-up. In-hotel: gym, public Wi-Fi, no-smoking rooms* ☰*AE, DC, MC, V* ☲*CP.*

$$–$$$$ 🖫 **Shipwright Inn B&B.** In a lovely 1860s home originally owned by the local shipbuilder James Douse are eight unique guest rooms and one apartment. The nautical theme is continued throughout the house in both construction and decoration. All rooms have original wood floors and Victorian memorabilia. Some units have fireplaces, whirlpool baths, and balconies. Enjoy the memorable breakfast and afternoon tea. ⊠*51 Fitzroy St., C1A 1R4* 🕾*902/368–1905 or 888/306–9966* 🖷*902/628–1905* ⊕*www.shipwrightinn.com* 🖙*8 rooms, 1 apartment* ♿*In-room: DVD (some), VCR (some). In-hotel: public Wi-Fi, no-smoking rooms* ☰*AE, MC, V* ☲*BP.*

$$–$$$ 🖫 **Elmwood Heritage Inn.** One of the Atlantic Provinces' leading archi-
★   tects, W. C. Harris, designed this handsome Victorian home in 1889, located down a tree-lined lane on a 1-acre estate. Elmwood was originally owned by Arthur Peters, grandson of Samuel Cunard, founder of the famous shipping line. The antiques-laden home has been restored, and the tastefully decorated rooms have either claw-foot tubs (in three rooms) or double whirlpools. Some rooms have a working fireplace.

A common living room has its own fireplace and second-floor balcony as well as a refrigerator, CD player, and video collection. Breakfast is an elegant candlelit affair. ✉ *121 N. River Rd., C1A 3K7* ☎ *902/368–3310 or 877/933–3310* 🖷 *902/628–8457* ⊕ *www.elmwoodinn.pe.ca* ⮑ *7 rooms* ♿ *In-room: VCR (some), DVD (some). In-hotel: public Wi-Fi, no-smoking rooms* ⊟ *AE, DC, MC, V* ⦿ *BP.*

$–$$$ ⊞ **Hillhurst Inn**. In the heart of downtown, this grand 1897 mansion was once the home of George Longworth, a prominent Charlottetown merchant who made a fortune from building and operating ships. The reception area, dining room, and living room are paneled with burnished oak and beech, the work of the shipwrights Longworth employed. Each of the unique guest rooms has period furniture, and many have exquisite handmade beds. Two rooms have whirlpool baths. ✉ *181 Fitzroy St., C1A 1S3* ☎ *902/894–8004 or 877/994–8004* 🖷 *902/892–7679* ⊕ *www.hillhurst.com* ⮑ *9 rooms* ♿ *In room: dial-up. In hotel: no-smoking rooms* ⊟ *AE, DC, MC, V* ⦿ *BP.*

¢–$ ⊞ **Sherwood Motel**. The friendly owners of this family-oriented motel help you reserve tickets for events and plan day trips. Don't be daunted by the Sherwood's proximity to the airport—very little traffic passes in front of this property. There are 28 motel rooms in the main building and 18 units in the newer motor inn behind the motel. ✉ *281 Brackley Point Rd.–Rte. 15, 5 km (3 mi) north of downtown Charlottetown, C1E 2A3* ☎ *902/892–1622 or 800/567–1622* ⊕ *www.canadaselect. com* ⮑ *46 rooms* ♿ *In-room: kitchen (some), Wi-Fi (some). In-hotel: some pets allowed, no-smoking rooms* ⊟ *MC, V.*

NIGHTLIFE & THE ARTS

☺ ★ **The Beaconsfield Children's Festival** (☎ *902/368–6603* ⊕ *www.peimuseum.com*), at Beaconsfield Historic House, features music and performances for children through July and August. The **Benevolent Irish Society Hall** (✉ *582 N. River Rd.* ☎ *902/892–2367*) stages concerts on Friday, mid-May through October. *Ceilidhs*, or live traditional entertainment combining dancing, fiddling, and stories, can be found in and around Charlottetown. For information on locations and times contact the **Visitor Information Center** (☎ *902/368–4444*). One of Canada's most popular attractions is the **Charlottetown Festival** (✉ *Grafton and Queen Sts.* ☎ *902/628–1864 or 800/565–0278* ⊕ *www.confederationcentre. com*), home to the nation's longest-running musical, *Anne of Green Gables—The Musical*. Professional comedies and musical theater are presented in three venues, and free outdoor performances take place on the property.

Eddie May Murder Mystery Dinner Theatre (✉ *Stanley Bridge Country Resort & Conference Centre, Rte. 6, 5 km [3 mi] west of Cavendish* ☎ *902/569–1999 or 902/886–2882*) combines madcap improvisation with sleuthing and dining. **Feast Dinner Theatre** (✉ *Rodd Charlottetown, Kent and Pownal Sts.* ☎ *902/629–2321*) from mid-June through August stages a lively show while you feast on a four-course meal with all the tea and coffee you can drink.

For complete and current listings of entertainment events pick up a free copy of *The Buzz,* available at most hotels and restaurants, and in many newstands. For a quiet drink with local young professionals, try **Mavor's** (⌧*Grafton St.* ☎*902/628–6107*), in Confederation Centre. Escape summer heat in the outdoor courtyard or retreat to the suave interior for a Starbucks coffee. A great place for live entertainment and good food is **St. James Gate** (⌧*129 Kent St.* ☎*902/892–4283*). **Bourbon's House of Blues** (⌧*65 University Ave.* ☎*902/892–4411*), Prince Edward Island's only blues bar, also features live entertainment, and caters to a music-friendly crowd.

SPORTS & THE OUTDOORS

BICYCLING

Bicycling is a favorite sport in Prince Edward Island. There are several companies in Charlottetown that offer bicycle repairs and rentals as well as offer helpful suggestions on good city bicycle tours, among them **Smooth Cycle** (⌧*308 Queen St.* ☎*902/566–5530*).

GOLF

The 27-hole **Dog River Golf Links** (⌧*472 Clyde River Road RR #2, off Route 1, Clyde River* ☎*902/675–2585, 902/675–4602 off-season*) is 13 km (8 mi) from town. The only 27-hole course on the Island is divided into a linked course of 18 (par 71) and a separate nine (par 35). Part of the scenery includes farmland and the Clyde River itself. The course, its clubhouse and its restaurant, are open from mid-April to the end of October.

The 18-hole **Fox Meadow Golf and Country Club** (⌧*167 Kinlock Rd., Stratford* ☎*902/569–4653*) is 5 km (3 mi) from town. The challenging par-72 championship course was designed by Rob Heaslip and overlooks the community of Stratford and Charlottetown Harbour.

WATER SPORTS

You can arrange pick-up service from your hotel for north-shore sea kayaking. A good way to discover the area's natural beauty is to contact **Outside Expeditions** (⌧*370 Harbourview Dr., 8 km [5 mi] east of Cavendish, North Rustico* ☎*902/963–3366 or 800/207–3899* ⊕*www.getoutside.com*). **Peake's Wharf Boat Tours/Seal Watching** (⌧*1 Great George St., Peake's Wharf* ☎*902/566–4458*) arranges harbor cruises and seal-watching tours.

SHOPPING

The most interesting shops are on Peake's Wharf, in Confederation Court Mall (off Queen Street), along Victoria Row (the section of Richmond Street between Queen and Great George streets), and on Water Street. There are also factory outlet stores along the Trans-Canada Highway at North River Causeway near the western entrance to the city.

The **Charlottetown Farmer's Market** (⊠*100 Belvedere Ave.* ☎*902/626–3733*), held Saturday year-round and also Wednesday during the summer months, offers island-made crafts, along with ethnic foods and local produce. At **Just Us Girls** (⊠*100 Queen St.* ☎*902/566–1285*) you'll find international clothing, gourmet food in the café, and imported Italian gelato. **Northern Watters Knitwear** (⊠*150 Richmond St.* ☎*902/566–5850*) carries fine quality knitted sweaters among other island-produced high-quality products. Next door, **Best of PEI** (⊠*156 Richmond St.* ☎*902/368–8835*) is your one stop for island-made pottery, woodwork, crafts, and glassware. **Moonsnail Soapworks and Aromatherapy** (⊠*85 Water St.* ☎*902/892–7627 or 888/771–7627*) produces handmade soaps using olive, coconut, and palm oils, and a full line of natural body-care products that contain herbs, spices, and pure essential oils for scent. **Firehorse Studios** (⊠*89 Water St.* ☎*902/368–3378*) features fused, custom, and stained glass from local artists, as well as paintings; they also run workshops.

BLUE HERON DRIVE

The Blue Heron Drive follows Route 15 north to the north shore then winds along Route 6 through north-shore fishing villages, past the spectacular white-sand beaches of Prince Edward Island National Park, through Anne of Green Gables country. That alone is enough for a full day, but it's worth continuing along the south shore, with its red–sandstone seascapes and historic sites. The drive takes its name from the great blue heron, a stately waterbird that migrates to Prince Edward Island every spring to nest in the shallow bays and marshes. The whole circuit roughly outlines Queens County and covers 190 km (118 mi). It circles some of the Island's most beautiful landscapes and best beaches. The northern section around Cavendish and the Green Gables farmhouse is cluttered with commercial tourist operations, but if you look beyond the fast-food outlets and tacky gift shops, you can envision the Island's simpler days. Unspoiled beauty still exists in the magnificent sunsets, refreshing open spaces, distinctive red headlands, white sandy beaches, and everchanging sculpted coastline.

PRINCE EDWARD ISLAND NATIONAL PARK

Fodor'sChoice
★
24 km (15 mi) north of Charlottetown.

Prince Edward Island National Park has been touched with nature's broadest brushstrokes—sky and sea meet red–sandstone cliffs, rolling dunes, and long stretches of sand. The national park, a narrow strip of mostly beach and dunes, stretches for more than 40 km (25 mi) along the north shore of the Island, from Cavendish to Tracadie Bay, plus a separate extension, about 24 km (15 mi) farther east at Greenwich. Greenwich was added in 1998 and features some of the most spectacular landscapes in the park. Walking trails show the progression from beach to dune to forest, and also include a boardwalk over a large pond. An interpretive center has extensive displays on the local

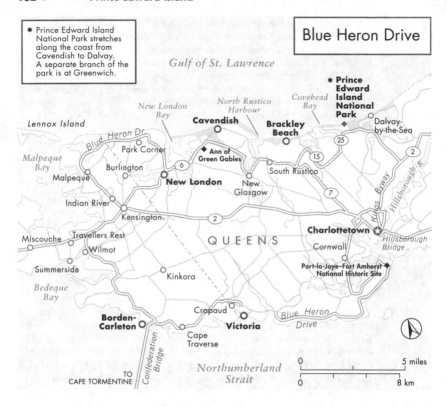

* Prince Edward Island National Park stretches along the coast from Cavendish to Dalvay. A separate branch of the park is at Greenwich.

Blue Heron Drive

Gulf of St. Lawrence

New London Bay

North Rustico Harbour

Covehead Bay

Cavendish

Brackley Beach

* **Prince Edward Island National Park**

Dalvay-by-the-Sea

Lennox Island

Blue Heron Dr.

Park Corner

♦ Ann of Green Gables

25

Malpeque Bay

Burlington

6

South Rustico

15

Malpeque

New London

New Glasgow

7

Indian River

Kensington

2

Q U E E N S

Charlottetown

Hillsborough Bridge

Miscouche

Travellers Rest

Wilmot

Cornwall

Kings Byway

Hillsborough R.

Summerside

Kinkora

Port-la-Joye–Fort Amherst National Historic Site

Bedeque Bay

Crapaud

Blue Heron Drive

Borden-Carleton

Victoria

Cape Traverse

Confederation Bridge

TO CAPE TORMENTINE

Northumberland Strait

0   5 miles

0   8 km

ecosystem and a multimedia presentation on local geology, archaeology, and history. If you're just looking to relax, head down to the supervised beach.

There are seven entrances to the park system off routes 6, 13, and 313. Cavendish Grove, off Route 6, occupies the former home of a 16-hectare amusement park, which Parks Canada bought in 2005. Park here and you have a pleasant 25-minute tree-lined walk to the beach. You can picnic in the grove, accompanied by a soundtrack of songbirds and honking Canada Geese, who call the nearby pond their home. The visitor center here is open mid-June to mid-October. Bicyclists, hikers, and cross-country skiers will enjoy the park's scenic trails. It's sometimes hard to reach Parks Canada staff during autumn and winter; call in spring and summer for rates and schedules if you are planning a camping trip. The national park has two campgrounds—Cavendish and Stanhope, which are in walking distance of beaches. Their fees and seasons vary. For campground reservations, visit www.pccamping.ca or call 877/737–3783. ☎902/672—6350 ⊕www.pc.gc.ca ✉$7, $17 for family ⊙Daily dawn–dusk.

WHERE TO STAY & EAT

$$–$$$$
Fodor's Choice
★

✕**Dayboat.** Sean Furlong is a young chef who has a budding master's eye for food combinations—textures, design, layout—combined with an appreciation for fresh produce, much of which comes off island farms or out of the waters nearby. The menu is surprising and the portions are generous. Steak, seafood, fresh vegetables—they're all treated with care and imagination. The desserts are scrumptious. An added bonus is the view up the Wheatley River, one of the best restaurant views on the Island. The inside is brightly decorated, and hung with art from local painters. In fine weather you can dine on the large deck, and you might just see an osprey stooping. ⌧*Rte. 6, Oyster Bed Bridge* ⌂*5033 Rustico Rd., Hunter River R.R. 3, C0A 1N0* ☎*902/963–3833* ⊟*AE, MC, V* ⊗*Oct.–May.*

$$$–$$$$
🖵**Dalvay-by-the-Sea.** Just within the eastern border of Prince Edward Island National Park is this Victorian house, built in 1895 as a private summer home. Rooms are furnished with antiques and reproductions. You can sip cocktails or tea on the porch while viewing the inn's gardens, Dalvay Lake, or the nearby beach. Canoes and rowboats are available. In addition to the rooms in the inn, Dalvay also has eight upscale overnight cottages. (There are no TVs in the rooms, and ocean breezes provide the only air-conditioning.) Park entrance fees apply. ⌧*Rte. 6, near Dalvay Beach* ⌂*Box 8, PEI National Park, Grand Tracadie C0A 1P0* ☎*902/672–2048 or 888/366–2955* ⊕*www.dalvaybythesea.com* 🛏*26 rooms, 8 cottages* ⌂*In-room: no a/c, no TV. In-hotel: restaurant, bar, tennis court, bicycles, no-smoking rooms* ⊟*AE, DC, MC, V* ⊗*Closed mid-Oct.–early June* ⦿*MAP.*

> ### SEA OF LOVE
>
> That newlywed couple saying their vows on the brown sands of Dalvay is among the growing number of lovebirds who are choosing Prince Edward Island for a destination wedding. Sun, sand, sea, calm breezes, and that particular hush found only in a country or seashore inn at dusk make an ideal potion for a wedding and a honeymoon.

$$–$$$$
🖵**Blue Heron Hideaways Beach Houses.** Blue Heron comprises one six-bedroom beach house (sleeps up to 10) and one studio cottage, both on Point DeRoche's 10 km (6 mi) of white-ocean beach. The private beach, perfect for beachcombing, has sand dunes and wildlife. The beach house has a pool, screened solarium, and double fireplace. The cottage is octagonal and painted pink. Units have gas barbecues, CD players, and whirlpool baths. Two other beach houses, located about 5 km (3 mi) away at Blooming Point on Tracadie Bay, have views of the bay, dunes, and lush sunsets, and come with kayaks. One sleeps up to 9, the other up to 12. From mid-June to mid-September, both properties are rented by the week only; off-season, rentals as short as three days will be considered. ⌧*Rte. 218, Point DeRoche C0A 1H0* ☎*902/566–2427* 🖷*902/368–3798* ⊕*www.blueheronhideaways.com* 🛏*3 houses, 1 cottage* ⌂*In-room: no a/c, kitchen, refrigerator, VCR* ⊟*No credit cards* ⊗*Closed mid-Oct.–early June.*

CAMPING   🏕 **Prince Edward Island National Park.** The park is on the north shore of PEI, running from Cavendish to Dalvay, and along part of the Greenwich Peninsula. Parks Canada runs two campsites right in the park, at Cavendish and Stanhope. Some sites are serviced with kitchen shelters, electricity, and water and sewer. National park fees apply. Both sites feature some of the best beaches on the Island, hiking trails, playgrounds, and park activities on natural and cultural history. ☎ 902/672–6350 ♿ *Flush toilets, guest laundry, showers, play area* ⊕ *www.pc.gc.ca* ▭ *AE, MC, V* ⊗ *Closed late Aug.–mid-June.*

SPORTS & THE OUTDOORS

The **Links at Crowbush Cove** (⊠ *Off Rte. 2 on Rte. 350, Lakeside* ☎ *902/961–7306 or 800/235–8909*), an 18-hole, par-72 Scottish-style course with ocean views, is about 40 km (25 mi) east of the national park. The 18 holes of the links-style, par-72 course at **Stanhope Golf and Country Club** (⊠ *Off Rte. 6, Stanhope* ☎ *902/672–2842*) are among the most challenging and scenic on the Island. The course is a couple of miles west of Dalvay, along Covehead Bay.

BRACKLEY BEACH

15 km (9 mi) north of Charlottetown.

Just outside Prince Edward Island National Park, Brackley Beach offers a variety of country-style accommodations and eating establishments. The town has a national park information service building about 2 km (1 mi) from the tollbooth at the actual park entrance. Its bays and waterways attract migratory birds and are excellent for canoeing or kayaking and windsurfing.

WHERE TO STAY & EAT

$$–$$$ ✕ **Dunes Café.** A pottery studio, art gallery, artisans outlet, and an annex
Fodor'sChoice   housing clothing, furniture, and jewelry, share a property with this
★   stunning café. Wood ceilings soar above the indoor dining room, and a deck overlooks the dunes and marshlands of Covehead Bay. Chef Emily Wells and her team offer an eclectic and delightful mix of seafood, lamb, beef, and succulent vegetables. A full menu is also offered in the lounge and on the patio overlooking the beautifully tended gardens with its amusing statuary. ⊠ *Rte. 15, 1 km (½ mi) south of the national park, The Dunes, R.R. #9, Brackley Beach C1E 1Z3* ☎ *902/672–2586 for the café, 902/672–2586 for the gallery* ▭ *AE, MC, V* ⊗ *Closed early Oct.–late May.*

$$$ ✕🛏 **Shaw's Hotel and Cottages.** Each
★   room is unique in this 1860s hotel with antique furnishings, hardwood floors, and country elegance. Shaw's is one of only two remaining hotels on the Island that have been operating for more than a century. The hotel and cottages have lovely bay vistas. Half the cottages have fireplaces; all have televisions.

> **WORD OF MOUTH**
>
> "[What are my top 6 things to do in PEI?] Three lobster dinners, two lobster lunches, and one lobster breakfast would be a good start. Each in a different location, of course." —BAK

Canoes and kayaks are available. The restaurant ($$–$$$) has four-course menus of seafood, meats, and pastas. Lobster is served twice weekly. Seafood is served at the Sunday-evening buffet ($$$$), a popular local tradition. ✉*Rte. 15, Brackley Beach C1E 1Z3* ☎*902/672–2022* 🖷*902/672–3000* ⊕*www.shawshotel.ca* ↩*14 rooms, 3 suites, 25 cottages* ♿*In-room: no a/c, no TV (some). In-hotel: restaurant, bar, beachfront, bicycles, children's program (ages 3–12), no-smoking rooms* ▤*AE, MC, V* ⊘*Closed early Oct.–May; 6 cottages open year-round* †◯*MAP.*

$$–$$$ 🛏**Barachois Inn.**Rustico is one of the oldest communities on the Island, and the Barachois Inn blends into the historic region with its 1880 Victorian elegance. Built as the stately home for a local merchant, the original heritage house (Gallant House) has four spacious suites with period antiques and fine art. The adjacent MacDonald House also has four suites, each with a fireplace, a kitchenette, and a whirlpool tub. The inn overlooks a Victorian garden and the lovely countryside as it leads to nearby Rustico Bay. ✉*Rte. 243, off Rte. 6, 8 km (5 mi) west of Brackley Beach, Rustico* ⌖*R.R. 3, Hunter River C0A 1N0* ☎*902/963–2194 or 800/963–2194* 🖷*902/963–2906* ⊕*www.barachoisinn.com* ↩*8 suites* ♿*In-room: kitchen (some), VCR, DVD, Wi-Fi. In-hotel: gym, no-smoking rooms* ▤*AE, MC, V* †◯*BP.*

SPORTS & THE OUTDOORS
Northshore Rentals (✉*Rte. 15 at Shaw's Hotel* ☎*902/672–2022*) rents canoes, river kayaks, peddleboats, and bicycles.

There's lots of room on Richard Watts's 45-foot boat, and **Richard's Deep Sea Fishing** (✉*Covehead Bay* ☎*902/672–2376*) will supply the fishing rods and clean and fillet your catch. Or just get something cooked from Richard's restaurant when you return to the wharf.

SHOPPING
Island Farmhouse Gouda, also known as **Cheeselady's Gouda** (✉*Rte. 223, 8 km [5 mi] off Rte. 2, Winsloe North* ☎*902/368–1506*), not only demonstrates how genuine Gouda is produced but also offers samples of uniquely flavored cheeses. **The Dunes Studio Gallery** (✉*Rte. 15 south of the national park* ☎*902/672–2586*), owned and run by Peter Jansons and his partner Nash, has expanded immensely in recent years. In its peaceful setting, you can buy clothing by Nash, with its unmistakable Indonesian stylishness; pottery and furniture by Peter; jewelry by Eve Llyndorah; works by leading local artists; and the products of craftspeople from around the world. Lose yourself among the glassware, plates, and many one-of-a-kind pieces. Throughout the summer, the pottery studio is open to the public.

CAVENDISH

21 km (13 mi) west of Brackley Beach.

Cavendish is the most-visited Island community outside Charlottetown because of the heavy influx of visitors to Green Gables, Prince Edward Island National Park, and amusement park–style attractions. Recre-

Who is Anne, anyway?

Well, the first thing to remember is that it's Anne, spelled with an "e"—not Ann.

In Lucy Maud Montgomery's classic novel, first published in 1908, Marilla Cuthbert and her brother Matthew live on a farm in Prince Edward Island. They're getting on in years and decide to adopt an orphan boy to help out with the chores. It's with some surprise, then, that Matthew comes back from the train station with a feisty, eleven-year old, redheaded girl, but it's not long before Anne—and her adventures and mishaps and friends—becomes an essential part of their lives.

Anne of Green Gables was made into a two-part television movie in 1985, starring Megan Follows. It was a huge success, airing first on the CBC in Canada, and then on PBS in the United States. It was followed by a television series which ran from 1990 to 1996.

ational options range from bumper-car rides and waterslides to pristine sandy beaches. In 1908, Lucy Maud Montgomery (1874–1942) entered immortality as a beloved Canadian writer of fiction. It was in that year that she created a most charming and enduring character, Anne Shirley, whom Mark Twain described as "the dearest and most lovable child in fiction since the immortal Alice [in Wonderland]." Montgomery's novel *Anne of Green Gables* is enjoyed today by more fans than ever, and thousands of them will flock to the Cavendish area this year to visit some of the homes associated with Montgomery and to explore the places described in the book.

The **Site of Lucy Maud Montgomery's Cavendish Home** is where the writer lived with her maternal grandparents after the untimely death of her mother. Though the foundation and surrounding white-picket fence of the home where Montgomery wrote *Anne of Green Gables* are all that remain, the homestead's fields and old apple-tree gardens provide lovely walking grounds. A bookstore and museum are also on the property, which is operated by descendants of the family. This is a National Historic Site of Canada. ⊠*Rte. 6, just east of Green Gables* ☎*902/963–2969* ⊕*www.peisland.com/lmm* ⊠*$4* ☉*Mid-May–mid-Oct., daily 9–5.*

★ **Green Gables,** ½ km (¼ mi) west of Lucy Maud Montgomery's Cavendish homesite, is the green-and-white farmhouse that served as the setting for *Anne of Green Gables*. Held dearly by Montgomery, it belonged to her grandfather's cousins. The house, farm buildings, and grounds re-create some of the settings found in the book, as do posted walking trails of the Haunted Wood (1 km [½ mi]) and Balsam Hollow (1 km [½ mi]). The Butter Churn Café sells scones, sandwiches, beverages (including raspberry cordial) and ice cream. The site has been part of Prince Edward Island National Park since 1937. There'll be special events running throughout 2008, which marks the 100th anniversary of the book's publication. ⊠*Rte. 6, west of Rte. 13* ☎*902/963–7874* ⊕*www.pc.gc.ca/lhn-nhs/pe/greengables/index_E.asp* ⊠*$5.50* ☉*May–*

late June, Sept., and Oct., daily 9–5; late June–Aug., daily 9–6; Oct. 31–Apr., call for hrs.

☺ **New Glasgow Country Gardens,** about 10 km (6 mi) south of Cavendish, overlooks Prince Edward Island's most beautiful river valley. The garden itself is 12 acres, with 2 km (1 mi) of walking trails past fountains and groomed garden beds and through natural woodland, with ample opportunity to sit and take in the beauty. ⊠ *Rte. 224, New Glasgow* ☎ *902/964–4300* ⊕ *www.preservecompany.com* ✉ *By donation* ⊙ *Call for hrs.*

3

WHERE TO STAY & EAT

Accommodations in the Cavendish area are often booked a year in advance for July and most of August. Don't despair—hotels in Charlottetown and elsewhere in the central region are still within easy driving distance of "Anne's Land."

$–$$$$ ✕ **New Glasgow Lobster Suppers.** Established in 1958, New Glasgow Lobster Suppers brings fresh lobster direct from a pound on the premises to your plate. Scallops, hot roast beef, haddock, and ham are other choices. All guests receive unlimited fresh-baked rolls, cultivated steamed mussels, seafood chowder, garden salad, homemade desserts, and beverages. Bar service is also available, and there's a children's menu. The dining area can seat up to 500 guests at one time, and it often fills up, but because turnover is fast, there isn't usually a long wait. ⊠ *Rtes. 604 and 258 at New Glasgow* ☎ *902/964–2870* 🖷 *902/964–3116* ⊕ *www.peilobstersuppers.com* ⊟ *AE, MC, V* ⊙ *No lunch. Closed mid-Oct.–late May.*

$–$$$ ✕ **Prince Edward Island Preserve Company.** One of the best spots on the Island to stop for tea, this restaurant serves wonderful desserts and has an extensive tea list. The dining room has a 25-foot ceiling, providing lots of room to hang handmade quilts. Two walls of windows look over Prince Edward Island's most beautiful river valley with its abundant bird life. The restaurant serves breakfast, lunch, and dinner, with a cuisine noted for freshness of ingredients. Notable items include the potato pie with maple-bacon cream and raspberry cream-cheese pie. The ice cream is homemade. A shop sells gourmet products and preserves made on-site. ⊠ *Rtes. 224 and 258, New Glasgow* ☎ *902/964–4300 or 800/565–5267* ⊕ *www.preservecompany.com* ⊟ *AE, DC, MC, V* ⊙ *Closed early Oct.–late May.*

$–$$$$ ⚏ **Cavendish Country Inn and Cottages.** Hosts Donald and Dale McKearney enjoy the family atmosphere of their cottage complex. There are several playgrounds on the site, outdoor hot tubs, horseshoes, and complimentary VHS movies. June visitors will be treated to trees heavy with apple blossoms. Lots of natural wood lends a rustic feel to the cottages, which vary from simply furnished one-bedrooms to deluxe four-bedrooms with whirlpool baths, fireplaces, and dishwashers. Rooms in the inn include breakfast; rooms in the motel have kitchenettes. ⊠ *Rte. 6, C0A 1N0* ☎ *902/963–2181 or 800/454–4853* ⊕ *www.cavendishpei. com* ⇝ *11 rooms, 35 cottages* ⬟ *In-room: no a/c (some), VCR. In-hotel: pools, no-smoking rooms, laundry facilities, public Wi-Fi* ⊟ *AE, MC, V* ⊙ *Closed late Oct.–May.*

$–$$$ ☷**Kindred Spirits Country Inn and Cottages.** Green hills surround this lovely country estate, a short walk from Green Gables House and Golf Course. You can relax by the parlor fireplace and then retreat to a large room or suite, decorated in country Victorian style with local antiques. Surrounding extensive lawns and gardens are 20 large cottages that range from economy to luxury (the upper-end cottages have fireplaces and hot tubs). All cottages are fully equipped for cooking; some have dishwashers and all have barbecues. You can play pool and Ping-Pong in the rec room. ⊠*Memory La. off Rte. 6, C0A 1N0* ☎*902/963–2434 or 800/461–1755* 🖷*902/963–2619* ⊕*www.kindredspirits.ca* ⇨*25 rooms, 20 cottages* ⚷*In-room: kitchen (some), VCR (some), Wi-Fi. In-hotel: pool, gym, no-smoking rooms* ☰*AE, MC, V* ☾*Closed mid-Oct.–mid-May* ¹⊚¹*BP.*

WORD OF MOUTH
"Our favorite part of our trip was PEI. We stayed at Kindred Spirits Inn in Cavendish and I loved it. They treated us like royalty. Ask for the romance package as they give you extras such as a chowder supper and picnic for the beach. The room was heavenly and breakfasts out of this world. They are the nicest people!" —Dorris

$ ☷**Bay Vista Motor Inn and Cottage.** This spotlessly clean and friendly motel caters to families. Parents can sit on the outdoor deck and take in the New London Bay panorama while keeping an eye on their children in the large playground. There's a good hiking trail opposite the motel. Beaches and all area attractions are nearby. A three-bedroom cedar cottage is available for weekly rental. ⊠*Rte. 6* ☝*9517 Cavendish Rd. W, Bayview C0A 1E0* ☎*902/963–2225 or 800/846–0601* ⊕*www.bayvistamotorinn.com* ⇨*28 rooms, 2 apartments, 1 cottage* ⚷ *In-room: refrigerator, ethernet. In-hotel: pool, laundry facilities, public Wi-Fi, no-smoking rooms, some pets allowed* ☰*AE, MC, V* ☾*Closed late Sept.–mid-June* ¹⊚¹*CP.*

CAMPING ⚐**Marco Polo Land Campground.** Of the many camping options in the Cavendish region—some inside national and provincial parks—this is one of the best private campgrounds. The site has supervised activities, including hayrides. The serviced lots are often reserved well in advance for July and August. A beach is a 2-km (1-mi) walk or a 4-km (2½-mi) drive away. Some tent sites have electricity and water. ⊠*Rte. 13* ☎*902/963–2352 or 800/665–2352* 🖷*902/963–2384* ⊕*www.marcopololand.com* ⇨*243 tent sites, 263 RV sites* ⚷*Flush toilets, full hookups, partial hookups, dump station, guest laundry, showers, fire pits, picnic tables, food service, general store, play area, swimming (2 pools)* ⚑*Reservations essential* ☰*MC, V* ☾*Closed late May–late Sept.*

SPORTS & THE OUTDOORS

GOLF The scenic, 18-hole, par-72 **Green Gables Golf Course** (⊠*Prince Edward Island National Park, Rte. 6* ☎*800/235–8909* ⊕*www.golflinkspei.com or www.peiplay.com*), with its original design by Stanley Thompson, is one of a half dozen golf courses in the north-shore region. Renowned golf-course architect Thomas McBroom worked to restore the course throughout 2007 to reflect many of Thompson's original design features. It's due to reopen in spring 2008, with the official grand opening

SEA KAYAKING

set for July 1 (Canada Day). The clubhouse lounge serves refreshments and light meals. The course is closed November through April.

Trips with **Outside Expeditions** (✉*370 Harbourview Dr., off Rte. 242, 8 km [5 mi] east of Cavendish, Rustico ☎902/963–3366 or 800/207–3899 ⊕www.getoutside.com*), in North Rustico Harbour, can be geared to suit beginning or experienced paddlers. Tours include food from light snacks to full-fledged meals, depending on the expedition.

3

NEW LONDON

11 km (7 mi) southwest of Cavendish.

This tiny picturesque fishing village overlooking New London Harbour is best known as the birthplace of Lucy Maud Montgomery. It's also home to several seasonal gift and crafts shops and a tea shop. The wharf area is a great place to stop, rest, and watch fishing boats come and go.

The **Lucy Maud Montgomery Birthplace** is a modest white-and-green house overlooking New London Harbour; the author of *Anne of Green Gables* was born here in 1874. The interior of the house has been furnished with Victorian antiques to re-create the era. Among memorabilia on display are a replica of Montgomery's wedding dress, and personal scrapbooks filled with many of her poems and stories. ✉*Rtes. 6 and 20 ☎902/886–2099 or 902/436–7329 ⊑$3 ⊗Mid-May–June and Sept.–mid-Oct., daily 9–5; July and Aug., daily 9–5.*

WHERE TO EAT

¢–$$$ ✕**Carr's Oyster Bar.** Sit on the deck, look down the Stanley River to the dunes of the national park, and after your first few oysters you may never want to leave. Some of the servers at this shellfish house are regional champion oyster shuckers. The pub-style menu includes swimming fish as well as chicken, burgers, fries, and steak, but the oysters on the half shell here could possibly be the best on the planet. Also on the premises is a small aquarium (admission $6.50). ✉*Rte. 6, Stanley Bridge ☎902/886–3355 ⊟MC, V ⊗Closed Nov.–mid-May.*

WHERE TO SHOP

Owners Aubrey Bell and Patricia Bennett oversee the tasteful **Gallery 18 Ltd.** (✉*10686 Rte. 6 ☎902/886–3201 or 866/963–3339*). They sell a finely chosen selection of antique maps and prints, old and collectible books, vintage posters, fine art, antiques, and ephemera. You can find first editions of Graham Greene, including signed copies, along with an impressive selection of woodblock prints from 19th-century illustrated newspapers. Much is related to Canada, particularly Prince Edward Island. The shop, in a converted century-old Beatty-style barn, has become a local landmark thanks to a row of giant Romanesque windows clearly visible from the road.

NORTHWEST CORNER

Blue Heron Dr. begins 12 km (7 mi) west of New London, and extends 66 km (41 mi) to Borden-Carleton.

Some of the most beautiful scenery on the Island is on Blue Heron Drive along the north shore. As the drive follows the coastline south to the other side of the Island, it passes rolling farmland and the shores of Malpeque Bay. There are a couple of lovely beaches in this area. Just north of Darnley, off Route 20, is a long sand beach with a number of sandstone caves at the end. This beach—Darnley Beach—does not have developed facilities and is often almost entirely deserted except for the seabirds.

Not far from the village of Malpeque is **Cabot Beach Provincial Park,** which has camping facilities and a playground. In summer the beach area is supervised during the day, and the playground is open dawn to dusk. ⊠*Rte. 20, 16 km (10 mi) north of Kensington* ☎*902/836–8945, 888/734–7529 camping reservations* ⊕*www.gentleisland.com* ⊠*Free for day use; camping prices subject to change, so check the Web site or call* ☽*June–Sept., daily dawn–dusk.*

⊙ **Woodleigh Replicas & Gardens,** in Burlington, southwest of New London, is a 45-acre park with 30 scale replicas of Great Britain's best-known architecture, including the Tower of London and Dunvegan Castle. The models, some large enough to enter, are furnished with period antiques. Children especially enjoy climbing to the top of the lookout tower that crowns a small hill surrounded by flower gardens. A medieval maze and 10 acres of English country gardens are also on the grounds, as is a picnic area, a children's playground, and a snack bar. ⊠*Rte. 234, Burlington* ☎*902/836–3401* ⊕*www.woodleighreplicas.com* ⊠*$10* ☽*June, Sept., and Oct., daily 9–5; July and Aug., daily 9–7.*

⊙ The **Anne of Green Gables Museum at Silver Bush** was once the home of Lucy Maud Montgomery's aunt and uncle. Montgomery herself lived here for a time and was married in the parlor in 1911. Inside the house, which is still owned by descendants of Montgomery, are mementos such as photographs and a quilt worked on by the writer. One of the highlights of a visit to Silver Bush is a ride in Matthew's carriage (Matthew is one of the characters in *Anne of Green Gables*). Short trips around the farm property are available as well as longer excursions. The property also includes a lovely crafts shop. ⊠*Rte. 20, Park Corner* ☎*902/886–2884* ⊕*www.annesociety.org/anne* ⊠*$3* ☽*Late May, daily 11–4; June and Sept., daily 10–4; July and Aug., daily 9–5; Oct., 1–4, days vary.*

WHERE TO STAY

$–$$$ ☷**Stanley Bridge Country Resort & Conference Centre.** This collection of high-quality cottages, lodge rooms, and inn rooms overlooks lovely New London Bay. The property's central location makes it an ideal base for exploring the whole island. The cottages, with pine interiors, open-beam ceilings, and private decks, are available in several price ranges, with or without kitchens and with one to three bedrooms. The lodge rooms have kitchenettes. ⊠ *Rte. 6, Stanley Bridge* ⌂ *Box 8203, Kensington C0B 1M0* ☎ *902/886–2882 or 800/361–2882* 🖷 *902/886–2940* ⊕ *www.stanleybridgeresort.com* ⌑ *16 cottages, 10 lodge rooms, 28 inn rooms* ♿ *In-room: kitchen (some). In-hotel: restaurant bar, pool, gym, laundry facilities, public Internet, Wi-Fi (inn), no-smoking rooms* ☰ *AE, MC, V* ⊘ *Closed late Oct.–early May* ⦿ *EP; complimentary CP for inn.*

$-$$ **⊞ Malpeque Cove Cottages.** Within walking distance of Cabot Beach Provincial Park and only 21 km (13 mi) from Cavendish, these two- and three-bedroom cottages sit in an open field and have magnificent views of the rising sun over Darnley Basin. The interiors are pine, and each unit has a barbecue and picnic table; some have a whirlpool bath, and all have a roofed patio overlooking the harbor. Oliver and Marian Joncourt preside over this family-owned vacation getaway. ⊠ *Rte. 105, Malpeque* ⌂ *Box 7614, Kensington C0B 1M0* ☎ *902/836–1072 or 888/283–1927* ⊕ *www.malpeque.ca* ⌑ *12 cottages* ♿ *In-room: no a/c, kitchen (some). In-hotel: laundry facilities, some pets allowed, no-smoking rooms* ☰ *MC, V.*

NIGHTLIFE & THE ARTS

St. Mary's Church (⊠ *Rte. 104, 5 km [3 mi] north of Kensington, Indian River* ☎ *902/836–4933 or 866/856 3733* ⊕ *www.indianriverfestival.com* ⦿ *$24–$32*) has performances by visiting artists in July and August as part of the Indian River Festival of Music. The church has very good acoustics and a beautiful pastoral setting, and the concerts here are often broadcast nationally by the Canadian Broadcasting Corporation.

BORDEN-CARLETON

35 km (22 mi) south of New London.

Once home port to the Marine-Atlantic car ferries, Borden-Carleton is now linked to the mainland via the Confederation Bridge. The 13-km (8-mi) behemoth spans the Northumberland Strait and ends in Cape Jourimain, New Brunswick.

⟲   The **Gateway Village** complex (⊠ *Foot of Confederation Bridge, near tollbooths* ☎ *902/437–8539 or 888/437–6565, info center: 902/437–8570*) has crafts and gift shops and food-service outlets, plus a government-run visitor information center (open year-round), with an interactive display about the Bridge and Prince Edward Island products and history. Watch the rolling floor on your way in—it's a neat way to get you accustomed to the dunes and waves, but it can catch you by surprise. Music is everywhere, from step-dancers outside the center to musicians playing to appreciative audiences. The Prince Edward Island section of the Trans-Canada Highway begins here and continues through Charlottetown to the Wood Islands Ferry Terminal. Many visitors to Prince Edward Island enter the province across the Confederation Bridge, explore the Island, then continue on to Nova Scotia via ferry from Wood Islands.

EN ROUTE

Before the late 1800s, when ferry service began, passengers and mail were taken across the Northumberland Strait in iceboats that were rowed and alternately pushed and pulled by men across floating ice. **The iceboat monument** (⊠ *Rte. 10, Cape Traverse*) commemorates their journeys. Route 10 also provides excellent views of the Confederation Bridge.

VICTORIA

22 km (14 mi) east of Borden-Carleton.

Victoria-by-the-Sea, as this charming community is known locally, is a fishing village filled with antiques, art galleries, and handicrafts shops. But the real beauty of Victoria is that it has retained its peace and integrity. The little shops and eateries are owned by local people. Many of the artists and craftspeople who live here do so to escape the hectic life of larger centers. To truly appreciate Victoria, park on one of its several streets and walk. Stroll about the community, browse its shops, watch the fishing boats beside the wharf, admire the harbor lighthouses, and take time to chat with the locals. Be sure to take in a performance at the Victoria Playhouse.

The usually uncrowded **Victoria Provincial Park** is just outside the village. Here beach lovers enjoy the warm, calm waters of the Northumberland Strait. You can walk on the sand flats at low tide. If you're lucky enough to be there when there's an electrical storm, the display over the water is quite something.

WHERE TO STAY & EAT

$–$$$ ✕ **Landmark Café.** This quirky, memorabilia-filled eatery specializes in quiche, seafood, and vegetarian dishes. Try Eugene's Cajun-style shrimp and scallops, or his steamed salmon and scallops in garlic butter and dill. Eat the walnut-filled brownie for dessert, and your mouth will thank you. You can count on great service, too. ⊠ *12 Main St.* ☎ *902/658–2286* ▭*MC, V* ⊘*Closed Oct.–May.*

$ ✕▣ **Victoria Village Inn and Restaurant.** The rooms in this three-story Victorian house, next to the Victoria Playhouse, feature original wood floors, large sash windows, and casual furnishings. The co-owner of the inn, Stephen Hunter, a culinary chef, offers casual meals ($$–$$$) of fresh seafood from the wharf a block away. ⊠*22 Howard St., Box 1, C0A 2G0* ☎*902/658–2483 or 866/658–2483* ⊕*www.victoriavillageinn. com* ➥*3 rooms, 1 suite (sleeps up to 4)* ☖*In-room: no a/c, no TV. In-hotel: restaurant, no-smoking rooms* ▭*AE, MC, V* ⦿|*BP.*

$ ▣ **Orient Hotel.** One of two hotels on Prince Edward Island that have
★   been in continuous operation for more than a century, this B&B has cozy guest rooms and suites. Most rooms have expansive water views, and they've been individually decorated with a fine eye for style, accessories, and colors. Breakfast is served in the downstairs breakfast room, called Mrs. Profitt's Tea Room. There you can also get a snack Tuesday to Sunday from 11:30 to 4. It's worth the trip to Victoria just for the scones with clotted cream, or the English trifle parfait. ⊠*34 Main St., Box 55, C0A 2G0* ☎*902/658–2503 or 800/565–6743* ⊕*www.*

theorienthotel.com ⤶*5 rooms, 3 suites* ⛹*In-room: no a/c. In hotel: restaurant, bicycles, no kids under 12, no-smoking rooms* ▭*MC, V* ⊘*Closed mid-Oct.–mid-May* ⍾*BP.*

NIGHTLIFE & THE ARTS

In summer, the historic **Victoria Playhouse** (⊠*Howard and Main Sts.* ☎*902/658–2025 or 800/925–2025* ⊕*www.victoriaplayhouse.com*) has a renowned professional theater program that celebrates Maritime comedy. From late June through September, the company mounts four plays plus a Monday-night Musical Showcase Series. In the Community Hall (circa 1914), the theater has just 150 seats and excellent acoustics. The world premiere of *Anne and Gilbert,* a musical covering the two L.M. Montgomery books that followed *Anne of Green Gables,* was held here in 2005.

SHOPPING

Island Chocolates (⊠*Main St.* ☎*902/658–2320 or 800/565–2320* ⊘*Closed mid-Oct.–mid-June*), a family-run chocolate factory in a 19th-century store, sells sweets handmade with Belgian chocolate, fresh fruit, nuts, and liqueurs. Espresso, teas, and other desserts are available. Sit on their deck and chat with the locals and other visitors.

PORT-LA-JOYE–FORT AMHERST NATIONAL HISTORIC SITE OF CANADA

36 km (22 mi) east of Victoria.

Today's verdant, peaceful grounds of Port-la-Joye–Fort Amherst hide much of its tumultuous history. In 1720, during the Franco-British struggle for control of North America, the French arrived to set up an administrative capital and military post in "Isle Saint-Jean"—establishing the first European settlement on the Island. Ownership of the land seesawed between England and France until 1758, when the British used Fort Amherst, as they renamed it, as a base from which to expel the Acadians. The 18th-century homestead of Michel Haché Gallant—harbor captain, property owner, and patriarch of the most respected family in Port La Joye—was rediscovered in 1987. You can stroll along the wooded trails and over the original earthworks of the fort. Bring a picnic to enjoy terrific panoramic views of Charlottetown's harbor. To book a tour, call ☎902/566–7626.

POINTS EAST COASTAL DRIVE

For 375 km (233 mi), the Points East Coastal Drive traces the coastline of green and tranquil Kings County on the eastern end of the Island. The route passes wooded areas, patchwork-quilt farms, fishing villages, historic sites, and long, uncrowded beaches; among these, Basin Head and the sands in the Greenwich section of Prince Edward Island National Park are standouts. In early summer, fields of blue, white, pink, and purple wild lupines slope down to red cliffs and blue sea. From Montague, you can take a seal-watching tour. To reach King County from Charlottetown, take Route 1 East and then follow the Point East Coastal Drive counterclockwise.

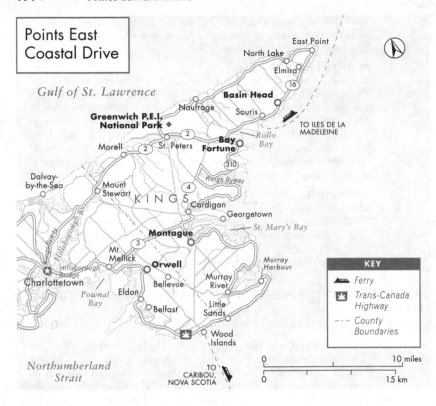

Points East Coastal Drive

Gulf of St. Lawrence

East Point
North Lake
Elmira
16
Basin Head
Naufrage   Souris
Greenwich P.E.I.
National Park ◆
TO ILES DE LA
MADELEINE
2
Bay
Morell   2   St. Peters   Fortune   *Rollo
Bay*
310
Dalvay-
by-the-Sea   Mount
Stewart   *Kings Byway*
K I N G S
4
Cardigan
Georgetown
— *St. Mary's Bay*
Montague
3
Mt.
Mellick
*Hillsborough
Bridge*   Orwell   Murray
River   Murray
Harbour
Charlottetown
*Pownal
Bay*   Eldon
Bellevue
Belfast   Little
Sands
Wood
Islands
*Northumberland
Strait*
TO
CARIBOU,
NOVA SCOTIA

KEY
🚢 Ferry
🍁 Trans-Canada Highway
- - - County Boundaries

0 ———— 10 miles
0 ———— 15 km

ORWELL

27 km (17 mi) east of Charlottetown.

For those who like the outdoors, Orwell, lined with farms that welcome guests and offer activities, is ideal.

The **Orwell Corner Historic Village** is a living-history farm museum that re-creates a 19th-century rural settlement by employing methods used by Scottish and Irish settlers. The village contains a beautifully restored 1864 farmhouse, a school, a general store, a church, a community hall, a blacksmith shop, a refurbished shingle mill, and barns with handsome Acadian horses and a draft horse. From spring to fall the site runs fairs and crafts shows, and in summer the community hall is the site of a ceilidh one evening a week. The village includes the Prince Edward Island Agriculture Museum, which displays a wide array of old farm implements, and shows a historical film of the tools in use, including commentary about old times on the farm by older Islanders. ⊠*Rte. 1 off Trans-Canada Hwy.* ☎*90/651–8515* ⊕*www.orwellcorner.isn.net* 🎫*$7.50* ⊙ *Late May–June, weekdays 9–4:30; July–Labour Day, daily 9:30–5; early Sept.–mid-Oct., Sun.–Thurs. 9–4:30.*

3

The **Sir Andrew Macphail Homestead,** a National Historic Site, is a 140-acre farm property that contains an ecological forestry project, gardens, and three walking trails. The restored 1829 house and 19th-century outbuildings commemorate the life of Sir Andrew Macphail (1864–1938), a writer, professor, physician, and soldier. Wednesday to Sunday when the house is open, a restaurant serves a traditional Scottish lunch with local produce, including the wine. There's occasional live entertainment. ⊠ *Off Rte. 1* ☎ *902/651–2789* ⊕ *www.islandregister. com/macphailfoundation.html* ✉ *Donations are appreciated* ⊙ *Farm: late June–early Oct., Wed. and Sun. 11–7:30, Thurs.–Sat. 11–4:30. Grounds: late June–early Oct., daily dawn–dusk.*

OFF THE BEATEN PATH

Ben's Lake Trout Fishing and Campground. This pleasant attraction is especially appreciated by aspiring young anglers. You're almost guaranteed a fish, and the staff cleans it and, for a small fee, supplies the barbecue and picnic table for a great meal. Fly-fishing can also be arranged. ⊠ *Rte. 24, Bellevue* ☎ *902/838–2706* ⊕ *www.benslake.com* ✉ *Free, catch $4 per pound* ⊙ *Apr.–Sept., daily 8–8; Oct., weekends 8–8 or by reservation; Nov.–Mar., by reservation only.*

WHERE TO STAY

$ ⚟ **Forest and Stream Cottages.** These one- and two-bedroom cottages in a forest grove provide a secluded stay overlooking a small lake. You can use one of the rowboats, canoes, or peddleboats to explore the lake, or you can take advantage of the property's nature trails. These traditional-style cottages have screened verandas, and each has a barbecue and picnic table. Also on the property is Country Charm Bed & Breakfast, which is open year-round. In winter, after a hearty breakfast, you can go snowshoeing or cross-country skiing and then return for a soak in the hot tub. ⊠ *Murray Harbour, C0A 1V0* ☎ *902/962–3537 or 800/227–9943* 🖷 *902/962–2130* ⊕ *www.forestandstreamcottages.com* ⤳ *6 cottages* ♿ *In-room: no a/c, kitchen (some), DVD. In-hotel: bicycles, laundry facilities, public Internet, some pets allowed, no smoking rooms* ☰ *MC, V* ⊙ *Cottages closed Nov.–Apr.*

EN ROUTE

One of the Island's oldest churches, **St. John's Presbyterian,** is in Belfast, off Route 1 on Route 207. This pretty white church on a hill was built by settlers from the Isle of Skye who were brought to the Island from Scotland in 1803 by Lord Selkirk.

At Little Sands, on Route 4, is Canada's only coastal winery, **Rossignol Estate Winery,** which has tastings for a small fee.

The lighthouse at **Cape Bear** is the site of the first wireless station in Canada to receive the distress call from the *Titanic.*

MONTAGUE

20 km (12 mi) northeast of Orwell.

The business hub of eastern Prince Edward Island, Montague is a lovely small town that straddles the Montague River and serves as a departure point for seal-watching boat tours.

☺ **Cruise Manada Seal-watching Boat Tours** (☎902/838–3444 or 800/986–3444 ⊕www.cruisemanada.com) sails past a harbor-seal colony and mussel farms. Boats leave from Montague Marina on Route 4 and Georgetown on Route 3 (select cruises only) from mid-May through September. The tour price is $22; call to reserve. There are ceilidhs on Friday nights.

> ### THE CONFEDERATION TRAIL
>
> The Confederation Trail, Prince Edward Island's section of the Trans Canada Trail, created along the roadbed of the abandoned railway networks, extends almost the complete length of the Island, from Tignish to Elmira. Its more than 350 km (217 mi) of flat surface is covered with rolled stone dust, making it an excellent path for hiking and bicycling. Plum-color entry gateways are near roadways at many points, and food and lodging is available at villages along the way.

The restored **railway station** overlooking the marina has a tourist information center and a number of small crafts shops inside. The Confederation Trail continues past the station and is ideal for a leisurely stroll.

WHERE TO STAY & EAT

$$–$$$ ✕**Windows on the Water Café.** Overlooking the former railway station is this old house furnished with antiques. In warm weather you can eat on the large deck with views of the Montague Marina. Winner of the Island Shellfish Chowder Competition, this lovely little eatery has tasty seafood, vegetarian fare, steak, and chicken dishes. Old-style desserts include apple crisp and bread pudding. ⊠106 Sackville St. ☎902/838–2080 ▤MC, V ⊙Closed early Oct.–mid-May.

$–$$ ⊞ **Roseneath Bed & Breakfast.**This fine heritage home, built in 1868, faces the Brudenell River. You can golf at the adjacent Brudenell and Dundarave courses, walk or bike the Confederation Trail (which crosses the property), go trout fishing, or explore the 90 acres of woodlands. All rooms have views of the river or the property's extensive gardens. Morning brings coffee delivered to your room and a home-cooked breakfast downstairs. A lobster dinner may be arranged in advance during May and June. ⊠R.R. 6, Cardigan C0A 1G0 ☎902/838–4590 or 800/823–8933 �🖷902/838–4590 ⊕www.rosebb.ca ⇄3 rooms, 1 suite ♿In-room: no a/c, no TV, Wi-Fi. In-hotel: bicycles ▤MC, V ⊙Closed Nov.–Apr.; open off-season by reservation ¶◎|BP.

BAY FORTUNE

23 km (14 mi) north of Montague.

The drive along Route 310 on the eastern shore is a tour through essential Prince Edward Island. Small wooded areas break up farm fields sloping away from the shore. Bays and rivers cut into the landscape, and fishing boats take shelter in every harbor. Bay Fortune, site of one of the larger of these harbors, has been a secret refuge of American vacationers for two generations; they return year after year to relax in the peace and quiet of this charming little community.

WORD OF MOUTH

"I love to hike and bike. The Confederation Trail on PEI is ideal for either. The beaches are gorgeous. The fresh seafood is wonderful."
—cmcfong

3

OFF THE
BEATEN
PATH

Souris. The Souris area, 14 km (9 mi) north of Bay Fortune, is noted for its fine traditional musicians. An outdoor Scottish concert at Rollo Bay in July, with fiddling and step dancing, attracts thousands every year. At Souris a car ferry links Prince Edward Island with Québec's scenic **Magdalen Islands** (☎ *887/624–4437*).

WHERE TO STAY & EAT

¢–$$ ✕**Sheltered Harbour Café.** Cheerfully decorated in a nautical theme, this roadside family restaurant is frequented mostly by locals. It serves basic fare—seafood, burgers, salads, liver and onions—well prepared and at ridiculously reasonable prices. The café is open year-round and is wheelchair accessible. ⊠*Rtes. 2 and 340, Fortune* ☎*902/687–1997* ⊟*AE, MC, V.*

$$–$$$$ ✕⊡**Inn at Bay Fortune.** Superb dining and genteel living await at this ★ enticing, unforgettable getaway, the former summer home of Broadway playwright Elmer Harris. The inn overlooks Fortune Harbour and the Northumberland Strait. Many of the rooms, furnished with Island antiques and crafts by local artists, have fireplace sitting areas; some have a balcony. Rooms from the top of the tower have views of Cape Breton, Nova Scotia. Tread Softly Cottage, a restored farmhouse, has two bedrooms; Howe Point Cottage, a modern wood-paneled lodge, has three bedrooms, a loft, and a view of the Northumberland Strait. Local fresh-caught and fresh-harvested ingredients are served in an old-time ambience at the restaurant ($$$–$$$$), where guests can dine on the veranda that wraps around the inn, providing breathtaking water views, or in the kitchen at the chef's table. Specialties include braised lobster with shiitake, tapioca, and lobster sauce, and maple-roast tenderloin of pork. Many of the herbs and fruits come right from the Inn's extensive gardens. ⊠*Rte. 310 off Rte. 2, C0A 2B0* ☎*902/687–3745, 860/563–6090 off-season* ⊕*www.innatbayfortune.com* ⤴*17 rooms, 2 houses* ⌂*In-room: kitchen (some). In-hotel: restaurant, public Internet, public Wi-Fi, no-smoking rooms* ⊟*AE, MC, V* ⊘*Closed late Oct.–mid-May* ⦿*BP.*

$$–$$$$ ✕⊡**Inn at Spry Point.** The sister property of the Inn at Bay Fortune, Fodor'sChoice this luxury retreat hugs the end of a 110-acre peninsula. In addition ★ to 4 km (2½ mi) of shoreline walking trails, the serene and beautifully appointed property has a 1-km (½-mi) sandy beach. Each of the rooms has a king bed and either a private balcony or a garden terrace. At lunch, seafood and locally grown fresh produce are served in the restaurant ($$$–$$$$); pan-seared scallops, halibut, and salmon take top billing. Desserts are glorious. Guests go to the Inn at Bay Fortune *(see above)* for dinner. The absence of TVs adds to the calm and

peacefulness, and the Inn, like the Inn at Bay Fortune, fits wonderfully into a lush, natural setting. ⊠*Spry Point Rd.* ☎*902/583–2400, 860/563–6090 off-season* ⊟*902/583–2176* ⊕*www.innatsprypoint. com* ⊠*15 rooms* ⚫*In-room: no TV. In-hotel: reestaurant, bicycle, public Wi-Fi, no-smoking rooms* ⊟*AE, MC, V* ⊗*Closed early Oct.– late May* ⍣*BP.*

$ ⟨∷⟩**Rollo Bay Inn.** This roadside inn, done up in a Queen Anne style, has spacious rooms and comfortable wing chairs, and a few extra dollars will buy you a water view. The local beach is a five-minute drive away, and there is no charge for the picturesque view of the bay from the breakfast room. The lone suite has a kitchenette. The inn is open year-round. ⊠*Rte. 2, 4 km west of Souris, Rollo Bay C0A 2B0* ☎*902/687–3350* ⊟*902/687–3570* ⊕*www.peisland.com/rollobayinn* ⊠*19 rooms, 1 suite* ⚫*In-room: Wi-Fi. In-hotel: no-smoking rooms* ⊟*AE, MC, V.*

¢–$ ⟨∷⟩**Lighthouse and Beach Motel.**This was never a real lighthouse; it's just made up to look like one. The rooms are tiny and the 1970s decor is faded, but the beach is a five-minute walk away. ⊠*Rte. 330, Lower Rollo Bay C0A 2B0* ☎*800/689–2339* ⊟*902/687–1566* ⊠*18 rooms, 1 suite* ⚫*In-room: no a/c, kitchen (some). In-hotel: no-smoking rooms* ⊟*AE, MC, V* ⊗*Early Sept.–mid-June* ⍣*CP.*

BASIN HEAD

13 km (8 mi) north of Souris.

This beach is noted for exquisite silvery sand that stretches northeast for miles, backed by high grassy dunes. The lovely sand beach has been "discovered," but it's still worth spending some time here. Scuff your feet in the sand and hear it squeak, squawk, and purr. Known locally as "singing sand," it is a phenomenon found in only a few locations worldwide. The high silica content in the sand helps produce the sound. A boardwalk leads from the **Basin Head Fisheries Museum** at the top of the hill down to the beach area. There's a small takeout next to the museum where fish-and-chips and other fast food may be purchased and eaten at picnic tables overlooking the ocean.

Red Point Provincial Park (⊠*Rte. 16, 13 km [8 mi] east of Souris, 2 km [1 mi] west of Basin Head* ☎*902/357–3075* ⊗*June–mid-Sept.*) makes an excellent base for campers. The park has a supervised ocean beach and an interpretive program.

⟳ The **Basin Head Fisheries Museum** is on a headland overlooking the

> **BEST BEACHES**
>
> In summer, thanks to the shallow waters of the Gulf of St. Lawrence, the ocean beaches have the warmest water north of the Carolinas, making for fine swimming. Basin Head Beach, near Souris—with its miles of singing sands—is one of the most popular beaches on the Island. Not as busy, and featuring ocean sunsets, is West Point, with lifeguards, nearby restaurants and showers. At Greenwich, near St. Peters Bay, a half-hour walk along the floating boardwalk brings you to an endless empty beach.

Northumberland Strait and has views of one of the most beautiful white-sand beaches on the Island. The museum depicts the ever-changing nature of Prince Edward Island's historic inshore fishing tradition through interesting displays of artifacts. On the wharf by the beach is an old cannery, which is a designated heritage building. ⊠ *Off Rte. 16, east of Souris, turn onto dirt road marked with sign indicating Basin Head Beach and Basin Head Fisheries Museum* ☎ *902/357–7233 or 902/368–6600 off-season* ⊕ *www.peimuseum.com* ▣ *$4* ⊙ *Early June–Oct., daily 9–5.*

GREENWICH (P.E.I. NATIONAL PARK)

19 km (12 mi) southwest of Basin Head.

The western portion of the Greenwich peninsula, known for its superior beach and massive sand dunes, became part of Prince Edward Island National Park in 1998. These dunes are moving, gradually burying the nearby woods. Here and there the bleached skeletons of trees thrust up through the sand like wooden ghosts. To get to the national park, follow Route 16 to St. Peters Bay and Route 313 to Greenwich. The road ends at an interpretive center (open mid-May to mid-September) whose programs explain the ecology of this rare land formation. Visitors are permitted to walk along designated pathways among sand hills and through beige dunes to reach the beach. Because of the rather delicate nature of the dune system, visitors must stay on the trails and refrain from touching the flora. ⊠ *Rte. 313, 6 km (4 mi) north of St. Peters Bay* ☎ *902/672–6350* ⊕ *www.pc.gc.ca* ▣ *$7, $17 for family* ⊙ *Daily dawn–dusk.*

WHERE TO STAY & EAT

¢–$ ✕ **Rick's Fish and Chips.** Possibly the best fish-and-chips on Prince Edward Island, Rick's chips are fresh cut and the fish is fresh caught. The menu includes other fried favorites, more healthful choices such as grilled salmon, and quiche and pizza for those who aren't seafood fans. With its spartan interior, Rick's is best enjoyed when you can sit at one of the picnic tables outside. ⊠ *Rte. 2, St. Peters* ☎ *902/961–3438* ⚠ *Reservations not accepted* ▭ *MC, V* ⊙ *Closed early Oct.–early May.*

$$$$ ✕ 📷 **The Inn at St. Peters.** Overlooking the serene waters of St. Peters Bay,
★ this idyllic inn is the only four-star property in the eastern part of the Island. It's situated on 13 acres filled with more than 25,000 flowers, near the beaches and sand dunes of Greenwich. All suites have a working fireplace, a rocking chair, and a deck facing the bay. Walkers and bicyclist can explore the nearby Confederation Trail, and owner Karen Davey will help arrange golf packages at area courses. Rates include breakfast and dinner in the top-notch McCulloch Room ($$$–$$$$), where you are treated to imaginative Continental cuisine with a contemporary flair and beautiful sunsets. Try the mussels with smoked tomato butter. ⊠ *Inn at St. Peters, 1668 Greenwich Rd., St. Peters Bay C0A 2A0* ☎ *902/961–2135 or 800/818–0925* ⊕ *www.innatstpeters. com* ↪ *16 suites* ⚐ *In-room: refrigerator, VCR, Wi-Fi. In-hotel: res-*

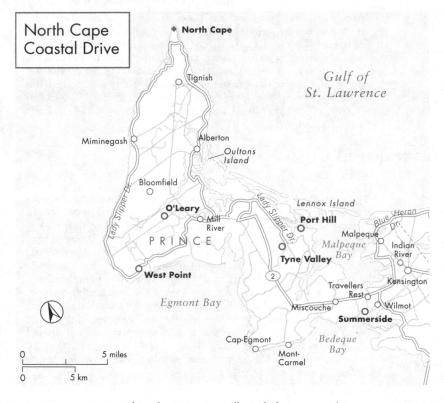

taurant, bicycles, some pets allowed (fee), no-smoking rooms ▤MC,
V ☉ *Mid-Oct.–late May* ﾂ◯MAP.

**EN
ROUTE**

Ships from many nations have been wrecked on the reef running northeast
from **East Point Lighthouse** (✉ *Rte. 16, East Point* ☎ *902/357–2106*). Guided tours are offered mid-June through August, and many books about life at
sea are available at the gift shop in the 1908 fog-alarm building. Because of
the high erosion in this area, caution should be used when approaching the
high cliffs overlooking the ocean.

NORTH CAPE COASTAL DRIVE

The North Cape Coastal Drive winds along the coast of the narrow,
indented western end of the Island, known as Prince County, through
very old and very small villages that still adhere to a traditional way of
life. Acadians, descendants of the original French settlers, inhabit many
of these hamlets. The area is known for its oysters and Irish moss (the
source of carrageenan, a thickener used in processing ice cream and
many other foods), but most famously for its potato farms. Visitors
tend to follow the straight, flat Route 2 most of the distance, which
gives a rather boring view of the Island. To truly appreciate what the

western region has to offer, divert along the coastline. Follow Route 14 to West Point and continue northward along the Northumberland Strait. Return along the Gulf of St. Lawrence via Route 12, which passes the lovely beach area of Jacques Cartier Provincial Park. Both of these highways are part of the North Cape Coastal Drive.

SUMMERSIDE

71 km (44 mi) west of Charlottetown.

3

Summerside, the second-largest city on the Island, has a beautiful waterfront area with a beach and boardwalk in the west end. A self-guided walking tour arranged by the Eptek Exhibition Centre is a pleasant excursion along leafy streets lined with large houses. A number of buildings in Summerside have murals painted on the sides, most depicting historical events. The Confederation Trail passes through the city, and the former railway station makes an excellent starting point for walking or biking excursions. It takes about a half hour to drive by car from Summerside to major attractions such as Cavendish in the central region of Prince Edward Island.

During the third week of July, all of Summerside celebrates the eight-day **Summerside Lobster Carnival,** with livestock exhibitions, harness racing, fiddling contests, and of course, lobster suppers.

The **International Fox Museum and Hall of Fame** describes some unique local history. Silver foxes were first bred in captivity in western Prince Edward Island, and for several decades Summerside was the headquarters of a virtual gold rush based on fox ranching. Some of the homes in Summerside and the surrounding area built with money from this enterprise are known as fox houses. ⊠ *33 Summer St.* ☎ *902/432–1332* ⌕ *Donation* ☉ *June–early Sept., daily 10–4.*

Eptek Art and Culture Centre, on the waterfront, has a spacious main gallery with changing Canadian-history and fine-arts exhibits, often with a strong emphasis on Prince Edward Island. In the same buildings are the 527-seat **Harbourfront Theatre** and the **PEI Sports Hall of Fame** ⊠ *130 Harbour Dr., Waterfront Properties* ☎ *902/888–8373* ☏ *902/888–8375* ⌕ *$4* ☉ *Days and hrs vary; call ahead.*

Spinnakers' Landing, a boardwalk along the water's edge, is lined with shops. The area has a good blend of shopping, history, and entertainment. The re-created lighthouse may be climbed for panoramic views of Bedeque Bay and the city. In summer, weather permitting, there's often free evening entertainment (usually at 7 PM) on the outdoor stage over the water. ⊠ *150 Harbour Dr.* ☎ *902/436–6692 or 902/888–8364* ⊕ *www.spinnakerslanding.com.*

Many descendants of the Island's early French settlers live in the Miscouche area, 10 km (6 mi) northwest of Summerside, and the **Acadian Museum** *(Musée Acadien)*, a National Historic Site, commemorates their history. There's a permanent exhibition on Acadian life as well as an audiovisual presentation depicting the history and culture of Island

Acadians. It also has a genealogical center and an Acadian gift shop. ✉ *23 Main Dr. E (Rte. 2), Miscouche* ☎ *902/432–2880* ⊕ *www.peimuseum.com* 🖃 *$4.50* ⏱ *July and Aug., daily 9:30–7; reduced hrs off-season.*

WORD OF MOUTH

"I took lots of pictures, but PEI was pretty in a way that defied my ability to photograph it. It wasn't dramatically pretty the way mountains and forests are pretty. It was all rolling green fields, acres of yellow flowers, bright blue skies, and little churches with their white steeples shining in the sun. It was those incredible red dirt roads through potato fields and woods, leading directly into the turquoise ocean. Can you tell that I liked it a lot, and I want to go back?"   —china_cat

Guided interpretive tours of the **1867 Wyatt Historic House** animate the heirlooms and stories of this restored Edwardian home of the prominent Wyatt family. The simple house was greatly embellished through the years: tours begin in the 1890s, and end in the authentic 1950s kitchen. ✉ *85 Spring St., Summerside* ☎ *902/432–1327* ⊕ *www.wyattheritage.com* 🖃 *Call for admission prices* ⏱ *June–Sept., Mon.–Sat. 10–5; Oct.–May, Tues.–Fri. by appointment.*

WHERE TO STAY & EAT

$–$$ ✕ **The Deckhouse Pub & Eatery.** Seafood is the specialty at this spot right on the historic and attractive waterfront. The menu includes beef, chicken, and lots of other dishes, so there's plenty to choose from. Dining on the deck offers a superb water view and the summer breeze. The friendly staff does their best to accommodate substitutions. The Deckhouse also hosts live musical performances. ✉ *150 Harbour Dr.* ☎ *902/436–0660* ▤ *AE, MC, V.*

$–$$ ✕ **The Home Place Inn and Restaurant.** This restaurant, which is licensed to sell alcohol, is in a home built in 1915 by local merchant Parmenus Orr. The dining room, which seats up to 45 people, has a varied menu of home cooking at its best. The panfried Malpeque oysters are not to be missed. ✉ *21 Victoria St., 13 km (8 mi) northeast of Summerside, Kensington* ☎ *902/836–5686* ▤ *MC, V* ⏱ *Closed mid-Oct.–mid-June.*

¢–$$ ✕ **Brothers Two Restaurant.** Next to the Quality Inn Garden of the Gulf, this restaurant is popular with local residents. Service is friendly and seating is in booths, at tables, and in a roofed-patio area in summer. As with most restaurants in Prince Edward Island, fish is a staple on the menu, and dishes such as fish-and-chips can be found along with more elaborate creations. The pride of the restaurant is the homemade bread served with each meal. ✉ *618 Water St.* ☎ *902/436–9654* ▤ *AE, DC, MC, V.*

$–$$$ 🏨 **Quality Inn and Suites Garden of the Gulf.** Close to the city's rich cultural attractions, this hotel has a high-ceiling courtyard with rooms on both sides. The sunlit courtyards will put you more in mind of the southern United States than eastern Canada. There is a separate lodge-style building next to the main structure; both are adjacent to the Brothers Two Restaurant. ✉ *618 Water St.* ✉ *Box 1627, Summerside C1N 2V5* ☎ *902/436–2295 or 800/265–5551* 🖶 *902/432–2911* ⊕ *www.quality-*

innpei.com ⇥*94 rooms* &*In room: refrigerator (some). In-hotel: golf course, pools, bicycles, public Wi-Fi, some pets allowed, no-smoking rooms* ⊟*AE, DC, MC, V.*

$$ ★ ⌶**Loyalist Country Inn–A Lakeview Resort.** Throughout this waterfront inn are detailed touches that create traditional elegance. The Loyalist combines the atmosphere of a country inn with the professionalism of a large hotel. In the heart of Summerside, the property overlooks the city waterfront, a yacht club, and a marina. The rear of the hotel faces the main downtown area, the former railway station, and the Confederation Trail—good for biking. The Prince William Dining Room has an innovative menu of seafood, steaks, and Island delicacies. Some rooms have whirlpool baths. Ask for one of the many light-filled rooms facing the harbor, so you can wake up to blue water, green land, and blue sky. ⊠*195 Harbour Dr., C1N 5R1* ☎*902/436–3333 or 800/361–2668* 🖷*902/436–4304* ⊕*www.lakeviewhotels.com/summerside* ⇥*100 rooms, 3 suites* &*In-hotel: restaurant, bar, pool, gym, public Wi-Fi, no-smoking rooms* ⊟*AE, DC, MC, V.*

$–$$ ⌶**Silver Fox Inn.** A fine old Victorian house and a designated historic property, this B&B houses a tearoom where homemade scones and Devonshire cream are served each afternoon. Breakfasts include homemade quiche, muffins, and croissants. If you make prior arrangements, the chef will prepare dinner. Outside, a two-tier deck provides a lovely view of the garden. Goldfish swim in ponds both in the garden and in the tearoom. ⊠*61 Granville St., Summerside C1N 2Z3* ☎*902/436–1664 or 800/565–4033* ⊕*www.silverfoxinn.net* ⇥*6 rooms* &*In-room: ethernet. In hotel: no children under 11, no-smoking rooms, Wi-Fi* ⊟*AE, MC, V* ⍟*BP.*

NIGHTLIFE & THE ARTS

The **College of Piping and Celtic Performing Arts of Canada** (⊠*619 Water St. E* ☎*902/436 5377 or 877/224–7473* ⊕*www.collegeofpiping. com*) puts on a summerlong Celtic Festival incorporating bagpiping, Highland dancing, step dancing, and fiddling. The **Harbourfront Theatre** (⊠*124 Harbour Dr.* ☎*902/432–3046 or 800/708–6505* ⊕*www. jubileetheatre.com*) celebrates the tradition and culture of the region with dramatic and musical productions year-round in the 527-seat main-stage theater. Call for information on current productions and schedule.

At **Feast Dinner Theatre** (⊠*Brothers Two Restaurant, 618 Water St.* ☎*902/888–2200*), established in 1978, musical comedy is served up with a four-course (seafood or chicken) mid-June through early September. There's a new show in the fall. From early September through late October, the new show is accompanied by a harvest buffet, including turkey, corn, pumpkin pie.

PORT HILL

35 km (22 mi) north of Miscouche on Rte. 12.

Port Hill was one of the many communities in the Tyne Valley that benefited from the shipbuilding boom of the 1800s, the era of tall-masted wooden schooners. Some beautifully restored 19th-century homes testify to the prosperity of those times.

By the mid-1840s, shipbuilder James Yeo Jr. was the most powerful businessman on the Island. His former home is here at the **Green Park Shipbuilding Museum and Yeo House.** The 19th-century mansion is topped by a cupola from which Yeo observed his nearby shipyard with a spyglass. The museum details the history of the shipbuilder's craft. Those skills are brought to life at a re-created shipyard with carpentry and blacksmithing shops. The museum has events and activities throughout the summer. ⊠ *Green Park Provincial Park, Rte. 12* ☎ *902/831–7947* ⊑ *$5* ⊙ *June, weekdays 9:30–5:30; July–Sept., daily 9:30–5:30.*

TYNE VALLEY

8 km (5 mi) south of Port Hill.

The charming community of Tyne Valley has some of the finest scenery on the Island. Watch for fisherfolk standing in flat boats wielding rakes to harvest the famous Malpeque oysters. A gentle river flows through the middle of the village, with lush green lawns and sweeping trees edging the water.

The **Tyne Valley Oyster Festival** takes place here the first week of August. This three-day event includes fiddling, step dancing, oyster shucking, a talent contest, and a community dance. The festival is a good time to sample a fried-oyster and scallop dinner. Call **Tourism PEI** (☎ *902/368– 7795 or 888/734–7529*) for dates and times.

WHERE TO STAY & EAT

¢ ✕⊞ **Doctor's Inn Bed & Breakfast.** Beautifully landscaped, this 1860s village home is a joy in summer with its garden of herbs and flowers. In winter cross-country skiers gather around the woodstove or living-room fireplace and share conversation over a warm drink. At the dining-room table, the local catch of the day is complemented by produce from the inn's own organic gardens. Dinner ($$$$) is prix fixe and available by reservation only. There are free tours of the inn's gardens. ⊠ *Rte. 167, 32 Allen Rd., Tyne Valley C0B 2C0* ☎ *902/831–3057* ⊕ *www.peisland.com/doctorsinn* ⇨ *2 rooms without bath* ⚇ *In-room: no a/c, no TV. In-hotel: restaurant, public Internet, some pets allowed, no-smoking rooms* ⊟ *MC, V* ⦿⊩ *BP.*

SHOPPING

Lennox Island has one of the largest communities in the province of Mi'Kmaq, the First Nations people who came to Malpeque Bay nearly 10,000 years ago. To get here, take Route 12 west to Route 163 and follow the road over the causeway leading to a large island projecting into Malpeque Bay. **Indian Art & Craft of North America** (⊠ *Rte. 163* ☎ *902/831–2653*) specializes in Mi'Kmaq ash-split baskets as well as pottery, jewelry, carvings, and beadwork. The shop, which sits on the edge of the water, has a screened-in porch where visitors may enjoy a complimentary cup of coffee along with the scenery. Call for hours.

O'LEARY

37 km (23 mi) northeast of Tyne Valley.

The center of Prince County is composed of a loose network of small towns; many are merely a stretch of road. In the tradition of their forebears, a majority of the local residents are engaged in farming and fishing. Farmers driving their tractors through fields of rich, red soil, and colorful lobster boats braving the seas are common scenes in this area. This region is well known for its magnificent red cliffs, majestic lighthouses, and glistening sunsets. Woodstock, north of O'Leary, has a resort where opportunities for outdoor activities abound. The town is also a good base from which to visit one of the Island's best golf courses and a rare woolen-crafts shop.

Many things in the friendly Acadian town of **Tignish** are cooperative, including the supermarket, insurance company, seafood plant, service station, and credit union. The imposing parish church of **St. Simon and St. Jude** (✉313 Church St. ☎902/882–2049) has a superb 1882 Tracker pipe organ, one of the finest such instruments in eastern Canada. The church is often used for recitals by world-renowned musicians. ✉Rte. 2; 12 km (7½ mi) north of O'Leary.

WHERE TO STAY & EAT

$–$$$ ✕⚏**Rodd Mill River—A Rodd Signature Resort.** With activities ranging from night skiing to golfing, canoeing, and kayaking, this is truly an all-season resort. One of the highlights of the resort, which is inside Mill River Provincial Park, is the Mill River Golf Course. Every table at the restaurant ($$–$$$) has a view of the course. Menu items include seafood specialties such as planked salmon and a lobster platter, plus pastas, steak, and chicken. The heated pool has a 90-foot slide. ✉Rte. 136, 5 km (3 mi) east of O'Leary, Box 399, Woodstock C0B 1V0 ☎902/859–3555 or 800/565–7633 📠902/859–2486 ⊕www.rodd vacations.com ⇆80 rooms, 10 suites ♿ In-room: dial-up. In-hotel: restaurant, bar, golf course, tennis court, pool, gym, spa, water sports, spa, bicycles public Wi-Fi, some pets allowed, no-smoking rooms ➟AE, DC, MC, V ⊗Closed Nov.–Jan. and Apr.

SPORTS & THE OUTDOORS

Among the most scenic and challenging courses in eastern Canada is the 18-hole, par-72 **Mill River Provincial Golf Course** (✉Mill River Provincial Park, Rte. 136, Woodstock ☎902/859–3920 or 800/235–8909 ⊗Closed late Oct.–early May). It is ranked among the country's top 50 courses and has been the site of several championship tournaments. Book in advance.

SHOPPING

The **MacAusland's Woollen Mill** (✉Rte. 2, Bloomfield ☎902/859–3005) has been producing famous MacAusland blankets since 1932. It's the only producer of 100% pure virgin wool blankets in Atlantic Canada.

NORTH CAPE

27 km (17 mi) north of O'Leary.

In the northwest, the Island narrows to a north-pointing arrow of land, at the tip of which is North Cape with its imposing lighthouse. At low tide, one of the longest reefs in the world gives way to tidal pools teeming with marine life. Seals often gather offshore here. The curious structures near the reef are wind turbines at the Atlantic Wind Test Site, set up on this breezy promontory to evaluate the feasibility of using wind power to generate electricity.

The **Interpretive Centre and Aquarium** has information about marine life, local history, and turbines and windmills. ⊠*End of Rte. 12* ☎*902/882–2991* ⌨*$5* ☉*July and Aug., daily 9–8; late May–June and Sept.–mid-Oct., daily 10–6.*

The **Irish Moss Interpretive Centre,** in the tiny ocean-side town of Miminegash, tells you everything you wanted to know about Irish moss, the fan-shaped red alga found in abundance on this coast and used as a thickening agent in foods and other products. "Seaweed pie," made with Irish moss, is served at the adjacent Seaweed Pie Café. ⊠*Rte. 14; 20 km (12 mi) south of North Cape* ☎*902/882–4313* ⌨*$2* ☉*Early June–Sept., daily 10–7.*

WHERE TO STAY & EAT

$$–$$$ ✕**The Boat Shop Steak & Seafood Restaurant.** An authentic renovated boat-building shop houses this restaurant with a panoramic view of the marina from its multilevel dining room and outdoor patio. The varied menu features local seafood, island beef, and island produce. ⊠*296 Harbourview Dr. (Rte. 152), 33 km (21 mi) south of North Cape, Northport* ☎*902/853–4510* ▭*MC, V* ☉*Closed Oct.–May.*

$–$$$ ✕**Wind & Reef Restaurant.** This restaurant serves good seafood, such as Island clams, mussels, and lobster, as well as steaks, prime rib, and chicken. There's a fine view of the Gulf of St. Lawrence and the Northumberland Strait. ⊠*End of Rte. 12, North Cape* ☎*902/882–3535* ▭*MC, V* ☉*Closed Oct.–May.*

$ ⬚**Tignish Heritage Inn.**Originally built as a convent in 1868, this large inn is close to North Cape, Mile 0 of the Confederation Trail, and the facilities offered in the town of Tignish. Rooms range in size from cozy to spacious, and all have wooden headboards. Each room has a view of the grounds, which include a quiet pathway weaving through tall maple trees. Some of the bathrooms have cast-iron, claw-foot tubs. The peaceful gardens are dotted with a gazebo, a fountain, and lovely flowers. ⊠*Maple St. behind St. Simon and St. Jude Church, Box 398, Tignish C0B 2B0* ☎*902/882–2491 or 877/882–2491* 🖷*902/882–2500* ⊕*www.tignish.com/heritageinn* ⌁*17 rooms, 1 suite* ⌂*In-room: no a/c. In-hotel: laundry facilities, public Wi-Fi, no-smoking rooms* ▭*AE, DC, MC, V* ☉*Closed mid-Oct.–mid-May, except for groups by reservation only* �‖CP.

WEST POINT

35 km (22 mi) south of Miminegash.

At the southern tip of the western shore, West Point has a tiny fishing harbor, campsites, and a supervised beach.

Fodor'sChoice
★ **West Point Lighthouse,** built in 1875, is the tallest lighthouse on the Island. When it was automated, the community took over the building and converted it into an inn and museum, with a moderately priced restaurant. The lighthouse is open daily, late May through late September, from 9 to 9; Admission is $2.50. Don't miss the sunsets here.

North Cape Coastal Drive meanders from West Point back to Summerside through the **Région Évangéline,** the Island's main Acadian district. At **Cap-Egmont** (✉ *72 km [45 mi] east of West Point*) stop for a look at the Bottle Houses, two tiny houses and a chapel built by a retired carpenter entirely out of glass bottles—more than 25,000 of them—mortared together like bricks. The chapel even has pews made from glass.

WHERE TO STAY & EAT

$–$$
Fodor'sChoice
★ ✕▦ **West Point Lighthouse.** Few people can say they've actually spent the night in a lighthouse, but here's your chance to do just that. This one was first lit in 1876. Rooms, most with ocean views, are pleasantly furnished with local antiques and cheerful handmade quilts. You can enjoy clam digging, a favorite local pastime, or perhaps try finding the buried treasure reputed to be hidden nearby. The restaurant ($–$$$) serves fresh lobster, scallops, mussels, chowder, and other seafood. Climb the 72 steps to the top of the lighthouse museum for a spectacular view of the Northumberland Strait. Make your reservations early. ✉*Rte. 14* 🕿*O'Leary R.R. 2, C0B 1V0* 🕿*902/859-3605 or 800/764-6854* 🖷*902/859-1510* ⊕*www.westpointlighthouse.com* ⇗*10 rooms* ⚭*In-hotel: restaurant, beachfront, no-smoking rooms* ▤*AE, DC, MC, V* ☽*Closed Oct.–May.*

PRINCE EDWARD ISLAND ESSENTIALS

To research prices, get advice from other travelers, and book travel arrangements, visit www.fodors.com.

TRANSPORTATION

BY AIR

Air Canada and its regional carriers offer daily nonstop service from Charlottetown to Halifax and Toronto, both of which have connections to the rest of Canada, the United States, and beyond. WestJet offers summer service to Toronto. Northwest flies directly from Detroit to Charlottetown during the summer season. Delta flies direct from Boston. Sunwing flies in from Toronto. Prince Edward Air is available for private charters.

Charlottetown Airport is 5 km (3 mi) north of town.

Contacts **Charlottetown Airport** (☎ *902/566–7997*).**Prince Edward Air** (☎ *902/566–4488* ⊕ *www.peair.com*). **Sunwing** (☎ *800/761–1711* ⊕ *www. sunwing.ca*).

BY BOAT & FERRY

Northumberland Ferries sails between Wood Islands and Caribou, Nova Scotia, from May to mid-December. The crossing takes about 75 minutes, and the round-trip costs approximately $60 per vehicle, $80 for a recreational vehicle; foot passengers pay $14 (you pay only when leaving the Island). A fuel surcharge is added. Ask about this when booking. There are 18 crossings per day in summer.

Contacts **Northumberland Ferries** (☎ *888/249–7245* ⊕ *www.nfl-bay.com*).

BY CAR

The 13-km-long (8-mi-long) Confederation Bridge connects Cape Jourimain, in New Brunswick, with Borden-Carleton, Prince Edward Island. The crossing takes about 12 minutes. The toll is about $41 per car, $47 for a recreational vehicle; it's collected when you leave the Island. The lack of public transportation on the Island makes having your own vehicle almost a necessity. There are more than 3,700 km (2,300 mi) of paved road in the province, including the three scenic coastal drives: North Cape Coastal Drive, Blue Heron Drive, and Points East Coastal Drive. A helpful highway map of the province is available from Tourism PEI and at visitor centers on the Island.

Designated Heritage Roads are surfaced with red clay, the local soil base. The unpaved roads meander through rural and undeveloped areas, where you're likely to see lots of wildflowers and birds. A four-wheel-drive vehicle is not necessary, but in spring and inclement weather the mud can get quite deep and the narrow roads become impassable. Keep an eye open for bicycles, motorcycles, and pedestrians.

Contacts **Tourism PEI** (☎ *888/734–7529 or 902/368–4444*).

CONTACTS & RESOURCES

EMERGENCIES

Emergency Services **Ambulance, fire, police** (☏ *911 or 0*).

Hospitals Prince County Hospital (✉ *65 Roy Boates Ave., Summerside* ☏ *902/438–4200*). **Queen Elizabeth Hospital** (✉ *60 Riverside Dr., Charlottetown* ☏ *902/894–2200 or 902/894–2095*).

SPORTS & THE OUTDOORS

BICYCLING   The Island is popular with bicyclists for its moderately hilly roads and stunning scenery, yet there are plenty of level areas, especially west of Summerside to Tignish and along the north shore. A 9-km (5½-mi) path near Cavendish Campground loops around marsh, woods, and farmland. The Confederation Trail allows people to cycle from one end of the Island to the other. Shoulderless, narrow secondary roads in some areas and summer car traffic can be challenging. Several tour companies rent bicycles and provide custom-made tours. Trailside Adventures in Mt. Stewart provides five suggested tours with maps (2 to 52 km [1 to 32 mi]) and will make suggestions for longer trips. A two-sided map and information sheet is available from Tourism PEI.

Contacts Tourism PEI (☏ *800/463–4734 or 902/368–4444*). **Trailside Adventures** (☏ *888/704–6595* ⊕ *www.trailside.ca*).

FISHING   Deep-sea fishing boats are available along the eastern end of the Island as well as in the north-shore region. Although some boats can be chartered for fishing bluefin tuna, most operators offer excursions to fish for mackerel. Freshwater sportfishing for trout or salmon is also an option. A nonresident three-day fishing license is the shortest one you can get. It costs $27. The season license costs $40. They can be purchased at many businesses (hardware, tackle, convenience stores) throughout Prince Edward Island. A few operations rent fishing tackle and offer "no license required" fishing on private ponds. The Government of Prince Edward Island Web site lists businesses that sell fishing licenses.

Contacts Government of Prince Edward Island (⊕ *www.gov.pe.ca/egovernment*).

GOLF   More than two dozen 9- and 18-hole courses are open to the public. Several of the more beautiful ones have scenic ocean vistas, and almost all have hassle-free golfing, with easily booked tee times, inexpensive rates, and uncrowded courses, particularly in fall. For a publication listing golf courses in Prince Edward Island, and to book online, contact Tourism PEI. Most courses may be booked directly or by contacting Golf PEI.

Contacts Golf PEI (☏ *866/465-3734* ⊕ *www.golfpei.com*). **Tourism PEI** (☏ *800/463–4734 or 902/368–4444 information, 800/235–8909 booking* ⊕ *www. golflinkspei.com*).

SEA KAYAKING   With its quiet coves and cozy bays, Prince Edward Island has become a haven for those who enjoy sea kayaking. Outside Expeditions provides rentals and tours designed for all levels of expertise.

Contacts Outside Expeditions (☎ *902/963–3366 or 800/207–3899* ⊕ *www. getoutside.com*).

SHOPPING For information on crafts outlets around Prince Edward Island, contact the Prince Edward Island Crafts Council.

Contacts Prince Edward Island Crafts Council (☎ *902/892–5152*).

TOURS

The Island has about 20 sightseeing tours, including double-decker bus tours, taxi tours, cycling tours, harbor cruises, and walking tours. Most tour companies are based in Charlottetown and offer excursions around the city and to the beaches.

DRIVING TOURS Yellow Cab can be booked for tours by the hour or day.

Contacts Yellow Cab (☎ *902/892–6561*).

WALKING TOURS Island Nature Trust sells a nature-trail map of the Island. Tourism PEI has maps of the 350-km (217-mi) multiuse Confederation Trail.

Contacts Island Nature Trust (☎ *902/892–7513* ⊕ *www.islandnaturetrust.ca*). Tourism PEI (☎ *800/463–4734 or 902/368–4444* 🖷 *902/566–4336* ⊕ *www. peiplay.com*).

VISITOR INFORMATION

Tourism PEI publishes an informative annual guide for visitors and maintains eight visitor information centers (VICs) on the Island. It also produces a map of the 350-km (217-mi) Confederation Trail. The main visitor information center is in Charlottetown and is open early-May to October daily and November to mid-May weekdays.

Contacts Tourism PEI (☎ *800/463–4734 or 902/368–4444* 🖷 *902/368–6613* ⊕ *www.peiplay.com*). Visitor Information Center (☎ *902/888–8364 in summer*).

Newfoundland
& Labrador

A humpback whale

WORD OF MOUTH

"Coastal Newfoundland has its charms in all seasons but for whales and puffins late June through mid August is the best time."

—gannetmusic

WELCOME TO NEWFOUNDLAND & LABRADOR

TOP REASONS TO GO

★ **The rugged beauty:** Magnificent mountains, sweeping vistas, wooden houses perched on rocky seacliffs, hidden fjords, and the deep blue sea. It's breathtaking.

★ **The people:** You'll never get lost here, because the people go out of their way to help visitors. They are the nicest and friendliest folks you're likely to ever meet.

★ **Wildlife:** Whales, puffins, caribou, and moose. Bird sanctuaries and ecological reserves. Thirty-three million seabirds can't be wrong.

★ **The culture:** Let us entertain you with our storytelling, Irish music, plays, festivals, writers and comedians.

★ **Amazing fish dishes:** Crab cakes, seafood chowder, lobster, shrimp, and cod, cod, cod: au gratin, pan-fried, or in the traditional Newfoundland dish of fish and brewis.

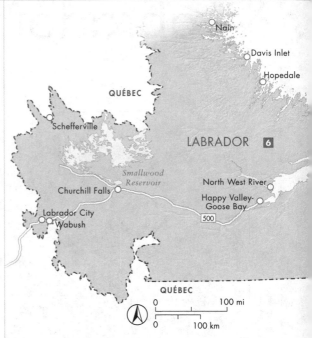

1 St. John's. The capital of Newfoundland is usually the starting point for visits to the province.

2 Avalon Peninsula. This picturesque region is home to about half of Newfoundland's population. Cape Spear National Historic Site is the furthest east point in North America.

3 Eastern Newfoundland. The Bonavista Peninsula has history and archaeological artifacts; the Burin Peninsula is more about stark landscapes. Clarenville, halfway between the two is a good base for exploring, though not much of destination in itself. Terra Nova Park was Newfoundland's first National Park.

4 Gander and around. Gander is known for its airport and aviation history; it's a good base for exploring fishing villages like Twillingate.

White-tailed Buck

5 **Western Newfoundland.** The wild and rugged Great North Peninsula is home to two Unesco World Heritage Sites (Gros Morne National Park and L'Anse aux Meadows), and the west coast is famed for its Atlantic salmon fishing, mountain ranges, winter sports, and the second largest city in the province, Corner Brook.

6 **Labrador.** This is "the big land," with towering mountains and a vast supply of rivers and lakes. The Northern Lights dance in the wide open sky.

GETTING ORIENTED

The province includes the island of Newfoundland and Labrador, which is on the mainland, bordering Québec. Most airlines fly in to the provincial capital on St. John's, on the Avalon Peninsula, making this the logical starting point for vistors to the island of Newfoundland. Moving clockwise around the perimeter of the peninsula, you traverse the Cape Shore. Farther west, on the main island, is the Burin Peninsula, and to the north, the Bonavista Peninsula and Notre Dame Bay. On the west side of Newfoundland, the Great Northern Peninsula stretches up toward Labrador; Corner Brook, the second-largest city, is a good starting point for exploring the mountains. You'll do much of your driving on Route 1, the Trans-Canada Highway.

NEWFOUNDLAND & LABRADOR PLANNER

Getting Around

A leisurely drive around the province is the best way to absorb its culture and beauty. Most tourists fly in to St. John's; major car-rental agencies have kiosks at the airport. Newfoundland has become a popular tourist destination, so you book at least your first night's accommodation and your car rental in advance. If you don't have a car, St. John's has Metrobus for travel in the capital city region, and DRL Coachlines travels across the island from St. John's to Port aux Basques, stopping at major towns on Route 1 (also known as the Trans-Canada Highway). Ferry services connect to Labrador as well as to Nova Scotia, and smaller ferries run to smaller island communities around the coast.

Making the Most of Your Time

On the far east coast of Canada, the province of Newfoundland and Labrador, as it is officially called, is a bit of a contradiction in terms: it's the youngest province—it joined the Confederation in 1949—but its timeline stretches back to AD 1000, when Vikings made first landfall on the Great Northern Peninsula. You won't meet Vikings today, but you can certainly soak up hundreds of years of history by walking around downtown St. John's. Take a stroll up Water Street, the oldest street in North America. Imagine a time when pirates like Blackbeard sailed around these shores and often made stops to get supplies and have a drink at the first pub in North America.

Across the island on the Great Northern Peninsula you won't want to miss the glacier-carved fjords and magnificent mountains at Gros Morne National Park, a UNESCO World Heritage Site. Take a boat tour, do a hike, and visit the Intrepretation Centre.

Farther up the Peninsula at L'Anse aux Meadows National Historic Park, another UNESCO World Heritage Site, visit the only authenticated Viking settlement in North America. Sit inside the Norse Longhouses and tale a look across the Labrador Strait.

Farther north, at St. Barbe, you can catch the ferry to Québec on the mainland and then drive a short distance to Labrador, which begins at The Straits. Moving west, make your way through some of the wildest parts of the country and finally to the twin towns of Labrador City and Wabush, combine natural phenomena, wilderness adventure, history, and culture.

A Unique Time

Newfoundland and The Straits in southeastern Labrador have their own time zone: Newfoundland standard time, a half hour ahead of the rest of Labrador and the other Atlantic Canada provinces. When time zones were established, the Dominion of Newfoundland was an independent country with its own time zone. The government tried to make the province conform to Atlantic Standard time in 1963, but the measure was quashed by public outcry.

Packing Tips

It's all about the layers in Newfoundland. You'll need shorts and short-sleeve shirts for when it's warm and sunny. Pack a fleece jacket or a hoodie in case the temperature drops. The next piece of clothing might be the most important: a windbreaker. You will need that to keep the chill out when the winds are up. To top off your ensemble, you'll need raingear, like a slicker. Throw in a pair of gloves. May the sun shine on your holidays, but if it doesn't, you'll be dressed for it.

Moose Warning

Newfoundland is home to more than 110,000 moose, and most highways run through their habitat. If possible, avoid night driving, as most moose-related vehicle accidents happen between dusk and dawn. Watch for vehicles that slow down or stop on the sides of roads: drivers may have spotted a moose. And pay attention to those caution signs, which are placed in areas where moose are known to cross frequently.

Dining & Lodging

Stay at least one night in a bed-and-breakfast. You'll get a chance to experience Newfoundland's world-renowned hospitality. All you may want is a place to lay down your head, you probably leave feeling like family. You'll also be treated to a wonderful home-cooked breakfast.

Seafood is an excellent value in Newfoundland and Labrador. Cod can be found panfried, baked, or poached; cold-water shrimp, snow crab, and lobster are also good choices. Many restaurants offer seasonal specialties with a wide variety of traditional wild and cultured species, such as steelhead trout, salmon, mussels, and sea scallops.

What It Costs In Canadian Dollars

	¢	$	$$	$$$	$$$$
Restaurants	under C$8	C$8–C$12	C$13–C$20	C$21–C$30	over C$30
Hotels	under C$75	C$75–C$125	C$126–C$175	C$176–C$250	over C$250

Restaurant prices are per person for a main course at dinner. Hotel prices are for two people in a standard double room in high season.

Festivals

Newfoundlanders love a party, and from the cities to the smallest towns they celebrate their history and unique culture with festivals and events throughout the summer. "Soirees" and "times"—big parties and small parties—offer a combination of traditional music, recitation, comedy, and local food, sometimes in a dinner-theater setting.

When to Go

Seasons vary dramatically in Newfoundland and Labrador. Most tourists visit between June and September, when the bogs and meadows turn into a colorful riot of wildflowers and greenery and the province is alive with festivals, fairs, concerts, and shows. Temperatures hover between 24°C (75°F) and 29°C (85°F). In spring, icebergs float down from the north, and in late spring, fin, pilot, minke, and humpback whales arrive to hunt for food along the coast, staying until August. Fall is also popular: the weather is usually fine, hills and meadows are loaded with berries, and the woods are alive with moose, caribou, partridges, and rabbits. In winter, ski hills attract downhillers and snowboarders; forest trails hum with snowmobiles and all-terrain vehicles taking anglers to lodges and lakes; and cross-country ski trails in provincial and national parks are oases of quiet.

4

Updated by
Wanita Bates

CANADA STARTS HERE, FROM THE east, on the island of Newfoundland in the North Atlantic. Known as Mile One, the province's capital of St. John's is North America's most easterly point and its oldest city. The province also includes Labrador to the northwest, on the mainland bordering Québec. Along Newfoundland and Labrador's nearly 17,699 km (11,000 mi) of coastline, humpback whales feed near shore, millions of seabirds nest, and 10,000-year-old icebergs drift by fishing villages.

The first European settlement in North America was established in Newfoundland with the arrival of Vikings from Iceland and Greenland more than 1,000 years ago. Vikings assembled a sod hut village at what is now a National Historic Site at L'Anse aux Meadows, calling their new home Vinland. They stayed less than 10 years and then disappeared into the mists of history for centuries. The site was discovered in the 1960s.

Early as they were, the Vikings were preceded by people who lived in the region 9,000 years ago, as the glaciers melted. A 7,500-year-old burial ground in southern Labrador is the oldest-known cemetery in North America. When explorer John Cabot arrived at Bonavista from England in 1497, he reported an ocean so full of fish they could be caught in a basket lowered over the side of a boat. Within a decade, St. John's had become a crowded harbor. Soon, fishing boats from France, England, Spain, and Portugal vied for a chance to catch Newfoundland's lucrative cod, which would shape the province's history.

At one time, 700 outports dotted Newfoundland's coast, devoted to the world's most plentiful fish. Today, only about 400 of these settlements survive. By 1992, cod had become so scarce from overfishing that the federal government called a moratorium, throwing thousands out of work. The cod have not yet returned, forcing generations of people to retrain for other industries or leave. The fishing industry has since diversified into other species, mainly crab. The development of one of the world's richest and largest nickel deposits at Voisey's Bay in northern Labrador, near Nain, holds hope for new prosperity, as does the growing offshore oil and gas industry.

In 1949, Newfoundland and Labrador joined the Canadian Confederation. Despite more than 50 years as a Canadian province, the people are still independent and maintain a unique language and lifestyle. Whether Confederation was a good move is still a matter of great debate. E. Annie Proulx's Pulitzer Prize–winning novel *The Shipping News* brought the province to the attention of the world. Now Newfoundland writers such as Wayne Johnston (*The Colony of Unrequited Dreams, The Navigator of New York*), Michael Crummey (*River of Thieves*), and Lisa Moore (*Open*) are bringing the province to an international audience.

Visitors find themselves straddling the centuries. Old Irish, French, and English accents and customs still exist in small towns and outports despite television and the Internet. The cities of St. John's in the east and Corner Brook to the west are very much part of the 21st century.

Wherever you travel in the province, you're sure to meet some of the warmest, wittiest people in North America. Strangers have always been welcome in Newfoundland. Your first task is to master the name of the island portion of the province—it's New-fund-*land,* and it rhymes with understand.

The effects of globalization and the changing economy are eroding the old dialects as young people leave for larger cities. Still, it's these same young people who are devoted fans of the Newfoundland band Great Big Sea and other modern exponents of traditional music breaking into the international market.

ST. JOHN'S, NEWFOUNDLAND

4

When Sir Humphrey Gilbert sailed into St. John's to establish British colonial rule for Queen Elizabeth in 1583, he found Spanish, French, and Portuguese fishermen working the harbor, all fighting for a spot in Newfoundland's lucrative cod fishery. For centuries, Newfoundland was the largest supplier of salt cod in the world, and St. John's Harbour was the center of the trade. As early as 1627, the merchants of Water Street—then known as the Lower Path—were doing a thriving business buying fish, selling goods, and supplying alcohol to soldiers and sailors.

Today, old meets new in the province's capital (population 100,646). Modern office buildings are surrounded by heritage shops and colorful row houses. St. John's mixes English and Irish influences, Victorian architecture and modern convenience, and traditional music and rock and roll into a heady brew. The arts scene is lively, but overall the city has a relaxed pace.

EXPLORING ST. JOHN'S

The city encircles St. John's Harbour, expanding past the hilly, narrow streets of old St. John's. Downtown has the most history and character. The city was destroyed by fire many times. Much of the row housing dates back to the last major blaze, known as the Great Fire, in 1892. Heritage houses on Waterford Bridge Road, winding west from the harbor along the Waterford River, and Rennies Mill Road and Circular Road to the east (backing onto Bannerman Park), were originally the homes of sea captains and merchants. Duckworth Street and Water Street, running parallel to the harbor, are where you find the shops and restaurants, but duck down the narrow lanes and paths as you get farther from the harbor to get the best sense of the city's history. A walk downtown takes in many historic buildings, but a car is needed to explore some farther-flung sights.

SIGHTS TO SEE

🔟 **Anglican Cathedral of St. John the Baptist.** A fine example of Gothic Revival architecture designed by Sir George Gilbert Scott, this church was first completed in the mid-1800s; it was rebuilt after the 1892 fire. Every

GREAT ITINERARIES

IF YOU HAVE 3 DAYS
Pick either the west or east coast of Newfoundland. On the west coast, after arriving by ferry at **Port aux Basques**, drive through the Codroy Valley, heading north to **Gros Morne National Park** and its fjords, and overnight in nearby Rocky Harbour or Woody Point. The next day, visit **L'Anse aux Meadows National Historic Site**, where the Vikings built a village a thousand years ago; there are reconstructions of the dwellings. Spend the night in **St. Anthony** or nearby.

On the east coast, the ferry docks at Argentia. Explore the Avalon Peninsula, beginning in **St. John's**, where you should spend your first night. The next day visit **Cape Spear**, the most easterly point in North America, and the **Witless Bay Ecological Reserve**, where you can see whales, seabirds, and icebergs. Drive through **Placentia** and spend your third day at **Cape St. Mary's Ecological Reserve**, known for its gannets and dramatic coastal scenery.

IF YOU HAVE 6 DAYS
On Newfoundland's west coast, add southern Labrador to your trip. A ferry takes you from St. Barbe to Blanc Sablon on the Québec-Labrador border. Drive 96 km (60 mi) to **Red Bay** to explore the remains of a 17th-century Basque whaling station; then head to **L'Anse Amour** to see Canada's second-tallest lighthouse. Overnight at **L'Anse au Clair**. Return

through Gros Morne National Park and explore **Corner Brook**, where you should stay overnight. The next day, travel west of **Stephenville** to explore the Port au Port Peninsula, home of Newfoundland's French-speaking population.

On the east coast add **Trinity** to your must-see list, and spend the night there or in **Clarenville**. The north shore of Conception Bay is home to many picturesque villages, including **Cupids** and **Harbour Grace**. Several half-day, full-day, and two-day excursions are possible from St. John's, and in each direction a different personality of the region unfolds.

IF YOU HAVE 9 DAYS
In addition to the places already mentioned on the west coast, take a drive into central Newfoundland and visit the lovely villages of Notre Dame Bay. Overnight in **Twillingate**. Catch a ferry to **Fogo** or the **Change Islands**. Accommodations are available on both islands, but book ahead.

On the east coast add the Burin Peninsula and a trip to France—yes, France—to your itinerary. You can reach the French territory of **St-Pierre and Miquelon** by passenger ferry from Fortune. Explore romantic **Grand Bank**, named for the famous fishing area just offshore, and climb Cook's Lookout in **Burin**, where Captain James Cook kept watch for smugglers from St-Pierre.

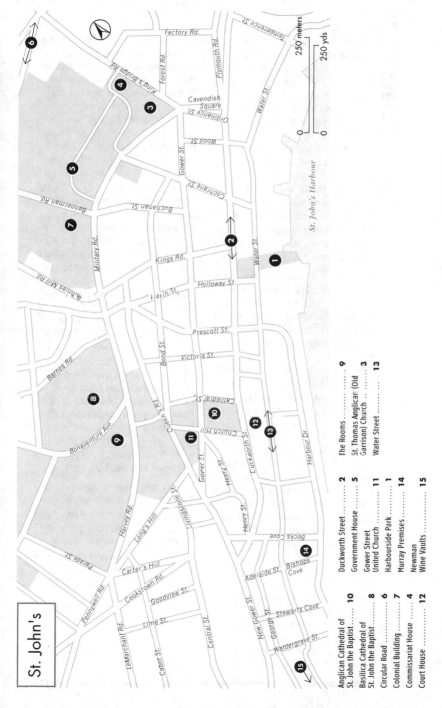

St. John's

Anglican Cathedral of
St. John the Baptist **10**
Basilica Cathedral of
St. John the Baptist **8**
Circular Road **6**
Colonial Building **7**
Commissariat House **4**
Court House **12**

Duckworth Street **2**
Government House **5**
Gower Street
United Church **11**
Harbourside Park **1**
Murray Premises **14**
Newman
Wine Vaults **15**

The Rooms **9**
St. Thomas Anglican (Old
Garrison) Church **3**
Water Street **13**

St. John's Harbour

250 meters
250 yds

A Good Walk

Begin at **Harbourside Park** ❶ on Water Street, where Gilbert planted the staff of England and claimed Newfoundland. When you leave, turn left on Water Street, right on Holloway Street, and then right onto **Duckworth Street** ❷. The east end of this street is full of crafts shops and other stores. After walking east for five blocks, turn left onto Ordnance Street, just one of several streets that recall St. John's military past. Cross Military Road to **St. Thomas Anglican (Old Garrison) Church** ❸, built in the 1830s as a place of worship for British soldiers.

Turn left as you leave St. Thomas and walk up King's Bridge Road. The first building on the left is **Commissariat House** ❹, an officer's house restored to the style of the 1830s and one of the oldest buildings in the province. North of Commissariat House, a shady lane on the left leads to the gardens of **Government House** ❺. **Circular Road** ❻, where the business elite moved after a fire destroyed much of the town in 1846, is across from the gardens in front of the house. Back on Military Road, cross Bannerman Road to the **Colonial Building** ❼, the former seat of government. Walk west on Military Road until it becomes Harvey Road. The Roman Catholic **Basilica Cathedral of St. John the Baptist** ❽, finished in 1855, is on the right; you pass the Basilica Museum in the Bishop's Palace just before you get there. Cross Bonaventure Avenue as you leave the Basilica to visit **The Rooms** ❾, the province's one-stop shopping for arts, culture, and heritage. The Rooms is the home of the provincial archives, museum, and art gallery.

Cross Harvey Road as you leave the Rooms and turn right down Garrison Hill, so named because it once led to Fort Townshend, now home to fire and police stations. Cross Queen's Road and walk down Cathedral Street to Gower Street and the Gothic Revival **Anglican Cathedral of St. John the Baptist** ❿. The entrance is on the west side on Church Hill. **Gower Street United Church** ⓫ is directly across from the cathedral on the west side of Church Hill. Continue to the bottom of Church Hill to see the Duckworth Street **Court House** ⓬, with its four turrets, each one different. Exit the courthouse and turn right; then go down the long set of steps to **Water Street** ⓭, one of the oldest commercial streets in North America. Turn right on Water Street to reach the **Murray Premises** ⓮, a restored mercantile complex with boutiques, a science center, offices, restaurants, a coffee bar, and a wine cellar. Exit Murray Premises and continue left on Water Street to the last stop, the historic **Newman Wine Vaults** ⓯, at 436 Water Street just west of the corner of Water and Springdale streets, where for 200 years the legendary Newman's Port has been aged.

TIMING: Downtown St. John's is compact but hilly. The walk avoids major uphill climbs. Expect to spend up to a full day visiting these sights, depending on how long you stay at each location and the number of stores you take in along the way. This walk is best undertaken from spring to fall.

Wednesday, there's a free lunchtime organ recital from 1:15 to 1:45. Women of the parish operate a tearoom in the crypt 2:30 to 4:30 daily in July and August, from 2 PM on Wednesday. Drop down for a cuppa with homemade scones, tea biscuits, and cookies ($8). ⊠ *22 Church Hill* ☎ *709/726–5677* ⊕ *www.infonet. st-johns.nf.ca/cathedral* ⊠ *Free* ⊙ *Tours June–Sept., weekdays 10–noon, 2–4; Sat. 10–noon; Sun., after 11 service.*

HOW'S THE WEATHER?

This rocky island perched on the edge of the cold North Atlantic Ocean might be the only place in the world where you can have four seasons in one day and where the saying "If you don't like the weather out your front door go look out the back door," rings true. St. John's is a weather champion in Canada. It holds the distinctions of being the foggiest, snowiest, wettest, windiest, and cloudiest of all major Canadian cities.

8 Basilica Cathedral of St. John the Baptist. This 1855 Roman Catholic cathedral in the Romanesque style has a commanding position above Military Road, overlooking the older section of the city and the harbor. A museum with vestments and religious objects is next door in the Bishop's Palace. ⊠ *200 Military Rd.* ☎ *709/726–3660* ⊕ *www.stjohnsarchdiocese.nf.ca* ⊠ *Museum $2* ⊙ *Museum June–mid-Sept., Mon.–Sat. 10–4, Sun. 11–4.*

6 Circular Road. After the devastating fire of 1846, the business elite of St. John's moved to Circular Road. The street contains some very fine Victorian houses and shade trees.

7 Colonial Building. This columned building (erected 1847–50) was the seat of the Newfoundland government from the 1850s until 1960, when the legislature moved to its current home, the Confederation Building, in the north end of the city. The limestone for the building was imported from Cork, Ireland. ⊠ *Military and Bannerman Rds.*

4 Commissariat House. The residence and office of the British garrison's supply officer in the 1830s has been restored to reflect that era. Interpreters dress in period costume. ⊠ *King's Bridge Rd.* ☎ *709/729–6730* or *709/729–0592* ⊕ *www.tcr.gov.nl.ca/tcr/historicsites* ⊠ *$3* ⊙ *Mid-May–Sept., daily 10–5:30.*

12 Court House. The late-19th-century courthouse has an eccentric appearance: each of its four turrets is a different style. ⊠ *Duckworth St. at bottom of Church Hill.*

2 Duckworth Street. Once called the Upper Path, this has been St. John's "second street" for centuries. (Water Street is the main street.) Stretching from the bottom of Signal Hill in the east to near City Hall in the west, Duckworth Street has restaurants, bars, antiques and crafts shops, and lawyers' offices. Lanes and stairways lead off the street down to Water Street and up to higher elevations.

5 Government House. This is the residence of the lieutenant governor, the queen's representative in Newfoundland. Myth has it that the moat around Government House was designed to keep out snakes, though Newfoundland is one of a handful of regions in the world (along with

Ireland and New Zealand) that does not have snakes. The house, so the story goes, was originally intended for the governor of a warmer colony, where serpents might be a problem. In fact, the moat was actually designed to allow more light into the basement rooms. Built in the 1830s, the house is not open for tours, but it has a marvelous garden you can explore. ⊠ *Military Rd.* ☎ *709/729–4494* ⊕ *www.mun.ca/ govhouse* 🈺 *Free* ☉ *Garden daily dawn–dusk.*

⑪ Gower Street United Church. This 1896 church has a redbrick facade, green turrets, 50 stained-glass windows, and a massive pipe organ. ⊠ *99 Gower St., at Queen's Rd.* ☎ *709/753–7286* ⊕ *www.gowerunited.ca* 🈺 *Free* ☉ *Sept.–May, weekdays 9–3; July and Aug., weekdays 9–12; tours available year-round during office hours.*

① Harbourside Park. Here Sir Humphrey Gilbert claimed Newfoundland for Britain in 1583, much to the amusement of the French, Spanish, and Portuguese fishermen in port at the time. They thought him a fool, a judgment borne out a few days later when he ran his ship aground and drowned. The small park is a good vantage point to watch the boats come and go and rest from your walk, but the larger parks have more green space and are better for picnics. This area, known as the Queen's Wharf, is where the harbor-pilot boat is docked. ⊠ *Water St. E.*

⑭ Murray Premises. One of the oldest buildings in St. John's, the Murray Premises dates from only 1846, because the city was destroyed many times by fire; the last and worst fire was in 1892. This restored warehouse now houses shops, offices, and restaurants. The **Newfoundland Science Centre** (☎ *709/754–0823*), open daily, with hands-on exhibits and special demonstrations, is within the Murray Premises. ⊠ *Water St. and Harbour Dr., at Beck's Cove* ☎ *709/754–0823* ⊕ *www.nlsciencecentre. com* 🈺 *$6* ☉ *Weekdays 10–5, Sat. 10–6, Sun. noon–6.*

⑮ Newman Wine Vaults. This 200-year-old building with stone barrel vaults is where the renowned Newman's Port was aged. According to legend, a Newman and Company vessel loaded with port wine was driven off course by pirates in 1679 and forced to winter in St. John's. Upon return to London, her cargo was found to have improved in flavor and the historic wine vaults on an island in the North Atlantic were built. The vaults are now a provincial historic site with guides who interpret the province's long and unique association with port. You can purchase more than 20 different brands of port on-site. ⊠ *436 Water St.* ☎ *709/739–7870* ⊕ *www.historictrust.com* 🈺 *Donations accepted* ☉ *June–Aug., daily 10–4:30 or by appointment.*

⑨ The Rooms. Provincial archives, a museum, and an art gallery are encom-

Fodor's Choice ★ passed in The Rooms, which opened in 2005. The design was inspired by traditional "fishing rooms," tracts of land by the waterside where fishing activities took place, and the views of St. John's from the third and fourth levels of this industrially designed building over the Narrows are awe inspiring. The two floors of galleries hold a collection of more than 7,000 contemporary works of art. A fourth-floor restaurant serves ($–$$) fabulous seafood dishes like crab cakes and chowder and desserts like Newfoundland Berry Cobbler and Sticky Toffee Pudding with Crème Anglaise. ✉*9 Bonaventure Ave.* ☎*709/757–8000* 💲*$5, free Wed. 6–9 PM and first Sat. of each month; special exhibits $12* 🕐*June–mid-Oct., Mon., Tues., Fri., and Sat. 10–5, Wed. and Thurs. 10–9, Sun. noon–5; mid-Oct.–May, Tues., Fri., and Sat. 10–5, Wed. and Thurs. 10–9, Sun. noon–5. Archives closed Sun.*

❸ St. Thomas Anglican (Old Garrison) Church. English soldiers used to worship at this black wooden church, the oldest in the city, during the early and mid-1800s. ✉*8 Military Rd.* ☎*709/576–6632* 💲*Free* 🕐*Late June–Aug., daily 9:30–5:30; call for off-season hrs.*

⓭ Water Street. Originally called the Lower Path, Water Street has been the site of businesses since at least the 1620s. The older architecture resembles that of seaports in southwest England and Ireland.

GREATER ST. JOHN'S

A number of must-see attractions can be found a short drive from the downtown core. When you stand with your back to the ocean at Cape Spear National Historic Site—the easternmost point of North America—the entire population is to the west of you. Cape Spear and the historic Signal Hill National Historic Site are excellent places to see icebergs and whales in spring and early summer. Plan to spend a full day exploring Greater St. John's to give yourself some time at each spot.

SIGHTS TO SEE

The Battery. This tiny fishing village perches precariously at the base of steep cliffs between Signal Hill and St. John's Harbour. Narrow lanes snake around the houses, which empty directly onto the street, making this a good place to get out and walk.

Bowring Park. An expansive Victorian park west of downtown, Bowring resembles the famous city parks of London, after which it was modeled. Dotting the grounds are ponds and rustic bridges; the statue of Peter Pan just inside the east gate was cast from the same mold as the one in Kensington Park in London. The wealthy Bowring family donated the park to the city in 1911. ✉*Waterford Bridge Rd.* ☎*709/576–6134* 💲*Free* 🕐*Daily dawn–dusk.*

Cabot Tower. This tower at the summit of Signal Hill was constructed in 1897 to commemorate the 400th anniversary of Cabot's landing in Newfoundland. The ride here along Signal Hill Road affords fine harbor, ocean, and city views, as does the tower. Guides lead tours in summer. ✉*Signal Hill Rd.* ☎*709/772–5367* ⊕*www.pc.gc.ca* 💲*Free* 🕐*Apr,–Dec., daily 9–5; mid-May–Labor Day, daily 8:30 AM–9 PM.*

★ Cape Spear National Historic Site. At the easternmost point of land on the continent, songbirds begin chirping in the dim light of dawn, and whales (in early summer) feed directly below the cliffs, providing an unforgettable start to the day. From April through July, you may see icebergs floating by. **Cape Spear Lighthouse,** Newfoundland's oldest such beacon, has been lovingly restored to its original form and furnishings. ✉*Rte. 11* ☎*709/772–5367* ⊕*www.pc.gc.ca* 💲*Site free,* *lighthouse $3.95* ⊘*Site daily dawn–dusk; lighthouse mid-May–mid-Oct., daily 10–6; Visitor Interpretation Centre and Heritage Gift Shop mid-May–Labor Day, daily 9:30–8, after Labor Day–Oct. 15, daily 10–6.*

🐚 **The Fluvarium.** Underwater windows look onto a brook at the only public facility of its kind in North America. In season you can observe spawning brown and brook trout in their natural habitat. Feeding time for the fish, frogs, and eels is 4 PM daily. ⊠*5 Nagle's Pl., C. A. Pippy Park* ☎*709/754–3474* ⊕*www.fluvarium.ca* 💲*$5.50* ⊘*May–Labor Day, daily 9–5; Labor Day–Apr., weekdays 9–4:30, weekends 9–5.*

> ### WORD OF MOUTH
>
> "Be sure to go out to Cape Spear (eastern most point on the NA continent) where you might want to take in a sunrise and watch the whales at play from the lighthouse point. Signal Hill is also a must and you would probably enjoy the challenging hiking trails there as well as the magnificent view from Cabot Tower."
>
> —Retired_teacher

🐚 **Johnson GEO CENTRE.** Built deep into the earth with only the entryway protruding aboveground, this geological shrine is literally embedded in Signal Hill, itself made up of 550-million-year-old rocks. (The province's oldest rocks date back 3.87 billion years.) Kids five and up love the theater with sounds of thunder and lightning, and kids under five love squirting water at the rocks and seeing the different rock formations. An exhibit, "The Titanic Story," displays some artifacts and submersible footage of the wreck site. ⊠*175 Signal Hill Rd.* ☎*709/737–7880 or 866/868–7625* ☎*709/737–7885* ⊕*www.geocentre.ca* 💲*$10.25* ⊘*Mid-May–mid-Oct., Mon.–Sat. 9:30–5, Sun. 1–5; mid-Oct.–mid-May, Tues.–Sat. 9:30–5, Sun. 1–5.*

Maddox Cove and Petty Harbour. These neighboring fishing villages lie along the coast between Cape Spear and Route 10. The wharves and sturdy seaside sheds, especially those in Petty Harbour, harken back to a time not long ago when the fishery was paramount in the economy and lives of the residents.

★ **Memorial University Botanical Garden.** The many gardens at this 110-acre natural area include rock gardens and scree, a Newfoundland historic-plants bed, peat and woodland beds, an alpine house, a medicinal garden, and native-plant collections. There are also four pleasant walking trails. You can see scores of varieties of rhododendron here, as well as many kinds of butterflies and the rare hummingbird hawkmoth. Guided walks are available with advance notice for groups of 10 or more. ⊠*C. A. Pippy Park, Oxen Pond, 306 Mt. Scio Rd.* ☎*709/737–8590* ⊕*www.mun.ca/botgarden* 💲*$3.50* ⊘*May–Nov., daily 10–5; Dec.–Apr., daily 10–4.*

NEED A BREAK?   **The Bloomin' Tea Pot** is on the grounds of the MUN Botanical Garden. If it's tea you like in your china cup, they have more than 30 to choose from, along with fresh-baked scones with clotted cream and soups, salads and sandwiches. They're liquor licensed and serve fine and dessert wines, as well as English and local beers. ☎ *709/753–8327* ◷ *Daily 10–5.*

Quidi Vidi. No one knows the origin of the name of this fishing village, one of the oldest parts of St. John's. The town is best explored on foot, as the roads are narrow and make driving difficult. In spring, the inlet, known as the Gut, is a good place to catch sea-run brown trout. The Gut is a traditional outport in the middle of a modern city, making it a contrast worth seeing. ✉ *Take the first right off Kings Bridge Rd. (left of the Fairmont Hotel) onto Forest Rd., which heads into the village.*

Quidi Vidi Battery. This small redoubt has been restored to the way it appeared in 1812 when soldiers stood guard to fight off a possible American attack during the War of 1812–14. Costumed interpreters tell you about the hard, unromantic life of a soldier of the empire. The site has no washroom facilities, so make a stop before you go. ✉ *Off Cuckold's Cove Rd.* ☎ *709/729–2977 or 709/729–0592* 💰 *$3* ◷ *Mid-May–Sept., daily 10–5:30.*

Fodor'sChoice ★ **Signal Hill National Historic Site.** In spite of its height, Signal Hill was difficult to defend: throughout the 1600s and 1700s it changed hands with every attacking French, English, and Dutch force. In 1762, this was the site of the final battle between the French and British in the Seven Years' War (called the French and Indian War in the United States). A wooden palisade encircles the summit of the hill, indicating the boundaries of the old fortifications. In July and August, cadets in 19th-century British uni-

> **DAY AT THE RACES**
>
> If you are in St. John's on the first Wednesday of August, head down to Quidi Vidi Lake and experience the Royal St. John's Regatta (⊕ www.stjohnsregatta.org), the oldest continuous sporting event in North America. The fixed-seat rowing shells hold a crew of six and the coxswain. This garden-party-reunion/sporting event draws more than 30,000 people.

form perform a tattoo of military drills and music. En route to the hill is the **Visitor Centre,** with exhibits describing St. John's history. In 1901 Guglielmo Marconi received the first transatlantic-wire transmission near **Cabot Tower,** at the top of Signal Hill, and today you can visit the Marconi Exhibit on the top floor. From the top of the hill it's a 500-foot drop to the narrow harbor entrance below; views are excellent. Walking trails take you to the base of the hill and closer to the ocean. Dress warmly; it's always windy. ✉ *Signal Hill Rd.* ☎ *709/772–5367* ⊕ *www.pc.gc.ca* 💰 *Site free; visitor center $3.95* ◷ *Site daily dawn–dusk. Visitor Centre mid-June–Labor Day, daily 8:30–8; Labor Day–Oct. and May–mid-June, daily 8:30–4:30; Nov.–Apr., weekdays 8:30–4:30.*

WHERE TO STAY & EAT

$$$–$$$$ **Fodor'sChoice** ★ ✕ **Bianca's Cuisine de Soleil.** Modern paintings lend this bright eatery the air of an art gallery. The menu changes seasonally but emphasizes fish dishes and prides itself in using fresh local ingredients such as mussels steamed in gin or snow-crab ravioli. Bianca's is known for its fine wines, and if you don't know what you want, Bianca herself might be around to help. ✉*171 Water St.* ☎*709/726–9016* ⚓*Reservations essential* ▤*AE, DC, MC, V* ◷*No lunch weekends.*

$$–$$$$ ✕**The Cellar.** This restaurant may have started out in the basement but has moved into a place of prominence in St. John's on Water Street, one of the oldest streets in North America. It has kept its recognizable name and reputation for fine dining. Menu selections include chicken, pork, lamb, beef, and delicious local seafood dishes. ✉*189 Water St.* ☎*709/579–8900* ▤*AE, MC, V* ◷*No lunch weekends.*

$–$$$ ✕**The Casbah.** A bright red exterior welcomes you into this trendy, trop-ical-looking spot. By day, large windows let in lots of sun, and in the evening, red fairy lights illuminate the open balcony. There is a bar on the main floor and a menu that includes soups, salads, panini sand-wiches, meats, and seafood. It's the weekend brunch, however, that takes the cake. For your money, you get a big feed of steak and eggs, potatoes, grilled vegetables, baked beans, and home-style toast. ✉*2 Cathedral St.* ☎*709/738–5293* ⚓*Reservations essential* ▤*MC, V.*

¢–$$$ ✕**Velma's Place.** For traditional Newfoundland fare such as fish and *brewis* (bread and fish soaked in water and boiled) and Jigg's dinner (boiled beef served with potatoes, carrots, cabbage, and turnips), Vel-ma's is the place to go. The service here is friendly, and the maritime look tastefully transcends the usual lobster-pot kitsch. ✉*264 Water St.* ☎*709/576–2264* ▤*AE, DC, MC, V.*

$–$$ ✕**The Big R.** Popular among locals, this fish-and-chips place with two locations in the city draws diners from all walks of life. Be warned: schoolkids eat at the Harvey Road location at lunchtime, and it can be noisy. ✉*69 Harvey Rd.* ☎*709/722–2256* ✉*201 Blackmarsh Rd.* ☎*709/722–6549* ▤*V.*

¢–$$ ✕**Pasta Plus Café.** Pasta is the specialty here, but the local chain also serves curries, salads, and pizza. If you're branching out, try a curry dish served with banana-date chutney, or a crepe stuffed with seasonally available seafood. ✉*233 Duckworth St.* ☎*709/739–6676* ✉*Avalon Mall, Thorburn Rd.* ☎*709/722–6006* ✉*Churchill Sq., Elizabeth Ave.* ☎*709/739–5818* ✉*The Village Shopping Centre* ☎*709/368–3481* ▤*AE, DC, MC, V.*

$ ✕**International Flavours.** This place may not look like much, but the curry dishes are delicious. ✉*4 Quidi Vidi Rd.* ☎*709/738–4636* ▤*V* ◷*Closed Sun.*

¢–$ ✕**Ches's.** Since the 1950s, this restaurant has been serving fish-and-

Fodor's Choice chips to a steady stream of customers from noon until after midnight.

★ They come from all walks of life to sample the flaky fish fried in a batter whose recipe the owner keeps under lock and key (literally). It's strictly laminated tabletops and plastic chairs, but the fish is hot and fresh. ✉*9 Freshwater Rd.* ☎*709/722–4083* ✉*655 Topsail Rd.* ☎*709/368–9473* ✉*29–33 Commonwealth Ave., Mount Pearl* ☎*709/364–6837* ✉*8 Highland Dr.* ☎*709/738–5022* ▤*MC, V.*

¢–$ ✕**The Sprout.** On the walls, local artists and craftspeople display their work, but the real works of art arrive at your table in the form of salads, soups (like the Me-So Hungry Miso soup), and sandwiches (the Bravocado is cheese, avocado, and sprouts on homemade grain bread). It's great vegetarian fare; in place of a burger, try the chickpea Give Peas a Chance or Thai One On (pad thai). The vegan chocolate mousse is decadent. Cows all over the Avalon Peninsula are smiling. The brick floor extends up one wall, and you can sit at tables or one of the four booths scattered around the room. ⊠ *364 Duckworth St.* ☎ *709/579–5485* ⚑ *No reservations* ═ *AE, DC, MC, V* ⊘ *Closed Mon. No lunch Sun.*

$$$-$$$$ ✕▥ **Fairmont Newfoundland.** Charming rooms overlook the harbor at
★ this nine-story hotel where uniformed bellhops meet you at the door. Ask for a south-facing room for a great view of Signal Hill and the Narrows. The hotel is noted for its Sunday and evening buffets in the Bonavista restaurant ($$-$$$), and the fine cuisine at the Cabot Club ($$$-$$$$), which serves Newfoundland specialties, seafood, and the best Caesar salad in town. An indoor garden atrium overlooks the Narrows and is an ideal spot for breakfast or afternoon tea. The Cabot Club is worth a visit whether you're staying at the hotel or not. ⊠ *115 Cavendish Sq., Box 5637, A1C 5W8* ☎ *709/726–4980* ☐ *709/725–2025* ⊕ *www.fairmont.com* ⟿ *301 rooms, 14 suites* ⚹ *In-room: refrigerator (some), dial-up. In-hotel: 2 restaurants, room service, bar, pool, gym, spa, laundry service, concierge, executive floor, parking (no fee), no-smoking rooms, some pets allowed* ═ *AE, DC, MC, V.*

$$$ ✕▥ **Blue on Water.** Natural flavors and a simplistic approach to organic fare is what this trendy restaurant (reservations essential; $$$-$$$$) is all about. Try the carrot ginger soup, and their cod tongues are to die for. If you want your fish fresh, this is the place, and customers rave about the freshness. Above is a modern boutique hotel with turquoise-colored walls and wide-screen flat-panel TVs. If you leave the windows open, you can catch a fresh whiff of the Atlantic Ocean. ⊠ *319 Water St., A1C 1B9* ☎ *709/754–2583* ⊕ *www.blueonwater.com* ⟿ *7 rooms* ⚹ *In-room: DVD, ethernet. In-hotel: restaurant, room service, no elevator, no-smoking rooms* ═ *D, DC, MC, V.*

$$-$$$ ▥ **Delta St. John's.** Rooms in this popular convention hotel in downtown St. John's are standard, but they overlook the harbor and the city. The staff is friendly and the lobby bright, with foliage, mahogany trim, and polished brass. Rooms facing New Gower Street have the best views. The restaurant, Quinn's Plate ($$-$$$$), serves steak and seafood, but restaurants of all types are in abundance nearby. ⊠ *120 New Gower St., A1C 6K4* ☎ *709/739-6404 or 800/563–3838* ☐ *709/570–1622* ⊕ *www.deltahotels.com* ⟿ *404 rooms, 30 suites* ⚹ *In-room: refrigerator (some), dial-up. In-hotel: restaurant, room service, bar, pool, gym, laundry service, parking (fee), no-smoking rooms, some pets allowed* ═ *AE, DC, MC, V.*

$$-$$$ ▥ **McCoubrey Manor.** This Queen Anne–style heritage home was built in 1904 for Henry T. McCoubrey, manager of a prominent St. John's merchant firm. The front veranda and back garden are perfect places to spend a quiet evening. The house is near the base of Signal Hill and within walking distance of shops, restaurants, and historical landmarks. Three suites have whirlpool tubs and fireplaces. Evening wine and cheese is included in the rate. ⊠ *6–8 Ordnance St., A1C 3K7* ☎ *709/722-7577 or 888/753-7577* ☐ *709/579-7577* ⊕ *www.*

4

mccoubrey.com ⟋6 suites ⟋In-room: kitchen (some), VCR, Wi-Fi. In-hotel: no elevator, laundry facilities, parking (no fee), no-smoking rooms ⊟AE, MC, V |Ol BP.

$$-$$$ 🖭**Murray Premises Hotel.** Set under original beamed ceilings, columns, and timber-slanted roofs, this boutique hotel abounds in luxurious extras. All rooms feature custom maple furniture and a bed adorned with a beautiful, warm duvet and high-quality linens. Large marble bathrooms have oversize Jacuzzis and towel warmers. ⊠5 Becks Cove, A1C 6H1 ☎709/738–7773 or 866/738–7773 🖷709/738–7775 ⊕www.murraypremiseshotel.com ⟋28 rooms ⟋In-room: DVD, refrigerator, ethernet. In-hotel: laundry service, parking (no fee), no-smoking rooms ⊟AE, DC, MC, V |Ol CP.

$-$$$ 🖭**Elizabeth Manor Bed & Breakfast.** Local artwork decorates the walls
★ of this 1894 Victorian, one of the city's most established and popular B&Bs. Helpful staff will help coordinate car rentals and tourist excursions. The inn tastefully blends the new and the old. It's central to shops and downtown attractions, but the return climb up the hill might leave you winded. ⊠21 Military Rd., A1C 2C3 ☎709/753–7733 or 888/263–3786 🖷709/753–6036 ⊕www.elizabethmanor.nl.ca ⟋8 rooms, 2 with shared bath ⟋In-room: no a/c, Wi-Fi, kitchen. In-hotel: no elevator, no-smoking rooms ⊟AE, MC, V |Ol BP.

$$ 🖭**Angel House Heritage Inn.** When William Hurt was in town filming a
Fodor'sChoice movie, he rented out this 1878 home, which sits on an acre of land and
★ is set back from the road for privacy. The house is impeccable, as is its park-like garden. The owner will pick you up at the airport and see that you arrive safely. The video library is stocked with over 850 titles. A generous breakfast is served in the dining room or outside on the patio. The original carriage house has been turned into a shop that features books, blooms, and antiques. ⊠146 Hamilton Ave., Box 2463, Stn. C, A1C 6E7 ☎709/739–4223 or 866/719–4223 🖷709/576–3367 ⊕www.angelhousebb.com ⟋4 rooms ⟋In-room: DVD, Wi-Fi. In-hotel: no-smoking rooms ⊟AE, MC, V |Ol BP.

$$ 🖭**Everton House.** Five-star luxury is what you'll find in this grand heri-
Fodor'sChoice tage home built in 1891, a few minutes' walk from the downtown
★ area. Its 12-foot-high ceilings, yellow kitchen with glass-door cupboards, and huge windows make it warm and welcoming. The rooms are carpeted and very elegantly decorated. The huge backyard is hung with hammocks in the summertime. ⊠25 Kingsbridge Rd., A1C 3K4 ☎709/739–1616 or 877/739–1616 🖷709/739–8726 ⊕www.everton-house.com ⟋4 rooms, 1 suite ⟋In-room: DVD, VCR, Wi-Fi. In-hotel: bar, no elevator, laundry service, parking (no fee), no-smoking rooms ⊟AE, DC, MC, V |Ol BP.

$$ 🖭**Holiday Inn.** The surprise at this chain hotel is the location: walking trails meander around small lakes and link into the Grand Concourse. Pippy Park, which has two golf courses, is directly across the street, and a miniature golf course is nearby. The in-house restaurant, East Side Mario's, serves Italian food and burgers. The hotel is in the center of the city near the airport and shopping mall. ⊠180 Portugal Cove Rd., A1B 2N2 ☎709/722–0506 🖷709/722–9756 ⊕www.holidayinnstjohns.com ⟋250 rooms ⟋In-room: refrigerator (some), dial-up. In-hotel:

restaurant, bar, pool, gym, laundry service, parking (no fee), no-smoking rooms, some pets allowed ⊟AE, D, DC, MC, V.

$$ ⊡**Quality Hotel—Harbourview.** This harbor-front hotel is in the downtown core, directly overlooking the harbor. Friendly staff immediately flash a welcoming smile when you enter the tiled, sand-color lobby. The five floors of rooms are clean and comfortable. The restaurant, Rumpelstiltskins, has a splendid view and an unpretentious menu. ⊠2 Hill O'Chips, A1C 6B1 ☎709/754–7788 ⊟709/754–5209 ⊕www. choicehotels.ca/cn246 ⊃160 rooms △In-room: dial-up (some), Wi-Fi. In-hotel: restaurant, room service, laundry service, parking (no fee), no-smoking rooms ⊟AE, D, DC, MC, V.

$–$$ ⊡**Bluestone Inn Bed & Breakfast.** In the heart of the city, this old grand Victorian lady is one of the few stone houses left standing in St. John's. It was built with the same stone used for the Basilica, Government House, Anglican Cathedral, and Cabot Tower. As B&Bs go, this one is a little more funky than frilly. All rooms have fireplaces, and some have whirlpool tubs. Breakfast starts with partridgeberry pancakes, banana French toast, or cereals in the exposed-stone-walled basement of the "Excess Baggage" Pub. The former servants' quarters has a door to the outside that the owners refer to as "the bed and shed"; it's for those who want to slip in early in the morning. The third-floor view over the city is grand, but if you feel like getting a real bird's-eye view of your surroundings, talk to the owner/pilot who has a float plane you can charter. ⊠34 Queen's Rd., A1C 1A5 ☎709/754–7544 or 877/754–9876 ⊕www.thebluestoneinn.com ⊃6 rooms △In-room: no a/c, Wi-Fi. In-hotel: no elevator, no-smoking rooms ⊟AE, DC, V ⦿⊦BP.

$–$$ ⊡**Park House Inn, Bed and Breakfast.** Three Newfoundland prime ministers lived at this house built in the late 1870s. It sits next to Colonial House, the former seat of government, and is in a great location for those who want to walk downtown St. John's. The grand foyer has 5-foot-high wainscoting and a circular mahogany staircase. The house is filled with antiques and Newfoundland art on the walls. A large white deck embraces the back of the house, and the rooms—with queen-size sleigh beds and fireplaces—are luxurious, warm, and inviting. ⊠112 Military Rd., A1C 2C9 ☎709/576–2265 or 866/303–0565 ⊟709/576–2268 ⊕www.newfoundlandbedandbreakfast.nl.ca ⊃4 rooms △In-room: DVD, dial-up. In-hotel: no elevator, laundry facilities, parking (no fee), no-smoking rooms ⊟AE, MC, V ⦿⊦BP.

$ ⊡**The Roses Bed and Breakfast.** This downtown Victorian home, within walking distance of the city's main attractions, features spacious rooms with old-fashioned decor. Be sure to catch the fabulous view of the city from the top-floor kitchen, where a full breakfast is served Monday to Saturday, and a Continental version on Sunday. ⊠9 Military Rd., A1C 2C3 ☎709/726–3336 or 877/767–3722 ⊕www.therosesbandb. com ⊃6 rooms △In-room: no a/c. In-hotel: no elevator, public Wi-Fi, no-smoking rooms ⊟AE, MC, V ⦿⊦BP.

4

CLOSE UP

Newfoundland English

Newfoundland English is made up from words that came here centuries ago when fertile fishing grounds brought sailors from all over Europe and the British Isles to these shores. Then in the late 16th century, colonies of people were brought here to settle, with very little—except, of course, for their culture in the form of words, sayings, and songs. Because of the province's relative isolation, accents remained strong and these archaic words took root to become New-foundland English.

There are words for everything, from food words such as *scoff* (a big meal), *touton* (fried bread dough), and *duff* (a pudding), to words to describe the fickle weather, such as *leeward* (a threatening storm), *airsome* (bracing cold), and *mauzy* (foggy and damp). "The sun is splitting the rocks!" is something you might hear on a fine day.

There are words that relate to the fishery: a *flake* is where you dry fish, perhaps after having caught them on

your *dory*, a small rowboat. A *bedlamer* is a young seal. And, of course, there are plenty of words to describe all manner of people: a *gatcher* is a show-off and a *cuffer* tells tall tales.

A *drung* is a narrow road, a *scuff* is a dance, to *coopy* means to crouch down, and if you are going for a *twack*, you're window-shopping. If you're from *Upalong*, that means you're not from here.

To help develop an ear for the provincial dialects, pick up a copy of the *Dictionary of Newfoundland English* (⊕ www.heritage.nf.ca/dictionary). The dictionary was first published in 1982; it's now in its second edition and has more than 5,000 words.

Twackwear Inc. by **2 Streels** (☎ *709/579–4671* ⊕ *www.twackwear. com*), a St. John's–based company, preserves old Newfoundland words by printing them on T-shirts and magnets. They're available at shops around Newfoundland and online.

NIGHTLIFE & THE ARTS

St. John's has tremendous variety and vitality for such a small population. Theater settings include traditional spaces, courtyards, and parks. Celtic-inspired traditional music and traditional rock are the city's best-known music genres, although there's also a vibrant blues and alternative-rock scene.

THE ARTS

The Arts and Culture Centre (⊠ *Allandale Rd.* ☎ *709/729–3650*) has a 1,000-seat main theater and a well-stocked library. The Centre is the site of musical and theatrical events from September through June. The library is open year-round, Tuesday through Thursday 10 to 9, and Friday and Saturday 10 to 5:30; it's closed Saturday, June through August. The **Resource Centre for the Arts** (⊠ *LSPU Hall, 3 Victoria St.* ☎ *709/753–4531*) is an innovative theater with professional main-stage and experimental second-space productions year-round. It has been the launching pad for the province's best-known and successful theatrical exports. The **Ship Inn** (⊠ *Solomon's La. between Duckworth and Water Sts., 265 Duckworth Str., A1C 2G9* ☎ *709/753–3870*) serves as the local arts watering hole. This is a great place to have a fish meal like panfried cod or cod au gratin; their fi & chi (fish-and-chips) are fabulous. Nighttime performances showcase local musical talent of all genres. The **Newfoundland and Labrador Folk Festival** (☎*866/576–8508* ⊕*www.sjfac.nf.net*), held in St. John's the first weekend in August, is the province's best-known traditional music festival.

NIGHTLIFE
St. John's well-deserved reputation as a party town has been several hundred years in the making. Downtown **George Street** is the city's most famous street, with more bars per capita than any other street in North America. The short cobblestone street has dozens of pubs and restaurants. Seasonal open-air concerts, which close off the street, are held here as well. When Russell Crowe comes to town, he jams at **O'Reilly's Pub** (✉*15–17 George St.* ☎*709/722–3735 or 866/307–3735* ⊕*www.oreillyspub.com*), famous for its live Irish and Newfoundland music. O'Reilley's also has a full pub-grub menu; the fish-and-chips are excellent.

SPORTS & THE OUTDOORS

GOLF
Neither high winds nor unforgiving temperatures can keep golfers off the links in St. John's. If you want to play, call several days in advance to book a tee time. The par-71, 18-hole Admiral's Green and the par-35, 9-hole Captain's Hill are adjacent public courses in **C. A. Pippy Park** (✉*460 Allandale Rd.* ☎*709/753–7110* ⊕*www.pippyparkgolf.com*) that overlook St. John's. **Clovelley** (✉*Off Stavanger Dr.* ☎*709/722–7170* ⊕*www.clovellygolf.com*) has two 18-hole courses: the 72-par Osprey and the 62-par Black Duck, in the east end of St. John's. **The Woods** (✉*Off Rte. 2 in the city's west end* ☎*709/368–4747* ⊕*www. thewoods.ca*) has wide, forgiving fairways on its 18-hole, par-71 layout. It caters to players of moderate skill.

HIKING
A well-developed, marked trail system, the **Grand Concourse** (☎*709/737–1077* ⊕*www.grandconcourse.ca*), crisscrosses the city of St. John's, covering more than 120 km (70 mi). Some trails traverse river valleys, parks, and other open areas, and others are sidewalk routes. Well-maintained trails encircle several lakes, including Long Pond and Quidi Vidi Lake, both of which are great for bird-watching. Detailed maps are available at tourist information centers and many hotels.

SCUBA DIVING
The ocean around Newfoundland and Labrador rivals the Caribbean in clarity, but certainly not in temperature. There are thousands of known shipwreck sites. One, a sunken whaling ship, is only several feet from the shore of the Conception Bay community of Conception Harbour. The wrecked ship and a wealth of sea life can be explored with a snorkel and wet suit. **Ocean Quest** (✉*Foxtrap Marina, Foxtrap* ☎*709/834–7234 or 866/623–2664* ⊕*www.oceanquestcharters.com*) offers classes for beginners and leads ocean tours aboard Zodiacs and a

38-foot custom boat to popular scuba-diving sites, including the WWII shipwrecks off Bell Island and Conception Harbor whaling wrecks.

SEA KAYAKING

One of the best ways to explore the coastline is by kayak, which lets you visit sea caves and otherwise inaccessible beaches. There's also a very good chance you'll see whales, icebergs, and seabirds. **O'Brien's Whitecap Adventures** (⊠ *Bay Bulls* ☎ *709/753–4850* ⊕ *www.obriens-boattours.com*), about 30 minutes outside St. John's, conducts half-day sea-kayaking trips. **Wilderness Newfoundland Adventures** (⊠ *67 Circular Rd.* ☎ *709/579–6353 or 888/747–6353* ⊕ *www.wildnfld.ca*) offers excursions leaving from Cape Broyle through world-famous sanctuaries, under waterfalls, and inside caves. In season, paddle with whales and icebergs.

WHALE-WATCHING

The east coast of Newfoundland, including the area around St. John's, provides spectacular whale-watching opportunities with up to 22 species of dolphins and whales visible along the coast. Huge humpback whales weighing up to 30 tons come close to shore to feed in late spring and early summer. You may be able to spot icebergs and large flocks of nesting seabirds in addition to whales on many boat tours. For tour times and rates, visit the tour company booths at harborside in summer, near Pier 7, or inquire at your hotel.

Iceberg Quest Ocean Tours (☎ *709/722–1888 or 866/720–1888* ⊕ *www. icebergquest.com*) has daily sailings at 9:30, 1, 4, and 7 of their two-hour fully narrated tour. You'll be entertained with traditional and local music aboard, as they head out through the narrows of the harbour between Signal Hill and Fort Amherst. Keep your eyes open for whales and icebergs and the beautiful scenery of the most easterly points in North America. There's also a licensed bar on board

SHOPPING

The **Art Gallery of Newfoundland and Labrador** (⊠ *The Rooms, 9 Bonaventure Ave.* ☎ *709/757–8000*) is the province's largest public gallery and exhibits historical and contemporary Canadian arts and crafts with an emphasis on local artists and artisans. **Christina Parker Gallery** (⊠ *7 Plank Rd.* ☎ *709/753–0580* ⊕ *www.christinaparkergallery.com*) carries mainly the work of local artists in all media, including paintings (Barbara, Christopher, and Mary Pratt), sculpture, drawing, and prints. The **Cod Jigger** (⊠ *245 Duckworth St.* ☎ *709/726–7422*) carries crafts and handmade wool sweaters and mittens. The **Devon House Craft Centre** (⊠ *59 Duckworth St.* ☎ *709/753–2749* ⊕ *www.craftcouncil.nl.ca*) displays local work and showcases innovative designs; it also headquarters the Craft Council of Newfoundland and Labrador. Check out the exhibits upstairs. The **Downhome Shoppe and Gallery** (⊠ *303 Water St.* ☎ *709/722–2970 or 888/588–6353* ⊕ *www.shopdownhome.com*) sells more than 5,000 items, each written, sung, or produced by a Newfoundlander or Labradorian. It has a large selection of local books, crafts, art, and souvenirs in two large storefront buildings from the late 1850s.

Eastern Edge Gallery (✉ *72 Harbour Dr., between Clift's-Baird's Cove and Prescott St., A1C 6K1* ☎ *709/739–1882* ⊕ *www.easternedge.ca*) is a contemporary artists' co-op that has everything from paintings and drawings to performance and video art from emerging artists. **Emma Butler Gallery** (✉ *111 George St. W* ☎ *709/739–7111* ⊕ *www.emmabutler.com*) represents some of the more prominent and established artists in the province. **Fred's Records** (✉ *198 Duckworth St.* ☎ *709/753–9191* ⊕ *www.freds.nf.ca*) has the best selection of local recordings, as well as other music. **The Lane Gallery** (✉ *Fairmont Hotel, 1st fl., Cavendish Sq.* ☎ *709/753–8946 or 877/366–5263* ⊕ *www.lanegallery.com*) has seascapes, landscapes, and other works by photographer Don Lane. **Living Planet** (✉ *116 Duckworth St.* ☎ *709/739–6810 or 877/739–6800* ⊕ *www.livingplanet.ca*) specializes in T-shirts printed in ecofriendly ways and designed by local artists. **Livyers** (✉ *202 Duckworth St.* ☎ *709/726–5650*) has a little of everything, from furniture and books to maps and prints. The **Newfoundland Weavery** (✉ *177 Water St.* ☎ *709/753–0496*) sells rugs, prints, lamps, books, crafts, and other gift items. **NONIA** (*Newfoundland Outport Nurses Industrial Association* ✉ *286 Water St.* ☎ *709/753–8062* ⊕ *www.nonia.com*) was founded in 1920 to give women in the outports a way to earn money to support nursing services in these remote communities. Homespun wool was used to create exquisite clothing. Today the shop continues to sell these fine homespun articles as well as lighter, more modern handmade items.

O'Brien's Music Store (✉ *278 Water St.* ☎ *709/753–6958* ⊕ *www.obriens.nf.ca*) is the oldest store on the oldest street in the oldest city in North America. Behind the counter, the O'Brien brothers, Roy and Gord, make you feel at home; it's worth a visit just to look at the accordions, tin whistles, and ugly sticks. **Rosemill Antiques** (✉ *556 Water St. W* ☎ *709/754–8224*) specializes in Newfoundland formal furniture, silver, glass, and china. **Wild Things** (✉ *124 Water St., A1C 5J9* ☎ *709/722–3123* ⊕ *www.wildlands.com/wildthings*) sells Newfoundland nature-theme crafts and jewelry, and Labradorite dolls.

AVALON PENINSULA

On the southern half of the peninsula, small Irish hamlets are separated by large tracts of wilderness. You can travel part of the peninsula's southern coast in one or two days, depending on how much time you have. Quaint towns line Route 10, and the natural sights are beautiful. La Manche and Chance Cove, both abandoned communities–turned–provincial parks, attest to the region's bounty of natural resources. At the intersection of routes 90 and 91 in Salmonier, you can head west and then south to Route 100 to Cape St. Mary's Ecological Reserve, or head north toward Salmonier Nature Park and on to the towns on Conception Bay. Both take about three hours. On the latter route, stop in Harbour Grace; if you plan to travel on to Bay de Verde, at the

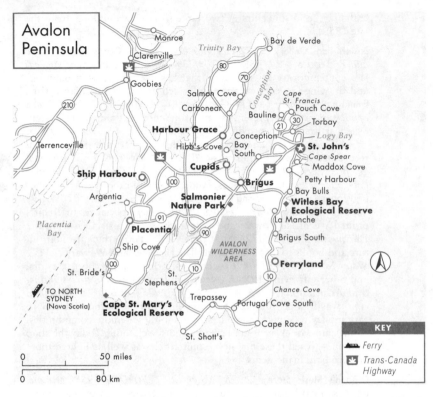

northern tip of the peninsula, and down the other side of the peninsula on Route 80 along Trinity Bay, consider overnighting in the Harbour Grace–Carbonear area. Otherwise turn around and follow the same route back to Route 1.

WITLESS BAY ECOLOGICAL RESERVE

29 km (18 mi) south of St. John's.

Four small islands and the water surrounding them make up the reserve, which is the summer home of millions of seabirds—puffins, murres, kittiwakes, razorbills, and guillemots. The birds, and the humpback and minke whales that linger here before moving north to the summer grounds in the Arctic, feed on capelin that swarm inshore to spawn.

This is an excellent place to see icebergs in late spring and early summer. Icebergs can linger in Newfoundland waters into June and sometimes July, cooling the temperature before falling victim to the milder climate. The loud crack as an iceberg breaks apart can be heard from shore, but a boat can get you a closer look at these natural ice sculptures. Icebergs have spawned a lucrative business in Newfoundland beyond tourism. Iceberg water and iceberg vodka are now on the market, made from ice chipped from the 10,000-year-old bergs as they float by. The best views of birds and icebergs are from tour boats that operate here ⊠*Rte. 10; take Pitts Memorial Dr. (Rte. 2) from downtown St. John's and turn right onto Goulds off-ramp, then left onto Rte. 10.*

SPORTS & THE OUTDOORS

From mid-May to mid-October, **Gatherall's Puffin and Whale Watch** (☎*709/334–2887 or 800/419–4253* ⊕*www.gatheralls.com*) leads six 90-minute trips per day into the reserve on a high-speed catamaran. The catamaran is quite stable in rough seas, so if you get queasy that might be the way to go. Shuttle service is available from St. John's hotels. **O'Brien's Whale and Bird Tours** (☎*709/753–4850 or 877/639–4253* ⊕*www.obriensboattours.com*) offers two-hour excursions in a 46-passenger boat to view whales, icebergs, and seabirds. They also lead sea kayak and Zodiac Coastal Explorer tours. Dress warmly.

> ### THE IRISH LOOP
>
> The Irish Loop (Route 10) loops around the southern shore of the Avalon Peninsula below St. John's. The highway hugs the coastline and takes you into the heart of Irish Newfoundland—to Bay Bulls, Witless Bay, Ferryland, Aquaforte, Fermeuse, Portugal Cove South, Trepassey, and Salmonier. It's a world filled with whales, caribou, and seabirds. Follow the loop around and you'll end up back in St. John's.

EN ROUTE Although there are many pretty hamlets along the way from Witless Bay to Ferryland on Route 10, **La Manche**, accessible only on foot, and **Brigus South** have especially attractive settings. La Manche is an abandoned fishing community between Tors Cove and Cape Broyle. The former residents moved to other towns after a storm destroyed part of the community in 1966; a suspension bridge that had been washed away by the storm's tides has since been rebuilt and is worth a visit. Brigus South, between Witless Bay and Cape Broyle, is a fishing village with strong traditional flavors whose name is derived from an old French word for "intrigue."

FERRYLAND

43½ km (27 mi) south of Witless Bay Ecological Reserve.

The main road into Ferryland hugs the coastline, where tiny bay houses dot the steep hills. Ferryland is one of the oldest European settlements in North America. The Englishman Lord Baltimore, Sir George Calvert, settled it in 1620. Calvert didn't stay long on this cold windswept shore—he left for a warmer destination and is more commonly credited with founding Maryland. In the summer this is a great spot to whale-watch.

The major ongoing **Colony of Avalon** archaeological dig at Ferryland has uncovered the early-17th-century colony of Lord Baltimore, who abandoned the area after a decade. The site includes an archaeology laboratory, exhibit center and museum, period gardens, and a reconstructed 17th-century kitchen. Guided tours are available. ⊠*Rte. 10, Ferryland* ☎*709/432–3200 or 877/326–5669* ⊕*www.heritage.nf.ca/*

avalon ⬛*$8 includes tour* ☉*Mid-May–Oct., daily 10–5; late June–Labor Day, daily 9–7.*

Ferryland Lighthouse. This historic lighthouse, built in 1871, now signals the spot for breathtaking views, worry-free picnics, and great food, such as crab cakes, green salads, and gooseberry fools. You bring the appetite, they pack everything else—even the blanket. Bread is baked daily in the lighthouse. There is also an optional guided walk when you prebook, and Saturday-evening picnics include dining with a local artist. There must be romance in the shadow of the lighthouse, because this has become a popular destination for weddings and engagement proposals. Check the Web site for menus (which vary day to day) and a list of events. Picnics start at $15 per person. ✉*Ferryland Lighthouse* ☎*709/363–7456* ⊕*www.lighthousepicnics.ca* ☉*June–Sept., Tues.–Sun. 11:30–6; call for off-season arrangements.*

OFF THE BEATEN PATH

Mistaken Point Ecological Reserve. One hundred sixty kilometers (100 mi) south on Route 10 from St. John's. At 620 million years old, this is one of the most significant fossil sites in the world. Fossil lovers from all over the world flock to Mistaken Point to see the oldest-multicelled fossils in North America. More than 30 species of ancient animals are found here, and most of them represent extinct groups unknown in our modern world. The road to the main reserve is 16 km (10 mi) along a dirt path to Cape Race; then be prepared to hike for 45 minutes over the barrens toward the ocean. ✉*Off Rte. 100* ☎*709/685–1823, 709/635–4520, 709/438–1100 call ahead for a tour and check on weather conditions* ⊕*www.env.gov.nl.ca/parks* ⬛*Site free, tours $10* ☉*Mid-May–mid-Oct., daily 9–5.*

While you're here, travel 5 kms (3 mi) farther along the road to the Cape Race Lighthouse (⊕*www.geocities.com/caperaceheritage/CapeRace*), the south-easternmost point in North America. The spot is most famous for receiving one of the first SOS messages from the Titanic.

SPORTS & THE OUTDOORS

Kayaking excursions with **Wilderness Newfoundland Adventures** (✉*67 Circular Rd., St. John's* ☎*709/579–6353, 888/747–6353, 709/432–3332 [Cape Broyle]* ⊕*www.wildnfld.ca*) leave from the old General Store on Harbour Road in Cape Broyle. They offer 2- and 4½-hour kayak trips as well as the "Go and Tow," a four-hour kayak trip out onto the ocean with return trip by motorized towboat. During whale season this is a great way to get up close and personal with humpbacks and minkes. Wilderness Newfoundland Adventures also runs guided hiking tours of the East Coast Trail.

SALMONIER NATURE PARK

🕊 *88 km (55 mi) northwest of Ferryland, 14½ km (9 mi) north of the intersection of Rtes. 90 and 91.*

Many indigenous animal species, including moose, caribou, lynx, and otters, can be seen at this 3,000-acre wilderness reserve area. An enclosed 100-acre exhibit allows up-close viewing. ✉*Salmonier Line, Rte. 90* ☎*709/229–7189* ⊕*www.gov.nl.ca/snp* ▣*$3.45, kids under 18 free* ☉*Early June–early Sept., daily 10–6; early Sept.–mid-Oct., weekdays 10–4.*

▌EN
ROUTE

From Salmonier Nature Park to Brigus, take Route 90, which passes through the scenic **Hawke Hills** before meeting up with the Trans-Canada Highway (Route 1). This reserve is the best representative of alpine barrens in Canada east of the Rockies. Turn off at Holyrood Junction (Route 62) and follow Route 70, which skirts Conception Bay.

BRIGUS

19 km (12 mi) north of intersection of Rtes. 1 and 70.

This historic village on Conception Bay has a wonderful public garden, winding lanes, and a teahouse. Brigus is best known as the birthplace of Captain Bob Bartlett, the famed Arctic explorer who accompanied Admiral Robert Peary on polar expeditions during the first decade of the 20th century.

Hawthorne Cottage, Captain Bartlett's home, is one of the few surviving examples of picturesque cottage style, with a veranda decorated with ornamental wooden fretwork. It dates from 1830 and is a National Historic Site. During July and August look for the **Live! On the Lawn Theatre,** a series of 25-minute vignettes about historic Brigus and its captain Bob Bartlett's adventures. ✉*South St. and Irishtown Rd.* ☎*709/753–9262, 709/528–4004 June–Aug.* ⊕*www.historicsites.ca* ▣*$3.75* ☉*Mid-May–June, Wed.–Sun., 9–5, July and Aug., daily 9–7, Sept.–mid-Oct., selected days 9–5, call ahead.*

The **John N. Leamon Museum (aka "Ye Olde Stone Barn")** displays historical town photos and artifacts that go back almost 200 years, with everything from household items to objects dealing with the fishery. ✉*4 Magistrate's Hill* ☎*709/528–3391* ▣*$1* ☉*June–Sept., daily 10–6.*

WHERE TO STAY

¢ 🏨**Brittoner Bed & Breakfast.** This 160-year-old restored home is in the heart of Brigus, near Hawthorne Cottage, the Olde Stone Barn Museum, and hiking trails. It has a large area for picnics, or to just sit outside and enjoy the splendid view. ✉*12 Water St., Box 163, A0A 1K0* ⊕*www.bbcanada.com* ☎*709/528–3412, 709/579–5995 Nov.–Apr.* 🛏*709/528–3412* ➪*3 rooms, 2 with bath* ♿*In-room: no a/c, no TV. In-hotel: no elevator, laundry facilities, some pets allowed, no-smoking rooms* ▬*No credit cards* ⏹*BP.*

¢ ⊡**Brookdale Manor.** This old farmhouse, in a quiet, country setting just outside town, is presided over by warm and friendly owners. A common area has a fireplace, television, and phone that you can use. Rooms are spacious, and the flower gardens are beautiful. It's a good value for your money. ⊠*Farm Rd., Box 121, A0A 1K0* ⊕*www.bbcanada.com/5274. html* 📠*709/528–4544 or 888/528–4544* ⤳*4 rooms* ⚿*In-room: no a/c, no phone, no TV. In-hotel: room service, no elevator, no-smoking rooms* ⊟*MC, V* �*CP.*

CUPIDS

5 km (3 mi) northwest of Brigus.

Cupids is the oldest English colony in Canada, founded in 1610 by John Guy, to whom the town erected a monument in 1910. Nearby flies a reproduction of the enormous Union Jack that flew during that 300th-anniversary celebration. When the wind snaps the flag, you can hear it half a mile away.

At **Cupids Museum,** in 1995, archaeologists began unearthing the long-lost remains of the original colony here. Some of the recovered artifacts—including pots, pipes, and trade beads—are on display in this community museum. ⊠*Main Rd.* ☎*709/528–3500 or 709/528–3477* ⌨*$3, includes museum and site* ☉*Call for an appointment to see the museum.*

WHERE TO STAY

¢ ⊡**Guy View Manor.** On a hillside overlooking the ocean, this ranch-style home is near the Cupids Archaeological Site and good hiking and walking trails. The brightly painted rooms each have their own entrance, giving you added privacy. A TV and telephone are available in the common room. ⊠*First Colony Dr., Box 122, A0A 2B0* ☎*877/728–4248* 📠*709/528–4248* ⊕*www.bbcanada.com/5438.html* ⤳*4 rooms* ⚿*In-room: no a/c, no phone, no TV. In-hotel: no elevator, no-smoking rooms* ⊟*V* ⊙*CP.*

¢ ⊡**Skipper Ben's.** This 113-year-old heritage home has been restored to maintain its original character, with wood ceilings and antique furnishings. The four spacious rooms of this B&B share two bathrooms. The dining room is open for lunch, afternoon tea, and dinner and well worth the visit as the owner is a great cook. ⊠*408 Seaforest Dr., Box 137, A0A 2B0* ☎*877/528–4436* 📠*709/528–4436* ⊕*www.skipper-bens.com* ⤳*4 rooms with shared bath* ⚿*In-room: no a/c, Wi-Fi. In-hotel: no elevator, no-smoking rooms* ⊟*No credit cards* ⊙*BP.*

HARBOUR GRACE

21 km (13 mi) north of Cupids.

Harbour Grace, once the headquarters of 17th-century pirate Peter Easton, was a major commercial town in the 18th and 19th centuries. Beginning in 1919, the town was the departure point for many attempts to fly the Atlantic. Amelia Earhart left Harbour Grace in 1932 to become the first woman to fly solo across the Atlantic. The town has two fine churches and several registered historic houses.

SHOPPING

You can't miss **Victoria Manor Shoppes & Gallery** (⊠*25 Victoria St.* ☎*709/596–8111* ⏱*Tues.–Sat. 10–5, Sun. noon–5, or by appointment*), a bright yellow heritage home–turned–antiques store trimmed in red. Inside, bright yellow walls and the old wood floors are a perfect backdrop for old Newfoundland knickknacks, outport furniture, and carnival glass. Funky knitted woolens are just one

ROUTE 100: THE CAPE SHORE

The Cape Shore area is the site of an outstanding seabird colony at Cape St. Mary's. It's also culturally and historically rich. The French settlers had their capital here in Placentia. Irish influence is also strong here, in music and manner. You can reach the Cape Shore on the western side of the Avalon Peninsula from Route 1, at its intersection with Route 100. The ferry from Nova Scotia docks in Argentia, near Placentia.

4

of the one-of-kind limited-edition crafts. If you're feeling bookish, have a gander at their used and antique bookstore. There's also a fine-art gallery with exhibits by emerging local artists. Well worth the stop.

WHERE TO STAY

$ 🏨**Rothesay House Inn Bed & Breakfast.** This Provincial Heritage Site B&B has a fascinating history. It was built in 1855 in Brigus, then dismantled, transported, and reconstructed in the Queen Anne style in Harbour Grace in 1906. The front of the house has a lovely porch, and the greens, yellows, and reds of the exterior are echoed in the room colors. ⊠*34 Water St., Box 577, A0A 2M0* ☎*709/596–2268* 🖷*709/596–0317* 🌐*www.rothesay.com* 🛏*4 rooms* 🛋*In-room: no a/c, no TV. In-hotel: restaurant, no elevator, no-smoking rooms* ▤*MC, V* 🍴*BP.*

PLACENTIA

48 km (30 mi) south of Rte. 1.

Placentia was Newfoundland's French capital in the 1600s. It was first settled by 16th-century Basque fishermen. The remains of an old fort built on a hill look out over Placentia and beyond to the placid waters and wooded, steep hillsides of the inlet.

Castle Hill National Historic Site, just north of town, is what remains of the French fortifications. The visitor center has a Life at Plaisance exhibit that shows the hardships endured by early English and French settlers. Performances of *Faces of Fort Royal,* a historical play about the French era, take place mid-July through August (call for show times). ⊠*Off Rte. 100* ☎*709/227–2401* 🎫*Site $3.95, play $5* ⏱*Site open year-round; visitor center mid-May–mid-Oct., daily 10–6.*

WHERE TO STAY

$ 🏨**Rosedale Manor Bed & Breakfast.** Wake up to the smell of home-baked bread and pastries prepared by the chef/host of this 1893 waterfront heritage home in the Second Empire style. The rooms are bright and cheery and the grounds are filled with flowers. There's no elevator, but there are two rooms on the ground floor. Don't miss the homemade partridgeberry truffles. Rosedale is well-located 1 km (½ mi) from Argentia Ferry, 50 km (31 mi) from Cape St. Mary's, and 1½ hours from St. John's. ⊠ *40 Orcan Dr., Box 329, A0B 2Y0* ☎ *709/227–3613 or 877/999–3613* ⊕ *www.rosedalemanor.ca* 📶 *5 rooms* ⚒ *In-room: no a/c, no phone, no TV, Wi-Fi. In-hotel: no elevator, no-smoking rooms* ⊟ *MC, V* 🍴 *BP.*

¢ 🔳 **Harold Hotel.** Minutes from the Argentia–Nova Scotia Ferry, the Harold Hotel is in the very heart of Placentia and a two-minute walk to the boardwalk and the ocean. Ask for one of the front-facing rooms, which look out over a rocky mountain. ⊠ *Main St., Box 142, A0B 2Y0* ☎ *709/227–2107 or 877/227–2107* 🖶 *709/227–7700* 📶 *19 rooms* ⚒ *In-room: no a/c. In-hotel: restaurant, bar, no elevator, laundry facilities, no-smoking rooms, some pets allowed* ⊟ *AE, DC, MC, V.*

SHIP HARBOUR

34 km (21 mi) north of Placentia.

An isolated, edge-of-the-world place, Ship Harbour has historic significance. In 1941, on a ship in these waters, Franklin Roosevelt and Winston Churchill signed the Atlantic Charter and formally announced the "Four Freedoms," which still shape the politics of the world's most successful democracies: freedom of speech, freedom of worship, freedom from want, and freedom from fear. Off Route 102, amid the splendor of Placentia Bay, an unpaved road leads to an Atlantic Charter monument.

CAPE ST. MARY'S ECOLOGICAL RESERVE

★ *65 km (40 mi) south of Placentia.*

Cape St. Mary's Ecological Reserve is the third-largest nesting colony of gannets in North America and the most accessible seabird colony on the continent. A paved road takes you within a mile of the colony. You can visit the interpretation center—guides are on-site in summer—and then walk to within 100 feet of the colony of nesting gannets, murres, black-billed kittiwakes, and razorbills. Most birds are March through August visitors. Call the weather line to check on conditions before heading out. The reserve has some of the most dramatic coastal scenery in Newfoundland and is a good place to spot whales. From July through September the interpretation center is the site of performances of traditional

> **WORD OF MOUTH**
>
> "Cape St. Mary's [Ecological Reserve] is an absolute must-see. Their Interpretive Centre is excellent, the scenery is superb, and the seabird colony—especially the 11,000 Northern Gannets—is awe-inspiring…. We are returning for the eighth time this summer—drawn back by the landscapes, incredible wildlife, the music, and especially by the wonderful people." —gannetmusic

music by local artists; call for information and times. ✉ *Off Rte. 100* ☎ *709/227–1666, 709/635–4520, 709/337–2473 weather line* ⊕ *www. gov.nl.ca/parks&reserves* ⛟ *Site free, center $5* ☉ *Mid-May–June and Sept.–mid-Oct., daily 9–5; July–Sept., daily 8–7.*

WHERE TO STAY

¢–$ 🏨 **Bird Island Resort.** This pleasant lodging is a half-hour drive from Cape St. Mary's. The motel units are standard, but cottages are carpeted, have decks and kitchens, and overlook the water, where you can watch the sun fall into the ocean at the end of the day. ✉ *Off Rte. 100, St. Bride's A0B 2Z0* ☎ *709/337–2450 or 888/337–2450* 🖶 *709/337–2903* ⊕ *www.birdislandresort.com* ⛱ *5 rooms, 15 cottages* ⛆ *In-room: no a/c, kitchen (some). In-hotel: gym, no elevator, laundry facilities, no-smoking rooms* ☰ *AE, MC, V.*

¢–$ 🏨 **Capeway Motel & Efficiency Units.** The main attraction of this basic motel is its proximity to the seabird sanctuary at Cape St. Mary's. Built in 1968, the two-story building was originally a convent. It was refurbished and opened as a motel in the 1990s. Rooms are very bright, but blinds effectively filter out the morning sun. In-room phones are available by request. ✉ *Main St., St. Bride's A0B 2Z0* ☎ *709/337–2163 or 866/337–2163* 🖶 *709/337–2028* ⊕ *www.thecapeway.ca* ⛱ *3 rooms, 7 efficiency units* ⛆ *In-room: no a/c, no phone, kitchen. In-hotel: no elevator, laundry facilities, no-smoking rooms* ☰ *AE, MC, V.*

EASTERN NEWFOUNDLAND

Clarenville, about two hours northwest of St. John's via the Trans-Canada Highway (Route 1), is the departure point for several different excursions: the Bonavista Peninsula with its Discovery Trail and the twin communities of Trinity and Bonavista; Terra Nova National Park; and the Burin Peninsula.

CLARENVILLE

189 km (117 mi) northwest of St. John's.

★ If history and quaint towns appeal to you, follow the **Discovery Trail,** which begins in Clarenville on Route 230A. The trail includes two gems: the old town of Trinity, famed for its architecture and theater festival, and Bonavista, one of John Cabot's reputed landing spots.

NEED A BREAK?

Clarenville Irving & Restaurant. In addition to fast, inexpensive food, and clean washrooms, this pit stop has a great view of Trinity Bay and Random Island. The homemade turkey soup is divine. ✉ *Clarenville* ☎ *709/466– 2073.*

WHERE TO STAY

$ 🏨 **Clarenville Inn.** This hotel on the Trans-Canada Highway has a million-dollar view of Random Sound. Rooms are standard, with wall-to-wall carpeting. It's a convenient home base for tourists looking to take day trips along the Discovery Trail, down the Burin Peninsula, or even

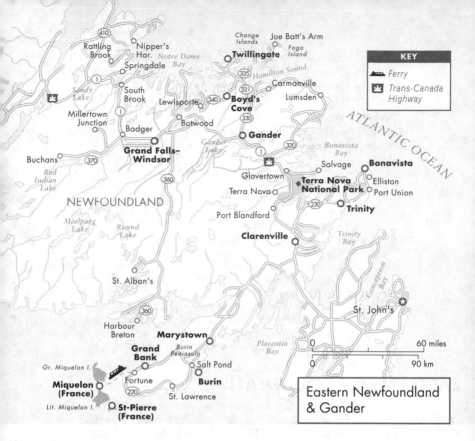

Eastern Newfoundland
& Gander

to the Avalon region. Rooms on the top floor are brighter, and the ones in the back have the better view. It's popular with families because children under 10 eat free in July and August, and there's a heated swimming pool. ⊠ *134 Transcanada Hwy., A5A 1Y3* ☎ *709/466–7911 or 877/466–7911* 🖷 *709/466–3854* ⊕ *www.clarenvilleinn.ca* 🛏 *62 rooms, 1 suite* ♿ *In-room: no a/c, ethernet. In-hotel: restaurant, room service, bar, pool, no elevator, laundry facilities, no-smoking rooms* 🗐 *AE, DC, MC, V.*

$ 🏨 **St. Jude Hotel.** Rooms are spacious and comfortable, if somewhat spartan, at this modern hotel. Rooms fronting the highway have a good view of the bay, but those in the back are quieter. The staff is extremely friendly and known for the quality of their service. Dustabella's restaurant has great homemade pea soup with dumplings and fabulous salt fishcakes. ⊠ *Rte. 1, Box 2500, A0E 1J0* ☎ *709/466–1717 or 800/563–7800* 🖷 *709/466–1714* ⊕ *www.stjudehotel.nf.ca* 🛏 *63 rooms* ♿ *In-room: Wi-Fi. In-hotel: restaurant, room service, bar, laundry service, some pets allowed, no-smoking rooms* 🗐 *AE, DC, MC, V.*

TERRA NOVA NATIONAL PARK

24 km (15 mi) north of Clarenville.

Newfoundland's first national park was Terra Nova Park, established in 1957. On Bonavista Bay, it has natural beauty, dramatic coastline, and rugged woods. Moose, black bear, and other wildlife move about freely in the forests and marshy bogs. Pods of whales play within sight of the shores, and many species of birds inhabit the cliffs and shores encompassed by the 396-square-km (246-square-mi) park.

Golf, sea kayaking, fishing, and camping are some of the draws here. Terra Nova also has the Marine Interpretation Center, nature walks, whale-watching tours, and a small but decent snack bar–cafeteria. Eight backcountry camping areas are accessible by trail or canoe. ⊠*Trans-Canada Hwy., Glovertown A0G 2L0* ☎*709/533–2801 or 709/533–2942* ⊕*www.pc.gc.ca* ☎*$5.45 mid-May–mid-Oct., free mid-Oct.–mid-May* ☉*Site daily dawn–dusk; center July and Aug., daily 9–8; May, June, Sept., and Oct., daily 10–5.*

WHERE TO STAY

$–$$ 🖺**Terra Nova Golf Resort.** Two of the most beautiful golf courses in Canada are at this resort at Port Blandford. The 18-hole Twin Rivers course, which is traversed by two salmon rivers, and the 9-hole Eagle Creek. Nestled in the beautiful Clode Sound near Terra Nova National Park, the high-end lodgings have all the big-city hotel luxuries rolled into the charm of a country inn. Rooms are large and bright with spectacular views. The property is sprawling, with lots to do, from hiking and swimming to an array of recreational activities. The golf courses are in high demand, so it's best to book two to three months in advance to be assured a tee time. Kids under 12 stay free, and there are children's programs in July and August. ⊠*Rte. 1, Box 160, Port Blandford A0C 2G0* ☎*709/543–2525, 709/543–2626 golf reservations* ☎*709/543–2201* ⊕*www.terranovagolf.com* ⇔*83 rooms, 6 suites* ⚶*In-room: refrigerator (some), dial-up. In-hotel: 3 restaurants, room service, bar, golf course, tennis court, pool, children's programs July and Aug. (ages 6 and up), no-smoking rooms* ⊟*AE, D, MC, V.*

TRINITY

71 km (44 mi) northeast of Clarenville.

Trinity is one of the jewels of Newfoundland. The village's ocean views, winding lanes, and snug houses are the main attractions. Several homes have been turned into museums and inns. In the 1700s, Trinity competed with St. John's as a center of culture and wealth. Its more contemporary claim to fame, however, is that its intricate harbor was a favorite anchorage for the British navy. Here, too, the smallpox vaccine was introduced to North America by a local rector. On West Street an information center with costumed interpreters is open daily mid-June through October. To get here, take Route 230 to Route 239.

The **Lester-Garland Premises Provincial Historic Site** takes you back over a century ago when merchant families ruled tiny communities. Next door the counting house has been restored to the 1820s, the retail store to the 1900s. An interpretation center traces the history of the town, once a mercantile center. ⊠ *West St.* ☎*709/464–2042 or 800/563–6353* ⊕*www.tcr.gov.nl.ca/tcr/historicsites* ◨*$3* ⊘*Mid-May–Sept., daily 10–5:30.*

The **Skerwink Trail** is a cliff walk with panoramic views of Trinity and the ocean. Along this historic footpath, you'll see sandy beaches, sea stacks (giant protruding rocks that have slowly eroded over time), and seabirds, and, in season, whales, icebergs, and bald eagles, too. This 5.3-km (3.3-mi) walk is not for the faint of heart. It takes about two hours and can be steep in places. Maps are available through the Discovery Trail Tourism Association, which maintains the hike; it begins across the harbor in Port-Rexton-Trinity East. ⊠ *Off Rte. 230, Port Rexton* ☎*709/466–3845* ⊕*www.thediscoverytrail.org/english/hikediscovery.*

WHERE TO STAY & EAT

¢–$$$ ✕**Dock Restaurant.** Right on the wharf, this restaurant is in a restored
★ 300-year-old fish merchant's headquarters. The menu includes traditional Newfoundland meals and seafood as well as the standard Canadian fare: burgers, chicken, and steak. Upstairs is an art gallery and crafts shop. ⊠*Trinity Waterfront* ☎*709/464–2133* ☰*AE, DC, MC, V* ⊘*Closed Nov.–Apr.*

$ ✕▦**Eriksen Premises.** This two-story mansard-style building was built in the late 1800s as a general store and tearoom. It has since been restored to its original elegance and character. The rooms here are larger than at its sister property, Bishop White Manor. They're also furnished with antiques and have views of the bay. The restaurant ($–$$; reservations essential) is known for its fish: it's a great spot to try cod tongues. For the faint of heart, you can't go wrong with a dish of fish chowder. ⊠ *West St., Box 58, Trinity Bay A0C 2S0* ☎*709/464–3698 or 877/464–3698* ▣*709/464–2104* ⊕*www.trinityexperience.com* ↹*7 rooms* ♿*In-room: no phone, no TV. In-hotel: restaurant, no elevator, no-smoking rooms* ☰*AE, MC, V* ⊘*Closed Nov.–Apr.* ⦿*BP.*

$–$$$ ▦**Campbell House B&B–Artisan House.** Owner Tineke Gow oversees this complex in the heart of Trinity. The mid-19th-century Campbell House is decorated with antiques and has low-ceilinged, light-filled rooms and a two-bedroom suite. The beds here are so comfortable you won't want to get out, but you should because there's lots to see around Trinity. Artisan House includes guest rooms and a working artist's studio. Guests can use the studio or watch a visiting artist at work. The Twine Loft Restaurant offers fine dining by reservation. Though there's no elevator, there's a wheelchair friendly ground-floor apartment. ⊠*49 High St., A0C 2S0* ☎*877/464–7700* ▣*709/464–3377* ⊕*www.trinityvacations.com* ↹*4 rooms, 1 suites, 1 studio* ♿*In-room: no a/c, kitchen (some), ethernet. In-hotel: restaurant, no elevator, laundry service, no-smoking rooms* ☰*AE, DC, MC, V* ⊘*Closed Nov.–Apr.* ⦿*BP.*

$–$$$ ▦**Fishers' Loft Inn.** Whales sometimes swim among small fishing boats in the harbor within sight of this inn, and icebergs drift by farther out in the bay. Rooms are bright and airy, with down duvets, handcrafted furniture, and original artwork. Four rooms have cathedral ceilings. The owners pack you a lunch and give you a map and guidance for hiking in the area. ⊠ *Mill Rd., 15 km (9 mi) northeast of Trinity, Box 36, Port Rexton A0C 2H0* ☎ *877/464-3240* ☎☎ *709/464-3240* ⊕ *www.fishersloft.com* ⇆ *21 rooms* ⚭ *In-room: no a/c, dial-up. In-hotel: no elevator, no-smoking rooms* ☰ *MC, V* ⊗ *Closed Nov.–Apr.*

¢–$ 🛏 **Sherwood Suites.** The cottages here are spacious and have living rooms and private patios. Opt for a cottage if you plan to do your own cooking. The motel rooms are large and bright with private entrances. ⊠ *Rocky Hill Rd., Box 2, Port Rexton A0C 2H0* ☎☎ *709/464-2130 or 877/464-2133* ⊕ *www.sherwoodsuites.com* ⇆ *4 rooms, 12 cottages* ⚭ *In-room: no a/c, kitchen (some). In-hotel: no elevator, laundry facilities, no-smoking rooms, some pets allowed* ☰ *AE, DC, MC, V* ⊗ *Closed Oct.–late May.*

NIGHTLIFE & THE ARTS

Shakespeare productions, dinner theater, and local dramas and comedies run throughout July and August at the Summer in the Bight festival at the **Rising Tide Theatre** (⊠ *Rte. 230 to Rte. 239, then left onto road into Trinity* ☎ *709/464-3232 or 888/464-3377* ⊕ *www.risingtidetheatre.com*). Check out the Web site for show information, dates, and times. The theater, on the waterfront, is styled like an old mercantile warehouse.

From mid-June through Labor Day, the company conducts New-Founde-Land Trinity Pageant plays, dinner theater, and walking tours of the lanes, roads, and sites of the town (Wednesday and weekends at 2), which are more theater than tour, with actors in period costume.

SPORTS & THE OUTDOORS

Atlantic Adventures Charters and Tours (☎ *709/464-2133 or 709/781-2255*) operates a 46-foot motorized sailboat for whale-watching or just cruising Trinity Bay. The boat departs daily at 10 AM and 2 PM, depending on the weather and on charter bookings. Tours are 2½ hours and cost about $40 per person. A group of six or more people can charter the boat for an 8- to 10-hour tour, which includes a meal, for about $85 per person. The vessel departs from the Dockside Marina.

BONAVISTA

28 km (17 mi) north of Trinity.

No one knows exactly where explorer John Cabot landed when he came to Atlantic Canada in 1497, but many believe it to have been at Bonavista, based on his descriptions of the newfound land.

The **Ryan Premises National Historic Site** on the waterfront depicts the almost 500-year history of the commercial cod fishery in a restored fish merchant's property. ⊠*Off Rte. 230* ☎*709/468–1600* ⊕*www.pc.gc. ca* ⊡*$3.95* ☼*Mid–May–Oct., daily 10–6.*

The **Cape Bonavista Lighthouse** on the point, about 1 km (½ mi) outside town, was built in 1843. It's been restored to the way it looked in 1870. ☎*709/468–7444 or 800/563–6353* ⊡*$3, includes Mockbeggar Plantation* ☼*Mid-May–Sept., daily 10–5:30.*

☽ The **Mockbeggar Plantation** teaches about the life of an outport merchant in the years immediately before Confederation. Guides in period costume lead you through an early-18th-century fish store, carpentry shop, and cod-liver-oil factory. ⊠*Off Rte. 230* ☎*709/468–7300 or 800/563–6353* ⊡*$3, includes Cape Bonavista Lighthouse* ☼*Mid-May–Sept., daily 10–5:30.*

WHERE TO STAY & EAT

$$ ✕⊞**The Harbour Quarters.** Built in the 1920s as a general store overlooking Bonavista Harbour, it's now a fabulous place to drop your anchor for the night. The rooms are comfortable and feature award-winning-local furniture. Skipper's restaurant has delicious seafood dishes and a great view of the harbor, where you can watch the sunset. ⊠*42 Campbell St., Box 399, Bonavista A0C 2S0* ☎*709/468–7982 or 866/468–7982* ⊞*709/468–7945* ⊕*www.harbourquarters.com* ⇆*11 rooms* ⌂*In-room: ethernet. In-hotel: restaurant* ⊟*AE, DC, MC, V* ⊙*CP.*

MARYSTOWN

283 km (175 mi) south of Bonavista.

Marystown, on the Burin Peninsula, is built around beautiful Mortier Bay, so big it was considered large enough for the entire British fleet during the early days of World War II. Shipbuilding is still the main industry, although it's certainly declined. Of note is the 20-foot statue of the Virgin Mary that looks out over the bay.

WHERE TO STAY

$ ⊞**Hotel Marystown.** This is the largest hotel on the Burin Peninsula; rooms are standard but comfortable. Rooms on the upper floors are a bit brighter. In the restaurant, P. J. Billington's, the peninsula's history of rum smuggling and connection to gangster Al Capone is told in photographs on the wall. ⊠*76 Ville Marie Dr., A0E 2M0* ☎*709/279–1600 or 866/612–6800* ⊞*709/279–4088* ⊕*www.cityhotels.ca* ⇆*131 rooms* ⌂*In-room: no a/c (some), kitchen (some), Wi-Fi. In-hotel: restaurant, room service, bar, gym, no elevator, laundry service, some pets allowed* ⊟*AE, DC, MC, V.*

BURIN

17 km (11 mi) south of Marystown.

A community built amid intricate cliffs and coves, Burin was an ideal setting for pirates and privateers, who used to lure ships into the rocky, dead-end areas to plunder them. When Captain James Cook was stationed here to chart the coast in the 1760s, one of his duties was to watch for smugglers bringing in rum from the island of St-Pierre. Smuggling continues to this day. Cook's Lookout, a hill overlooking Burin, is where Cook kept watch.

Heritage Museum, considered one of the best community museums in Newfoundland, gives you a sense of what life used to be like in this fishing community. It has a display of the 1929 tidal wave that struck Burin and the surrounding coastal communities, and information on the famous gangster Al Capone, who helped raise money for the local cottage hospital and arts center when he ran rum through the Burin Peninsula during prohibition. ⊠*Seaview Dr. off Rte. 221* ☎*709/891– 2217* ⊕*www.burin.ca* ⊠*Free* ⊙*Mar.–June, weekdays 8–4; July and Aug., daily 9–7.*

OFF THE BEATEN PATH

Cashel's Cove Crafts. Tucked away in the woods overlooking Mortier Bay is this little treasure of a store filled with only 100% Newfoundland-made products: some include traditional outport hooked and poked rugs, locally made quilts, pottery, homespun knits, jewelry, and native juniper-wood turnings. The owner encourages visitors to walk down the footpaths to the woodlands or to the beach. ⊠ *Take Rte. 210 (Burin Peninsula) at Goobies, make an immediate right turn as you enter Spanish Room, and follow signs to Cashel's Cove.* ⌂ *Box 665, Marystown* ☎ *709/279–1846* ⊕ *www.cashelscovecrafts.com.*

WHERE TO STAY

¢–$ ▥**Sound of the Sea Bed and Breakfast.** The sound of waves crashing on the shore drifts into this three-story B&B to create an utterly relaxing experience. The owners restored this 70-year-old merchant's house and have decorated it with antiques from the area. One room is furnished all in antiques. The proprietors can help plan the day's itinerary or arrange boat tours. ⊠*11A Seaview Dr. Rte. 221, A0E 1E0* ☎*709/891–2115 or 866/891–2115* ▤*709/891–2377* ⋩*3 rooms* ⌖*In-room: no a/c. In-hotel: no elevator, laundry facilities, public Internet, no-smoking rooms* ▤*MC, V* ⎆*BP.*

GRAND BANK

62 km (38 mi) west of Burin.

One of the loveliest communities in Newfoundland, Grand Bank has a fascinating history as an important fishing center. Because of trading patterns, the architecture here was influenced more by Halifax, Boston, and Bar Harbor, Maine, than by the rest of Newfoundland.

A sail-shaped building holds the **Provincial Seamen's Museum,** a memorial to the many Newfoundlanders who lost their lives at sea. ⊠*54 Marine Dr.* ☎*709/832–1484* ⊕*www.therooms.ca/museum/prov_museums. asp* ⊜*$2.50* ⊙*May–mid-Oct., daily 9:30–4:45.*

WHERE TO STAY

$ ⛨**Granny's Motor Inn.** The rooms here may be small, but they're clean and cozy and the owners are friendly. Each room has teak furnishings, carpeting, and a private entrance. The location is convenient, with easy access to the ferry to St-Pierre. The town's soccer field is also nearby—take a five-minute walk after dinner to catch the most popular sport on the Burin Peninsula. ⊠*33 Grandview Blvd., A0E 1W0* ☎*709/832–2355 or 888/275–1098* 🖷*709/832–0009* ⤹*10 rooms* ☖*In-room: Wi-Fi. In-hotel: restaurant, room service, bar, no elevator, laundry service, no-smoking rooms* ▤*AE, DC, MC, V.*

$ ⛨**Thorndyke Bed & Breakfast.** This 1917 Queen Anne–style mansion,
FodorsChoice a former sea captain's house, is a designated historic structure. The
★   blown-glass objects, colored panels, and sunporch have been part of the house since it was first built. This elegant home is filled with antique furniture and nice touches. The dining room walls are painted warm red, and a licensed dinner (i.e., one at which alcohol is served) is available by prebooking. Sea captains knew where to build houses so they had great views; this house is no exception. The ferry to St-Pierre is a five-minute drive away. ⊠*33 Water St., A0E 1W0* ☎*709/832–0820 or 866/882–0820* ⊕*www.thethorndyke.com* ⤹*5 rooms* ☖*In-room: no a/c, DVD. In-hotel: no elevator, no-smoking rooms* ▤*AE, D, DC, MC, V* ⊙*Closed mid-Sept.–Apr.* ⛨*BP.*

ST-PIERRE & MIQUELON

70-min ferry ride from Fortune, which is 10 km (6 mi) south of Grand Bank.

The islands of St-Pierre and Miquelon, France's only territory in North America, are a ferry ride away if you crave French cuisine or a bottle of perfume. Shopping and eating are both popular pastimes here. The bakeries open early, so there's always piping-hot fresh bread for breakfast. Bargain hunters can find reasonably priced wines from all over France. An interesting side trip via boat takes you to see seals, seabirds, and other wildlife, plus the huge sandbar (formed on the bones of shipwrecks) that now connects formerly separate Great and Little Miquelon. Visitors to the islands must carry proof of citizenship—even U.S. citizens must have a passport, and Canadians should have a passport or a government-issued photo ID. Because of the ferry schedule, a trip to St-Pierre means an overnight stay in a hotel or a pension, the French equivalent of a B&B.

Call the **St-Pierre Tourist Board** (☎*011/50841–02–00 or 800/565–5118) for information about accommodations.*

A passenger ferry operated by **St-Pierre Tours** (☎*709/832–2006, 709/722–4103, or 800/563–2006)* leaves Fortune (south of Grand

Bank) daily from mid-June to late September; the crossing takes a little over an hour. Call for schedule and rates.

WHERE TO STAY

$$ ☒ **Hotel Robert.** Gangster Al Capone stayed in a wing of this place when he ran rum through St-Pierre during prohibition. The rooms are spacious, but be warned that smoke lingers in the air. The owner is fluently bilingual and eager to educate tourists about St-Pierre. The hotel, a short walk from where the boat docks, is popular because of its tour packages. If you book your reservation through St-Pierre Tours, listed above, you'll get a deal that includes transportation and a cheaper room rate than if you book with the hotel directly. ☒ *Rue du 11 Novembre, St-Pierre, 97500* 📞 *508/41–2879, 709/832–2006, 800/563–2006 reservations, 011/50841–2879* ⟿*43 rooms* ♿ *In-room: no a/c, no phone. In-hotel: restaurant, no elevator, laundry facilities* ☰*MC, V* ⦿*CP.*

GANDER & AROUND

Gander, in east-central Newfoundland, is known for its airport and its aviation history. North of it is Notre Dame Bay, an area of rugged coastline and equally rugged islands that were once the domain of the now extinct Beothuk tribe. Only the larger islands are currently inhabited. Before English settlers moved into the area in the late 18th and early 19th centuries, it was seasonally occupied by French fisherfolk. Local dialects preserve centuries-old words that have vanished elsewhere. The bay is swept by the cool Labrador Current that carries icebergs south through Iceberg Alley; the coast is also a good whale-watching area.

GANDER

367 km (228 mi) north of Grand Bank.

Gander, a busy town of 9,651 people, is notable for its aviation history. It also has many lodgings and makes a good base for travel in this part of the province. After September 11, 2001, Gander gained international attention for having sheltered thousands of airline passengers whose planes were rerouted to this small town.

During World War II, **Gander International Airport** (☒*James Blvd.* 📞*709/256–6677* ⊕*www.ganderairport.com*) was chosen by the Canadian and U.S. air forces as a major strategic air base because of its favorable weather and secure location. After the war, the airport became an international hub for civilian travel; today it's a major air-traffic control center.

The **North Atlantic Aviation Museum** gives an expansive view of Gander's and Newfoundland's roles in aviation. In addition to viewing the expected models and photographs, you can climb into the cockpit of a real DC-3 parked outside next to a World War II Hudson bomber and a Canadian jet fighter. ☒*135 Trans Canada Hwy. (Rte. 1), between hos-*

pital and visitor information center ☎709/256–2923 ⊕www.naam.ca
☒$4 ⊙June–Sept., daily 9–9; Oct.–May, weekdays 9–5.

The **Silent Witness Memorial** marks the spot where, on December 12, 1985, an Arrow Air DC-8 carrying the 101st Airborne Division home for Christmas crashed, killing 256 soldiers and civilian flight crew. The memorial, eastbound on the Trans-Canada Highway 4 km (2½ mi) from Gander, is minutes off the main highway and worth a look.

From April to November, **Gander River Tours** (☎709/679–2271 ⊕www.
ganderrivertours.com) organizes salmon-fishing and hunting trips as well as guided tours of the river and wilderness areas around Gander.

WHERE TO STAY

$ 🏨 **Hotel Gander.** The view at this hotel on the Trans-Canada Highway is unremarkable, but rooms are spacious, modern, and clean. The largest hotel in Gander, it has a decent restaurant that serves standard Canadian fare. Children under 12 stay and eat for free. ⊠*100 Trans-Canada Hwy., A1V 1P5* ☎*709/256–3931 or 800/563–2988* 🖶*709/651–2641* ⊕*www.hotelgander.com* ⇆*152 rooms, 4 suites* ⼕*In-room: no a/c (some), dial-up. In-hotel: restaurant, room service, bar, pool, laundry facilities, no-smoking rooms* ☰*AE, DC, MC, V.*

$ 🏨 **Sinbad's Hotel and Suites.** Near nightclubs and restaurants, Sinbad's is popular with young couples. The hotel also has a lively bar of its own. Rooms are spacious but standard. ⊠*Bennett Dr., Box 450, A1V 1W6* ☎*709/651–2678 or 800/563–8330* 🖶*709/651–3123* ⊕*www.
steelehotels.com* ⇆*112 rooms* ⼕*In-room: kitchen (some). In-hotel: restaurant, bar, laundry service, public Internet, no-smoking rooms, some pets allowed* ☰*AE, DC, MC, V.*

BOYD'S COVE

66 km (41 mi) north of Gander.

Between 1650 and 1720, the Beothuks' main summer camp on the northeast coast was at the site of what is now Boyd's Cove. The coastline in and near Boyd's Cove is somewhat sheltered by Twillingate Island and New World Island. Short causeways link the shore to the islands.

The **Boyd's Cove Beothuk Interpretation Centre** offers a fresh look at the lives of the Beothuks, an extinct First Nations people who succumbed in the early 19th century to a combination of disease and battle with European settlers. The center uses traditional Beothuk building forms and adjoins an archaeological site that was inhabited from about 1650 to 1720, when pressure from settlers drove the Beothuks from this part of the coast. ⊠*Rte. 340* ☎*709/656–3114 or 800/563–6353* ⊕*www.
tcr.gov.nl.ca/tcr/historicsites* ☒$3 ⊙Mid-May–Sept., daily 10–5:30.

TWILLINGATE

31 km (19 mi) north of Boyd's Cove.

The inhabitants of this scenic old fishing village make their living from the sea and have been doing so for nearly two centuries. Colorful houses, rocky waterfront cliffs, a local museum, and a nearby lighthouse add to the town's appeal. One of the best places on the island to see icebergs, Twillingate is known to the locals as Iceberg Alley. These majestic and dangerous mountains of ice are awe inspiring to see when they're grounded in early summer.

Every year on the last full weekend in July, the town is the site of the **Fish, Fun & Folk Festival** (☎ 709/884–2678 ⊕ *www.fishfunfolkfestival. com*), where fish are cooked every possible way.

WHERE TO STAY

$ 🛏 **Paradise Bed & Breakfast.** Watch icebergs and whales from the patio of this modern, one-story home. The B&B is a five-minute walk to the beach and has an amazing view of Twillingate Harbour. ⊠ *192 Main St., A0G 4M0* ☎ *709/884–1999, 709/884–5683 off-season* ⊕ *www. bbcanada.com* ➦ *3 rooms* ⚭ *In-room: no phone, no TV. In-hotel: nosmoking rooms* ☰ *No credit cards* ⊘ *Closed Oct.–mid-May* ⦿|*BP.*

$ 🛏 **Ioulinguet Inn Bed & Breakfast.** In this 1920s-era home on the harbor front, rooms are old-fashioned, bright, and airy. Each room has two windows, and two of the rooms have views of the harbor. A secondstory balcony looks out over the Atlantic Ocean. You can wind down in the living room or den and admire the antiques and original character of the heritage house. ⊠ *56 Main St., A0G 4M0* ☎ *709/884–2080 or 888/447–8687* 🖷 *709/884–1274* ⊕ *www.bbcanada.com/9127.html* ➦ *3 rooms* ⚭ *In-room: no a/c. In-hotel: no elevator, laundry facilities, public Internet, some pets allowed, no-smoking rooms* ☰ *V* ⊘ *Closed Oct.–Apr.* ⦿|*CP.*

SPORTS & THE OUTDOORS

Twillingate Adventure Tours (☎ *709/884–5999 or 888/447–8687* ⊕ *www. twillingateadventuretours.com*) conducts two-hour guided cruises ($35 plus tax) on the M.V. *Daybreak* to see icebergs, whales, and seabirds. **Twillingate Island Boat Tours/Iceberg Craft Shop** (☎ *709/884–2242 or 800/611–2374* ⊕ *www.icebergtours.ca*) offers two-hour cruises to see whales, icebergs, and birds. Iceberg photography is the company's specialty, and there are tours that take amateur photographers out to get that perfect shot. Tours are $30 plus tax.

GRAND FALLS–WINDSOR

95 km (59 mi) west of Gander.

This central Newfoundland town is an amalgamation of two towns that were joined in 1991. The papermaking town of Grand Falls is the quintessential company town, founded by British newspaper barons early in the 20th century. Windsor was once an important stop on the

252 <   **Newfoundland & Labrador**

railway. The paper mill still ships newsprint all over the world, but the railway is no more.

A Logger's Life Provincial Museum. The hard lives of those who supplied wood for the paper mill are explored in this re-created 1920s-era logging camp. ✉ *Off Rte. 1, Exit 17, 2 km (1 mi) west of Grand Falls–Windsor* ☎ *709/292–4522* 🖥 *$2.50, includes Mary March Provincial Museum* ⊙ *Late Apr.–mid-Oct., daily 9–4:45.*

Mary March Provincial Museum. Mary March was the European name given to Demasduit, one of the last Beothuks. Displays trace the lives and customs of aboriginal cultures in Newfoundland and Labrador. ✉ *16 St. Catherine's St.* ☎ *709/292–4522* ⊕ *www.therooms. ca/museum/prov_museums.asp* 🖥 *$2.50, includes A Logger's Life Museum* ⊙ *May–late Oct., daily 9:30–4:45.*

OFF THE BEATEN PATH

Change Islands and Fogo Island. These outposts of the past give the impression of a place frozen in time. Modernity came arrived late here, and old expressions and accents still survive. Change Islands, with its outbuildings built on rock outcrops and on stilts, is a nice place for a quiet walk. Tilting, on the far end of Fogo Island, is famous for its "vernacular" architecture, two-story houses with typically one of three varying floor plans. The Dwyer Fishing Premises won an award for preservation of the architectural heritage of Newfoundland and Labrador; it's one part of the Tilting National Historic Site (☎ *709/658-7236 or 709/658-7381* ⊕ *www.townoftilting.com*) along with the Lane House Museum, the Old Irish Cemetery, and Sandy Cove Park. Open mid-June through mid-September, 10 to 8. In Tilting, there's overnight lodging at the four-room Foley's Place B&B (☎ *709/658-7244 or 866/658-7244*). You can take a ferry (☎ *709/627-3492 or 709/627-3448* ⊕ *www.gov.nl.ca/ ferryservices*) from Farewell to either the Change Islands or Fogo Island. To get to Farewell from Grand Falls–Windsor, go east on the Trans-Canada Highway to get to Route 340. Take Route 340 from Grand Falls–Windsor to Route 335, which takes you through scenic coastal communities.

WHERE TO STAY

$ 🖾 **Mount Peyton Hotel.** This lodging establishment has hotel and motel rooms, apartments with kitchenettes, and a good steak house. The hotel rooms have more services than the motel rooms, and easy access to the restaurant and bar. The motel rooms are across a divided highway from the hotel, making accessing the bar and restaurants tricky. ✉ *214 Lincoln Rd., A2A 1P8* ☎ *709/489-2251 or 800/563-4894* 🖨 *709/489-6365* ⊕ *www.mountpeyton.com* 💬 *150 rooms, 16 housekeeping units, 4 suites* ♿ *In-room: kitchen (some), Wi-Fi. In-hotel: 2 restaurants, bar, no elevator, laundry service, some pets allowed, no-smoking rooms* ▭ *AE, DC, MC, V* ⊙ *Motel rooms closed Sept.–Mar.*

WESTERN NEWFOUNDLAND

The Great Northern Peninsula is the northernmost visible extension of the Appalachian Mountains. Its eastern side is rugged and sparsely populated. The Viking Trail—Route 430 and its side roads—snakes along its western coast through a national park, fjords, sand dunes, and communities that have relied on lobster fishing for generations. At the tip of the peninsula, the Vikings established the first European settlement in North America a thousand years ago. For thousands of years before their arrival, the area was home to native peoples who hunted, fished, and gathered berries and herbs.

Western Newfoundland is known for the unlikely combination of world-class Atlantic salmon fishing and papermaking at two newsprint mills. This area includes Corner Brook, a major center. To the south, the Port au Port Peninsula west of Stephenville shows the French influence in Newfoundland, distinct from the farming valleys of the southwest, which were settled by Scots. A ferry from Nova Scotia docks at Port aux Basques in the far southwest corner.

DEER LAKE

208 km (129 mi) west of Grand Falls–Windsor.

Deer Lake was once just another small town on the Trans-Canada Highway, but the opening of Gros Morne National Park in the early 1970s and the construction of Route 430, a first-class paved highway passing right through to St. Anthony, changed all that. Today, with an airport and car rentals available, Deer Lake is a good starting point for a fly–drive vacation.

The **Newfoundland Insectarium** holds an intriguing collection of live and preserved insects, spiders, scorpions, and the like. A big attraction is the greenhouse, with live tropical butterflies. Check out the gift shop, which at times sells chocolate-covered crickets to eat. It's in a suburb of Deer Lake. ⊠*Rte. 430, Reidville* ☎*709/635-4545 or 866/635-5454* ⊕*www.nfinsectarium.com* ✆*$10* ⊙*Mid-Apr.–June and Sept.–mid-Oct., Tues.–Fri. 9–5, weekends 10–5; July and Aug., daily 9–9.*

WHERE TO STAY & EAT

¢–$ ✕**Deer Lake Irving Big Stop.** Good home-cooked meals and clean washrooms make this chain a welcome pit stop. The standard burgers and fries are available, but you can also eat a little more healthfully here with pita pockets and grilled–chicken burgers. ⊠*Rte. 1, Deer Lake* ☎*709/635-2129* ⊟*No credit cards.*

$$ 🖳**Deer Lake Motel.** The motel is clean and comfortable, but it's best to request a room in the back, because the front rooms face the highway and can be noisy. ⊠*15 Trans-Canada Hwy., A8A 2E5* ☎*709/635-2108, 800/563-2144 in Newfoundland* 📠*709/635-3842* ⊕*www.deerlakemotel.com* ➵*54 rooms, 2 suites* ♿*In-room: ethernet. In-hotel: 2 restaurants, room service, bar, no elevator, laundry service, parking (no fee), no-smoking rooms* ⊟*AE, MC, V.*

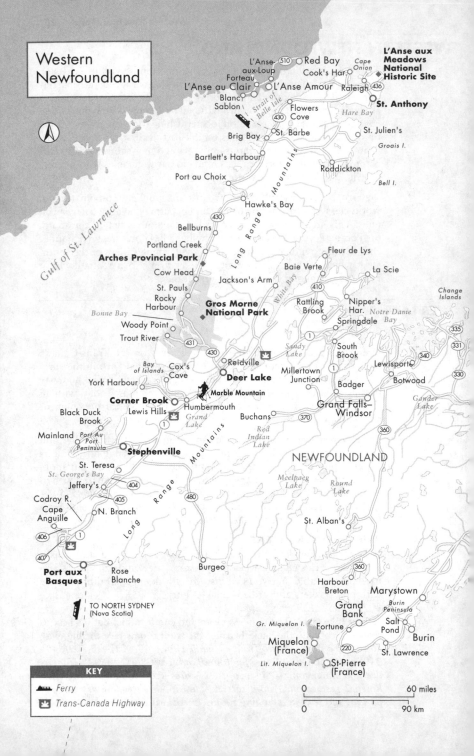

Western Newfoundland

L'Anse aux Meadows National Historic Site

L'Anse-aux-Loup · Red Bay · 510 · Cape Onion

Forteau · Cook's Har. · Raleigh · 436

L'Anse au Clair · L'Anse Amour · St. Anthony

Blanc Sablon · Flowers Cove · *Hare Bay*

Strait of Belle Isle · Brig Bay · St. Barbe · St. Julien's · *Groais I.*

Bartlett's Harbour · Roddickton

Port au Choix · *Bell I.*

Hawke's Bay

Bellburns

Portland Creek · Fleur de Lys

Arches Provincial Park · Baie Verte · La Scie

Cow Head · Jackson's Arm · *Change Islands*

St. Pauls · *White Bay*

Rocky Harbour · **Gros Morne National Park** · Rattling Brook · Nipper's Har. · *Notre Dame Bay* · 335

Bonne Bay · Springdale · 331

Woody Point · *Sandy Lake* · South Brook · 340

Trout River · Reidville · Millertown Junction · Lewisporte · 330

Bay of Islands · Cox's Cove · **Deer Lake** · Badger · Botwood · *Gander Lake*

York Harbour · Marble Mountain · Buchans · Grand Falls–Windsor · 370

Corner Brook · Humbermouth · 360

Black Duck Brook · Lewis Hills · *Grand Lake* · *Red Indian Lake*

Mainland · *Port Au Port Peninsula* · **NEWFOUNDLAND**

Stephenville · *Meelpaeg Lake* · *Round Lake*

St. Teresa

St. George's Bay · Jeffery's · 404

Codroy R. · 405 · 480

Cape Anguille · N. Branch · St. Alban's

406 · *Long Range Mountains*

407 · Burgeo · 360

Port aux Basques · Rose Blanche · Harbour Breton · Marystown

TO NORTH SYDNEY (Nova Scotia) · Grand Bank · *Burin Peninsula*

Gr. Miquelon I. · Fortune · Salt Pond · Burin

Miquelon (France) · 220 · St. Lawrence

Lit. Miquelon I. · St-Pierre (France)

Gulf of St. Lawrence

KEY

🚢 *Ferry*

⛷ *Trans-Canada Highway*

0 — 60 miles
0 — 90 km

GROS MORNE NATIONAL PARK

Fodor's Choice ★ *46 km (29 mi) north of Deer Lake on Rte. 430.*

Because of its geological uniqueness and immense splendor, this park has been named a UNESCO World Heritage Site. Among the more breathtaking visions are the expanses of wild orchids in springtime. Camping and hiking are popular recreations, and boat tours are available. To see Gros Morne properly you should allow yourself at least two days. An excellent **interpretation center** (⊠ *Rocky Harbour* ☎ *709/458–2417 or 709/458–2066* ⊕ *www.pc.gc.ca*) has displays and videos about the park. Scenic **Bonne Bay,** a deep, mountainous fjord, divides the park in two. You can drive around the perimeter of the fjord on Route 430 going north.

WORD OF MOUTH

"When I started planning my trip to Newfoundland two years ago, I started reading about Gros Morne National Park, with people describing its beauty with words normally used for places like Yosemite. I was EXTREMELY skeptical—and even MORE wrong. This place is like Yosemite and Big Sur combined. As I said to my wife, this place has a lot of 'OMG!' moments." —PaulRabe

4

Woody Point, a charming community of old houses and imported Lombardy poplars, is in the south of the park, on Route 431.

The **Tablelands,** rising behind Norris Point, is a unique rock massif that was raised from the earth's mantle through tectonic upheaval. Its rocks are toxic to most plant life, and Ice Age conditions linger in the form of persistent snow and moving rock glaciers. The **Discovery Centre** (⊠ *Rte. 431 on the outskirts of Woody Point heading west toward Trout River* ☎ *709/453–2490*) is the main interpretation center for the park and has educational programs on its geology and natural history.

The small community of **Trout River** is at the western end of Route 431 on the Gulf of St. Lawrence. You pass the scenic Trout River pond along the way.

The **Green Gardens Trail,** a spectacular hike, is also nearby, but be prepared to do a bit of climbing on your return journey. The trail passes through the Tablelands barrens and descends sharply to a coastline of eroded cliffs and green meadows.

Head to the northern side of the park, along coastal Route 430, to visit **Rocky Harbour** with its range of restaurants, lodgings, and a luxurious indoor public pool and large hot tub—the perfect place to soothe tired limbs after a strenuous day.

The most popular attraction in the northern portion of Gros Morne is the boat tour of **Western Brook Pond.** You park at a lot on Route 430 and take a 45-minute walk to the boat dock through an interesting mix of bog and woods. Cliffs rise 2,000 feet on both sides of the gorge, and high waterfalls tumble over ancient rocks. Hikers in good shape can tackle the 16-km (10-mi) hike up **Gros Morne Mountain,** at

2,644 feet the second-highest peak in Newfoundland. Weather permitting, the reward for your effort is a unique arctic landscape and spectacular views. The park's **northern coast** has an unusual mix of sand beaches, rock pools, and trails through tangled dwarf forests (which are locally called tuckamore forests). Sunsets seen from **Lobster Head Cove Lighthouse** are spectacular. Keep an eye out for whales, and visit the lighthouse museum, devoted to the history of the area. ⊠ *Viking Trail (Rte. 430) from Deer Lake* ☎ *709/458–2417* 🖷 *709/458–2059* ⊕ *www.pc.gc.ca* 🖃*$8.90* ☯ *Mid-May–mid-Oct., 10–5:30.*

WHERE TO STAY & EAT

$–$$$ ✕ **Seaside Restaurant.** This restaurant overlooking the ocean prepares fresh seafood in traditional Newfoundland style. Try scallops and shrimp sautéed or in a stir-fry, or choose from a wide selection of seafood dinners, including salmon, catfish, and cod tongue. ⊠ *Main St., Trout River* ☎ *709/451–3461* ☰ *MC, V* ☯ *Closed Nov.–late May.*

$–$$ ✕ **Fisherman's Landing.** The food is good here and ranges from seafood dishes (in season) to standard Canadian fare such as club and hot turkey sandwiches or pork chops and steak. ⊠ *Main St., Rocky Harbour* ☎ *709/458–2060* ☰ *AE, MC, V.*

$–$$ ✕ **Java Jack's.** The coffee is strong and freshly brewed, and this is a great
Fodor'sChoice place to pick up a take-away bag lunch, such as shredded pork with
★ partridgeberry-honey mustard for the boat trip to Western Brook Pond. On dine in and enjoy a great view of the harbor. For dinner, try their seafood bubbly bake, with seasonal fish in a cream sauce. The restaurant doubles as a gallery; work by Atlantic Canadian artists (all for sale) decorates the walls. ⊠ *88 Main St. N, Box 250, Rocky Harbour A0K 4N0* ☎ *709/458–3004* ☰ *AE, MC, V* ☯ *Closed mid-Oct.–mid-May.*

$$ 🖃 **Fisherman's Landing Inn.** This resort has two arms of rooms radiating from the sides of the main complex. The rooms are spacious and bright and have private outside entrances. They're set up like modern hotel rooms, with a country charm. The coffee shop–bar is the nerve center, where you can get three meals a day and linger for a few drinks. Kids 16 and under stay for free. ⊠ *West Link Rd., off Rte. 430, Box 124, Rocky Harbour A0K 4N0* ☎ *709/458–2711 or 866/458–2711* 🖷 *709/458–2168* ⊕ *www.fishermanslandinginn.com* ⇨ *40 rooms* ⟁ *In-room: dial-up. In-hotel: restaurant, room service, bar, laundry facilities, no-smoking rooms* ☰ *AE, DC, MC, V.*

$–$$ 🖃 **A-1 Wildflowers Country Inn.** Surrounded by wildflowers, this grand 80-year-old wood house overlooks the ocean and is central to boat tours and walking trails. Lace curtains and colorful quilts give the rooms a country feel. ⊠ *Main St. N, Box 291, Rocky Harbour A0K 4N0* ☎ *709/458–3000 or 888/811–7378* ⊕ *www.bbcanada.com/1622. html* ⇨ *5 rooms, 1 cottage* ⟁ *In-room: no a/c, Wi-Fi. In-hotel: no elevator, laundry service, no-smoking rooms* ☰ *MC, V* ☷*BP.*

$–$$ 🖃 **Frontier Cottages.** These rustic log cabins can hold up to six people and are ideal if you wish to do your own cooking while visiting Gros Morne. The cabins are close together, but the view of the hills from the deck is spectacular, and the cabins are clean, spacious, and private. The grocery store stocks most items, but for greater variety, pick up your staples at a larger store beforehand. ⊠ *Rte. 430, Box 172, Wilton-*

dale A0K 4N0 ☎709/453–7266 or 800/668–2520 📠709/453–7272
⟿7 cabins 🏊In-room: no a/c, no phone, kitchen. In-hotel: restaurant,
laundry facilities ⊟AE, DC, MC, V.

$–$$ 🖿 **Gros Morne Cabins.** These modern log chalets, which overlook the
Gulf of St. Lawrence, are near restaurants and stores in Rocky Harbour. Cabins have hardwood floors, log walls, and a tremendous ocean
view. They can accommodate up to four people. ✉Main St., Rocky
Harbour A0K 4N0 ☎709/458–2020 or 888/603–2020 📠709/458–
2882 ⊕www.grosmornecabins.com ⟿22 cabins 🏊In-room: no a/c,
kitchen, Wi-Fi. In-hotel: laundry facilities, no-smoking rooms ⊟AE,
DC, MC, V.

$–$$ 🖿 **Gros Morne Resort.** Rooms in the front of this hotel overlook the
ocean; those in the rear face the Long Range mountains and St. Pauls
Inlet. The rooms are spacious and have private balconies or patios.
Some suites have whirlpool tubs. Guests can choose from a restaurant
serving traditional meals or fine dining. The resort is in St. Pauls, a
small community encircled by Gros Morne Park. ✉Rte. 430, Box 100,
St. Pauls A0K 4Y0 ☎709/243–2606 or 888/243–2644 📠709/243–
2615 ⟿8 rooms, 12 suites 🏊In-hotel: 2 restaurants, bar, refrigerator
(some), no-smoking rooms ⊟AE, DC, MC, V.

$–$$ 🖿 **Ocean View Motel.** This large two-story motel is right on the water
and has an on-site kiosk for Bon Tours, which conducts sightseeing
boat trips on Western Brook Pond and Bonne Bay. A pub on the premises features a house band. The brightly decorated standard rooms
are clean; the rooms at the front of the building have water views.
✉Main St., Box 129, Rocky Harbour A0K 4N0 ☎709/458–2730 or
800/563–9887 📠709/458–2841 ⊕www.oceanviewmotel.com ⟿48
rooms, 4 suites 🏊In-hotel: restaurant, bar, no-smoking rooms ⊟AE,
DC, MC, V.

$–$$ 🖿 **Sugar Hill Inn.** Host Vince McCarthy's culinary talents and educated
palate has earned this inn a reputation for fine wining and dining.
There's only one sitting, at 7:30 PM, for the three-course meal in the
dining room. Afterward sit back under the vaulted cedar ceiling of the
common room, or relax in the cedar-lined hot-tub room with attached
sauna. A stay here is a delight. ✉115–129 Sexton Rd., Box 100, Norris
Point A0K 3V0 ☎709/458–2147 or 888/299–2147 📠709/458–2166
⊕www.sugarhillinn.nf.ca ⟿3 rooms, 3 suites, 1 cottage 🏊In-hotel:
room service, no elevator, laundry facilities, no-smoking rooms ⦿ICP,
BP ⊟AE, MC, V ⊘Closed Nov.–Feb.

$ 🖿 **Crocker Cabins.** These spacious two-bedroom cabins with two double
beds are in Trout River in the quieter, less-developed southern part of
Gros Morne National Park. They're in a wooded area between the
boundary of the community and the park. Each building contains two
cabins, which share a common deck. Rooms are standard, clean, and
can accommodate up to four people. There's a playground on-site.
✉57 Duke St., Trout River A0K 5P0 ☎709/451–3236 or 877/951–
3236 ⊕www.crockercabins.com ⟿4 cabins 🏊In-room: no a/c, no
phone, kitchen. In-hotel: laundry facilities, some pets allowed, no-
smoking rooms ⊟AE, MC, V.

4

¢   ⚏**Blanchard House.** Built in 1904, this heritage home has since been renovated but has retained its original character, accented by antique furniture. The owners also run the nearby Granite Coffee Shop. ✉*12 Blanchard La., Woody Point A0K 1P0* ☎*709/451–3236 or 877/951–3236* ⊕*www.crockercabins.com* ⟿*4 rooms* ⚇*In-room: no TV. In-hotel: no elevator, laundry facilities, no-smoking rooms* ▭*AE, MC, V* ⎆*CP.*

CAMPING   To make reservations at Gros Morne campgrounds listed below, contact **Parks Canada at Gros Morne** (☎*877/737–3783* 🖷*709/458–2059* ⊕*www.pccamping.ca*). For more info on the various campsites, go to www.pc.gc.ca. The campsite prices are in addition to the $8.90 park admission fee.

⚠**Berry Hill Campground.** These wooded sites are near the recreation complex, visitor center, and Lobster Cove Head Lighthouse. If you like hikes, there are three trails from the campground. ⚇*Flush toilets, dump station, showers, fire pits, play area* ⟿*146 drive-in, 6 walk-in sites* ✉*Rte. 430, 10 km (6 mi) north of Rocky Harbour* ▭*AE, MC, V* ⊗*Closed mid-Sept.–mid-June.*

⚠**Green Point Campground.** This year-round campground, 10 km (6.2 mi) north of Rocky Harbour, is the only campground that operates on a first-come, first-served basis. The campsites are high on a cliff, and from some you can see the ocean through the trees. ⚇*Fire pits* ⟿*31 drive-in sites* ✉*Rte. 430* ▭*AE, MC, V.*

⚠**Lomond Campground.** Trees and a view of Bonne Bay and the Long Range Mountains surround this nice campground. ⚇*Flush toilets, dump station, showers, fire pits, play area* ⟿*25 drive-in, 4 walk-in sites* ✉*Rte. 431* ▭*AE, MC, V* ⊗*Closed early Oct.–early May.*

⚠**Shallow Bay Campground.** The campsites themselves may be a little too close together, but with a long stretch of sandy beach, and washrooms, showers, and dishwashing facilities nearby, Shallow Bay is a great place to camp nonetheless. It's also close to Western Brook Pond. ⚇*Flush toilets, dump station, showers, picnic tables, play area, fireplaces* ⟿*62 drive-in sites* ✉*Rte. 430, near Cow Head* ▭*AE, MC, V* ⊗*Closed mid-Sept.–early June.*

⚠**Trout River Campground.** This is camping in the wilderness with clean shower facilities, a great outdoor cooking hut, and fabulous views of Trout River Pond and the Tablelands. The campsites are nicely sheltered and spaced. It's 18 km (11 mi) from the Discovery Centre. ⚇*Flush toilets, showers, play area, fireplaces* ⟿*40 drive-in, 4 walk-in sites* ✉*50 km (31 mi) from park entrance at Wiltondale, off Rte. 431* ▭*AE, MC, V* ⊗*Open mid-Sept.–early June.*

NIGHTLIFE & THE ARTS

The **Gros Morne Theatre Festival** (☎*877/243–2899* ⊕*www.theatrenew foundland.com*) provides summer entertainment in Cow Head and other venues throughout the park. Most productions are comedies, though there are some dramas based on local stories, plus an outdoor children's show.

SPORTS & THE OUTDOORS

BonTours (☎709/458–2730 or 800/563–9887 ⊕*www.bontours.ca*) runs sightseeing boat tours of Western Brook Pond in Gros Morne National Park and of Bonne Bay and Seal Island. **Gros Morne Adventures** (☎709/458–2722 or 800/685–4624 ⊕*www.grosmorneadventures.com*) has sea kayaking up the fjords and landlocked ponds of Gros Morne National Park, as well as a variety of hikes and adventures in the area. **Trout River Pond Boat Tour** (☎866/751–7500 ⊕*www.troutriverpondboattour.com*) leads tours on Trout River Pond near the southern boundary of Gros Morne National Park.

ARCHES PROVINCIAL PARK

4

20 km (12 mi) north of Gros Morne National Park.

Arches Provincial Park is a geological curiosity: its rock formations were made millions of years ago by wave action and undersea currents. The succession of caves through a bed of dolomite was later raised above sea level by tectonic upheaval. ⊠*Rte. 430* ☎*800/563–6353* ⊕*www.gov.nl.ca/parks&reserves* 🎫*Free* ☉*Early June–mid-Sept.*

EN ROUTE

Continuing north on Route 430 parallel to the Gulf of St. Lawrence, you find yourself refreshingly close to the ocean and the wave-tossed beaches. The **Long Range Mountains** to your right reminded Jacques Cartier, who saw them in 1534 as he was exploring the area on behalf of France, of the long, rectangular-shaped farm buildings of his home village in France. Small villages are interspersed with rivers where salmon and trout grow to be "liar size."

The remains of Maritime Archaic and Dorset people have been found in abundance along this coast, and **Port au Choix National Historic Site** has an interesting interpretation center about them. An archaeological dig also has discovered an ancient village. Ask at the interpretation center for directions to the site of the dig. ⊠*Off Rte. 430* ☎*709/458-2417, 709/861-3522* mid-June–Aug. ⊕*www.pc.gc.ca.* 🎫*$7.15* ☉*June-early Oct., daily 9–6.*

L'ANSE AUX MEADOWS NATIONAL HISTORIC SITE

FodorsChoice *210 km (130 mi) northeast of Arches Provincial Park.*
★

Around the year AD 1000, Vikings from Greenland and Iceland founded the first European settlement in North America near the northern tip of Newfoundland. They arrived in the New World 500 years before Columbus, but stayed only a few years and were forgotten for centuries. It was only in 1960 that the Norwegian team of Helge and Anne Stine Ingstad discovered the remains of the Viking settlement's long sod huts. Today L'Anse aux Meadows is a UNESCO World Heritage Site. Parks Canada has a fine visitor center and has reconstructed some of the huts to give you a sense of centuries past. An interpretation program introduces you to the food, games, and way of life of that long-ago time. ⊠*Rte. 436* ☎*709/623-2608* 🖨*709/623-2028 summer only*

⊕*www.pc.gc.ca/lhn-nhs/nl/meadows* ▢*$10.40* ⊙*June–early Oct., daily 9–6.*

⟳ Two kilometers (1 mi) east of L'Anse aux Meadows is a Viking attraction, **Norstead.** This reconstruction of an 11th-century Viking port has a chieftain's hall, church, and ax-throwing arena. Much of the site is aimed at kids, but the Viking boatbuilding course is designed for all ages. Interpreters in period dress can answer questions as they go about their Viking business. ⊠*Rte. 436* ☎*709/623–2828 or 877/620–2828* ⊕*www.norstead.com* ▢*$8* ⊙*June–late-Sept., daily 9–6.*

WHERE TO STAY & EAT

$$–$$$$ ✕**Norseman Restaurant.** This restaurant on the harbor front allows you
Fodor's Choice to pick your own lobster from a crate. An extensive wine list accom-
★ panies a menu ranging from seafood and pasta to caribou tenderloins. There's a dinner-theater performance every Tuesday and Friday in July and August. ⊠*Turn right at end of Rte. 436; Box 265, L'Anse aux Meadows* ☎*877/623–2018* ▤*DC, MC, V.*

¢–$$$ ✕**Fisherman's Galley.** Don't let the modest facade and roadside location fool you—inside, huge windows frame a magnificent view of a shallow harbor protected by an island dotted with grazing sheep, and with seabirds circling overhead. The food's not bad, either. Try the cod chowder or halibut, and walk it off with a stroll on the deck. The attached store sells crafts and books. ⊠*Rte. 436, St. Lunaire–Griquet* ☎*709/623–2431* ▤*AE, DC, MC, V* ⊙*Closed Oct.–Apr.*

$ ▥**Southwest Pond Cabins.** These basic cabins are a 10-minute drive from L'Anse aux Meadows. There are two cabins under one roof, but the units are totally self-contained and private. The exterior is log, with the interior spacious, bright, and clean. There's a playground and convenience store on the property. ⊠*Rte. 436, Box 58, St. Lunaire–Griquet A0K 2X0* ☎*709/623–2140 or 800/515–2261* ▤*709/623–2145* ⊕*www.southwestpondcabins.com* ▱*8 cabins* ☍*In-room: no a/c, no phone, kitchen. In-hotel: laundry facilities, no-smoking rooms* ▤*AE, MC, V* ⊙*Closed Nov.–mid-May.*

$ ▥**Valhalla Lodge Bed & Breakfast.** On a hill overlooking iceberg alley,
Fodor's Choice the Valhalla is 8 km (5 mi) from L'Anse aux Meadows. Some fossils
★ are part of the rock fireplace in the common room. The owner quickly becomes known by her guests for her pancakes with local berry sauce. Rooms are quiet and brightly painted, with large windows, pine Scandinavian furniture, and handmade quilts. The rooms all have Viking names. Pulitzer Prize winner E. Annie Proulx, author of *The Shipping News,* stayed here while writing the novel. The owners of this lodge have bought and now rent out two homes in which Proulx lived; you can even take her dory for a row. The "Quoyle's" is an three-bedroom A-frame house with a view of the ocean, and "Wavey's" is a low-ceilinged Newfoundland Saltbox with two bedrooms. ⊠*Box 10 Gunner's Cove, St. Lunaire–Griquet A0K 2X0* ☎*709/623–2018, 877/623–2018, 709/754–3105 off-season* ▤*709/623–2144* ⊕*www.valhalla-lodge.com* ▱*5 rooms* ☍*In-room: no a/c, DVD, VCR. In-hotel: no elevator, laundry facilities, public Internet, no-smoking rooms* ▤*DC, MC, V* ▯◌*BP* ⊙*Closed mid-Oct.–early May.*

¢–$ ⌨ **Viking Nest/Viking Village Bed & Breakfast.** Thelma Hedderson owns and oversees these two B&Bs on the same property. Each of the four rooms at the Viking Nest is named after a famous person or boat from Viking legends or history. Only one of the rooms has a private bathroom. The Viking Village is a five-room inn, with doors opening onto a fenced patio. Rooms here have spruce walls and Scandinavian furniture. Room phones are available only by request. The Viking settlement at L'Anse aux Meadows is 1 km (½ mi) away. ⌂ *Box 127, Hay Cove A0K 2X0* ☎ *877/858–2238* 🖶 *709/623–2238* ⊕ *www.vikingvillage. ca and www.bbcanada.com/vikingnest* ⏏ *9 rooms, 6 with bath* ♿ *In-room: no phone, no TV. In-hotel: no elevator, laundry service, airport shuttle* ☰ *AE, MC, V* ⊙| *BP.*

¢   ⌨ **Tickle Inn at Cape Onion.** This refurbished, century-old fisherman's house on the beach is probably the northernmost residence on the island of Newfoundland. Relax by the Franklin stove in the parlor after exploring the coast or L'Anse aux Meadows (about 45 km [28 mi] away). The kitchen serves seafood, baked goods, and homemade jams. Licensed evening dining (i.e., a meal with alcohol) is provided at additional cost. ✉ *R.R. 1, Box 62, Cape Onion A0K 4J0* ☎ *709/452–4321, 866/814–8567 June–Sept., 709/739–5503 Oct.–May* ⊕ *www.tickleinn. net* ⏏ *4 rooms with shared bath* ♿ *In-room: no a/c. In-hotel: no elevator, no-smoking rooms* ☰ *MC, V* ☙ *Closed Oct.–May* ⊙| *CP.*

ST. ANTHONY

16 km (10 mi) south of L'Anse aux Meadows.

The northern part of the Great Northern Peninsula served as the setting for *The Shipping News*, E. Annie Proulx's Pulitzer Prize–winning novel. St. Anthony is built around a natural harbor on the eastern side of the Great Northern Peninsula, near its tip. If you take a trip out to the lighthouse, you may see an iceberg or two floating by.

The **Grenfell Mission** was founded by Sir Wilfred Grenfell, a British medical missionary who established nursing stations and cooperatives and provided medical services to the scattered villages of northern Newfoundland and the south coast of Labrador in the early 1900s. It remains the town's chief employer. The main foyer of the **Charles S. Curtis Memorial Hospital** (✉ *178–200 West St.* ☎ *709/454–4010*) has a decorative tile mural depicting scenes from Grenfell's life.

The **Grenfell Historic Properties** comprise a museum, house, and interpretation center, all focusing on Grenfell's life and work. ✉ *Maraval Rd.* ☎ *709/454–4010* ⊕ *www.grenfell-properties.com* 🎟 *$5* ⊙ *May–Sept., daily 9–8.*

WHERE TO STAY & EAT

¢–$$ ✕ **The Light Keeper's Seafood Restaurant.** Good seafood and solid Canadian fare are served in this former lighthouse keeper's home overlooking the ocean. Halibut, shrimp, and cod are usually good bets, as is the seafood chowder. They have an incredible bakeapple cheesecake for dessert. ⊠*Fishing Point Rd.* ☎*709/454–4900* ▤*MC, V* ⊘*Closed Nov.–Apr.*

$–$$ ⊡**Tuckamore Lodge & Country Inn.** The Scandinavian-style cedar lodge with a lofty ceiling provides a luxurious base from which to explore the natural bounty of the area, which is about an hour away from St. Anthony. Lunch and dinner (corn chowder, cod fondue, chocolate macaroon pie, etc.) are offered for an additional price. Activity packages include fishing, sea kayaking, wilderness adventures, and snowmobiling. There are eight rooms in the lodge, which is for guests on package tours, and four rooms in the pine A-frame country inn. In both lodges, meals are served at big communal tables. ⊠ *1 Southwest Pond Rd., Box 100, Main Brook A0K 3N0* ☎*709/865–6361 or 888/865–6361* 🖷*709/865–2112* ⊕*www.tuckamorelodge.com* ⇆*9 rooms, 3 suites* ⌂*In-room: no a/c, no TV, Wi-Fi. In-hotel: laundry service, airport shuttle, no-smoking rooms* ▤*AE, DC, MC, V* �1○�11*BP.*

$ ⊡**Vinland Motel.** These are standard rooms, but the motel is in the center of town, so what it lacks in a view it makes up for in convenience. Two rooms and the suite have whirlpool baths. Rooms are clean, and the staff is friendly and helpful. ⊠*19 West St., A0K 4S0* ☎*709/454–8843 or 800/563–7578* 🖷*709/454–8468 vinlandmotel@nf.sympatico. ca* ⇆*43 rooms, 1 suite* ⌂*In-hotel: restaurant, bar, gym, laundry facilities, some pets allowed, no-smoking rooms* ▤*AE, DC, MC, V.*

SPORTS & THE OUTDOORS
Northland Discovery Boat Tours (⊠*Behind the Grenfell Interpretation Centre off West St.* ☎*709/454–3092 or 877/632–3747* ⊕*www. discovernorthland.com*) leads specialized trips to see whales, icebergs, and seabirds, as well as salmon-fishing excursions.

SHOPPING
Be sure to visit **Grenfell Handicrafts** (⊠*227A West St.* ☎*709/454–3576* ⊕*www.grenfell-properties.com*) in the Grenfell Historic Properties complex. Training villagers to become self-sufficient in a harsh environment was one of Grenfell's aims. A windproof cloth that they turned into well-made parkas came to be known as Grenfell cloth. Mittens, caps, and coats are embroidered with motifs such as polar bears; the selection of items for sale is extensive.

CORNER BROOK

50 km (31 mi) southwest of Deer Lake.

Newfoundland's second-largest city, Corner Brook is the hub of the island's west coast. Mountains fringe three sides of the city, which has beautiful views of the harbor and the Bay of Islands. The town is also home to one of the largest paper mills in the world (you'll probably smell it while you're here). Captain James Cook, the British explorer, charted the coast in the 1760s, and a memorial to him overlooks the bay.

Corner Brook is a convenient hub and point of departure for exploring the west coast. It's only a three-hour drive (allowing for traffic) from

4

the Port aux Basques ferry from Nova Scotia. The town enjoys more clearly defined seasons than most of the rest of the island, and in summer it has many pretty gardens. The nearby Humber River is the best-known salmon river in the province.

The north and south shores of the Bay of Islands have fine paved roads—Route 440 on the north shore and Route 450 on the south—and both are a scenic half-day drive from Corner Brook. On both roads, farming and fishing communities exist side by side.

> ### BERRY, BERRY GOOD
>
> In July and August, Newfoundland's wild berries ripen. Partridgeberries, also called mountain cranberries, cowberries, and lingonberries (among other names), are used for pies, jams, cakes, pancakes, and as a meat sauce. Bakeapples, also known as cloudberries, look like yellow raspberries and grow on low plants in bogs. Pickers sell them by the side of the road in jars. If the ones you buy are hard, wait a few days and they'll ripen into rich-tasting fruit. The berries are great on ice cream, cheesecake, or spread on bread.

OFF THE BEATEN PATH

The Newfoundland Emporium. Crammed from wall to wall with Newfoundland stuff is the best way to describe this place. The main store is full of books, art, crafts, music, and souvenirs. A three-level adjoining building is filled with antique furniture and Newfoundland collectibles, topped off by an art gallery. And if you want to meet a real Newfoundlander, look for Moosie, the 175-pound dog that makes the Emporium his home. ⊠ *7 Broadway* ☎ *709/634–9376* ☐ *AE, MC, V.*

WHERE TO STAY & EAT

$$ $$$$ ✕ **13 West.** Start your meal off with oysters and chase them down with
★ one of the wonderful salmon specials: strawberry salmon, mango salmon, blackened salmon, or salmon with rosemary and peppercorns. For those not interested in seafood, the rack of lamb and pork tenderloin are good choices. ⊠ *13 West St.* ☎ *709/634–1300* ☐ *AE, D, DC, MC, V* ⊗ *No lunch weekends.*

$$–$$$ ✕ ⊞ **Strawberry Hill Resort.** Once an exclusive retreat for the owner of the Corner Brook Mill, this resort has Newfoundland's finest salmon fishing, hiking, skiing, and snowmobiling. At the end of the day you can relax in the hot tub or sauna and retire to your room or chalet. Some rooms in the manor house have fireplaces and sitting areas; all come with a Continental breakfast. Chalets ($$$–$$$$), which sleep up to seven, have all the conveniences of home, with washers and dryers, kitchens, several bedrooms, and full-size living rooms. The resort has boat, helicopter, and snowmobile tours of the area, plus guided fishing, sea-kayaking, hiking, and spelunking trips. The dining menu changes daily and the salmon dishes are delectable. ⊠ *Rte. 1, Box 2200, 12 km (7 mi) east of Corner Brook, Little Rapids A2H 2N2* ☎ *709/634–0066 or 877/434–0066* ☎ *709/639–7604* ⊕ *www.strawberryhill.net* ⇆ *6 rooms, 8 chalets* ⚿ *In-room: Wi-Fi, no a/c, kitchen (some). In-hotel: restaurant, no elevator, no-smoking rooms* ☐ *AE, D, DC, MC, V* ⦿ *CP.*

$ ✕▦ **Glynmill Inn.** This Tudor-style inn was once the staff house for the
★ visiting top brass of the paper mill. Rooms are cozy, and the dining
room serves basic and well-prepared Newfoundland seafood, soups,
and specialty desserts. There's also a popular steak house ($$–$$$) in
the basement. ✉*1B Cobb La., Box 550, A2H 6E6* ☎*709/634–5181,
800/563–4400 in Canada* 🖷*709/634–5106* ⊕*www.glynmillinn.ca*
🗬*58 rooms, 23 suites* &*In-hotel: 2 restaurants, bar, Wi-Fi, gym, no-
smoking rooms, some pets allowed* ▤*AE, DC, MC, V.*

$ ✕▦ **Mamateek Inn.** The restaurant (¢–$$$) here is well known for its
exquisite view of the city and serves a wide selection of cuisines from
Tex-Mex and seafood to chicken and steak. The sunsets are remark-
able, so get a table close to the window. Rooms are standard, bright,
and clean, but it's the panoramic view of the city and the Bay of Islands
that is the selling point for this hotel. ✉*Maple Valley Rd., Box 787,
A2H 6G7* ☎*709/639–8901 or 800/563–8600* 🖷*709/639–7567* 🗬*55
rooms* &*In-room: Wi-Fi. In-hotel: restaurant, bar, gym, no elevator,
some pets allowed, no-smoking rooms* ▤*AE, DC, MC, V.*

SPORTS & THE OUTDOORS

The growing **Marble Mountain Resort** (✉*Rte. 1, 5 km [3 mi] east of Cor-
ner Brook, Steady Brook* ☎*709/637–7600 or 888/462–7253* ⊕*www.
skimarble.com*) has 35 downhill runs and four lifts capable of moving
6,500 skiers an hour, as well as a large day lodge, ski shop, day-care
center, and restaurant. The vertical drop is 1,700 feet. A full-day lift
ticket is $45.

STEPHENVILLE

77 km (48 mi) south of Corner Brook.

The former Harmon Air Force Base is in Stephenville, a town best
known for its summer festival. Stephenville is the only airstrip in Can-
ada able to land the space shuttle. It also has a large modern paper mill.
To the west of town is the Port au Port Peninsula, which was largely
settled by the French, who brought their way of life and language to
this small corner of Newfoundland.

The **Stephenville Theatre Festival** (☎*709/643–4982* ⊕*www.stf.nf.ca*),
held in July and August, is the province's major annual summer theat-
rical event, with a mix of light musicals and serious drama.

EN ROUTE
As you travel down the Trans-Canada Highway toward Port aux Basques,
routes 404, 405, 406, and 407 bring you into the small Scottish communities
of the **Codroy Valley.** Some of the most productive farms in the province are
nestled in the valley against the backdrop of the Long Range mountains and
the Lewis Hills, from which gales strong enough to stop traffic hurtle down to
the coast—winds in the area known as Wreckhouse have overturned tractor
trailers. The Codroy Valley is great for bird-watching, and the Grand Codroy
River is ideal for kayaking. Walking trails, a golf course, and mountain hikes
make the area an appealing stop for nature lovers.

CAMPING   ⚠ **Little Paradise RV Park.** Beautiful scenery, large campsites, great walking trails, and canoeing on the Little Codroy River make this an ideal spot to pull off the road and stay for a bit. There's a playground in a big field, where kids can hide in the fort and jump on the trampoline. ♿ *Flush toilets, dump station, drinking water, showers, fire pits, picnic tables, play area* ⛺*78 RV and tent sites* ✉*500 feet off Rte. 1(TCH)* ☎*709/955–2682* ⊟*AE, MC, V* ☉*Closed Oct.–May.*

PORT AUX BASQUES

166 km (103 mi) south of Stephenville.

Port aux Basques was one of seven Basque ports along Newfoundland's west coast and in southern Labrador during the 1500s and early 1600s and was given its name by the town's French successors. It's now the main ferry port connecting the island to Nova Scotia. In J. T. Cheeseman Provincial Park, 15 km (9 mi) north of town on the Trans-Canada Highway, and at Grand Bay West you may see the endangered piping plover, which nests in the sand dunes along this coast.

WHERE TO STAY

$-$$ ⊞ **St. Christopher's Hotel.** This clean, comfortable two-story hotel is minutes from the ferry and has good food. The quiet rooms are bright and modern, with heavy curtains to keep out the light if desired. The suites are spacious, with hardwood flooring and fireplaces. ✉*146 High St., Box 2049, A0M 1C0* ☎*709/695–7034 or 800/563–4779* 🖷*709/695–9841* ⊕*www.stchrishotel.com* ⛺*83 rooms* ♿*In-room: ethernet (some). In-hotel: restaurant, room service, bar, gym, laundry facilities, public Internet, some pets allowed, no-smoking rooms* ⊟*AE, DC, MC, V.*

$ ⊞ **Hotel Port aux Basques.** There's nothing special about the rooms here, but this is a good choice for families, because children stay free. The food in the restaurant is good, with a choice of local dishes and seafood. This modern hotel is closer to the ferry than any other in town. Suites have whirlpool baths. ✉*1 Grand Bay Rd., A0M 1C0* ☎*709/695–2171 or 877/695–2171* 🖷*709/695–2250* ⊕*www.hotelpab.com* ⛺*47 rooms 3 suites* ♿*In-room: kitchen (some), Wi-Fi. In-hotel: restaurant, room service, bar, no elevator, some pets allowed, no-smoking rooms* ⊟*AE, DC, MC, V.*

¢   ⊞ **Caribou Bed and Breakfast.** The Caribou tends to be a quiet B&B because most people have an early breakfast before catching the nearby ferry. The rooms are small and plain. Three rooms have a double and a single bed. Evening tea is served daily. ✉*42 Grand Bay Rd., A0N 1K0* ☎*709/695–3408* ⊕*www.visitnewfoundland.ca* ⛺*5 rooms, 3 with bath* ♿*In-room: no a/c, no phone, no TV. In-hotel: no-smoking rooms, no elevator* ⊟*MC, V* ☉*Closed Oct.–Apr.* ¶*CP.*

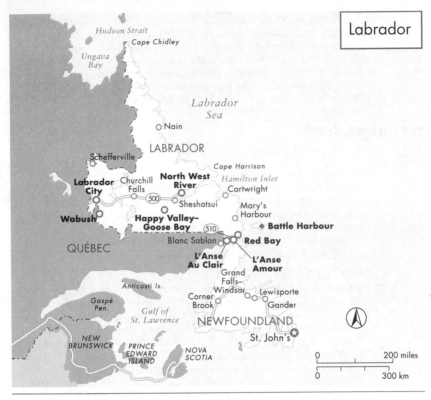

LABRADOR

The Straits in southeastern Labrador were a rich hunting-and-gathering ground for the area's earliest peoples, the Maritime Archaic tribes. The oldest industrial site in the New World is here—the 16th-century Basque whaling station at Red Bay.

Along the southern coast, most villages are inhabited by descendants of Europeans, whereas farther north they are mostly Inuit and Innu. Over the years the European settlers have adopted native skills and survival strategies, and the native peoples have adopted many European technologies. In summer the ice retreats and a coastal steamer delivers goods, but in winter small airplanes and snowmobiles are the only ways in and out.

Labrador West's subarctic landscape is challenging and unforgettable. The two towns here, Wabush and Labrador West, were built in the 1960s to accommodate employees of the Iron Ore Company of Canada. The area is home to the largest iron ore deposits in the world.

L'ANSE AU CLAIR

5 km (3 mi) from Blanc Sablon, Québec (ferry from St. Barbe, New-foundland docks in Blanc Sablon).

In L'Anse au Clair—French for "clear water cove"—anglers can try their luck for trout and salmon on the scenic Forteau and Pinware rivers. The French place-name dates from the early 1700s when this area was settled by French speakers from Québec. Ask at the local museum for directions to the Doctor's Path where, in the 19th century, the local doctor searched out herbs and medicinal plants.

WHERE TO STAY

$-$$ 🏨 **Northern Light Inn.** Loads of bus-tour passengers make this a stop in summer because the Northern Light is the only accommodation of any size along Route 510. The hotel is pretty ordinary, but breakfasts, lunches, and dinners are decent, the rooms spacious, and the furnishings of good quality. ⊠ *58 Main St. (Rte. 510), A0K 3K0* 🕾 *709/931–2332 or 800/563–3188* 🖷 *709/931–2708* ⊕ *www.northernlightinn. com* 🛏 *54 rooms, 5 cottages* ♿ *In-room: kitchen (some). In-hotel: restaurant, bar, laundry facilities, no elevator, no-smoking rooms* ⊟ *AE, DC, MC, V.*

L'ANSE AMOUR

19 km (12 mi) east of L'Anse au Clair.

The elaborate **Maritime Archaic Indian burial site** (⊠ *Rte. 510*), discovered near L'Anse Amour, is 7,500 years old. A plaque marks a site that is the oldest-known aboriginal–funeral monument in North America.

Constructed in 1857, the **Point Amour Lighthouse,** at 109 feet tall, is the second-tallest lighthouse in Canada. Interpreters in period costume tell the story of the lighthouse and the history of southern Labrador. You can climb to the top. ⊠ *Off route 510, Forteau and L'Anse au Loup* 🕾 *709/931–2013* ⊕ *www.pointamourlighthouse.ca* 🎫 *$3* ⊙ *Mid-June–mid-Oct., daily 10–5:30.*

EN
ROUTE
The **Labrador Straits Museum and Craft Store** has exhibits themed "150 years on the Labrador" and explores women's roles in Labrador Straits history. ⊠ *Rte. 510, between Forteau and L'Anse au Loup* 🕾 *709/931-2067 or 709/927-5733* 🎫 *$5* ⊙ *Mid-June-mid-Sept., Mon.-Sat. 9:30-5:30* ⊟ *MC, V.*

RED BAY

35 km (22 mi) northeast of L'Anse Amour.

The area's main attraction lies at the very end of Route 510: Red Bay, the site of a 16th-century Basque whaling station and a National Historic Site. Basque whalers began harpooning migrating whales from flimsy boats in frigid waters a few years after Cabot's discovery of the coast in 1497. Between 1550 and 1600 Red Bay was the world's whaling capital.

★ The **Red Bay National Historic Site** has a visitor center that interprets the Basque heritage with film and artifacts. A boat takes you on a five-minute journey to the excavation site on Saddle Island. ⊠ *Rte. 510* ☎ *709/920–2142* ⊕ *www.pc.gc.ca* ⊜ *Site $7, boat $2* ⊙ *Mid-June–early Oct., daily 9–6.*

COASTAL LABRADOR

To get to the south coast of Labrador, you can catch the ferry (July to December) at St. Barbe on Route 430 in Newfoundland to Blanc Sablon, Québec. From here you can drive to Mary's Harbour, and on to Cartwright, along Route 510. **Tourism Newfoundland and Labrador** (☎ *800/563–6353*) has information about ferry schedules.

Canadian Sailing Expeditions (☎ *902/429–1474 or 877/429–9463* ⊕ *www. canadiansailingexpeditions.com*) offers in July and August a "Fjords, Bays & Tickles" cruise, which travels up the coast of Western Newfoundland. The tour includes hands-on sail training while at sea, a stay in cruise ship–style cabins, local gourmet cuisine, guest lecturers and entertainers, as well as sea kayaks and bicycles for excursions.

A coastal boat takes passengers into a number of small communities. For information and schedules, call **Coastal Labrador Marine Services** (☎ *866/535–2567*) or visit the government Web site at ⊕ www.gov. nl.ca/ferryservices.

BATTLE HARBOUR NATIONAL HISTORIC SITE

★ *12 km (7 mi) by boat from Mary's Harbour.*

This near-shore island site has the only remaining intact outport fishing merchant's premises in the province. Settled in the 18th century, Battle Harbour was the main fishing port in Labrador and the economic and social center of the southern Labrador coast until the first half of the 20th century. After fires destroyed some of the community, the people moved to nearby Mary's Harbour. The Battle Harbour Historic Trust has restored the community to its former glory with historical structures and artifacts. The oldest Anglican church in Labrador is also at this site. You can stay overnight on the island at accommodations that range from individual cottages to a hostel-type bunkhouse. There is a restaurant on the Battle Harbour site. Information is available from the **Battle Harbour Historic Trust** (☎ *709/921–6677* ⊕ *www.battleharbour. com*). To get to the site, go to Government Wharf in Mary's Harbour and board the **MV** *Trinity Pride,* which leaves daily at 11 AM and 7 PM for the one-hour trip from Mary's Harbour. The boat returns from Battle Harbour at 9 AM and 4 PM daily. Tickets are $40 round-trip, and can be purchased at the wharf. There's no need to buy tickets in advance; space is not an issue. ⊠ *Southern Labrador coast, accessible by boat from Mary's Harbour* ☎ *709/921–6325* ⊕ *www.battleharbour.com* ⊜ *$8 includes optional guided tour* ⊙ *Mid-June–mid-Sept., daily 8–5.*

WHERE TO STAY

$ 🏨**Battle Harbour Inn.** Perched on a hilltop with a commanding view of the Labrador Straits from every window, this fully restored two-story house overlooks the merchant premises and Great Caribou Island. The rooms share two baths. The house is furnished with antiques and has a sunporch from which to relax and soak up the view. The inn doesn't have a phone or television, in keeping with the idea of taking visitors back to the 18th century, but there is a phone at the general store. ⊠*Battle Harbour Historic Site, Box 140, Mary's Harbour A0K 3P0* ☎*709/921–6216* 📠*709/921–6325* ⊕*www.battleharbour.com* 🛏*5 rooms without bath, 3 cottages* ♿*In-room: no a/c, no phone, no TV. In-hotel: no-smoking rooms, no elevator* ☰*MC, V* ⊘*Closed mid-Sept.–mid-June.*

4

HAPPY VALLEY–GOOSE BAY

525 km (326 mi) east of Labrador City.

Happy Valley–Goose Bay is the chief service center for coastal Labrador. Anyone coming to Labrador to fish will probably pass through here. The town was founded in the 1940s as a top-secret air base used to ferry fleets of aircraft to Europe. It's still used as a low-level flying training base by the British, Dutch, and German air forces.

WHERE TO STAY

$–$$ 🏨**Hotel North.** Rooms at this newly renovated hotel, though basic, are the best of the limited selection in this town. All are clean and comfortable, and the hotel is a two-minute drive from the airport. ⊠*25 Loring Dr., A0P 1C0* ☎*709/896–9301 or 877/996–9301* 📠*709/896–9302* ⊕*www.atyp.com/hotelnorth* 🛏*54 rooms, 3 suites* ♿*In-room: refrigerator, Wi-Fi. In-hotel: restaurant, laundry facilities, no-smoking rooms, no elevator* ☰*AE, DC, MC, V* ◉*CP.*

NORTH WEST RIVER

32 km (20 mi) northeast of Happy Valley–Goose Bay.

North West River was founded as a Hudson's Bay trading post in the 1830s. The town was also the starting point for the Wallace-Hubbard expedition of 1903. Leonidas Hubbard and Dillon Wallace were American adventurers who attempted a journey from Lake Melville to Ungava Bay along a previously untraveled route. They took a wrong turn, got lost, and Hubbard died in the wilderness from starvation. His wife, Mina, never forgave Wallace and completed her husband's journey in 1905. Her book, *A Woman's Way Through Unknown Labrador,* is still considered a classic.

The Wallace-Hubbard expedition and other historic events are examined at the **Labrador Heritage Society Museum,** in the 1923 Hudson Bay Company Building. Artifacts and displays relay the history of the Hudson's Bay Company and International Grenfell Association, trapping, and the trappers' families. ✉*Main St.* ☎*709/497–8858* ⊕*www.lab-heritage.ca* ✎*$2* ⊙*Mid-June–mid-Sept., Wed.–Sun. 8:30–4:30.*

WABUSH

525 km (326 mi) west of Happy Valley–Goose Bay.

The modern town of Wabush has all the amenities of larger centers, including accommodations, sports and recreational facilities, good shopping, and some of the warmest hospitality found anywhere. Labrador City and Wabush—or the "twin towns," as they are called—exist because of the rich iron-ore deposits, and the Iron Ore Company of Canada offers tours of the IOCC mine. Another highly recommended tour is the one for Churchill Falls, one of the world's largest underground hydro-generating stations. Both tours take place July and August on Wednesday and Sunday at 1:30 PM, and cost $11.50 each.

Arrangements for both tours can be made through the **Labrador West Tourism Association** (✉*Gateway Building, Rte. 500, Wabush* ☎*709/944–7631* ⊕*www.exploringlabrador.com*).

SPORTS & THE OUTDOORS

The **Smokey Mountain Ski Club** (✉*Rte. 500* ☎*709/944–2129* ⊕*www.smokeymountain.ca*), west of Wabush, is open mid-November to late April and has 18 groomed runs to accommodate beginners and advanced skiers. The vertical drop is 1,000 feet. A full-day lift ticket is about $30.

LABRADOR CITY

525 km (326 mi) west of Happy Valley–Goose Bay.

Labrador City has all the facilities of nearby Wabush, but more of them. At just fewer than 10,000 people, the city has more than three times the population of Wabush.

SPORTS & THE OUTDOORS

The **Carol Curling Club** (✉*Booth St.* ☎*709/944–5889* ⊕*www.carolcurlingclub.ca*) is the home club of two members of the 2005 Olympic Gold Medal curling team. The club has four sheets of ice, has produced some of the province's finest curlers, and has been the site of the provincial finals. From mid- to late March, the **Labrador Winter Odyssey** (✉*Rte. 500, Labrador City* ☎*709/944–3602*) is a winter carnival and festival rolled up into one. There are sliding parties, snowmobile races, and dogsled rides and to keep you warm, bonfires, and music.

NEWFOUNDLAND & LABRADOR ESSENTIALS

To research prices, get advice from other travelers, and book travel arrangements, visit www.fodors.com.

TRANSPORTATION

BY AIR

Air Canada flies into St. John's. Regional connectors are Air Canada Jazz (Québec to Wabush), Air Labrador, and Provincial Airlines. CanJet Airlines and WestJet have flights into the province from most Canadian cities. Continental Airlines has direct flights from Newark to St. John's. Air Transat operates some charter flights. At this writing, the reliability of air travel to cities around Newfoundland—other than to St. John's—is in a state of flux, so call airlines for up-to-date information.

The province's main airport is St. John's International Airport, though another international airport is at Gander, farther north. Domestic airports in Newfoundland are at Stephenville, Deer Lake, and St. Anthony. Airports in Labrador are in Happy Valley–Goose Bay, Wabush, and Churchill Falls.

4

Contacts **Air Labrador** (☎ 800/563-3042 ⊕ www.airlabrador.com). **Churchill Falls Airport** (☎ 709/925-3405). **Deer Lake Regional Airport** (☎ 709/635-3601). **Gander International Airport** (☎ 709/256-6677 ⊕ www.ganderairport.com). **Goose Bay Airport** (☎ 709/896-5445). **Provincial Airlines** (☎ 709/576-1666, 800/563-2800 in Atlantic Canada ⊕ www.provincialairlines.com). **St. John's International Airport** (☎ 709/758-8515 ⊕ www.stjohnsairport.com). **Stephenville Airport** (☎ 709/643-8444 ⊕ www.cyjt.com). **Wabush Airport** (☎ 709/282-5412).

BY BOAT & FERRY

Marine Atlantic operates a car ferry from North Sydney, Nova Scotia, to Port aux Basques, Newfoundland (crossing time is 6 hours), and, from June through September, from North Sydney to Argentia, three times a week (crossing time 12 to 14 hours). In all cases, reservations are required. To explore the south coast of Labrador, catch the ferry at St. Barbe on Route 430 in Newfoundland to Blanc Sablon, Québec. From here you can drive to Cartwright along Route 510. Tourism Newfoundland and Labrador has information about ferry schedules. Canadian Sailing Expeditions offers weeklong sailing trips aboard tall ships up the Northern Peninsula. Coastal Labrador Marine Services takes passengers to smaller communities in Labrador.

Contacts **Canadian Sailing Expeditions** (☎ 902/429-1474 or 877/429-9463 ⊕ www.canadiansailingexpeditions.com). **Coastal Labrador Marine Services** (☎ 866/535-2567 ⊕ www.tw.gov.nl.ca/ferryservices). **Marine Atlantic** (☎ 800/341-7981, 902/794-8109 TTY ⊕ www.marine-atlantic.ca). **Tourism Newfoundland and Labrador** (☎ 800/563-6353 ⊕ www.newfoundlandandlabrador.com).

BY BUS

DRL Coachlines runs a trans-island bus service in Newfoundland. Buses leave daily at 8 AM from St. John's and Port aux Basques. Outport taxis connect the major centers with surrounding communities.

Contacts **DRL Coachlines** (☎ 888/263-1854 ⊕ www.drlgroup.com).

BY CAR

In winter, some highways close during and after severe snowstorms. The Government of Newfoundland and Labrador's Department of Transportation & Works Web site has up-to-date information on road conditions and closures. Newfoundland and Labrador Tourism can help with any travel-related problems.

Newfoundland has an excellent highway system, and all but a handful of secondary roads are paved. The province's roads are generally uncrowded. Travel time along the Trans-Canada Highway (Route 1) from Port aux Basques to St. John's is about 13 hours, with time out for a meal. The trip from Corner Brook to St. Anthony at the northernmost tip of the island is about five hours. The drive from St. John's to Grand Bank on the Burin Peninsula takes about four hours. If you're heading for the southern coast of the Avalon Peninsula, pick up Route 10 just south of St. John's and follow it toward Trepassey.

The southeastern coast of Labrador is becoming more accessible by car. Route 510 now goes all the way to Cartwright. Route 500 links Labrador City with Happy Valley–Goose Bay via Churchill Falls. Conditions on this 526-km (326-mi) wilderness road are best from June through October. Labrador's road system is being extended and upgraded. If you plan to do extensive driving in Labrador, contact Newfoundland and Labrador Tourism for advice on the best routes and road conditions.

Contacts Newfoundland and Labrador Tourism (☎ 709/729–2830, 800/563–6353 in North America ⊕ www.newfoundlandandlabrador.com). **Department of Transportation & Works** (☎ 709/635–4144 in Deer Lake, 709/292–4444 in Grand Falls–Windsor and Central Newfoundland, 709/466–4160 in Clarenville, 709/729–7669 in St. John's, 709/896–7888 in Happy Valley–Goose Bay ⊕ www.roads.gov.nl.ca).

CONTACTS & RESOURCES

EMERGENCIES

Emergency Services Ambulance, fire, police (☎ 911 or 0).

Hospitals Captain William Jackman Hospital (✉ 410 Booth Ave., Labrador City ☎ 709/944–2632). **Charles S. Curtis Memorial Hospital** (✉ West St., St. Anthony ☎ 709/454–3333). **General Hospital** (✉ 300 Prince Philip Dr., St. John's ☎ 709/777–6300). **George B. Cross Hospital** (✉ Manitoba Dr., Clarenville ☎ 709/466–3411). **James Paton Memorial Hospital** (✉ 125 Trans-Canada Hwy., Gander ☎ 709/651–2500). **St. Clare's Mercy Hospital** (✉ 154 Le Marchant Rd., St. John's ☎ 709/777–5000). **Western Memorial Regional Hospital** (✉ Brookfield Ave., Corner Brook ☎ 709/637–5000).

SPORTS & THE OUTDOORS

FISHING Newfoundland has more than 200 salmon rivers and thousands of trout streams, and fishing these unpolluted waters is an angler's dream. The Atlantic salmon is king of the game fish. Top salmon rivers in Newfoundland include the Gander, Humber, and Exploits, and Labrador's top-producing waters are the Sandhill, Michaels, Flowers, and Eagle rivers. Lake trout, brook trout, and landlocked salmon are other favorite species. In Labrador, northern pike and arctic char can be added to that list. Seasonal and regulatory fishing information can be obtained from Newfoundland and Labrador Tourism. Nonresidents must hire a guide or outfitter for anything other than roadside angling. Big River Camps operates two remote fishing lodges in Labrador open during July and August; Eureka Outdoors has a salmon fishing lodge on the Humber River in Newfoundland.

Outfitter Big River Camps (☎ *709/686–2242* ⊕ *www.bigrivercamps.ca*).**Eureka Outdoors** (☎ *709/785–1992* ⊕ *www.eurekaoutdoors.nf.ca*).

HIKING The island portion of the province is a hiker's paradise, with a vast network of trails, some of which cut through resettled communities. Many provincial parks and both of the national parks have hiking and nature trails, and coastal and forest trails radiate out from most small communities. The East Coast Trail on the Avalon Peninsula covers 540 km (336 mi) of coastline; the trail stretches from Fort Amherst, in St. John's, to Cappahayden, on the beautiful southern shore. The trail begins in Conception Bay South and moves north to Cape St. Francis and then south all the way down to Trepassey. It passes through two dozen communities and along cliff tops that provide ideal lookouts for icebergs and seabirds. Call individual parks or the tourist information line for specifics. East Coast Trail Association helps hikers navigate the 540 km (336 mi) East Coast Trails, which hug the coastline of the Avalon Peninsula. Gros Morne Adventures runs guided day hikes and a six-day hiking adventure in Gros Morne National Park.

Outfitter East Coast Trail Association (☎ *709/738–4453* ⊕ *www.eastcoasttrail. com*).**Gros Morne Adventures** (☎ *709/458-2722* ⊕ *www.grosmorneadventures. com/hiking.html*).

TOURS

ADVENTURE TOURS Local operators offer sea kayaking, ocean diving, canoeing, wildlife viewing, mountain biking, white-water rafting, heli-hiking, and interpretive walks in summer. In winter, snowmobiling and caribou- and seal-watching expeditions are popular. In spring and early summer, a favored activity is iceberg-watching.

Eastern Edge Kayak Adventures leads east-coast sea-kayaking tours and gives white-water kayaking instruction. Maxxim Vacations in St. John's organizes packaged adventure and cultural tours. Tuckamore Lodge, in Main Brook, uses its luxurious lodge on the Great Northern Peninsula as a base for viewing caribou, seabird colonies, whales, and icebergs, and for winter snowmobile excursions. Wildland Tours in St. John's has three weeklong guided tours that view wildlife and visit historically and culturally significant sites across Newfoundland.

Contacts Eastern Edge Outfitters Ltd. (☎ *709/ 773–2201 or 866/782–5925* ⊕ *www.kayakjim.com*). **Maxxim Vacations** (☎ *709/754–6666 or 800/567– 6666* ⊕ *www.maxximvacations.com*). **Newfoundland and Labrador Tourism** (☎ *709/729–2830, 800/563–6353 in North America* ⊕ *www.newfoundland andlabrador.com*). **Tuckamore Lodge** (☎ *709/865–6361 or 888/865–6361* ⊕ *www.*

tuckamorelodge.com). **Wildland Tours** (☎ *709/722–3123, 888/615-8279* ⊕ *www. wildlands.com)*.

BUS TOURS Local tours are available for Port aux Basques, the Codroy Valley, Corner Brook, the Bay of Islands, Gros Morne National Park, the Great Northern Peninsula, and St. John's. Local information chalets—provincially run tourist centers located strategically along the Trans-Canada Highway—have contact names and numbers. Newfoundland and Labrador Tourism can help out here as well. McCarthy's Party in St. John's has guided bus tours across Newfoundland, learning vacations, and charter services. Wildland Tours also offers charters and learning vacations, including whale-study weeks and culinary tours of the island.

Contacts McCarthy's Party (☎ *709/579–4444 or 888/660-6060* ⊕ *www. mccarthysparty.com)*. **Newfoundland and Labrador Tourism** (☎ *709/729–2830, 800/563-6353 in North America* ⊕ *www.newfoundlandandlabrador.com)*. **Wildland Tours** (☎ *709/722–3123, 888/615-8279* ⊕ *www.wildlands.com)*.

On the St. John's Haunted Hike, the Reverend Thomas Wickam Jarvis (actor Dale Jarvis) leads several different and very popular walking tours of the city's haunted sites and urban legends on summer evenings; tours begin at the west entrance of the Anglican Cathedral on Church Hill. Look for the crowd of people standing in the dark.

Contacts St. John's Haunted Hike (☎ *709/576–2087 or 709/685-3444* ⊕ *www. hauntedhike.com)*.

VISITOR INFORMATION

Newfoundland and Labrador Tourism distributes brochures from its offices. The province maintains a 24-hour tourist-information line year-round that can help with accommodations and reservations.

From June until Labor Day, a network of visitor information centers, open daily 9 to 9, dots the province. These centers have information on events, accommodations, shopping, and crafts stores in their areas. The airports in Gander and St. John's operate in-season visitor-information booths. The city of St. John's operates an information center in a restored railway carriage next to the harbor.

Tourist Information City of St. John's Economic Development, Tourism & Culture (☎ *709/576-8106* ⊕ *www.stjohns.ca/visitors/index.jsp)*.

Newfoundland and Labrador Tourism (☎ *709/729–2830, 800/563–6353 in North America* ⊕ *www.newfoundlandandlabrador.com)*.

Nova Scotia & Atlantic Canada Essentials

PLANNING TOOLS, EXPERT INSIGHT,
GREAT CONTACTS

There are planners and there are those who, excuse the pun, fly by the seat of their pants. We happily place ourselves among the planners. Our writers and editors try to anticipate all the issues you may face before and during any journey, and then they do their research. This section is the product of their efforts. Use it to get excited about your trip to Nova Scotia & Atlantic Canada Essentials, to inform your travel planning, or to guide you on the road should the seat of your pants start to feel threadbare.

GETTING STARTED

We're really proud of our Web site: Fodors.com is a great place to begin any journey. Scan "Travel Wire" for suggested itineraries, travel deals, restaurant and hotel openings, and other up-to-the-minute info. Check out "Booking" to research prices and book plane tickets, hotel rooms, rental cars, and vacation packages. Head to "Talk" for on-the-ground pointers from travelers who frequent our message boards. You can also link to loads of other travel-related resources.

▪ RESOURCES

ONLINE TRAVEL TOOLS

All About Atlantic Canada Atlantic Canada Cycling, ⊕ *www.atl-canadacycling.com, outlines week-long* cycling trips in each of the four Atlantic provinces with routes, distances, difficulty, and location. Atlantic Canada Tourism, ⊕ *www.atlanticcanadatourism.com,* brings together all four Atlantic province information under one site. Canada's East Coast, ⊕ *www.canadaeastcoast.com,* a site provided by the Atlantic Canada Tourism Partnership, is offered in English, French, and German. Each of the provinces have good individual sites for getting information.

The Canadian Museums Association, ⊕ *www.museums.ca,* is a sort of cultural tour of the country.

The Globe and Mail, ⊕*www.theglobeandmail.com,* is one of Canada's two national newspapers; it's published in Toronto. The National Post, ⊕ *www. canada.com/nationalpost,* is the younger of Canada's competing newspapers; it's part of a chain that publishes dailies across the country. Magazines Canada, ⊕ *www.magazinescanada.ca,* offers a link on their homepage to over 300 magazines currently published in the country.

Parks Canada, ⊕ *www.pc.gc.ca/pn-np/ list_e.asp,* provides a province-by-province list of parks. Vision: The Atlantic Canada Company, ⊕ *www.visionatlantic.net,* has touring opportunities in PEI, Nova Scotia, New Brunswick, and Newfoundland and Labrador.

For festivals, check out Canada Events, ⊕ *www.canadaevents.ca,* which allows you to search by date, place, and type of event. Canada Events Calendar, ⊕ www.canadaeventscalendar.ca, helps you find out what's going on in several major centers. There's also ⊕*www.festivalseeker.com.*

Currency Conversion Google (⊕www. google.com) does currency conversion. Just type in the amount you want to convert and an explanation of how you want it converted (e.g., "14 Swiss francs in dollars"), and then voilà. **Oanda.com** (⊕www.oanda.com) also allows you to print out a handy table with the current day's conversion rates. **XE.com** (⊕www.xe.com) is a good currency conversion Web site.

Safety Transportation Security Administration (TSA; ⊕www.tsa.gov)

Time Zones Timeanddate.com (⊕www.timeanddate.com/worldclock) can help you figure out the correct time anywhere.

Weather Accuweather.com (⊕www. accuweather.com) is an independent weather-forecasting service with good coverage of hurricanes. **Weather.com** (⊕www.weather.com) is the Web site for the Weather Channel. **Environmment Canada** (⊕www.weatheroffice.g

c.ca) has the Canadian government's forecast for the entire country.

Other Resources CIA World Factbook (⊕www.odci.gov/cia/publications/factbook/index.html) has profiles of every country in the world. It's a good source if you need some quick facts and figures.

VISITOR INFORMATION
For information about provincial tourism offices, see the Essentials sections in individual chapters.

Contacts Canadian Tourism Commission (☎613/946–1000 ⊕www.canadatourism.com).

GEAR
If you plan on camping or hiking in the deep woods in summer, particularly in northern Canada, always carry insect repellent, especially in June, which is blackfly season. Mosquitoes are prevalent in May and June, especially at dusk and dawn and considerably heavier around swamps and standing water. Consider investing in specially designed hats, jackets, and pants constructed of very fine mesh material.

Atlantic Canada experiences a wide range of weather and temperatures throughout the year. Even an August evening can be quite cool, especially if you are close to the water. A waterproof wind-breaking jacket is essential.

▌PASSPORTS & VISAS

Citizens of the United States now need a passport to re-enter the United States from Canada. Passport requirements apply to minors as well.

Anyone under 18 traveling alone should carry a signed and dated letter from both parents or from all legal guardians authorizing the trip. It's also a good idea to include a copy of the child's birth certificate, custody documents if applicable, and death certificates of one or both parents, if applicable. (Most airlines do not allow children under age 5 to travel alone,

and on Air Canada, for example, children under age 12 are allowed to travel unaccompanied only on nonstop flights. Consult the airline, bus line, or train service for specific regulations if using public transport.)

Citizens of the United States, United Kingdom, Australia, and New Zealand do not need visas to enter Canada for a period of six months or fewer.

PASSPORTS
U.S. passports are valid for 10 years. You must apply in person if you're getting a passport for the first time; if your previous passport was lost, stolen, or damaged; or if your previous passport has expired and was issued more than 15 years ago or when you were under 16. All children under 18 must appear in person to apply for or renew a passport. Both parents must accompany any child under 14 (or send a notarized statement with their permission) and provide proof of their relationship to the child.

■TIP➜ Before your trip, make two copies of your passport's data page (one for someone at home and another for you to carry separately). Or scan the page and e-mail it to someone at home and/or yourself.

There are 13 regional passport offices in the United States, as well as 7,000 passport-acceptance facilities in post offices, public libraries, and other governmental offices. If you're renewing a passport, you can do so by mail. Forms are available at passport acceptance facilities and online.

The cost to apply for a new passport is $97 for adults, $82 for children under 16; renewals are $67. Allow six weeks for processing, both for first-time passports and renewals. For an expediting fee of $60 you can reduce this time to about two weeks. If your trip is less than two weeks away, you can get a passport even more rapidly by going to a passport office with the necessary documentation. Private expediters can get things done in as little as 48 hours, but charge hefty fees for their services.

U.S. Passport Information U.S. Department of State (☎877/487–2778 ⊕http://travel. state.gov/passport).

U.S. Passport & Visa Expediters A. Briggs Passport & Visa Expeditors (☎800/806–0581 or 202/338–0111 ⊕www. abriggs.com). **American Passport Express** (☎800/455–5166 or 800/841–6778 ⊕www. americanpassport.com). **Passport Express** (☎800/362–8196 ⊕www.passportexpress. com). **Travel Document Systems** (☎800/ 874–5100 or 202/638–3800 ⊕www. traveldocs.com). **Travel the World Visas** (☎866/886–8472 or 301/495–7700 ⊕www. world-visa.com).

TRIP INSURANCE

What kind of coverage do you honestly need? Do you even need trip insurance at all? Take a deep breath and read on.

We believe that comprehensive trip insurance is especially valuable if you're booking a very expensive or complicated trip (particularly to an isolated region) or if you're booking far in advance. Who knows what could happen six months down the road? But whether or not you get insurance has more to do with how comfortable you are assuming all that risk yourself.

Comprehensive travel policies typically cover trip-cancellation and interruption, letting you cancel or cut your trip short because of a personal emergency, illness, or, in some cases, acts of terrorism in your destination. Such policies also cover evacuation and medical care. Some also cover you for trip delays because of bad weather or mechanical problems as well as for lost or delayed baggage. Another type of coverage to look for is financial default—that is, when your trip is disrupted because a tour operator, airline, or cruise line goes out of business. Generally you must buy this when you book your trip or shortly thereafter, and it's only available to you if your operator isn't on a list of excluded companies.

If you're going abroad, consider buying medical-only coverage at the very least. Neither Medicare nor some private insurers cover medical expenses anywhere outside of the United States (including time aboard a cruise ship, even if it leaves from a U.S. port). Medical-only policies typically reimburse you for medical care (excluding that related to pre-existing conditions) and hospitalization abroad, and provide for evacuation. You still have to pay the bills and await reimbursement from the insurer, though.

Expect comprehensive travel-insurance policies to cost about 4% to 7% or 8% of the total price of your trip (it's more like 8% to 12% if you're over age 70). A medical-only policy may or may not be cheaper than a comprehensive policy. Always read the fine print of your policy to make sure that you are covered for the risks that are of most concern to you. Compare several policies to make sure you're getting the best price and range of coverage available.

BOOKING YOUR TRIP

Unless your cousin is a travel agent, you're probably among the millions of people who make most of their travel arrangements online.

But have you ever wondered just what the differences are between an online travel agent (a Web site through which you make reservations instead of going directly to the airline, hotel, or car-rental company), a discounter (a firm that does a high volume of business with a hotel chain or airline and accordingly gets good prices), a wholesaler (one that makes cheap reservations in bulk and then re-sells them to people like you), and an aggregator (one that compares all the offerings so you don't have to)?

Is it truly better to book directly on an airline or hotel Web site? And when does a real live travel agent come in handy?

ONLINE

You really have to shop around. A travel wholesaler such as Hotels.com or Hotel Club.net can be a source of good rates, as can discounters such as Hotwire or Priceline, particularly if you can bid for your hotel room or airfare. Indeed, such sites sometimes have deals that are unavailable elsewhere. They do, however, tend to work only with hotel chains (which makes them just plain useless for getting hotel reservations outside of major cities) or big airlines (so that often leaves out upstarts like jetBlue and some foreign carriers like Air India).

Also, with discounters and wholesalers you must generally prepay, and everything is nonrefundable. And before you fork over the dough, be sure to check the terms and conditions, so you know what a given company will do for you if there's a problem and what you'll have to deal with on your own.

■ TIP➜ To be absolutely sure everything was processed correctly, confirm reservations made through online travel agents, discounters, and wholesalers directly with your hotel before leaving home.

Booking engines like Expedia, Travelocity, and Orbitz are actually travel agents, albeit high-volume, online ones. And airline-travel packagers like American Airlines Vacations and Virgin Vacations—well, they're travel agents, too. But they may still not work with all the world's hotels.

An aggregator site will search many sites and pull the best prices for airfares, hotels, and rental cars from them. Most aggregators compare the major travel-booking sites such as Expedia, Travelocity, and Orbitz; some also look at airline Web sites, though rarely the sites of smaller budget airlines. Some aggregators also compare other travel products, including complex packages—a good thing, as you can sometimes get the best overall deal by booking an air-and-hotel package.

WITH A TRAVEL AGENT

If you use an agent—brick-and mortar or virtual—you'll pay a fee for the service. And know that the service you get from some online agents isn't comprehensive. For example Expedia and Travelocity don't search for prices on budget airlines like jetBlue, Southwest, or small foreign carriers. That said, some agents (online or not) *do* have access to fares that are difficult to find otherwise, and the savings can more than make up for any surcharge.

A knowledgeable brick-and-mortar travel agent can be a godsend if you're booking a cruise, a package trip that's not available to you directly, an air pass, or a complicated itinerary including several overseas flights. What's more, travel agents that specialize in a destination may have exclusive access to certain deals and insider information on things such as charter flights. Agents who specialize in types of travelers (senior citizens, gays and lesbians, naturists) or types of trips (cruises, luxury travel, safaris) can also be invaluable.

■TIP➔ Remember that Expedia, Traveloc- ity, and Orbitz are travel agents, not just booking engines. To resolve any problems with a reservation made through these com- panies, contact them first.

A top-notch agent planning your trip to Russia will make sure you get the correct visa application and complete it on time; the one booking your cruise may get you a cabin upgrade or arrange to have bottle of champagne chilling in your cabin when you embark. And complain about the surcharges all you like, but when things don't work out the way you'd hoped, it's nice to have an agent to put things right.

■ ACCOMMODATIONS

In the cities of the Maritime provinces, you have a choice of luxury hotels, mod- erately priced modern properties, and smaller older hotels with perhaps fewer conveniences but more charm. Options in smaller towns and in the country include large full-service resorts, small privately owned inns, roadside motels, and bed-and-breakfasts.

Expect accommodations to cost more in summer than in the off-season (except for places where winter is high season, such as ski resorts). Book well in advance for high-season accommodations. When making reservations, ask about special deals and packages. Big-city hotels that cater to business travelers often offer weekend packages. Discounts are com- mon when you book for a week or longer, and many city hotels offer rooms at up to 50% off in winter. Also be aware of any special events or festivals that may coin- cide with your visit and fill every room for miles around.

The lodgings we list are the cream of the crop in each price category. We always list the facilities that are available, but

we don't specify whether they cost extra; when pricing accommodations, always ask what's included and what costs extra. Properties are assigned price cat- egories based on the range between their least and most expensive standard dou- ble rooms at high season (excluding holi- days). Properties marked ╳⌂ are lodging establishments whose restaurants warrant a special trip. Check the planner page at the front of each province chapter for the price chart.

Most hotels and other lodgings require your credit-card details before they will confirm your reservation. If you don't feel comfortable e-mailing this information, ask if you can fax it (some places even prefer faxes). However you book, get confirmation in writing and have a copy of it handy when you check in.

Be sure you understand the hotel's can- cellation policy. Some places allow you to cancel without any kind of penalty— even if you prepaid to secure a discounted rate—if you cancel at least 24 hours in advance. Others require you to cancel a week in advance or penalize you the cost of one night. Small inns and B&Bs are most likely to require you to cancel far in advance. Most hotels allow children under a certain age to stay in their par- ents' room at no extra charge, but others charge for them as extra adults; find out the cutoff age for discounts.

■TIP➔ Assume that hotels operate on the European Plan (EP, no meals) unless we specify that they use the Breakfast Plan (BP, with full breakfast), Continental Plan (CP, Continental breakfast), Full American Plan (FAP, all meals), Modified American Plan (MAP, breakfast and dinner) or are all-inclu- sive (AI, all meals and most activities).

APARTMENT & HOUSE RENTALS
Rental cottages are common in the four Atlantic provinces, more so in Nova Scotia and Prince Edward Island. Most of the properties are family-owned but only used by the owners for a few weeks

Online Booking Resources

AGGREGATORS

Kayak	www.kayak.com	also looks at cruises and vacation packages.
Mobissimo	www.mobissimo.com	
Qixo	www.qixo.com	also compares cruises, vacation packages, and even travel insurance.
Sidestep	www.sidestep.com	also compares vacation packages and lists travel deals.
Travelgrove	www.travelgrove.com	also compares cruises and packages.

BOOKING ENGINES

Cheap Tickets	www.cheaptickets.com	a discounter.
Expedia	www.expedia.com	a large online agency that charges a booking fee for airline tickets.
Hotwire	www.hotwire.com	a discounter.
lastminute.com	www.lastminute.com	specializes in last-minute travel; the main site is for the U.K., but it has a link to a U.S. site.
Luxury Link	www.luxurylink.com	has auctions (surprisingly good deals) as well as offers on the high-end side of travel.
Onetravel.com	www.onetravel.com	a discounter for hotels, car rentals, airfares, and packages.
Orbitz	www.orbitz.com	charges a booking fee for airline tickets, but gives a clear breakdown of fees and taxes before you book.
Priceline.com	www.priceline.com	a discounter that also allows bidding.
Travel.com	www.travel.com	allows you to compare its rates with those of other booking engines.
Travelocity	www.travelocity.com	charges a booking fee for airline tickets, but promises good problem resolution.

ONLINE ACCOMMODATIONS

Hotelbook.com	www.hotelbook.com	focuses on independent hotels worldwide.
Hotel Club	www.hotelclub.net	good for major cities worldwide.
Hotels.com	www.hotels.com	a big Expedia-owned wholesaler that offers rooms in hotels all over the world.
Quikbook	www.quikbook.com	offers "pay when you stay" reservations that let you settle your bill at checkout, not when you book.

OTHER RESOURCES

Bidding For Travel	www.biddingfortravel.com	a good place to figure out what you can get and for how much before you start bidding on, say, Priceline.

each summer. That leaves week after week available for rental potential, with most owners leaving the booking to an agency on-line, an enterprising neighbor or through the newspaper.

Canadian Resources Canada Vacation Rentals (⊕www.canadavacationrentals.ca/Atlantic/) has rental listings for Newfoundland, PEI, New Brunswick, and Nova Scotia. **Atlantic Canada Vacation Rentals** (⊕www.atlantic canada.worldweb.com/WheretoStay/Vacation HomeRentals/) has dozens of local destinations to choose from. **Canada Cottage and Cabin Rentals** (⊕www.cottage-canada-usa.com/Canada.htm) is an international site but has a surprising number of local Canadian rental properties. **At the Cottage** (⊕www.atthe cottage.com) is a North-American-wide Web site with a focus on Ontario but has some excellent properties in the Atlantic region. Halifax Chronicle-Herald (☎902/426-2811 ⊕www.herald.com.ca).

More Online-Booking Resources At Home Abroad (☎212/421-9165 ⊕www.athome abroadinc.com). **Barclay International Group** (☎516/364-0064 or 800/845-6636 ⊕www.barclayweb.com). **Vacation Home Rentals** Worldwide (☎201/767-9393 or 800/633-3284 ⊕www.vhrww.com). **Villanet** (☎206/417-3444 or 800/964-1891 ⊕www.rentavilla.com). **Villas & Apartments Abroad** (☎212/213-6435 or 800/433-3020 ⊕www.vaanyc.com). **Villas International** (☎415/499-9490 or 800/221-2260 ⊕www.villasintl.com). **Villas of Distinction** (☎707/778-1800 or 800/289-0900 ⊕www.villasofdistinction.com). **Wimco** (☎800/449-1553 ⊕www.wimco.com).

BED & BREAKFASTS

B&Bs are a wonderful way to meet people who are passionate about their communities and who are well versed in local events and history. Bed & Breakfasts are prevalent in Nova Scotia, especially in the Annapolis Valley and the South Shore, where you can stay in the magnificent homes of the province's first ship builders, doctors, and town officials. Prince Edward Island and New Brunswick also have a number of stately B&Bs.

For assistance in booking B&B rooms, contact the appropriate provincial tourist board (⇨ *Visitor Information*), which will either have a listing of B&Bs or be able to refer you to an association that can help you secure reservations.

Reservation Services B&B Canada (⊕www. bbcanada.com) helpfully divides each province into tourist regions.**Bed & Breakfast.com** (☎512/322-2710 or 800/462-2632 ⊕www. bedandbreakfast.com) also sends out an online newsletter. **Bed & Breakfast Inns Online** (☎615/868-1946 or 800/215-7365 ⊕www. bbonline.com). **BnB Finder.com** (☎212/432-7693 or 888/547-8226 ⊕www.bnbfinder. com). **The Canadian Bed & Breakfast Guide** (☎905/262-4597 or 877/213-0089 ⊕www. canadianbandbguide.ca) is the oldest B&B guide in Canada. **Nova Scotia Bed & Breakfast Guide** (☎902/423-4480 or 800/948-4267 ⊕www.nsbedandbreakfast.com) has a list of properties that are inspected annually by Tourism Nova Scotia.**Prince Edward Island Inns and Bed and Breakfasts** (⊕www. peislandbedandbreakfast.com) has a quick-list reference of accommodations organized by price and region.**Select Inns of Atlantic Canada** (⊕www.selectinns.ca) has links and information to many local inns and B&Bs.

HOME EXCHANGES

With a direct home exchange you stay in someone else's home while they stay in yours. Some outfits also deal with vacation homes, so you're not actually staying in someone's full-time residence, just their vacant weekend place.

Exchange Clubs Home Exchange.com (☎800/877-8723 ⊕www.homeexchange. com); $59.95 for a 1-year online listing. **HomeLink** (☎800/638-3841 ⊕www. homelink.ca); this property exchange service has properties all over the world but this portal focuses on Canad. It's $90 yearly for Web-only membership; $140 includes Web access and two catalogs. **Intervac U.S.** (☎800/756-4663 ⊕www.intervacus.com); $78.88 for Web-only membership; $126 includes Web access and a catalog.

HOSTELS

Hostels offer bare-bones lodging at low, low prices—often in shared dorm rooms with shared baths—to people of all ages, though the primary market is young travelers, especially students. Most hostels serve breakfast; dinner and/or shared cooking facilities may also be available. In some hostels you aren't allowed to be in your room during the day, and there may be a curfew at night. Nevertheless, hostels provide a sense of community, with public rooms where travelers often gather to share stories. Many hostels are affiliated with Hostelling International (HI), an umbrella group of hostel associations with some 4,500 member properties in more than 70 countries. Other hostels are completely independent and may be nothing more than a really cheap hotel.

Membership in any HI association, open to travelers of all ages, allows you to stay in HI-affiliated hostels at member rates. One-year membership is about $28 for adults; hostels charge about $10 to $30 per night. Members have priority if the hostel is full; they're also eligible for discounts around the world, even on rail and bus travel in some countries.

Information Hostelling International—USA (☎301/495-1240 ⊕www.hiusa.org).

HOTELS

Canada doesn't have a national government rating system for hotels, but many provinces do rate their accommodations. Most hotel rooms have air-conditioning, private baths with tubs and showers, and two double beds; all hotels we list have air-conditioning and private bath unless otherwise noted.

▌AIRLINE TICKETS

Most domestic airline tickets are electronic; international tickets may be either electronic or paper. With an e-ticket the only thing you receive is an e-mailed receipt citing your itinerary and reservation and ticket numbers. The greatest

10 WAYS TO SAVE

1. Join "frequent-guest" programs. You may get preferential treatment in room choice and/or upgrades.

2. Call direct. You can sometimes get a better price if you call a hotel's local toll-free number (if available) rather than a central reservations number.

3. Check online. Check hotel Web sites, as not all chains are represented on all sites.

4. Look for specials. Always inquire about packages and corporate rates.

5. Look for price guarantees. For overseas trips, look for guaranteed rates. With your rate locked in you won't pay more, even if the price goes up in the local currency.

6. Look for weekend deals at business hotels. High-end chains catering to business travelers are often busy only on weekdays; to fill rooms they often drop rates dramatically on weekends.

7. Ask about taxes. Verify whether local taxes are included the rates. In some places taxes can add 20% or more to your bill.

8. Read the fine print. Watch for add-ons, including fees, surcharges, and "convenience" fees for such things as unlimited local phone service you won't use or a free newspaper in a language you can't read.

9. Know when to go. If your destination's high season is December through April and you're trying to book, say, in late April, you might save money by changing your dates by a week or two. Ask when rates go down. If your dates straddle peak and nonpeak seasons, a property may still charge peak-season rates.

10. Weigh your options (we can't say this enough). Weigh transportation times and costs against the savings of staying in a hotel that's cheaper because it's out of the way.

10 WAYS TO SAVE

1. Nonrefundable is best. If saving money is more important than flexibility, then non-refundable tickets work. Just remember that you'll pay dearly (as much as $200) if you change your plans.

2. Comparison shop. Web sites and travel agents can have different arrangements with the airlines and offer different prices for exactly the same flights.

3. Beware the listed prices. Many airline Web sites—and most ads—show prices *without* taxes and surcharges. Don't buy until you know the full price.

4. Stay loyal. Stick with one or two frequent-flier programs. You'll rack up free trips and accumulate the perks that make trips easier. On some airlines these include a special reservations number, early boarding, access to upgrades, and more roomy economy-class seating.

5. Watch those ticketing fees. Surcharges are usually added when you buy your ticket anywhere but on an airline Web site. (That includes by phone—even if you call the air-line directly—and paper tickets regardless of how you book).

6. Check often. Start looking for cheap fares from three months out. Keep looking until you find a price you like.

7. Don't work alone. Some Web sites have tracking features that will e-mail you immediately when good deals are posted.

8. Jump on the good deals. Waiting even a few minutes might mean paying more.

9. Be flexible. Look for departures on Tuesday, Wednesday, and Saturday, typically the cheapest days to travel. And check on prices for departures at different times and to and from alternative airports.

10. Weigh your options. What you get can be as important as what you save. A cheaper flight might have a long layover, or it might land at a secondary airport, where your ground transportation costs might be higher.

advantage of an e-ticket is that if you lose your receipt, you can simply print out another copy or ask the airline to do it for you at check-in. You usually pay a surcharge (up to $50) to get a paper ticket, if you can get one at all.

The sole advantage of a paper ticket is that it may be easier to endorse over to another airline if your flight is canceled and the air-line with which you booked can't accommodate you on another flight.

■ RENTAL CARS

When you reserve a car, ask about cancellation penalties, taxes, drop-off charges (if you're planning to pick up the car in one city and leave it in another), and surcharges (for being under or over a certain age, for additional drivers, or for driving across state or country borders or beyond a specific distance from your point of rental). All these things can add substantially to your costs. Request car seats and extras such as GPS when you book.

Rates are sometimes—but not always—better if you book in advance or reserve through a rental agency's Web site. There are other reasons to book ahead, though: for popular destinations, during busy times of the year, or to ensure that you get certain types of cars (vans, SUVs, exotic sports cars).

■TIP→ Make sure that a confirmed reservation guarantees you a car. Agencies sometimes overbook, particularly for busy weekends and holiday periods.

Renting a car is probably the best way to get around in Atlantic Canada. There is no inter-provincial bus system so the schedules don't synchronize and airplane jaunts are limited except for the most major destinations. In Nova Scotia, for example, there are only two commercial airports—in Halifax and in Sydney—leaving an entire province full of towns and villages in between. Because

Car-Rental Resources

AUTOMOBILE ASSOCIATIONS

U.S.: American Automobile Association (AAA)	315/797-5000	www.aaa.com
	most contact with the organization is through state and regional members.	
National Automobile Club	650/294-7000	www.thenac.com
	membership is open to California residents only.	

MAJOR AGENCIES

Alamo	800/522-9696	www.alamo.com
Avis	800/331-1084	www.avis.com
Budget	800/472-3325	www.budget.com
Hertz	800/654-3001	www.hertz.com
National Car Rental	800/227-7368	www.nationalcar.com

all four Atlantic provinces have a major (TransCanada Highway) and minor highway system, travelers can opt for the more direct route or the more interesting, meandering one. Using a rental allows you to see the country side and shoreline as you go exploring. Be warned that in Newfoundland, the major highway lies somewhat in the interior of the province so glimpses of the coastline are limited. Four-wheel drive vehicles are not required although most agencies offer two and four-wheel drive vehicles. If you cancel your reservation within 24 hours of your expected pick up time, you may be charged a day's rate.

Rental car prices in the four Atlantic provinces range from about C$39–$60 a day. Weekend-only car renters will be hit with higher prices and a better rate is offered to by-the-week customers.

If you require a car seat for your trip—most Atlantic Canadian provinces require the children up to nine be seated in a booster, then plan ahead. You can reserve a car seat online when booking your rental, or, if booking by phone, there is a 24-hour advance booking required. Car seats can run anywhere from about $10 a day to $60 per month. Some companies, such as Avis, don't rent manual-transmission cars in Canada.

Price local car-rental companies—whose prices may be lower, although their service and maintenance may not be as good as those of major rental agencies—and research rates on the Internet. Remember to ask about required deposits and cancellation penalties. If you're traveling during a holiday period, also make sure that a confirmed reservation guarantees you a car.

You must be 21 years old to rent an economy or midsize car and 25 years old to rent an SUV or other specialty vehicle. Rental-car companies have not set an upper age limit.

CAR-RENTAL INSURANCE
Everyone who rents a car wonders whether the insurance that the rental companies offer is worth the expense. No one—including us—has a simple answer. It all depends on how much regular insurance you have, how comfortable you are with risk, and whether or not money is an issue.

If you own a car, your personal auto insurance may cover a rental to some degree, though not all policies protect

10 WAYS TO SAVE

1. Beware of cheap rates. Those great rates aren't so great when you add in taxes, surcharges, and insurance. Such extras can double or triple the initial quote.

2. Rent weekly. Weekly rates are usually better than daily ones. Even if you only want to rent for five or six days, ask for the weekly rate; it may very well be cheaper than the daily rate for that period of time.

3. Don't forget the locals. Price local companies as well as the majors.

4. Airport rentals can cost more. Airports often add surcharges, which you can sometimes avoid by renting from an agency whose office is just off airport property.

5. Wholesalers can help. Investigate wholesalers, which rent in bulk, and which frequently offer better rates (note that you must usually pay for such rentals before leaving home).

6. Look for rate guarantees. With your rate locked in, you won't pay more, even if the price goes up in the local currency.

7. Fill up farther away. Avoid hefty refueling fees by filling the tank at a station well away from where you plan to turn in the car.

8. Pump it yourself. Don't prepay for rental-car gas. The savings isn't that great, and unless you coast in on empty upon return, you wind up paying for gas you don't use.

9. Get all your discounts. Find out whether a credit card you carry or organization or frequent-renter program to which you belong has a discount program. And confirm that such discounts really are a deal. You can often do better with special weekend or weekly rates offered by a rental agency.

10. Check out packages. Adding a car rental onto your air-/hotel-vacation package may be cheaper than renting a car separately.

you abroad; always read your policy's fine print. If you don't have auto insurance, then seriously consider buying the collision- or loss-damage waiver (CDW or LDW) from the car-rental company, which eliminates your liability for damage to the car. Some credit cards offer CDW coverage, but it's usually supplemental to your own insurance and rarely covers SUVs, minivans, luxury models, and the like. If your coverage is secondary, you may still be liable for loss-of-use costs from the car-rental company. But no credit-card insurance is valid unless you use that card for *all* transactions, from reserving to paying the final bill. All companies exclude car rental in some countries, so be sure to find out about the destination to which you are traveling.

Some rental agencies require you to purchase CDW coverage; many will even include it in quoted rates. All will strongly encourage you to buy CDW—possibly implying that it's required—so be sure to ask about such things before renting. In most cases it's cheaper to add a supplemental CDW plan to your comprehensive travel-insurance policy (*see* Trip Insurance under Things to Consider in Getting Started, above) than to purchase it from a rental company. That said, you don't want to pay for a supplement if you're required to buy insurance from the rental company.

A "no fault" policy is offered by all major car-rental companies for about $30 a day and will cover virtually any mishap.

■ TIP→ **You can decline the insurance from the rental company and purchase it through a third-party provider such as Travel Guard (⊕ www.travelguard.com)—$9 per day for $35,000 of coverage. That's sometimes just under half the price of the CDW offered by some car-rental companies.**

▮ GUIDED TOURS

Guided tours are a good option when you don't want to do it all yourself. You travel along with a group (sometimes large, sometimes small), stay in prebooked hotels, eat with your fellow travelers (the cost of meals sometimes included in the price of your tour, sometimes not), and follow a schedule.

But not all guided tours are an if-it's-Tuesday-this-must-be-Belgium experience. A knowledgeable guide can take you places that you might never discover on your own, and you may be pushed to see more than you would have otherwise. Tours aren't for everyone, but they can be just the thing for trips to places where making travel arrangements is difficult or time-consuming (particularly when you don't speak the language).

Whenever you book a guided tour, find out what's included and what isn't. A "land-only" tour includes all your travel (by bus, in most cases) in the destination, but not necessarily your flights to and from or even within it. Also, in most cases prices in tour brochures don't include fees and taxes. And remember that you'll be expected to tip your guide (in cash) at the end of the tour.

SPECIAL-INTEREST TOURS

The companies listed below offer multiday tours in Canada. Additional local or regionally based companies that have different-length trips with these themes are listed in each chapter, either with information about the town or in the Essentials section that concludes the chapter.

ADVENTURE

Contacts Atlantic Canada Nature Safaris (☎902/455-3595 or 877/455-3595 ⊕www.atlanticcanadasafaris.com).**Gorp Travel** (☎303/444-2622 or 800/444-0099 ⊕www.gorptravel.com).**Ocean Quest Adventure Resort** (☎866/623-2664 or 709/834-7234 ⊕www.oceanquestcharters.com).

BIKING

▮**TIP**➔Most airlines accommodate bikes as luggage, provided they're dismantled and boxed.

Contacts Atlantic Canada Cycling (☎902/423-2452 ⊕www.atlanticcanada-cycling.com).**Backroads** (☎510/527-1555 or 800/462-2848 ⊜510/527-1444 ⊕www.backroads.com). **Bike Riders Tours** (☎617/723-2354 or 800/473-7040 ⊕www.bikeriderstours.com). **Butterfield & Robinson** (☎416/864-1354 or 800/678-1147 ⊕www.butterfield.com). **Eastwind Cycle** (☎902/471-4424 ⊕www.eastwindcycle.com).**Easy Rider Tours** (☎978/463-6955 or 800/488-8332 ⊕www.easyridertours.com). **Freewheeling Adventures** (☎902/857-3600 or 800/672-0775 ⊕www.freewheeling.ca). **Pedal & Sea Adventures** (☎902/857-9319 or 877/777-5699 ⊕www.pedalandseaadventures.com).**Vermont Bicycle Touring** (☎800/245-3868 or 802/453-4811 ⊕www.vbt.com)

CULINARY

Contacts Culinarti (☎902/757-1865 ⊕www.culinarti.com).**Trout Point Lodge Cooking Vacation** (☎902/482-8360 ⊕www.foodvacation.com)

ECO TOURS

Contacts Black Spruce Tours (☎631/725-1493 ⊕www.blacksprucetours.com).**East Coast OutfittersS**(☎902/852-2567 or 877/852-2567 ⊕www.eastcoastoutfitters.com).

FISHING

Contacts Country Haven Lodge (☎877/359-4877 or 877/539-9655 ⊕www.grayrapids.com).**Fishing International** (☎707/542-4242 or 800/950-4242 ⊕www.travelsource.com/fishing).

GOLF

Contacts Cape Breton's Fabulous Foursome (☎902/539-0044 ⊕wwwgolf.capebreton.com).**Golf New Brunswick** (☎877/833-4662 ⊕www.golfnb.ca).**Golf Newfoundland** (☎709/722-2470 ⊕www.golfnewfoundland.ca).**Golf Nova Scotia**

(☎800/565-0000 ⊕www.golfnovascotia.com).
Golf Prince Edward Island (☎902/566-4653
or 866/465-3734 ⊕www.golfpei.ca).

WALKING/HIKING

Contacts Backroads (☎510/527-1555
or 800/462-2848 ⊕www.backroads.com).
Butterfield & Robinson (☎416/864-1354
or 800/678-1147 ⊕www.butterfield.com).
Country Walkers (☎802/244-1387 or
800/464-9255 ⊕www.countrywalkers.
com). **New England Hiking Holidays**
(☎603/356-9696 or 800/869-0949 ⊕www.
nehikingholidays.com). **Scott Walking Adventures** (☎902/858-2060 or 800/262-8644
⊕www.scottwalking.com). **Walking the World**
(☎970/498-0500 or 800/340-9255 ⊕www.
walkingtheworld.com); specializes in tours for
ages 50 and older.

SEA KAYAKING

Contacts Coastal Adventures (☎902/772-
2774 or 877/404-2774 ⊕www.coastalad-
ventures.com). **Coastal Safari Adventures**
(☎709/579-3977 or 877/888-3020 ⊕www.
coastalsafari.com). **Fresh Air Adventure**
(☎506/877-2249 or 800/545-0020 ⊕www.
freshairadventure.com). **Long Range Adventure** (☎709/458-3104 ⊕www.longrangead-
ventures.com).

WINE

Contacts Bear River Vineyards (☎902/467-
4156 ⊕www.winetravel.com). **Valley Wine
Tours** (☎902/404-9463 or 866/504-9463
⊕www.valleywinetours.ca).

∎ CRUISES

Every season (April to October), more
than 100 ships from New York, Boston,
and Montréal make Halifax a port of
call. About half of them stop in at Sydney,
Cape Breton's multimillion-dollar cruise
pavilion, where visitors are greeted by the
world's largest fiddle. Halifax Harbour's
proximity to downtown makes the city
ideal for short stopovers. All cruise ships

entering the harbor are scheduled by the
Halifax Port Authority.

In Prince Edward Island, about 25 cruise
ships call in at historic Charlottetown,
where an $18 million expansion was
completed in 2007.

Next door in New Brunswick, about 55
major cruise ships (and their 140,000
passengers) visit Saint John every year
from June through October.

Cruise ships are also an emerging element
of the Newfoundland and Labrador tourism sector. Right now, the province plays
host to a relatively small number of major
cruise lines and they must first dock at
either Corner Brook or St. John's, the
only ports with customs officers. However, more than 30 smaller ports all over
Newfoundland and Labrador now get at
least one visit from a cruise ship and the
province is making a push to lure more
tourists to well-known locations such as
L'Anse aux Meadows and Gros Morne
and to lesser-known ports such as Leading Tickles, Wonderstrands, and Tilting.

There are several companies, including
Pearl Seas Cruises, that offer complete
Canadian itineraries, stopping at several
ports in Atlantic Canada.

Contacts Pearl Seas Cruises (☎800/983-
7463 ⊕www.pearlseascruises.com)

TRANSPORTATION

■ BY AIR

Flying time to Halifax is 1½ hours from Montréal, 2 hours from Boston, 2½ hours from New York, 4½ hours from Chicago (with connection), 8 hours from Los Angeles (with connection), and 6 hours from London. The flying time from Toronto to both Charlottetown and St. John's is about 3 hours; a flight from Montréal to St. John's is 2 hours. Visitors from New York can expect a four-hour flight to St. John's, while Bostonians can expect a three-hour trip to the Newfoundland capital. Inside the Atlantic provinces, a jump from Halifax to Charlottetown takes only 25 minutes while a trip from Halifax to St. John's is about 90 minutes.

Departing passengers at all major airports must pay a $10 airport improvement fee and a $24 security fee before boarding. All major and regional airlines and charter lines that serve Atlantic Canada prohibit smoking. All Canadian airports are also nonsmoking, with the exception of Québec, where smoking is allowed in designated areas only.

Airlines & Airports Airline and Airport Links.com (⊕ www.airlineandairportlinks.com) has links to many of the world's airlines and airports.

Airline-Security Issues Transportation Security Administration (⊕ www.tsa.gov) has answers for almost every question that might come up.

AIRPORTS

The major airport is Halifax International Airport (YHZ). *For information about smaller airports, see the Essentials sections in individual chapters.*

Airport Information Halifax Robert L. Stanfield International Airport (☎ 902/873-4422 ⊕ www.hiaa.ca).

FLIGHTS

National flag carriers have the greatest number of nonstops. Domestic carriers may have better connections to your hometown and serve a greater number of gateway cities. Foreign third-party carriers may have a price advantage.

Air Canada serves every major city in Atlantic Canada, and within Canada it has flights to most smaller cities via its regional feeder airlines. Other major airlines that serve Halifax are American Airlines (via Boston); Continental (via Newark, NJ); Delta (via Boston); and Northwest (via Detroit). Among smaller regional carriers, Air Labrador and CanJet serve Newfoundland and Labrador; CanJet flies to Moncton, New Brunswick, and Fredericton, New Brunswick.

Air Canada dominates 90% of Canada's airline industry. Small carriers are worth investigating, especially when flying short distances between major centers. Contact regional travel agencies for charter companies. Private pilots should obtain information from the Canada Map Office, which has the *Canada Flight Supplement* (lists of airports with Canada Customs services) as well as aeronautical charts.

Airline Contacts Air Canada (☎ 888/247-2262 ⊕ www.aircanada.ca). **Air Labrador** (☎ 800/563-3042). Alaska Airlines (☎ 800/252-7522 or 206/433-3100 ⊕ www.alaskaair.com) American Airlines (☎ 800/433-7300 ⊕ www.aa.com). British Airways (☎ 800/403-0882 in North America, 0870/850-9850 in U.K. ⊕ www.ba.com). CanJet (☎ 800/809-7777). Continental Airlines (☎ 800/523-3273 for U.S. and Mexico reservations, 800/231-0856 for international reservations ⊕ www.continental.com). Delta Airlines (☎ 800/221-1212 for U.S. reservations, 800/241-4141 for international reservations ⊕ www.delta.com). Northwest Airlines (☎ 800/225-2525 ⊕ www.nwa.com). Provincial Airlines (☎ 709/576-1666, 800/563-

2800 in Atlantic Canada ⊕www.provair.com).
United Airlines (☎800/864–8331 for U.S.
reservations, 800/538–2929 for international
reservations ⊕www.united.com). **USAirways**
(☎800/428–4322 for U.S. and Canada reservations, 800/622–1015 for international
reservations ⊕www.usairways.com). **WestJet**
(☎877/929–8646 ⊕www.westjet.com).**Zoom**
(☎866/359–9666 ⊕www.flyzoom.com).

▌ BY BOAT

Car ferries provide essential transportation on the east coast of Canada. They
connect Nova Scotia with Maine and
New Brunswick: Bay Ferries Ltd. sails
from Bar Harbor and Portland Maine
to Yarmouth, and from Saint John,
New Brunswick, to Digby, Nova Scotia, between two and three times daily
in July–August and once daily May–June
and September–October. Bay Ferries' Bar
Harbor–Yarmouth and Portland–Yarmouth service uses a high-speed catamaran, which makes the crossings in 3
hours and 5½ hours, respectively. Known
as *The Cat*, this catamaran is very popular for both its convenience and speed, so
reserve ahead.

Weather permitting, from May through
December, Northumberland Ferries operates between Caribou, Nova Scotia, and
Wood Islands, Prince Edward Island,
making the trip several times a day.
Marine Atlantic operates regular, year-
round between North Sydney and Port
aux Basques, on the west coast of Newfoundland, and a three-times-a-week service between North Sydney and Argentia,
on Newfoundland's east coast, runs from
mid-June through September.

Metro Transit runs frequent passenger
ferries from the Halifax ferry terminal at
Lower Water Street to Alderney Gate in
downtown Dartmouth and to Woodside
Terminal (near Dartmouth Hospital).
Ferries are more frequent during weekday
rush hours; they also operate on Sunday
in summer (10–6, June through Septem-

ber). Free transfers are available from the
ferry to the bus system (and vice versa). A
single crossing costs $2 and is worth it for
the up-close view of both waterfronts.

*For additional information about regional
ferry service, see Essentials sections in
individual chapters.*

Schedules are available through Tourism
Nova Scotia outlets or online. Reservations can also be made online. Smaller
independent ferries within the province
that cross rivers take cash only, but the
fare is usually less than $5.

Information Bay Ferries, Ltd. (☎902/566–
3838 or 888/249–7245 ⊕www.nfl-bay.
com). **Marine Atlantic** (☎902/794–5200
or 800/341–7981 ⊕www.marine-atlantic.
ca). **Northumberland and Bay Ferries Ltd.**
(☎888/249–7245 or 800/565–0201).

▌ BY BUS

If you don't have a car, bus travel is essential in Atlantic Canada, especially to visit
out-of-the-way towns that don't have airports or rail lines. Buses usually depart
and arrive only once a day from any given
departure or destination. Greyhound
Lines and Voyageur offer interprovincial
service. Acadian Lines operates bus service throughout Atlantic Canada. Buses
are quite comfortable, have clean bathrooms, and make occasional rest stops.

Bus terminals in major cities and even
in many smaller ones are usually efficient operations with service all week
and plenty of agents on hand to handle
ticket sales. In villages and some smaller
towns, the bus station is simply a counter
in a local convenience store, gas station,
or snack bar. If you ask, the bus driver
will usually stop anywhere on the route
to let you off, even if it is not a designated
terminal.

Greyhound Lines from New York and
Montréal connect with Acadian through
New Brunswick. Acadian also provides
service between urban centers within

FLYING 101

■ Flying may not be as carefree as it once was, but there are some things you can do to make your trip smoother.

■ Minimize the time spent standing line. Buy an e-ticket, check-in at an electronic kiosk, or—even better—check-in on your airline's Web site before leaving home. Pack light and limit carry-on items to only the essentials.

■ Arrive when you need to. Research your airline's policy. It's usually at least an hour before domestic flights and two to three hours before international flights. But airlines at some busy airports have more stringent requirements. Check the TSA Web site for estimated security waiting times at major airports.

■ Get to the gate. If you aren't at the gate at least 10 minutes before your flight is scheduled to take off (sometimes earlier), you won't be allowed to board.

■ Double-check your flight times. Do this especially if you reserved far in advance. Schedules change, and alerts may not reach you.

■ Don't go hungry. Ask whether your airline offers anything to eat; even when it does, be prepared to pay.

■ Get the seat you want. Often, you can pick a seat when you buy your ticket on an airline Web site. But it's not guaranteed; the airline could change the plane after you book, so double-check. You can also select a seat if you check-in electronically. Avoid seats on the aisle directly across from the lavatories. Frequent fliers say those are even worse than back-row seats that don't recline.

■ Got kids? Get info. Ask the airline about its children's menus, activities, and fares. Sometimes infants and toddlers fly free if they sit on a parent's lap, and older children fly for half price in their own seats. Also inquire about policies involving car seats; having one may limit seating options. Also ask about seat-belt extenders for car seats. And note that you can't count on a flight attendant to produce an extender.

■ Check your scheduling. Don't buy a ticket if there's less than an hour between connecting flights. Although schedules are padded, if anything goes wrong you might miss your connection. If you're traveling to an important function, depart a day early.

■ Bring paper. Even when using an e-ticket, always carry a hard copy of your receipt; you may need it to get your boarding pass, which most airports require to get past security.

■ Complain at the airport. If your baggage goes astray or your flight goes awry, complain before leaving the airport. Most carriers require this.

■ Beware of overbooked flights. If a flight is oversold, the gate agent will usually ask for volunteers and offer some sort of compensation for taking a different flight. If you're bumped from a flight *involuntarily*, the airline must give you some kind of compensation if an alternate flight can't be found within one hour.

■ Know your rights. If your flight is delayed because of something within the airline's control (bad weather doesn't count), the airline must get you to your destination on the same day, even if they have to book you on another airline and in an upgraded class. Read the Contract of Carriage, which is usually buried on the airline's Web site.

■ Be prepared. The Boy Scout motto is especially important if you're traveling during a stormy season. To quickly adjust your plans, program a few numbers into your cell: your airline, an airport hotel or two, your destination hotel, your car service, and/or your travel agent.

Nova Scotia. Shuttle van services also offer a few choices between urban centers in all four provinces.

There are a number of small, regional bus services; however, connections are not always convenient. On larger touring buses, there's no differentiation between classes (i.e., executive vs. economy). Instead, the entire bus is considered executive. For amenities, the executive coach usually seats about two dozen people instead of four dozen, and the seats are leather instead of cloth upholstered.

Bus companies do not accept reservations. Pick up your tickets at least 45 minutes before the bus's scheduled departure time.

Bus Information Acadian Lines (☎506/870–4852, 800/567–5151 within Nova Scotia, New Brunswick, and PEI ⊕www.smt bus.com). **Voyageur** (☎514/842–2281). **Greyhound Canada** (☎800/661–8747 ⊕www. greyhound.ca). **Greyhound International** (☎0134/231–7317 in U.K).

∎ BY CAR

In Atlantic Canada your own driver's license is acceptable for up to three months. Atlantic Canada's highway system is excellent. It includes the Trans-Canada Highway, the longest highway in the world—running about 8,000 km (5,000 mi) from Victoria, British Columbia, to St. John's, Newfoundland, with ferries bridging coastal waters at each end.

FROM THE U.S.

Drivers must carry owner registration and proof of insurance coverage, which is compulsory in Canada. The Canadian Non-Resident Inter-Provincial Motor Vehicle Liability Insurance Card, available from any U.S. insurance company, is accepted as evidence of financial responsibility in Canada. The minimum liability coverage in Atlantic Canada is C\$200,000. If you are driving a car that

is not registered in your name, carry a letter from the owner that authorizes your use of the vehicle.

The U.S. Interstate Highway System leads directly into Canada along Interstate 95 from Maine to New Brunswick. There are many smaller highway crossings between the two countries as well.

Insurance Information Insurance Bureau of Canada (☎416/362–2031 in Canada ⊕www. ibc.ca).

GASOLINE

At this writing, the per-liter price of gas is \$1.15 (\$4.37 per gallon) in Nova Scotia, \$1.25 (\$4.75 per gallon) in Newfoundland, \$1.09 (\$4.14 per gallon) in New Brunswick, and \$1.06 (\$4.03 per gallon) in PEI. To investigate where prices are lower before you fill up the tank, try ⊕*www.gastips.com.*

Distances are always shown in kilometers (a mile is 1.6 kilometers), and gasoline is always sold in liters. (A gallon has 3.8 liters.)

ROADSIDE EMERGENCIES

In case of an accident or emergency call 911. If you're a member of the American Automobile Association, you're automatically covered by the Canadian Automobile Association while traveling in Canada.

Emergency Services Canadian Automobile Association (☎800/222–4357).

Rules of the Road By law, you are required to wear seat belts (and to use infant seats). Some provinces have a statutory requirement to drive with vehicle headlights on for extended periods after dawn and before sunset. Radar-detection devices are illegal. Speed limits, given in kilometers, vary from province to province, but they are usually within the 90- to 110-kph (50- to 68-mph) range outside cities. Speed limits are strictly enforced, and tickets start at \$75. Drinking and driving (anything over .08 blood-alcohol level) is considered a serious crime with serious penalties, including loss of driving privileges, impoundment of your vehicle, and jail. In all four Atlantic provinces, your car can be confiscated for 24 hours if you are found to have a .05 blood alcohol level. Roadblock checks are not unusual, especially on holiday weekends. Parking tickets start at $12 and are common, especially in larger urban centers.

Always strap children under 40 pounds into approved child-safety seats. Children must wear seat belts regardless of where they're seated. In Nova Scotia, even children over 40 pounds who are less than 145 cm (57 inches) in height and are under the age of nine must still be in a booster seat. These rules do not apply, however, if you are visiting Nova Scotia from another province or country and you are driving your own vehicle, provided your vehicle complies with the child restraint safety laws of the province or country where it is registered.

At this writing, Newfoundland is the only province to have banned hand-held cell phone use while driving; drivers in other provinces are currently permitted to be holding a cell phone while driving but this may change. You may turn right at a red light after stopping if there is no oncoming traffic. When in doubt, wait for the green.

▌BY TRAIN

VIA Rail, Canada's Amtrak counterpart, provides transcontinental rail service to Atlantic Canada. However, train service in Atlantic Canada is limited to a Montreal-to-Halifax trip, called The Ocean, which runs six times per week. There are three service classes: comfort class—an upright seat with foot- and head-rest—is the most economical price; comfort sleeper is the middle-of-the-road with a sleeping berth or bedroom; and Easterly class (offered mid-June to mid-October) offers up educational presentations and workshops and luxury-class accommodations including double sleeping cars and private showers. Expect to pay almost double for accommodations in Easterly over seats in comfort class. This train service is now non-smoking (including the washrooms, lounges, and bedrooms), but smokers get a few breaks along the way when the train pulls into stations at Charny, and Campbellton and Moncton in New Brunswick. Tickets are available on-line (credit card payment only), over the phone or in person at VIA RAIL counters.

If you're planning to travel a lot by train, look into the Canrail pass. It allows 12 days of coach-class travel within a 30-day period; sleeping cars are available, but they sell out very early and must be reserved at least a month in advance during the high season (June to mid-October), when the pass is $837, plus applicable taxes. The low season rate (October 16 to May) is $523, plus taxes. The pass is not valid during the Christmas period (December 15 through January 5). For more information and reservations, contact a travel agent in the United States.

Train travelers can check out the 30-day North American RailPass offered by VIA Rail. It allows unlimited coach-economy travel in the United States and Canada. You must indicate the itinerary when purchasing the pass. The cost is $1,149, plus tax, from June to October 15; $815, plus tax, at other times.

Information Long-Haul Leisurail (⌂ Box 113, Peterborough, PE3 8HY U.K. ☎ 01733/335599). **VIA Rail Canada** (☎ 800/561–3949 or 888/842–7245 ⊕ www. viarail.ca).

ON THE GROUND

■ COMMUNICATIONS

INTERNET

It's the norm in most hotels—and many inns and B&Bs—to provide either a public computer or wireless capabilities to guests. In the larger centers, like Halifax, Saint John, St. John's, and Charlottetown, wireless coffee shops are sprouting up so you can surf while you sip. Airports and ferry terminals have also jumped on the wireless bandwagon, offering travelers an option for computer time while they wait for their next flight or boat ride

Contacts Cybercafes (⊕ www.cybercafes. com) lists over 4,000 Internet cafés worldwide. **Ji-Wire** (⊕ www.jiwire.com) has more than 150,000 Wi-Fi hot spots in 136 countries, including dozens in the Atlantic provinces.

PHONES

The good news is that you can now make a direct-dial telephone call from virtually any point on earth. The bad news? You can't always do so cheaply. Calling from a hotel is almost always the most expensive option; hotels usually add huge surcharges to all calls, particularly international ones. In some countries you can phone from call centers or even the post office. Calling cards usually keep costs to a minimum, but only if you purchase them locally. And then there are mobile phones *(⇨ below)*; as expensive as mobile-phone calls can be, they are still usually a much cheaper option than calling from your hotel.

Like the United States, phone numbers have seven numbers. In most cases, the prefix of phone numbers denotes a certain geographical area within the province you are calling. Area codes are three numbers and are the following: for Prince Edward Island and Nova Scotia (902), New Brunswick (506), and Newfoundland and Labrador (709). Pay phones, which cost 25¢ for each call, are quite

common in airports, hotels, on some street corners in downtown areas, and at gas stations. They can be used to make long distance calls either by calling the operator ("0") to reverse the charges, by depositing several coins to pay for the first minute of talk, or by credit or phone card (some pay phones, especially in airports, are equipped to handle cards directly).

Phone cards are readily available at grocery and drug stores, as well as some convenience stores and gas stations. Cellular phone stores are readily accessible all over Atlantic Canada.

CALLING OUTSIDE CANADA

The country code for the United States is 1.

MOBILE PHONES

If you have a multiband phone (some countries use different frequencies from what's used in the United States) and your service provider uses the world-standard GSM network (as do AT&T and Verizon), you can probably use your phone abroad. Roaming fees can be steep, however: 99¢ a minute is considered reasonable. It's almost always cheaper to send a text message than to make a call, since text messages have a very low set fee (often less than 5¢).

If you just want to make local calls, consider buying a new SIM card (note that your provider may have to unlock your phone for you to use a different SIM card) and a prepaid service plan in the destination. You'll then have a local number and can make local calls at local rates.

You can also rent a phone in Canada before you go, through Cellular Abroad or Planet Omni. This is likely to be cheaper than relying on your own phone and paying the high roaming costs on a U.S. number because these companies let you take advantage of the low local rates, regardless of the length of your trip.

However, rental prices vary drastically in price based on style and features. With a cell phone rental, you will also need to purchase a Canada SIM card.

■ TIP→ If you travel internationally frequently, save one of your old mobile phones or buy a cheap one on the Internet; ask your cell-phone company to unlock it for you, and take it with you as a travel phone, buying a new SIM card with pay-as-you-go service in each destination.

Contacts Cellular Abroad (☎800/287-5072 ⊕www.cellularabroad.com) rents and sells GMS phones and sells SIM cards that work in many countries. Mobal (☎888/888-9162 ⊕www.mobalrental.com) rents mobiles and sells GSM phones (starting at $49) that will operate in 140 countries. Per-call rates vary throughout the world. Planet Fone (☎888/988-4777 ⊕www.planetfone.com) rents cell phones, but the per-minute rates are expensive. Planet Omni (☎888/988-4777 ⊕www.planetomni.com) rents cell phones, but the per-minute rates are expensive.

▌ CUSTOMS & DUTIES

You're always allowed to bring goods of a certain value back home without having to pay any duty or import tax. But there's a limit on the amount of tobacco and liquor you can bring back duty-free, and some countries have separate limits for perfumes; for exact figures, check with your customs department. The values of so-called "duty-free" goods are included in these amounts. When you shop abroad, save all your receipts, as customs inspectors may ask to see them as well as the items you purchased. If the total value of your goods is more than the duty-free limit, you'll have to pay a tax (most often a flat percentage) on the value of everything beyond that limit.

U.S. Customs and Immigration (⇨In the U.S.) has preclearance services at international airports in Calgary, Edmonton, Montréal, Ottawa, Vancouver, and Winnipeg.

American and British visitors may bring the following items into Canada duty-free: 200 cigarettes, 50 cigars, and 7 ounces of tobacco; 1 bottle (1.1 liters or 40 imperial ounces) of liquor or wine, or 24 355-ml (12-ounce) bottles or cans of beer for personal consumption. Any alcohol and tobacco products in excess of these amounts is subject to duty, provincial fees, and taxes. You can also bring in gifts up to a total value of C$750.

A deposit is sometimes required for trailers (refunded upon return). Cats and dogs must have a certificate issued by a licensed veterinarian that clearly identifies the animal and certifies that it has been vaccinated against rabies during the preceding 36 months. Guide dogs are allowed into Canada without restriction. Plant material must be declared and inspected. There may be restrictions on some live plants, bulbs, and seeds. With certain restrictions or prohibitions on some fruits and vegetables, visitors may bring food with them for their own use, providing the quantity is consistent with the duration of the visit.

Canada's firearms laws are significantly stricter than those in the United States. Only sporting rifles and shotguns may be imported, provided they are to be used for sporting, hunting, or competition while in Canada. All firearms must be declared to Canadian Customs at the first point of entry. Failure to declare firearms will result in their seizure, and criminal charges may be made. Regulations require visitors to have a confirmed "Firearms Declaration" to bring any guns into Canada; a fee of $50 applies, good for one year. For more information contact the Canadian Firearms Centre.

Information in Canada Canada Border Services Agency (☎800/461-9999 in Canada, 204/983-3500, 506/636-5064 ⊕www.cbsa.gc.ca). Canadian Firearms Centre (☎800/731-4000). Revenue Canada (☎800/461-9999 in Canada).

U.S. Information U.S. Customs and Border Protection (⊕ www.cbp.gov).

▌EATING OUT

The Atlantic Provinces are a preferred destination for seafood lovers. Excellent fish and shellfish are available in all types of dining establishments. The restaurants we list are the cream of the crop in each price category. Properties indicated by a ✕⊡ are lodging establishments whose restaurant warrants a special trip. This book has a price chart at the start of each province chapter.

MEALS & MEALTIMES
Unless otherwise noted, the restaurants listed in this guide are open daily for lunch and dinner. Pubs generally serve food all day and into the wee hours of the night. The dinner meal at restaurants usually begins around 5 PM with seating through 9 or 10 PM.

RESERVATIONS & DRESS
Regardless of where you are, it's a good idea to make a reservation if you can. We only mention them specifically when reservations are essential (there's no other way you'll ever get a table) or when they are not accepted. We mention dress only when men are required to wear a jacket or a jacket and tie.

SMOKING
In Nova Scotia *all* public indoor smoking is banned. In late 2007, cigarettes will also disappear from view in convenience stores. Store owners will be required to remove public display cases, stocking them under counters and out of reach of customers. Similar legislation has been in place in the other Atlantic provinces and only in Prince Edward Island are you still able to smoke, albeit in designated smoking rooms (some of which are outdoor patios).

WINES, BEER & SPIRITS
Locally produced wines, ranging from young table wines to excellent vintages, are offered in most licensed restaurants

and are worth a try. Provincially owned liquor stores, as well as private outlets, are operated in Atlantic Canada. Stores selling alcohol are permitted to be open on Sundays (as of 2007), but some provinces, like Prince Edward Island, limit their Sunday openings to just the summer months. Most are open from noon to 5 PM. Private store owners are open longer, especially on Friday and Saturday nights. PEI has a few beer-only stores and in Newfoundland, you can buy beer at many convenience stores. For a list of government-operated stores (including private store "agents" who sell beer in Newfoundland), check out the Web site for each province.

▌ELECTRICITY

Canada uses the same voltage as the United States, so all of your electronics should make the transition without any fuss at all. No need for adapters.

▌EMERGENCIES

All embassies are in Ottawa. There is a United States consulate in Halifax.

Foreign Consulates U.S. Consulate (✉1969 Upper Water St., Halifax, NS ☎902/429-2480). **U.S. Embassy** (✉490 Sussex Dr., Ottawa ☎613/238-5335).

HEALTH

Infectious diseases can be airborne or passed via mosquitoes and ticks and through direct or indirect physical contact with animals or people. Some, including Norwalk-like viruses that affect your digestive tract, can be passed along through contaminated food. Speak with your physician and/or check the CDC or World Health Organization Web sites for health alerts, particularly if you're pregnant, traveling with children, or have a chronic illness.

HOURS OF OPERATION

Most banks are open Monday through Friday 10 to 5 or 6. All banks are closed on national holidays. Nearly all banks have automatic teller machines (ATMs) that are accessible around the clock.

Hours at museums vary, but most open at 10 or 11 and close in the evening. Many are closed on Monday; some stay open late one day a week, and admission is sometimes waived during those extended hours.

Stores, shops, and supermarkets usually are open Monday through Saturday 9 to 6, and Sunday 12 to 5, although in major cities supermarkets are often open 7:30 AM to 11 PM, and some food stores are open around the clock. Stores often stay open Thursday and Friday evenings, most shopping malls until 9 PM. Drugstores in major cities are often open until midnight, and convenience stores tend to be open 24 hours a day, or at least until midnight, seven days a week.

HOLIDAYS

Canadian national holidays are as follows: New Year's Day (January 1), Good Friday (late March or early April), Easter Monday (the Monday after Good Friday), Victoria Day (late May), Canada Day (July 1), Labour Day (first Monday in September), Thanksgiving (mid-October), Remembrance Day (November 11), Christmas, and Boxing Day (December 26).

The following are provincial holidays and observances: New Brunswick Day (first Monday in August); St. Patrick's Day (March 17), St. George's Day (April 23), Discovery Day (June 26), Memorial Day (July 1), and Orangemen's Day (July 10) in Newfoundland; and Civic Holiday (the first Monday in August) in Nova Scotia.

MAIL

In Canada you can buy stamps at the post office or from convenience stores, hotel lobbies, railway stations, airports, bus terminals, many retail outlets, and some newsstands. Note that the suite number often appears before the street number in an address, followed by a hyphen.

Following are postal abbreviations for provinces and territories: Alberta, AB; British Columbia, BC; Manitoba, MB; New Brunswick, NB; Newfoundland and Labrador, NL; Northwest Territories and Nunavut, NT; Nova Scotia, NS; Ontario, ON; Prince Edward Island, PE; Québec, QC; Saskatchewan, SK; Yukon, YT.

Within Canada, postcards and letters cost 52¢ for up to 30 grams, 93¢ for between 31 and 50 grams, and $1.10 for between 51 and 100 grams. Letters and postcards to the United States cost 93¢ for up to 30 grams, $1.10 for between 31 and 50 grams, and $1.86 for up to 100 grams.

International mail and postcards are $1.55 for up to 30 grams, $2.20 for between 31 and 50 grams, and $3.60 for between 51 and 100 grams.

MONEY

ATMS & BANKS

Your own bank will probably charge a fee for using ATMs abroad; the foreign bank you use may also charge a fee. Nevertheless, you'll usually get a better rate of exchange at an ATM than you will at a currency-exchange office or even when changing money in a bank. And extracting funds as you need them is a safer option than carrying around a large amount of cash.

■TIP➜ PIN numbers with more than four digits are not recognized at ATMs in many countries. If yours has five or more, remember to change it before you leave.

Most banks, gas stations, malls, and convenience stores have automatic-teller machines (ATMs) that are accessible around the clock.

CREDIT CARDS

Throughout this guide, the following abbreviations are used: **AE,** American Express; **DC,** Diners Club; **MC,** Master-Card; and **V,** Visa.

It's a good idea to inform your credit-card company before you travel, especially if you're going abroad and don't travel internationally very often. Otherwise, the credit-card company might put a hold on your card owing to unusual activity—not a good thing halfway through your trip. Record all your credit-card numbers—as well as the phone numbers to call if your cards are lost or stolen—in a safe place, so you're prepared should something go wrong. Both MasterCard and Visa have general numbers you can call (collect if you're abroad) if your card is lost, but you're better off calling the number of your issuing bank, since MasterCard and Visa usually just transfer you to your bank; your bank's number is usually printed on your card.

If you plan to use your credit card for cash advances, you'll need to apply for a PIN at least two weeks before your trip. Although it's usually cheaper (and safer) to use a credit card abroad for large purchases (so you can cancel payments or be reimbursed if there's a problem), note that some credit-card companies *and* the banks that issue them add substantial percentages to all foreign transactions, whether they're in a foreign currency or

not. Check on these fees before leaving home, so there won't be any surprises when you get the bill.

■TIP➜ Before you charge something, ask the merchant whether or not he or she plans to do a dynamic currency conversion (DCC). In such a transaction the credit-card *processor* (shop, restaurant, or hotel, not Visa or MasterCard) converts the currency and charges you in dollars. In most cases you'll pay the merchant a 3% fee for this service in addition to any credit-card company and issuing-bank foreign-transaction surcharges.

Dynamic currency conversion programs are becoming increasingly widespread. Merchants who participate in them are supposed to ask whether you want to be charged in dollars or the local currency, but they don't always do so. And even if they do offer you a choice, they may well avoid mentioning the additional surcharges. The good news is that you *do* have a choice. And if this practice really gets your goat, you can avoid it entirely thanks to American Express; with its cards, DCC simply isn't an option.

Reporting Lost Cards American Express (☎800/528–4800 in the U.S. or 336/393–1111 collect from abroad ⊕www.americanexpress.com). **MasterCard** (☎800/627–8372 in the U.S. or 636/722–7111 collect from abroad ⊕www.mastercard.com). **Visa** (☎800/847–2911 in the U.S. or 410/581–9994 collect from abroad ⊕www.visa.com).

CURRENCY & EXCHANGE

At this writing, the exchange rate is, for the first time in 30 years, favorable for the Canadian dollar.

Throughout this book, unless otherwise stated, all prices are given in Canadian dollars.

U.S. dollars are accepted in much of Canada (especially in communities near the border). However, to get the most favorable exchange rate, exchange at least some of your money into Canadian funds. Traveler's checks (some are available in Canadian dollars) and major U.S. credit cards are accepted in most areas.

The units of currency in Canada are the Canadian dollar (C$) and the cent, in almost the same denominations as U.S. currency ($5, $10, $20, 1¢, 5¢, 10¢, 25¢, etc.). The $1 and $2 bill are no longer used; they have been replaced by $1 and $2 coins (known as a "loonie," because of the loon that appears on the coin, and a "toonie," respectively).

Prices throughout this guide are given for adults. Substantially reduced fees are almost always available for children, students, and senior citizens.

TRAVELER'S CHECKS & CARDS
Some consider this the currency of the cave man, and it's true that fewer establishments accept traveler's checks these days. Nevertheless, they're a cheap and secure way to carry extra money, particularly on trips to urban areas. Both Citibank (under the Visa brand) and American Express issue traveler's checks in the United States, but Amex is better known and more widely accepted; you can also avoid hefty surcharges by cashing Amex checks at Amex offices. Whatever you do, keep track of all the serial numbers in case the checks are lost or stolen.

Contacts American Express (888/412-6945 in the U.S., 801/945-9450 collect outside of the United States to add value or speak to customer service ⊕www.americanexpress.com).

▮ TAXES

A goods and services tax (GST) of 5% (it was 6% until January 1, 2008) applies on virtually every transaction in Canada except for the purchase of basic groceries. Newfoundland and Labrador, Nova Scotia, and New Brunswick have a 14% single harmonized sales tax (HST), which combines the GST and the provincial sales tax.

WORST-CASE SCENARIO

All your money and credit cards have just been stolen. In these days of real-time transactions, this isn't a predicament that should destroy your vacation. First, report the theft of the credit cards. Then get any traveler's checks you were carrying replaced. This can usually be done almost immediately, provided that you kept a record of the serial numbers separate from the checks themselves. If you bank at a large international bank like Citibank or HSBC, go to the closest branch; if you know your account number, chances are you can get a new ATM card and withdraw money right away. **Western Union** (800/325-6000 ⊕ www.westernunion.com) sends money almost anywhere. Have someone back home order a transfer online, over the phone, or at one of the company's offices, which is the cheapest option. The U.S. State Department's **Overseas Citizens Services** (⊕www.travel.state.gov/travel 202/501-4444) can wire money to any U.S. consulate or embassy abroad for a fee of $30. Just have someone back home wire money or send a money order or cashier's check to the state department, which will then disburse the funds as soon as the next working day after it receives them.

As of April 2007, the Canadian government canceled the GST refund program.

You must pay a $10 airport-improvement tax and a $24 security tax at airports when you leave Canada, but the cost is usually rolled into the price of your airline ticket.

Information Canada Customs and Revenue Agency (☎902/432–5608, 800/668–4748 in Canada ⊕www.ccra-adrc.gc.ca).

▌ TIME

New Brunswick, Nova Scotia, and Prince Edward Island are on Atlantic time, which is (during daylight saving time) three hours earlier than Greenwich mean time (GMT) and one hour later than eastern daylight time (EDT). Newfoundland and Labrador are on Newfoundland time, which is –2:30 GMT and +1:30 EDT.

▌ TIPPING

Tips and service charges are not usually added to a bill in Canada. In general, tip 15% of the total bill (before tax). This goes for waiters and waitresses, barbers and hairdressers, and taxi drivers. Porters and doormen should get about $2 a bag. For maid service, leave at least $2 per person a day ($3 in luxury hotels).

UNDERSTANDING NOVA SCOTIA & ATLANTIC CANADA

OF SEA & LAND

BOOKS & MOVIES

FRENCH VOCABULARY

OF SEA & LAND

Canada's Atlantic provinces are bound to the sea by tradition and geography. Each province has a distinct personality, but the Atlantic Ocean and the other great bodies of water that flow into it from farther inland—the Bay of Fundy with its mighty tides, the warm Baie des Chaleurs, and the Gulf of St. Lawrence, which in pioneer days was part of Canada's nautical highway to the world—have influenced the lifestyle and culture of the more than 2 million people who live in the Maritime provinces—Nova Scotia, New Brunswick, and Prince Edward Island—along with the province of Newfoundland and Labrador.

The culture manifests itself in the region's language, art, and music. It has been shaped by strong ties to Europe, decades of economic hardship, and a struggle to tame the land. Celtic music, for example, a strong tradition in Cape Breton and other parts of Nova Scotia, has thrived for centuries. The haunting melodies of a lost homeland traveled over the Atlantic in the 18th century when the first Highlanders arrived from Scotland, and mingled with musical influences from the Acadians and Irish. Today Celtic music is being "exported" in a modern form, via young avant-garde performers, to the Scottish homeland from whence it came. In New Brunswick the toe-tapping fiddle music of the French-speaking Acadians echoes the rhythms of the jigs and reels of Ireland, Scotland, and France. In Newfoundland, too, a lively musical tradition is tempered with folkloric, humorous tales of yesteryear and a vocabulary full of twists and turns that delight the ear.

The Atlantic provinces are strongly rooted in the past, but they are not isolated from the rest of North America—far from it. Those who live in the region have always looked beyond their own borders to wheel and deal with the outside world. The bounty of the ocean (now sadly in decline in certain areas, in part because of mismanagement of resources), marine commerce, and shipbuilding once provided the economic lifeblood of the region, and people sold (and continue to sell) their catches and their expertise around the globe.

Tourism and other service industries have taken over where some of the more traditional occupations have left off. Many national and international technology companies have set up shop here (especially in New Brunswick, which has a large bilingual workforce), attracted by the quality of life and by labor and housing costs that are lower than those in the rest of Canada.

Even Prince Edward Island, Canada's smallest province and a rural enclave of manicured farmland and picturesque villages, is no longer the sleepy backwater of yesteryear. Connected, since 1997, to the mainland by the Confederation Bridge, it is visited by more than 1 million people annually, almost half the entire population of Atlantic Canada.

The Island offers a multitude of outdoor attractions in scenic surroundings, as do all the Atlantic provinces. Gently rolling roads (no hill is higher than 500 feet) make it ideal for cycling. Beaches, many in spectacular settings, abound throughout the region. The Bay of Fundy, which divides Nova Scotia from New Brunswick, is renowned for its whale-watching. On Newfoundland, the birdlife is abundant, and moose are so plentiful (125,000 at last count) that locals may warn you not to drive at night.

Atlantic Canada isn't all moose and maritime landscapes, though. Its cities, although small, are attractive, safe, clean, and historic. Charlottetown, on Prince Edward Island, is an intimate, walkable community with old wooden houses and quiet tree-lined streets. Fredericton, New Brunswick's capital, is a university town on the St. John

River. It, too, has gracious old buildings, as well as an exceptional regional
art museum—the Beaverbrook Art Gallery—named after its benefactor and
one of New Brunswick's most famous
citizens, Lord Beaverbrook, a renowned
Canadian and British press magnate.

St. John's, Newfoundland, has terrific
crafts stores (many locals still while
away the long winters by knitting sweaters, socks, and woolen hats) and lively
pubs, many of them housed in colorfully
painted, renovated wooden buildings
that march up from the waterfront.

Halifax, Nova Scotia, is the self-proclaimed "capital" of Atlantic Canada.
The business center of the region, it is
also the area's most populous and sophisticated city. Old and new blend comfortably here. Gracing its harbor skyline are
a 19th-century fortress (the Citadel),
high-rise hotels, a renovated waterfront
collectively known as Historic Properties, and several glass-wall office towers.
The present is here, but, as in the rest of
the region, the past is not forgotten.

—Helga Loverseed

BOOKS & MOVIES

BOOKS

Newfoundland & Labrador For contemporary fiction, pick up *The Shipping News,* the Pulitzer Prize–winning novel by E. Annie Proulx: it's an atmospheric and moving tale of fishing and family, set in Newfoundland (the author is American); the book is much better than the movie. Wayne Johnston is a native Newfoundlander and The Colony of Unrequited Dreams is a comic epic about the history of the province. His *Baltimore's Mansion* is a memoir depicting his childhood on the Avalon Peninsula. *The North Bay Narrative,* by Walter Staples (Peter E. Randall), is the true story of the evolution of a remote outpost into a bustling fishing town.

New Brunswick David Adams Richards is one of New Brunswick's best-known writers. His novels *Mercy Among the Children* and *Bay of Love and Sorrows,* both set in northern New Brunswick, explore bleak themes. Richards has also authored *Lines on the Water,* a tale of the fishing community on the Miramichi River. In the memoir *Home: Chronicle of a North Country Life,* by Beth Powning, the author and her husband relocate from Connecticut to a farm near the Bay of Fundy.

Nova Scotia The sweeping novel *Fall on Your Knees,* by Ann-Marie MacDonald, takes place partly on Cape Breton Island; it was an Oprah book club selection. Henry Wadsworth Longfellow's poem *Evangeline* tells the story of lovers separated when the British deported the Acadians in 1755. The poem has been the inspiration for a number of tourist attractions in the province. *Island: The Complete Stories,* by Alistair MacLeod, is a collection of tales about everyday life in Nova Scotia. His first novel, *No Great Mischief,* is the story of a Scottish family that builds a new life on Cape Breton.

Prince Edward Island It almost goes without saying that *Anne of Green Gables* is a must-read.

General Acadian culture is unique to this region and Clive Doucet's *Notes from Exile: On Being Acadian* is a thoughtful memoir that explores what it means to be Acadian and incorporates the history of Acadie and the Acadians.

MOVIES

Rain, Drizzle, and Fog (1998) is a documentary about Newfoundland through the eyes of a "townie," or resident of St. John's. *The Shipping News* (2001), set in Newfoundland, was filmed primarily in Corner Brook, New Bonaventure, and Trinity, Newfoundland. The documentary *Ghosts of the Abyss* (2003) has excellent footage of the *Titanic,* which sank off the coast of Newfoundland. Canadian director James Cameron's *Titanic* (1997) was filmed partly in Halifax.

Many lesser-known movies filmed and set in the Atlantic provinces show more of the landscape and culture. Some are *The Bay of Love and Sorrows* (2002; Miramichi, New Brunswick); *The Bay Boy* (1984; Cape Breton, Nova Scotia); *Margaret's Museum* (1995; Cape Breton, Nova Scotia); *New Waterford Girl* (1999; Cape Breton, Nova Scotia); *A Rumor of Angels* (2000; Crescent Beach, Halifax, Lunenburg, and Sambro, Nova Scotia); and *Rare Birds* (2001; Cape Spear, Petty Harbour, and St. John's, Newfoundland).

FRENCH VOCABULARY

One of the trickiest French sounds to pronounce is the nasal final *n* sound (whether or not the *n* is actually the last letter of the word). You should try to pronounce it as a sort of nasal grunt—as in "huh." The vowel that precedes the *n* will govern the vowel sound of the word, and in this list we precede the final *n* with an *h* to remind you to be nasal.

Another problem sound is the ubiquitous but untransliterable *eu*, as in *bleu* (blue) or *deux* (two), and the very similar sound in *je* (I), *ce* (this), and *de* (of). The closest equivalent might be the vowel sound in "put," but rounded.

Words and Phrases

	English	French	Pronunciation
Basics			
	Yes/no	Oui/non	wee/nohn
	Please	S'il vous plaît	seel voo **play**
	Thank you	Merci	mair-**see**
	You're welcome	De rien	deh ree-**ehn**
	That's all right	Il n'y a pas de quoi	eel nee ah pah de **kwah**
	Excuse me, sorry	Pardon	pahr-**dohn**
	Sorry!	Désolé(e)	day-zoh-**lay**
	Good morning/ afternoon	Bonjour	bohn-**zhoor**
	Good evening	Bonsoir	bohn-**swahr**
	Goodbye	Au revoir	o ruh-**vwahr**
	Mr. (Sir)	Monsieur	muh-**syuh**
	Mrs. (Ma'am)	Madame	ma-**dam**
	Miss	Mademoiselle	mad-mwa-**zel**
	Pleased to meet you	Enchanté(e)	ohn-shahn-**tay**
	How are you?	Comment ça va?	kuh-mahn-sa-**va**
	Very well, thanks	Très bien, merci	tray bee-ehn, mair-**see**
	And you?	Et vous?	ay **voo**?

Numbers

one	un	uhn
two	deux	deuh
three	trois	twah
four	quatre	**kaht**-ruh
five	cinq	sank
six	six	seess
seven	sept	set
eight	huit	wheat
nine	neuf	nuff
ten	dix	deess
eleven	onze	ohnz
twelve	douze	dooz
thirteen	treize	trehz
fourteen	quatorze	kah-**torz**
fifteen	quinze	kanz
sixteen	seize	sez
seventeen	dix-sept	deez-**set**
eighteen	dix-huit	deez-**wheat**
nineteen	dix-neuf	deez-**nuff**
twenty	vingt	vehn
twenty-one	vingt-et-un	vehnt-ay-**uhn**
thirty	trente	trahnt
forty	quarante	ka-**rahnt**
fifty	cinquante	sang-**kahnt**
sixty	soixante	swa-**sahnt**
seventy	soixante-dix	swa-sahnt-**deess**
eighty	quatre-vingts	kaht-ruh-**vehn**
ninety	quatre-vingt-dix	kaht-ruh-vehn-**deess**
one-hundred	cent	sahn
one-thousand	mille	meel

Colors

black	noir	nwahr
blue	bleu	bleuh
brown	brun/marron	bruhn/mar-**rohn**
green	vert	vair

orange	orange	o-**rahnj**
pink	rose	rose
red	rouge	rooje
violet	violette	vee-o-**let**
white	blanc	blahnk
yellow	jaune	zhone

Days of the Week

Sunday	dimanche	**dee**-mahnsh
Monday	lundi	**luhn**-dee
Tuesday	mardi	**mahr**-dee
Wednesday	mercredi	**mair**-kruh-dee
Thursday	jeudi	**zhuh**-dee
Friday	vendredi	**vawn**-druh-dee
Saturday	samedi	**sahm**-dee

Months

January	janvier	**zhahn**-vee-ay
February	février	**feh**-vree-ay
March	mars	marce
April	avril	a-**vreel**
May	mai	meh
June	juin	zhwchn
July	juillet	**zhwee**-ay
August	août	oot
September	septembre	sep-**tahm**-bruh
October	octobre	awk-**to**-bruh
November	novembre	no-**vahm**-bruh
December	décembre	day-**sahm**-bruh

Useful Phrases

Do you speak . . . English?	Parlez-vous . . . anglais?	par-lay **voo** **ahn**-glay
I don't speak . . . French	Je ne parle pas . . . français	zhuh nuh parl **pah** frahn-**say**
I don't understand	Je ne comprends pas	zhuh nuh kohm-prahn **pah**
I understand	Je comprends	zhuh kohm-**prahn**
I don't know	Je ne sais pas	zhuh nuh say **pah**
I'm American/	Je suis américain/	zhuh sweez a-may-

British	anglais	ree-**kehn**/ahn-**glay**
What's your name?	Comment vous appelez-vous?	ko-mahn voo za-pell-ay-**voo**
My name is . . .	Je m'appelle . . .	zhuh ma-**pell** . . .
What time is it?	Quelle heure est-il?	kel air eh-**teel**
How?	Comment?	ko-**mahn**
When?	Quand?	kahn
Yesterday	Hier	yair
Today	Aujourd'hui	o-zhoor-**dwee**
Tomorrow	Demain	duh-**mehn**
This morning/ afternoon	Ce matin/cet après-midi	suh ma-**tehn**/set ah-pray-mee-**dee**
Tonight	Ce soir	suh **swahr**
What?	Quoi?	kwah
What is it?	Qu'est-ce que c'est?	kess-kuh-**say**
Why?	Pourquoi?	**poor**-kwa
Who?	Qui?	kee
Where is . . .	Où se trouve . . .	oo suh **troov**
the train station?	la gare?	la gar
the subway?	la station de?	la sta-**syon** duh
station?	métro?	may-**tro**
the bus stop?	l'arrêt de bus?	la-**ray** duh **booss**
the airport?	l'aérogare?	lay-ro-**gar**
the post office?	la poste?	la post
the bank?	la banque?	la bahnk
the hotel?	l'hôtel?	lo-**tel**
the store?	le magasin?	luh ma-ga-**zehn**
the cashier?	la caisse?	la **kess**
the museum?	le musée?	luh mew-**zay**
the hospital?	l'hôpital?	lo-pee-**tahl**
the elevator?	l'ascenseur?	la-sahn-**seuhr**
the telephone?	le téléphone?	luh tay-lay-**phone**
Where are the rest rooms?	Où sont les toilettes?	oo sohn lay twah-**let**
Here/there	Ici/là	ee-**see**/la
Left/right	A gauche/à droite	a goash/a drwaht
Straight ahead	Tout droit	too drwah
Is it near/far?	C'est près/loin?	say pray/lwehn
I'd like . . .	Je voudrais . . .	zhuh voo-**dray**
a room	une chambre	ewn **shahm**-bruh

the key	la clé	la clay
a newspaper	un journal	uhn zhoor-**nahl**
a stamp	un timbre	uhn **tam**-bruh
I'd like to buy . . .	Je voudrais acheter . . .	zhuh voo-**dray ahsh**-tay
a cigar	un cigare	uhn see-**gar**
cigarettes	des cigarettes	day see-ga-**ret**
matches	des allumettes	days a-loo-**met**
dictionary	un dictionnaire	uhn deek-see-oh-**nare**
soap	du savon	dew sah-**vohn**
city map	un plan de ville	uhn plahn de **veel**
road map	une carte routière	ewn cart roo-tee-**air**
magazine	une revue	ewn reh-**vu**
envelopes	des enveloppes	dayz ahn-veh-**lope**
writing paper	du papier à lettres	dew pa-pee-**ay** a **let**-ruh
airmail writing paper	du papier avion	dew pa-pee-**ay** a-vee-**ohn**
postcard	une carte postale	ewn cart pos-**tal**
How much is it?	C'est combien?	say comb-bee-**ehn**
It's expensive/cheap	C'est cher/pas cher	say share/pa share
A little/a lot	Un peu/beaucoup	uhn peuh/bo-**koo**
More/less	Plus/moins	plu/mwehn
Enough/too (much)	Assez/trop	a-say/tro
I am ill/sick	Je suis malade	zhuh swee ma-**lahd**
Call a . . . doctor	Appelez un . . . médecin	a-play uhn mayd-**sehn**
Help!	Au secours!	o suh-**koor**
Stop!	Arrêtez!	a-reh-**tay**
Fire!	Au feu!	o fuh
Caution!/Look out!	Attention!	a-tahn-see-**ohn**

Dining Out

A bottle of . . .	une bouteille de . . .	ewn boo-**tay** duh
A cup of . . .	une tasse de . . .	ewn **tass** duh
A glass of . . .	un verre de . . .	uhn **vair** duh
Ashtray	un cendrier	uhn sahn-dree-**ay**
Bill/check	l'addition	la-dee-see-**ohn**
Bread	du pain	dew pan

Breakfast	le petit-déjeuner	luh puh-**tee** day-zhuh-**nay**
Butter	du beurre	dew burr
Cheers!	A votre santé!	ah vo-truh sahn-**tay**
Cocktail/aperitif	un apéritif	uhn ah-pay-ree-**teef**
Dinner	le dîner	luh dee-**nay**
Special of the day	le plat du jour	luh plah dew **zhoor**
Enjoy!	Bon appétit!	bohn a-pay-**tee**
Fixed-price menu	le menu	luh may-**new**
Fork	une fourchette	ewn four-**shet**
I am diabetic	Je suis diabétique	zhuh swee dee-ah-bay-**teek**
I am on a diet	Je suis au régime	zhuh sweez oray-**jeem**
I am vegetarian	Je suis végé-tarien(ne)	zhuh swee vay-zhay-ta-ree-**en**
I cannot eat . . .	Je ne peux pas manger de . . .	zhuh nuh **puh** pah mahn-**jay** deh
I'd like to order	Je voudrais commander	zhuh voo-**dray** ko-mahn-**day**
I'm hungry/thirsty	J'ai faim/soif	zhay fahm/swahf
Is service/the tip included?	Le service est-il compris?	luh sair-**veess** ay-teel com-**pree**
It's good/bad	C'est bon/mauvais	say bohn/mo-**vay**
It's hot/cold	C'est chaud/froid	say sho/frwah
Knife	un couteau	uhn koo-**toe**
Lunch	le déjeuner	luh day-zhuh-**nay**
Menu	la carte	la cart
Napkin	une serviette	ewn sair-vee-**et**
Pepper	du poivre	dew **pwah**-vruh
Plate	une assiette	ewn a-see-**et**
Please give me . . .	Merci de me donner . . .	Mair-**see** deh meh doe-**nay**
Salt	du sel	dew sell
Spoon	une cuillère	ewn kwee-**air**
Sugar	du sucre	dew **sook**-ruh
Waiter!/Waitress!	Monsieur!/ Mademoiselle!	muh-**syuh**/ mad-mwa-**zel**
Wine list	la carte des vins	la **cart** day van

INDEX

PHOTO CREDITS

ABOUT OUR WRITERS

Wanita Bates has lived in five different Canadian provinces but, since 1992, has become a self-proclaimed "NBC'er"—a Newfoundlander By Choice—and loves it. Based in St. John's and the Southern Shore, Wanita spends her time traveling around the easternmost province telling people's stories, in words, photographs and on radio. Her work has appeared in *Canadian Geographic, Chatelaine, Today's Parent,* and *Border Crossings.*

Jeff Bursey has only ever lived on islands, including PEI and Newfoundland and Labrador. He's written tourism pieces on PEI for national and international vacationers. His fiction, book reviews and articles have appeared throughout North America and England.

Amy Pugsley Fraser, a reporter at the *Halifax Herald,* updated the Nova Scotia Essentials and Nova Scotia and Atlantic Canada Essentials sections for this edition. Her writing has been published in local books such as *Hurricane Juan: The Story of a Storm* and *Halifax Street Names,* as well as in *Canadian House & Home* and other national magazines. Amy lives in Halifax with her husband and three young sons.

Sandra Phinney writes from her perch in Yarmouth, Nova Scotia where she's penned two books and hundreds of article in over 60 publications. She's happiest when meeting people and exploring off-the-beaten-track places in Atlantic Canada.